Cambridge Medieval Textbooks

Edward III is usually remembered for his stirring victories over the French and Scots. Yet these triumphs occurred against a domestic backdrop of economic upheaval, crime, high taxation, and the Black Death. Edward's ability to pursue his ambitions amid such challenges shows the effectiveness of his leadership and the resilience of English institutions. This book examines the strains on English life in this remarkable era, beginning with village society and moving up through towns, the church, nobility, and government. Professor Waugh shows how an interlocking network of hierarchies at each level enabled Edward to reach into local communities to get what he needed. Compliance, however, required hard bargaining as subjects chafed under incessant taxes and royal demands. During Edward's reign parliament, particularly the House of Commons, became for the first time the primary arena for negotiations between the king and the community of the realm and the focal point of national politics.

Professor Waugh's incisive account of these tumultuous events also contains an extensive guide to further reading, in addition to a glossary of the more abstruse medieval terms. It will make an important addition to the highly successful series of Cambridge Medieval Textbooks, and will appeal both to students encountering medieval studies for the first time, and that broad general audience with an interest in the reign of one of England's most celebrated monarchs.

Cambridge Medieval Textbooks

This is a series of specially commissioned textbooks for teachers and students, designed to complement the monograph series 'Cambridge Studies in Medieval Life and Thought' by providing introductions to a range of topics in medieval history. The series combines both chronological and thematic approaches, and will deal equally with British and European topics. All volumes in the series will be published in hard covers and in paperback.

Already published

Other titles are in preparation

ENGLAND IN THE REIGN
OF EDWARD III

SCOTT L. WAUGH

Department of History
University of California, Los Angeles

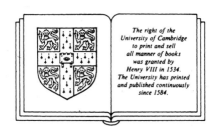

The right of the
University of Cambridge
to print and sell
all manner of books
was granted by
Henry VIII in 1534.
The University has printed
and published continuously
since 1584.

CAMBRIDGE UNIVERSITY PRESS

Cambridge
New York   Port Chester
Melbourne   Sydney

Published by the Press Syndicate of the University of Cambridge
The Pitt Building, Trumpington Street, Cambridge CB2 1RP
40 West 20th Street, New York, NY 10011, USA
10 Stamford Road, Oakleigh, Melbourne 3166, Australia

First published 1991

Printed in Great Britain at the University Press, Cambridge

British Library cataloguing in publication data
Waugh, Scott L.
England in the reign of Edward III – (Cambridge medieval textbooks)
1. England, 1327–1377
1. Title
942.037

Library of Congress cataloguing in publication data
Waugh, Scott L. 1948–
England in the reign of Edward III/Scott L. Waugh
p.   cm. – (Cambridge medieval textbooks)
Includes bibliographical references.
ISBN 0-521-32510-2. – ISBN 0-521-31039-3 (paperback)
1. Great Britain – History – Edward III, 1327–1377. 2. England –
Civilization – Medieval period, 1066–1485. 1. Title. 11. Series.
DA233.W29 1991
942.03'7–DC20   90–1566
CIP

ISBN 0 521 32510 2 hardback
ISBN 0 521 31039 3 paperback

CONTENTS

v

FIGURES AND TABLES

FIGURES

TABLES

ACKNOWLEDGEMENTS

My principal debt is to Dr Jim Bolton who kindly suggested to Cambridge University Press that I might like to write this book. Richard Fisher took up the suggestion and has been supportive, indeed enthusiastic, throughout. Professor Richard Rouse and Professor Eleanor Searle generously read some parts and offered helpful criticism, though any errors are entirely my own. Joan Waugh provided insightful commentary and spirited encouragement during the conception and writing of the book. Dr Chase Langford drew the maps and figures. I am especially grateful to have had the opportunity to use the excellent unpublished doctoral dissertations of Maryanne Kowaleski, William Ormrod, and Simon Walker. Assistance in the form of the University of California President's Research Fellowship in the Humanities and from the Academic Senate of UCLA enabled me to complete the book over the past year. Anyone who writes a survey is quickly made aware of the extent to which history is a collaborative enterprise. Historical understanding depends on the findings and insights of many different scholars working in many different areas. One of the pleasures of writing this book has been to acquaint and re-acquaint myself with so much excellent work. The field has produced scholarship equal to the excitement of the age.

Map 1. Towns and villages mentioned in Chapters 3–6.

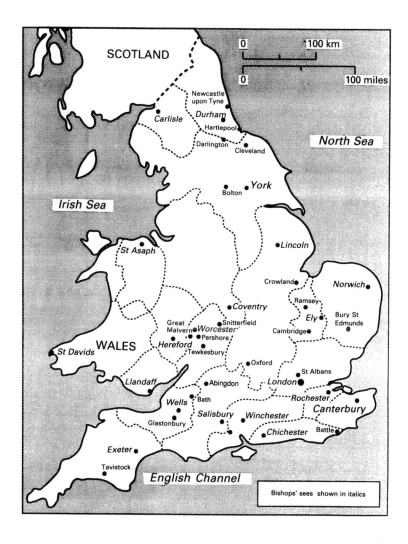

Map 2.   Ecclesiastical sites mentioned in Chapter 9.

PART I

OVERVIEW

I

INTRODUCTION

·

As it is said that running water is the most powerful thing that can be, because all the particles of water take effect equally in the current, wherefore water pierces the hard rock; just so it is with a nation which exerts itself with a single spirit to maintain the dignity of its lords, who desire nothing but the welfare of the community and individually follow no other design.

(*Scalacronica*)

For a generation between 1330 and 1370 England was exceptionally unified and with a 'single spirit' achieved some of the greatest military victories of the middle ages. The image of Edward III and his time is inextricably linked to war. Crécy, Calais, and Poitiers, the Black Prince, Henry of Lancaster, and John Chandos, and Edward himself bring to mind valour and chivalry and have occupied centre stage in most histories of the period.

Yet the domestic backdrop is equally compelling. Edward's military accomplishments are especially impressive because they occurred at a time of remarkable change. The first half of the century saw pitiful harvests, famine, and severe deflation in quick succession. Then the Black Death struck, not just in 1348, but again in 1360, 1373, and periodically thereafter. The resulting drop in population, loss of tenants, and rise in wages battered the economy that undergirded lordship and government. Crime and corruption sparked anxiety and protest. These dislocations made the difficult job of mobilizing manpower and wealth even more formidable than in ordinary times.

Edward's reign, moreover, lay between two periods of extreme political

3

disorder, under his father, Edward II, and his grandson, Richard II. Writers were pessimistic about the chances for unity. Thomas Gray's paean to solidarity follows a warning about the dire consequences of disunity; dangers that were realized in Edward II's reign. *The Brut* chronicler and Ranulf Higden likewise disparaged the English character and were unhopeful about the political outlook. Thomas Brinton and John Gower decried the moral decay they saw in the 1370s, as the country was torn once again by factions and rivalry. Yet in between, from roughly 1330 to 1370, there was only one period of severe political unrest, 1340–1. Neatly symbolized in the camaraderie of the Order of the Garter, harmony between the monarch and nobility made it possible for Edward to direct English energies toward foreign wars.

This book focuses on these domestic issues. From 1330 to 1369, England witnessed an extraordinary fulfilment of the potential of the medieval state, founded on cooperation and trust between the king, the landed elite, and the church. Because of that trust, Edward was able to extract more from his subjects than any other medieval king. He was able to field armies far from home for extended periods. He delegated extensive authority to the highest aristocrats and greatest churchmen. He consulted regularly with gentry, merchants, and burgesses.

Domestic developments set government and politics on a path different from the one they had followed over the previous century. No longer was political opposition largely a baronial pursuit. The house of commons matured into an accepted fixture of English politics, giving the gentry and local communities a direct voice in politics. With the crown and nobility in close alliance, attacks on the government after 1330 emanated largely from the commons. Similarly, the office of the justices of the peace gave the county gentry a firm platform for rule in the English countryside. War was Edward's primary aim, but those who governed his subjects were primarily concerned about order and justice and were quick to complain when crown policies produced upheaval.

The crown was linked to communities and subjects through a series of social hierarchies. Whether in village, town, county, or country as a whole, English society was dominated by small cliques which controlled office-holding and social institutions. Overwhelmingly male and wealthy, they exercised both formal and informal power from the family to the royal council. Whether serving as jurors, reeves, bailiffs, constables, members of parliament, or royal councillors, they mediated relations between the crown and its subjects. As members of elites, they also shared an interest in maintaining their authority. To do so, they depended on those in power above and below them. The most powerful groups in England were the aristocrats, or magnates as they were called (earls and barons), and the higher gentry (bannerets, knights, and some esquires). Though they were numerically small – numbering approximately 75 aristocrats and 2,500 higher gentry out of a population of about 5 to 6 million before 1348 – and though their influence stretched across counties and the kingdom as a whole, they did not exercise power in ways essentially different from those elites at other levels of society. The sources of power and techniques of rule were largely the same. Linkages between elites at all levels made possible the maintenance of their authority as well as the transmission of commands from crown to subjects.

The fourteenth-century English state, therefore, had two important characteristics: it was one in which, first, authority and responsibility for law, order, and defence were concentrated in a single ruler, the king, yet in which, secondly, effective power was widely diffused through the social, economic, and intellectual elites.

Government was in the king's hands. He set policy, conducted diplomacy, received public revenues, and had charge of law and justice. He had, for the middle ages, a sophisticated bureaucracy. He also had obligations, which were usually expressed in Christian terms. His coronation oath thus emphasized that he ruled for the benefit of his community. Thomas Gray, author of the *Scalacronica*, expressed this principle nicely by saying that kings would do well

to attribute their benefits to God and to the good behaviour of their people, in whose welfare consists their treasure; for God holds things in due governance as the executive government of their people. For the people often suffer for the sins of kings; wherefore [kings] ought to take good heed lest their actions bring about general and widespread disaster, as has often been seen; so that their [high] estate should be regulated towards God by virtue and towards the people by morality.

These same ideals turned up in a variety of forms in the early fourteenth century. *De speculo regis*, written early in Edward's reign to warn him of the evils of purveyance, opens with a statement about the ideal king, centring on the notion of justice and equity. Thomas Brinton stated in a sermon that the honour of kings rested on three things: military power, prudent counsel, and the just governing of the people.

Brinton alluded to a feudal ideal of kingship, not entirely distinct from Christian teachings, which stressed the duty of counsel. A king should not act wilfully, that is, on his own without advice. Edward recognized this. In his first, independent statement as king in 1330, he announced: 'We wish all men to know that henceforth, we wish to govern our people according to right and reason, as befits our royal dignity. And that business which touches us and the state of our realm shall be conducted by common counsel with the lords of our realm, and in no other manner.'

He reiterated the importance of counsel upon taking the title of king of France in 1340:

> [In] the affairs of the kingdom we do not intend to act precipitately and arbitrarily, but, holding our will in check, we will be guided by the counsel and advice of the peers, prelates, magnates and faithful vassals of the kingdom, as shall seem best for the honour of God, the protection and advancement of the Church, which we revere in the fullness of devotion, and the furtherance of both the public and private good.

Because these words were propaganda designed to get the Flemings to support his cause, they must be treated with caution. Yet Edward was not necessarily being duplicitous. The themes of counsel, consent, and common good reverberated throughout his reign. Whether Christian or feudal, the principles expressed the reality of medieval governing in which the monarchy and leaders of the communities of the realm were interdependent.

Each needed the other and none was all powerful. Elites wanted the king to adjudicate disputes, provide favours, and sanction their authority. Prone to bickering and factionalism, they could not rule by themselves. As a sovereign and suzerain, the king had broad theoretical powers but in practice they were limited. He could go to war as he pleased, but he needed the earls, barons and knights to lead and organize his armies. He could halt trade in and out of the country but needed the consent of merchants or the entire country to tax that trade. He could prohibit the alienation of any lands held of him in chief but could not unjustly deprive any person of his or her land. He could appoint and remove officers at will but if those officers did not have the respect of the nobility and church they would not be obeyed. He needed the consent of the population before he could tax them. This was scarcely autocratic kingship.

The king's success depended on his ability to rally the nobility and gentry to his cause and through them mobilize the resources of his kingdom. Edward had to work through interlocking elites to implement his policies. Special assemblies of merchants and burgesses, county gentry, or clerics brought these local authorities together to consider royal demands. But such assemblies opened the door to other issues, as those who met took the opportunity to discuss matters of common concern. Politics in such a small, face-to-face community thus involved constant bargaining between the king and individuals, communities, or coalitions. It occurred over taxation, an obvious example, but it was just as likely to be concerned with other thorny issues such as privileges or grievances. The process found its highest expression in the house of commons. Frequent meetings of parliament, called by Edward to rally support and levy taxes, made negotiation a national concern. The commons transmitted local worries to the centre and provided an outlet for discontent. Because this interchange was so important in shaping the political events of Edward's reign, an understanding of politics demands a prior understanding of the conditions in which the government had to work.

After a brief narrative of the highlights of Edward's reign, Part II lays out this economic and social context. The patterns of wealth and power essential to the maintenance of authority began in the peasant family and the village community. They had to bear the weight of seigneurial demands and royal policy while enduring economic change. Towns and markets were likewise crucial for peasants, lords, and king alike. Providing mechanisms for the distribution of goods and for earning sorely needed cash, they were also centres of wealth and authority, hierarchically structured with institutions and elites of their own. Edward seized on those merchant elites to help him finance war and gain compliance with his policies. They provided further the first links in an economic chain that bound England into continental commerce and production. Wool was England's prime export commodity earning valuable profits for producers and merchants and offering a tempting target for taxation. It was also crucial to England's balance of payments. The flow of specie into and out of the country and the consequent activity of the royal mints had a significant impact throughout the English economy. These basic elements of agriculture, marketing, and overseas trade form the topics of Chapters 3, 4, and 5.

The last two chapters of Part II view these elements dynamically and take up the startling economic and demographic changes that beset England between 1300 and 1377. Prices, population, and lordship were the crucial determinants. The dramatic rise and fall of prices early in the century followed at once by the calamities of the plague upset what people had come to regard as 'normal' economic conditions and ushered in a period of uncertainty. The consequences were immediately apparent and landlords fought to retain the advantages that they had enjoyed for centuries. Legislation, seigneurial determination, and a remarkable degree of class cohesion meant that the landlord class enjoyed a couple of decades of prosperity before the effects of the demographic collapse really took hold in the 1370s. The period was important as well because it witnessed the high point of English conquests in France. The economic health of the military classes allowed them to carry out Edward's enterprise while the buoyancy of production and trade buttressed government finances.

Part III concentrates on the landholding elite and government. The 'single spirit' that Gray thought essential to the success of a nation was not always evident among the landlords. Indeed, to contemporaries they seemed riven with competition. War, chivalry, and the common threat of economic change helped them to close ranks. The peerage and gentry, nevertheless, further evolved into distinct social and political groupings, centred on the houses of lords and commons. The clergy were woven into this elite, though they had particular concerns that sometimes put them at odds with their lay colleagues. The English church was torn between the worldly demands of patronage and preferment and its pastoral mission. In the fourteenth century, the issue became magnified as the crown, papacy, English clergy, and landlords vied for control of church patronage.

The instruments of rule are discussed in Chapters 10 and 11. The success of any state depends on the degree to which its authority can penetrate to local communities and secure compliance with its commands. The medieval English government did so by ruling through the leading men of the community, whether in the village, hundred, county, or country as a whole. As the scope of Edward's demands increased, so did the number of officials scouring the countryside for money, goods, and men. This combination of forces made the problem of corruption acute. Crime and official misconduct merged into one another, posing a serious threat to local order early in the century. Thus tested by war, crime, and economic upheaval, the crown experimented with its administration. Taxation was altered. Innovative financial schemes abounded as the government endeavoured to find resources to match Edward's ambitions. For the first time, laymen occupied the most important posts, those of chancellor and treasurer. Various criminal tribunals were set up to restore order. And justices of the peace were introduced, giving local elites an even firmer hold than they had had over law and order in their communities. Edwardian government was highly successful for its time, but its success brought on problems for itself.

All of these issues preoccupied the inner counsels of government and influenced the politics of Edward's reign. His policies reached deep into the population. Taxation, purveyance, military obligations, and criminal inquests affected all of his subjects at a time when economic setbacks made it hard for them to meet their ordinary obligations. Edward, therefore, had to negotiate for the country's support, a process that is taken up in Part IV. The council had been the traditional arena of discussion between king and aristocracy, but it grew into an executive body in the fourteenth century as parliament attained greater political prominence. The two houses of parliament, the lords and commons, gradually took shape and the commons began to flex their political muscle in earnest. Politics in Edward's reign is notable for two reasons. First, it was largely contained in parliament without spilling over into armed conflict. Secondly, the commons took a leading part. Their role was indicative of the growing maturity of parliament and a sign of how profoundly Edward's policies affected his subjects. Despite pride in English victories, there was an undercurrent of unrest throughout

Edward's reign which helped spark political conflict in the late 1330s and again in the 1370s.

Battlefield glories were therefore not the only events that marked Edward's long reign. Within England, change was evident at every level of society and the economy. In the long run, these domestic issues proved to be of far greater consequence than the ephemeral victories in France.

2

SURVEY OF EVENTS 1307–1377

The highlights of Edward III's reign can be briefly narrated. Because his father's rule had been such a calamity, leaving a residue of mistrust that had to be cleared up before Edward could undertake any serious military campaigning, it is important to begin with Edward II's misfortunes.

He came to the throne on his father's death in July 1307. Though regal in appearance and welcomed at first, Edward displayed few of his father's statesmanlike qualities. By the end of the year, his favouritism toward Piers Gaveston and his abandonment of the war in Scotland caused grumbling among the barons. His coronation in February 1308 was carried out under a cloud and included an additional clause to the customary oath which stated that the king would uphold the laws chosen by his people.

Storms followed. Angered by Edward's lavish gifts to Gaveston, the barons secured Gaveston's exile in 1308, but by July 1309 Edward had succeeded in bringing him back, at the price of certain concessions. Edward and Gaveston did not change their ways so that in December 1310, under baronial pressure, Edward appointed a baronial committee to draw up reforms. When the Ordinances, as they were called, the most complete reform programme since the Provisions of Oxford in 1258, were finally issued in August 1311, they amounted to a comprehensive attack on Edward and his government. They called not only for the exile of Gaveston and other associates, but for stringent controls on royal appointments and policy making. Parliament was envisaged as the instrument of restraint. Gaveston duly left the country but soon returned to Edward's side. Some of the barons had had enough. Under the direction of the earl of Warwick and Thomas earl of Lancaster, Gaveston was seized and beheaded on 19 June

1312. The destruction of his favourite deeply embittered Edward and made complete reconciliation with the barons impossible. The two most powerful components of the state, the monarchy and baronage, were hopelessly alienated and distrustful of one another. The only bright spot in the year was the birth of Edward's eldest son Edward on 13 November.

Only the Scots benefited from this turmoil. Led by Robert Bruce, they extended their grip on their homeland and even plundered deep into northern England. Edward finally launched a major campaign in 1314, but it was a fiasco. The Scots triumphed at Bannockburn on 24 June, driving the English from Scotland. The earl of Gloucester and forty knights were killed. It was the most humiliating defeat that English armies suffered during the later middle ages.

It also put Edward at the mercy of his baronial opponent, Thomas of Lancaster. During the next six years, power seesawed back and forth between the two as they attracted or lost adherents. Lancaster continually pushed for the enforcement of the Ordinances, which Edward despised, but gradually alienated many of his peers, who saw his insistence on reform as a veiled attempt to take power for himself. For his part, Edward once again lavished wealth and power on favourites. This clash of personalities proved fatal. Meanwhile, harsh weather and poor harvests drove up grain prices producing widespread famine beginning in 1315. The north of England was nearly in anarchy, torn apart by private wars and feuds. Part of the problem was the threat of invasion by the Scots, who had again consolidated their power under the cover of political unrest.

Just prior to 1320, the two Hugh Despensers, father and son, became preeminent at court. The younger Hugh owed his power to his position as household chamberlain and to his marriage to Eleanor, one of the three coheiresses to the vast estate of the last earl of Gloucester, killed at Bannockburn. After 1318, when the estate was finally divided up, Hugh, buttressed by royal authority, began enlarging his wife's share by intimidating his rivals, particularly in the Welsh Marches. The campaign galvanized the Marchers into action, and they forced the Despensers into exile. It was not enough. They soon returned and Edward defeated his opponents, called the Contrariants, at the battle of Boroughbridge on 16 March 1322. Several leaders, including Thomas of Lancaster, were executed, though others, such as Roger de Mortimer of Wigmore, were imprisoned. The triumph gave the Despensers undisputed control of the government. Yet their personal aggrandizement and Edward's amassing of a huge treasure deepened the mistrust between the king and the community of the realm.

Few, therefore, rallied to Edward when his queen, Isabella, invaded England in the autumn of 1326. The opportunity for renewed opposition arose because of changes overseas. In 1323, Edward concluded a thirteen

year truce with the Scots. Trouble then erupted in France. As the duke of
Gascony, Edward owed homage to the French king. This peculiar relationship, in which the king of England was a vassal of the king of France because
of the remaining territories from his twelfth-century inheritance, had been
a source of friction for over a century. Whenever relations between the two
sovereigns soured, the king of France would declare Gascony forfeit and
move to seize it. The last time, in 1294, harassment of French shipping by
English and Gascon mariners had been the source of conflict. In 1324 it was
the construction of a fortified town, a *bastide*, by the French at Saint Sardos
and its swift destruction by the English. Edward, however, was unable to
defend Gascony. The following year, he sent Isabella to France to sue for
peace, and his son Edward joined her shortly thereafter to perform homage
for Gascony.

Isabella and Edward refused to return. She became the centre of opposition to her husband, having formed a liaison with Roger de Mortimer,
who had managed to escape from the Tower. With the aid of the count of
Hainault, they invaded England in September 1326 and overthrew Edward
and his friends. Deposition was the last option available to baronial opponents and one that had not been exercised since the Conquest. Trust in the
monarch had reached a nadir. The nobility accused him of spurning wise
counsel, losing Scotland and Gascony, harming the nobility and church,
impoverishing the realm for his own gain, and failing to do justice to all
regardless of their position. Their complaints reveal the standards by which
they measured royal government: counsel, justice, and the common good.
Yet they betrayed their uneasiness over the novelty of their actions in the
way in which they groped for a legal formula for the deposition and in their
painstaking efforts to enlist support as widely as possible. The procedure was
convoluted. A parliament was summoned in January 1327 and Edward was
asked to attend, but he refused. Opinion was divided. A majority first swore
homage to Edward's son, then deposed Edward, and then sent a delegation
to him that asked him to resign in favour of his son. They renounced their
homage to Edward, dissolved the royal household, and accepted Edward's
son as king.

Legal formulae barely cloaked the military force that made deposition
possible. The proceedings were conducted in London where the previous
October the citizens had murdered the treasurer and bishop of Exeter,
Walter Stapledon. They prodded parliament to action whenever it
appeared to drag its feet. Magnates with their armed retinues and Isabella's
force of Hainaulters were equally intimidating.

Edward III, only fourteen when he came to the throne, was completely
under the authority of his mother and her lover. He had been betrothed at
their insistence to Philippa, daughter of the count of Hainault who had been

so instrumental in the invasion, and finally married her a year after becoming king. A regency council was set up to guide the government, but it was pushed aside. Mortimer and Isabella proved to be as grasping as the Despensers. They hoarded wealth, enlarged Mortimer's retinue, and trounced their enemies. Mortimer had himself created earl of March, a novel title, in October 1328. Resistance to Isabella and Mortimer rose at first outside the court. Henry of Lancaster and Edward's uncle Edmund earl of Kent participated in an abortive rebellion in 1328, and Edmund was executed in 1330 for plotting against the regime. Tension mounted as the crown tried to root out conspiracies and opposition. Tournaments were prohibited and sweeping powers of arrest were given to officials.

Lancaster plotted with two younger courtiers, Richard de Bury and William Montagu, to overthrow the regime. They put the young king in contact with the pope who gave the enterprise his blessing. In a dramatic coup, they seized Mortimer at Nottingham castle on 19 October 1330, tried him in parliament, and executed him. Isabella received gentler treatment. After giving up much of her plunder, she was left with a generous dower and lived in luxury until she died in 1358.

In the aftermath of the coup, the government first directed its efforts toward restoring order in England. The time was not right for an ambitious foreign policy, though tensions were building in France, Scotland, and Flanders which would eventually plunge England into war. Immediately on Edward's accession in 1327, a truce had been concluded with the French, though events seemed to invite intervention. Charles IV of France died in 1328 without direct descendants of his own, leaving the inheritance of the kingdom in doubt. Philip of Valois, son of Charles' uncle Charles, stepped forward and took possession, but a case could also be made for Edward's right to the throne through his mother, Charles IV's sister. Though the issue was raised and Isabella may have dreamed of asserting the claim, England with its internal problems could hardly mount an invasion of France. Edward, therefore, performed homage to Philip at Amiens in 1329 and again in 1331. Nevertheless, two factors henceforth bedevilled Anglo-French relations: the English king's traditional position as duke of Gascony and the new possibility of his right to be king of France.

Edward's first military ventures occurred in Scotland. Ironically, Mortimer, like Edward II, was condemned for his failure there. He had resumed the war in 1327 only to meet with disaster at Stanhope Park where the Scots managed to elude a superior English force. The treaty of Northampton in 1328 established peace by conceding much of what Robert Bruce had sought and arranging for a marriage between Edward III's sister and Robert's son David. The terms were deeply resented in

England. Mortimer was blamed for the humiliation and the treaty was one of the factors contributing to his fall.

Robert Bruce died in 1329, leaving the Scottish throne to his young son David. The minority tempted Bruce's old enemies to revive their plotting. Edward Balliol, a pretender to the throne whose father had lost out to Bruce, along with several English lords called the 'disinherited' because they had lost territory in Scotland on Bruce's victory, invaded Scotland and defeated the regency forces at Dupplin Moor in 1332. The 'disinherited' had lobbied Edward for assistance and he had covertly supported them. Once he was crowned, Balliol acknowledged Edward's lordship and promised him a huge portion of Scottish territory. We can believe the *Scalacronica* when it states that Edward, 'being eager for arms and glory, and his council being enterprising and burning for war, . . . soon came to an agreement . . . all the sooner because they desired to retrieve their prestige from those by whom they had forfeited it'. The memories of English failures under his father and Mortimer were still fresh. Edward, therefore, openly aided Balliol after Bruce's adherents rallied and drove him from the country. In 1333, Edward launched an invasion of Scotland, defeated the Scots at Halidon Hill, and seized Berwick. It was the first English victory in Scotland in a generation and helped restore English confidence, though it failed to wipe out Scottish resistance. The Scots rallied and Edward brought armies northward again and again for the next four years to no avail.

The Scottish danger had been amplified when Scotland and France concluded the treaty of Corbeil in 1326. They promised one another mutual aid, especially in the event of a war with England. In 1334, Philip, the king of France, made it clear that he would support David Bruce, who had been exiled, and that a settlement of Anglo-French relations would have to include Scotland. He was determined to aid the Scots in their resistance.

On the continent, the king of France also had to deal with an unruly vassal, Flanders. For the time being, Philip was in command. With his assistance, the count of Flanders, Louis de Nevers, had defeated a coalition of rebellious towns at Cassel in 1328. Louis was not inclined to desert his protector. Nevertheless, English wool was vitally important to the towns, whose livelihood centred on textile manufacturing. Edward thus had an economic lever which he did not hesitate to use in trying to pry the Flemings away from the French king. Further, he enjoyed close relations with the count of Hainault, one of Flanders' neighbours.

Such were the convoluted relations between England, Scotland, Flanders, France, and the papacy when Edward decided to embark on war. The first steps may have been taken as early as August 1336 when Edward declared an embargo on the export of wool, a move perhaps calculated to force Flanders to ally with England. In the autumn, he raised the alarm against an anticipated invasion by the French. Progress toward war became even clearer in January 1337 when Edward discussed his claim to the French throne in council. In March, according to subsequent reports, parliament endorsed Edward's plans and confirmed his grants of new titles and honours, designed to strengthen the nobility. Therefore, when Philip acted to confiscate Gascony in May 1337, because Edward had given shelter to Robert of Artois, a fugitive from French justice, war was a foregone conclusion. The following October, Edward publicly put forth his claim to the French throne, though it was not until January 1340 that he actually styled himself 'king of France'.

Edward's motives have been much disputed. Was he sincere in his claim? Or was it a ploy to pressure the French into concessions on Gascony? Or an effort to break the stalemate in Scotland? Each of these considerations undoubtedly played some part in the formulation of Edward's policy, but no definitive answer can be given to any. The surest conclusion is that Edward was determined to fight. That determination powered English policy for forty years, from 1337 to 1377.

The war can be divided into three phases, 1337 to 1341, 1341 to 1360, and 1360 to 1377. In the first, Edward followed the examples of his father and king John who had built up grand coalitions of allies before attacking the French in 1214 and 1294. He enlisted the aid of the emperor, Ludwig of Bavaria, as well as of a host of princes from the region around northern France. He accepted the title of Vicar of the Empire from Ludwig and spent vast sums to seal his alliances. In July 1338, he arranged for a home government in the Ordinances of Walton and then embarked, full of hope. The outcome was disappointing to say the least. Edward and his allies were unable to engage the French, even though they came close to it at Buironfosse in October 1339. Their soldiers indulged in some vicious plundering in the countryside, but no battle was fought. Even though revolt in Flanders forced the count to flee to France in 1339 and the leader of the revolt, James van Artevelt of Ghent, sealed an alliance with Edward full of promises of assistance, Edward could make no headway. Thomas Gray, in his *Scalacronica*, sneered that Edward stayed for 'fifteen months without making any war, only jousting and leading a jolly life'.

The expense of buying allies and maintaining his army proved catastrophic. Though he secured new taxes from parliament, his ministers had difficulty collecting them because his demands had exacerbated an already severe shortage of coinage in England. England suffered directly from French raids along the south-eastern coasts in 1338 and 1339. In June 1340, Edward won an impressive naval victory at Sluys which destroyed the French fleet and brought a respite from plundering. Despite the triumph, Edward was short of money. He had been forced to pawn his crown in 1339, while the earls of Derby, Northampton and Warwick were imprisoned for his debts in 1340. The earls of Suffolk and Salisbury were captured in a skirmish and held for ransom. In September, Edward had to halt the siege of Tournai and conclude the truce of Espléchin. The whole enterprise had broken down, wrecked by lack of finance.

The political repercussions were felt immediately. Edward slipped back into England in December 1340, removed his leading ministers, and blamed John Stratford, the archbishop of Canterbury, for betraying him and his enterprise. Stratford had been entrusted with the unenviable tasks of leading the government at home and raising money and supplies. The issues were debated in parliament, which enacted legislation imposing controls on the king's choice of ministers. Edward, however, retained the support of most of the nobility and by the autumn was able to set aside the statute. The year 1341 was the first time a political crisis was conducted almost entirely in parliament, a sign of the commons' growing stature.

When Edward resumed the war, he changed his approach. The financial and political costs of his earlier effort had been too high. He dropped the policy of enlisting costly allies and concentrated instead on smaller, shorter campaigns. A dispute over the succession to the duchy of Brittany in 1342 gave Edward an excuse to fight and added another source of hostility between Edward and Philip. Fighting erupted before the end of the year and lasted on and off until 1343. Edward led an army and successfully campaigned up and down the duchy until the French dug in their heels at Vannes and the weather turned foul, convincing him to conclude another truce in January 1343.

During the truce, the two sides negotiated through the mediation of the papacy, but no compromise could be reached. Edward stuck by his claim to the French throne while the French insisted on the traditional feudal relationship between the two kings. If Edward was to surrender his claim, he wanted full sovereignty over his French territory in return. The talks broke down and both sides prepared for war.

Edward planned to invade France with three forces in 1345–6. One led by the earl of Northampton was dispatched to Brittany and achieved some notable victories by 1346. A second led by Henry of Lancaster sailed to Gascony. Lancaster proved to be an able commander by winning back substantial territory from the French. Edward commanded the third force himself which was destined for Flanders. The situation there, however, deteriorated with the overthrow of van Arteveldt. The country became inhospitable to the English and the enterprise was abandoned. In July 1346, Edward set out again, perhaps to aid Lancaster who was meeting stiff opposition in Gascony. Whatever the intention, the force landed in Normandy taking the French by surprise. Edward marched eastward and almost reached Paris before the French army came up and gave pursuit. On 26 August 1346, the English turned and fought at Crécy. Though heavily outnumbered, they won a brilliant victory with the aid of good defences and the longbow. Edward then turned his attention to Calais. The French army failed to relieve the town and it fell to the English nearly a year later on 4 August 1347. In the meantime, the Scots had invaded the north of England in 1346. They were defeated by the English at Neville's Cross on 17 October and David II was taken prisoner.

The achievements of the English were stunning. They had humbled the most powerful monarchy in Europe and won considerable territory. They had won a resounding victory over their bitter enemies in Scotland. Yet they could not capitalize on their accomplishments. The Black Death marched through Europe between 1348 and 1350, killing as much as a third of the population and making military campaigning unrealistic. Neville's Cross did not resolve the Scottish issue. Resistance continued despite the imprisonment of the king, forcing Edward to conclude a truce with a demand for a ransom. He made as little headway in France. At the beginning of the new decade, there was only desultory fighting. Philip VI died in 1350, and his son John came to the throne. The two sides resumed negotiations but they faltered on the same obstacles of sovereignty and lordship that had wrecked the earlier talks.

At home, parliament was restive. The financial appetite of the war threatened to devour everything, forcing Edward to ask again and again for taxes. Parliament in 1344, 1346, 1348, and 1352 expressed its displeasure with his demands, though he largely got what he wanted.

The war resumed in 1355 with a new ferocity. Edward's eldest son, Edward 'the Black Prince', conducted a highly successful raid across southern France from Gascony to the Mediterranean, reaping plunder and ransoms and leaving a trail of destruction in his wake. Known as a *chevauchée*, it became England's preferred form of military campaigning. Smaller and less expensive than a full invasion force, it was also safer since the purpose was not to engage the enemy but to create havoc. In 1356, the technique was used for a two-pronged attack on France. Leading a force south from Normandy, Henry of Lancaster was to meet up with the Black Prince who was moving his own army northward from Gascony. Lancaster's *chevauchée* was quick and successful, but he failed to link up with the Black Prince. After enjoying considerable success of his own, the Black Prince turned back to Gascony but was soon pursued by the French under king John's leadership. The two forces met near Poitiers and after ferocious fighting, the English emerged victorious with king John and many of the French nobility their prisoners. The French monarchy had reached its lowest ebb. The Black Prince conducted John to England with the utmost chivalry and courtesy, where he was held while the English demanded a ransom of nearly £667,000. Edward III pressed his demands for the ransom and full sovereignty over his French territories in return for his claim to the throne, but the French refused. He therefore led yet another campaign in 1359, intending to put himself on the French throne by force. He marched to Rheims where French kings were crowned, but the city closed its gates and refused to yield. The English were forced to withdraw and suffered terribly in the harsh January weather and a devastating storm on 13 April.

Fighting was halted by the treaty of Brétigny, ratified on 24 October 1360. For the English, it was a disappointment. Edward gave up his claim to be king of France in return for sovereignty over an enlarged duchy of Aquitaine. Yet the ransom was reduced by a quarter, the French did not surrender all the territories they promised, and their offer of sovereignty proved hollow.

This phase of the war none the less ended on a high note. English conquests in France had reached their widest extent in generations and English armies had prevailed over much larger French forces. Praised by English and French writers alike, Edward reaped the rewards of victory. The plan to create a round table in 1344 and foundation of the Order of the Garter in 1347 burnished his image as a chivalric hero. Arthurian romance and chivalry were woven into the realities of war as knights strove to win reputations for themselves. Edward built on this to strengthen his court. His family added to his fame. He and Philippa produced eleven surviving children in these years, and the Black Prince, born in 1330, had gained the reputation of a valiant and fearsome captain.

Direct conflict between France and England did not break out again until 1369. In the meantime, the scope of the war widened to bring in additional combatants. In France, bands of soldiers, *routiers*, plundered the countryside. In the south, the kingdom of Castile became involved in the hostilities as France and England lined up behind two rival candidates to the throne, Henry of Trastamara and Pedro the Cruel. The Black Prince came to Pedro's aid in 1367 and won another great victory at the battle of Nàjera. It would be the last of his career. The victory, moreover, was short lived for Henry killed Pedro in 1369 and secured Castile as a French ally. Most importantly, France gained access to the Castilian navy, the finest in Europe. England's shores were once again threatened.

The Black Prince had been named prince of Aquitaine in 1362, but his rule was marked by bickering and ineptitude. By 1369, disgruntled subjects appealed to the king of France, Charles V, for relief. After some hesitation, Charles took up the issue in the *parlement* of Paris, thereby denying Edward's claim of sovereignty and reviving the pattern of appeal and forfeiture that had caused so much trouble in the past.

This time English fortunes crumbled. French attacks in Gascony pushed the English back to the coasts. The naval defeat at La Rochelle in 1372 was a decisive blow. With Edward old and enfeebled and the Black Prince incapacitated by disease, leadership fell to Edward's son, John of Gaunt. Yet he could not inspire the same enthusiasm nor instil the same sense of purpose as his father and elder brother had done. Expeditions in 1369 and 1373 under Gaunt's leadership were expensive but futile. The government's military goals were not clear. Castle after castle fell and by 1375 Gaunt agreed to a two-year truce.

Matters at home were no better. The government was in the hands of a small group of self-interested courtiers under the influence of the king's mistress, Alice Perrers. While the war went badly, they provided for themselves. Initially, the resumption of war was not burdensome, because the crown had sufficient reserves to pay the costs. But that changed and the commons began to resent the combination of taxes and favouritism. The situation exploded in the Good Parliament of 1376, when the commons took the momentous step of impeaching several of the courtiers. It signalled the culmination of a long period of political apprenticeship for the commons and their emergence as a real political force.

Edward, however, was only a bystander at these events. He assented to parliament's demands, but was not really in command. The centre of power was shifting. During the parliament, the Black Prince died. Edward's death followed a year later. The incredible triumphs of his early years had given way to defeat and disillusionment. The restoration of trust between the crown and nobility had been replaced by suspicion about the court and uncertainty about Edward's successor, his ten-year-old grandson Richard II.

PART II

ECONOMIC CHALLENGES

— • —

Paying for war in medieval England was problematic for three reasons. One was that there was no routine taxation, a problem that will be taken up later. Another was that the medieval economy did not produce a huge surplus over and above what was strictly necessary to keep society going. Finally, there was a brisk competition among the crown, barons, and church for a share of that surplus. Early fourteenth-century England was prosperous, but the wealth was limited. In this section, England's economic base, from village agriculture to overseas trade, will be examined in order to understand the economic constraints that Edward faced when he embarked on war.

The crucial fact was that the surplus was no longer growing. War, weather, and disease caused violent economic shifts and brought a long period of expansion to a close. A decade and a half of strong economic performance ended in 1315 with poor weather and famine. Grain production soon recovered, but a severe deflation between 1336 and 1342 hurt producers and made it harder to pay taxes. Yet these events paled in comparison to the plague, which first arrived in 1348 and struck again in 1360–1, 1369, and 1374. Altogether, nearly one-half of the population perished. In the 1350s, between bouts, the economy was buoyed by high prices and favourable trade conditions. During the 1360s and 1370s, however, the effects of the population loss began to make themselves felt. Tension mounted between different social groups and finally erupted in the English rising of 1381. From that point onward, many aspects of the medieval economy changed radically, conclusively ending the period of high population and high farming (see glossary).

While trends such as these are easily identified, it is less easy to specify their precise causes and consequences. Several features of the medieval economy have to be taken into account. Above all, it was an *agrarian* economy, in which most men and women invested the greater portion of their labour and from which the greatest profits were obtained. In such an economy, the balance between resources and population was crucial. As population grew, in the absence of widespread technological improvements in farming, it pressed on resources, producing scarcity. By the time of the Black Death, population growth had reached the point of diminishing returns. The addition of extra labour did not produce a corresponding increase, resulting in hardship for large numbers of people. Yet scarcity was also socially determined. The demands of landlords and, to a lesser extent, of the king, for rents, services, taxes, and fines aggravated 'natural' conditions, further shrinking the pool of wealth to be divided among peasants and townsfolk. Within every village, moreover, disparities in personal wealth as well as communal controls over agriculture affected productivity and the market. Finally, transportation, management, marketing, and money supply played a part in determining economic performance.

The economic contrasts stand out. On the one hand, a large portion of the English population lived precariously. Changes in harvest levels could have disastrous consequences, as the famine of 1315–21 demonstrated. Meaningful population decrease did not occur until the onslaughts of plague beginning in 1348. Only then was poverty somewhat ameliorated. On the other hand, the economy was resilient. The population stayed high until the Black Death, and poor weather and plague did not stop fortunes being made and spent in lavish consumption. Wool production remained high and profitable, harvests eventually stabilized and provided reasonable incomes for producers, and a native cloth industry began to grow and even make noticeable inroads into imports. In assessing the English economy in this period, these contrasting features must be kept in mind.

They will be examined by looking first at the village community and agricultural production, then at towns, internal trade, the overseas trade in wool and cloth, and, finally, at the overall trends in the English economy during the first three-quarters of the fourteenth century.

3

THE PEASANT FAMILY
AND VILLAGE SOCIETY

It is important to begin with the fundamental units of agricultural production and consumption: the peasant family and village community. England was, and is, characterized by the diversity of its geography, soil, and weather. Over natural variations, humans imposed the diversification of settlement and practices. The patterns of habitation tended to follow the geography: from the scattered hamlets and sparse population of the uplands and woodlands to the nucleated villages of the midlands and the dense communities of the east coast. In all, agriculture was a communal venture, though the degree and precise nature of co-operation differed. Villagers' customs were as varied as village plans. On top of these cultural differences, power imposed further distinctions, demarcating one lordship or jurisdiction from another, even within a single village. The crown and church drew additional boundaries to organize their own functions and dues.

Individuals were differentiated economically and legally. Medieval people had traditionally classified themselves according to their functions in the well-known concept of the three orders: those who work, those who fight, and those who pray. The scheme came into use around the year 1000 but it was still alive in the fourteenth century. Thus, William Langland could have his ploughman proclaim that 'for my part I'll sweat and toil for us both [himself and the knight] as long as I live, and gladly do any job you want. But you must promise in return to guard over Holy Church, and protect me from thieves and wasters who ruin the world.' It expresses the ideal of a functional reciprocity, in which the work of each member makes it possible for others to do theirs. The same desire for an organic unity was expressed in another commonplace image of the mystical social body.

Thomas Brinton, the bishop of Rochester, expressed this ideal in a sermon
in 1373:

Many are members of this mystical body, because the head are kings, princes, and
prelates; the eyes are wise judges and truthful counsellors; the ears are the religious
orders; the tongue good doctors; the right hands are knights ready for defending; the
left hands are merchants and faithful artisans; the heart are citizens and burgesses as
though placed in the middle; the feet are peasants and labourers as though firmly supporting the entire body. And although unity is watched over anxiously in all of these
members it is nevertheless chiefly observed in two principal members, that is in
heads for discretely and justly ruling and in hearts for loving perfectly.

Both of these images were moral idealizations. They expressed a desired
social unity and reciprocity. Yet they also masked great differences in power
and wealth that characterized actual social relations. Both hint, for example,
at the power of the knightly elite and speak hopefully that their force would
be used solely in defending the social order rather than in preying on it.

The images, however, also underplay the tremendous diversity of status
and function that had blossomed in English society since the early middle
ages. For that reason, the image of the social body was perhaps preferred in
the later middle ages to the older one of the three orders because it came
closer to representing the new social complexity. Social unity for Brinton
thus depended on the interaction of scholars, merchants, and citizens as well
as the traditional knights, prelates, and peasants. Chaucer painted this social
complexity through deft character portraits in his General Prologue to the
Canterbury Tales. William Langland drew a similar picture in the 'plain full
of folk' that opened *Piers Plowman*. Still, orders were differentiated on the
basis of the work they performed.

Not only was society functionally complex, but each group was highly
stratified, even agricultural communities. Despite moralists' portraits, the
peasantry did not constitute an economically homogeneous class.
Inequality had come about in various ways over the preceding centuries.
Population growth had fragmented individual holdings, leaving a large
corps of small holders and near-landless peasants. Land clearance or assarting
(carving arable from woodland) continued into the fourteenth century, but
the best soils had been brought under cultivation well before 1300. Newly
added land was of only marginal quality. The population thus expanded on
an essentially fixed base, so that there was less to go around. Family practices
abetted inequality. The endowment of new families, younger sons, widows
or widowers sliced up family holdings, while the buying and selling of
peasant land, evident from the twelfth century onward, exacerbated the
fragmentation of tenements. The village land market shifted resources from
those families struggling to survive and seeing some hope in selling segments

of their holdings to those whose surpluses allowed them the luxury of accumulating land. It also created a mosaic of subtenancies and leaseholds. The results are evident throughout England. A survey of midland manors from the hundred rolls in the late thirteenth century found 46 per cent of the peasant population holding seven to ten acres or less. Fifty per cent of the tenants on twenty-five manors belonging to the bishopric of Winchester held ten acres or less at the end of the thirteenth century. Parts of Norfolk had experienced extreme fission by 1300, the mean size of holdings ranging from only two to five acres. On one manor, 85 per cent of the tenantry held less than five. The other side of the coin was that only a handful of families in each village amassed holdings larger than thirty acres. Throughout England, land was distributed in inverse proportion to the population. Thus, 15 per cent of the freeholders on twenty-two manors in Gloucestershire in 1322 held 61 per cent of all the free land. At the opposite end, 27 per cent held just 7 per cent, and some of those held only a cottage with no arable at all.

This inequality takes on greater importance when measured against the minimum amount of land necessary for a family to survive. It was not the same everywhere. Soil conditions, the type of crops, crop rotation, agricultural practices, family size, the availability of supplementary food sources, and the amount of rent affect the calculation. For midland regions it is assumed that around ten acres represented bare subsistence, while in notably fertile areas of Kent and East Anglia, this was possible on around five acres. A study of an East Midlands village, Holywell-cum-Needingworth, found that the majority of villagers held only about ten acres of land yet many prospered and even advanced. Subsistence means just that, not starvation. However subsistence is calculated, it is clear from manorial surveys that roughly half of the peasantry lived perilously close to hunger, based on their landholdings alone. It is not surprising that mortality rates surged whenever harvests failed and grain prices soared.

These poor villagers had just enough land to commit them to farming but not enough to guarantee their prosperity. Their stake in the land, however meagre, tied them to the village. It would have been foolhardy to abandon it altogether. They were forced therefore into a ceaseless quest for extra earnings through wage labour or other enterprises to make up what their holdings could not supply. Some served the landlord, but most worked for their wealthy neighbours. Brewing, small crafts, service with other families, hunting and gathering, cutting and collecting wood, underbrush or peat, perhaps even crime, made up the economic inventory of smallholding families. The village economy was thus composed of a vast array of petty enterprises involving many different kinds of work. The community thrived on the one commodity available to everyone: labour. But, in a market as saturated with workers as these villages must have been and in an agrarian economy in which the demand for labour rises and falls with the farming seasons, returns could not have been as great or as consistent as people wanted.

Not surprisingly, wealthy families had a much wider array of economic options than poor ones. They could accumulate larger holdings, lease land, or lend money. Wealthy freeholders on the estate of Peterborough abbey, for instance, acted as entrepreneurs, buying or leasing land from villagers as well as the abbot, obtaining permission to build on the land, and then, presumably, leasing the parcels back to their neighbours. The profits from leases, farming, or labour, enabled the wealthy to hire workers to help increase the output of the land and to release husband and wife from less profitable activities, such as child-rearing. The experience of servitude was not the same for rich and poor families, since the poor were more likely than the rich to send children away for service and less likely to hire servants. It created a dependency of one class of villager on another. Barbara Hanawalt has conjectured that conditions in the early fourteenth century favoured these practices. With a high population, the cost of hiring servants was low while the extra money generated by servants would have been very welcome to families with marginal incomes.

Although customs, laws, and norms were applied uniformly at every level of village society, their meaning changed radically for families of different economic means. Everyone in England, for example, lived under the umbrella of church law, which dictated that a valid marriage was formed by words of present consent between a man and a woman. Yet, the choices of spouses, the contractual terms of marriages, and the ways in which they were celebrated differed according to the circumstances of the partners. As a general rule, the poor married later in life and less often. When they did marry, they had fewer children. Whether that was the result of later marriage or restraint in the face of economic realities cannot be resolved. That the former may have been more decisive than the latter is suggested by the fact that the rate of illegitimacy was higher for the poor than for the rich. The daughter of a wealthy peasant could anticipate a dowry in land, given to her and her husband by her family on marriage. In contrast, the dowries of poor women often consisted only of goods or a few coins. Poor families exercised less control over the choice of marriage partners. And the poor could not expect to live as long as their wealthy neighbours. These differences remind us that while it is correct to emphasize the power of the peasant family, it is just as important to note that conditions forced many villagers to act on their own. Economic need, illness, or death broke up families, and widows often remarried, changing the composition of the family.

The logic of the peasant economy thus created a particular kind of community. To begin with, the goal of virtually every family was to maintain the property, extend it if possible, and pass it on to their children. Maintenance involved meeting the obligations tied to the holding, such as rents, services, and fines, as well as farming the land year in year out. Losses caused by centrifugal forces, such as land sales or gifts to family members, had to be counteracted. By necessity, therefore, a second feature of this community was its intense economic activity. Villages bustled with enterprise. Craftsmen and other specialists subsisted on wages. Most tenants looked to work and small enterprises to help make ends meet while the better off bought petty luxuries and hired servants.

A final characteristic was the hierarchy of power. Village elites were essential to the king and landlords. For the latter, they ensured the collection of rents, the performance of services, and the levying of fines. They ran the manorial court, a hybrid of seigneurial and communal authority. It met every three weeks or so and regulated lordship and landholding for the lord while also dealing with village issues such as agriculture and social order. A handful of rich families repeatedly supplied court officers and jurors, personal pledges for debts and misdemeanours, and witnesses to transactions. This public power gave them even greater leverage over their neighbours. Their relations with their lords were not always harmonious, but they were firmly woven into the fabric of seigneurial authority. They formed the bottom tier of the administrative hierarchy stretching between king and subjects. As royal officers and jurors, they assessed lands, levied taxes, settled disputes, recruited soldiers, and investigated a host of questions.

At all levels of village society, the family represented the basic unit of production, kinship, and social interaction. It is difficult to see into peasants' households because they did not leave records opening their personal lives to view. What can be known must be reconstructed from sources compiled for other purposes, usually for the benefit of the landlord. Yet village studies are casting more and more light on this obscure area. Family meant the nuclear group of parents and children. Grandparents usually did not live long enough to form multi-generational households. When they did, it was likely, at least among the moderately well-off and wealthy families, that their children had established their own residences. A powerful cultural bias towards independent residences for each couple has been found in every study of village communities. Marriage was therefore as crucial a moment in the household's life-cycle as in the couple's.

Marriage meant the subordination of the wife to the husband. Just as the village as a whole was structured hierarchically, so were the lives of individuals There was a clear and important distinction between the rights and powers of men and women. Men led public, communal lives centred on working the land and governing the community. Women's lives centred on the household, child-rearing, and work. They were barred from public office. They did not appear in court as often as men. They did not usually hold property and only inherited land when there were no male heirs. One study has shown that they were more often sellers than buyers of land, and in any case participated in the land market far less frequently than men. Widowhood brought somewhat greater independence. A widow held her dower for her lifetime, usually a third of her deceased husband's property though it could amount to the entire holding in some villages. Many widows successfully worked their dower-holdings, calling on their sons or hiring men to do the ploughing when necessary. Community leaders and landlords, however, pressured widows to remarry, to reassure themselves that the holding would produce its share of communal agriculture and manorial services. Studies of the sixteenth and seventeenth centuries, moreover, show that widows, especially those with young children, tended to be amongst the poorest members of the community and most in need of assistance.

Labour was similarly differentiated according to gender. *Piers Plowman* catches the flavour of this division when Piers decides to set out on pilgrimage after he has done his ploughing. The women ask how they can help, and he replies that they can sew up sacks, mend garments, spin flax, and teach their daughters how to do likewise. Indeed, Piers' wife is named 'Workwhile-there-is-time'. Meanwhile, Piers and a gang of men dig, ditch, plough, and weed. Farming thus absorbed most of their energy, and families depended on the contribution of the entire household, including women, children, and servants. Heavy work, such as ploughing, carting, or land clearing, as well as specialized crafts such as carpentry, masonry, thatching, or smithing were performed almost exclusively by males. Women ordinarily worked in the fields planting or weeding, but turned out in larger numbers when the season demanded many hands, such as at harvest time, to stack or bind the sheaves. Only a few women lived as full-time agricultural labourers, moving with the work and receiving the same wages as men. Most worked close to home, particularly if they had small children. Women cultivated the family croft, a garden attached to the house, to add fruit, vegetables, and eggs to the family's diet. They supplemented the family income with earnings from dairying, spinning, or other tasks. Judith Bennett has found that a surprisingly large number of unfree (see below, p. 35) women on Ramsey abbey's estate bought their marriage rights themselves, rather than have their fathers pay, and probably earned the money independently. Brewing is a good example of women's work. It required only simple tools found in every household so that women could do it either full- or part-time in the home. In the end, however, it was men who regulated the enterprise, for women were never 'aletasters', those responsible for assessing the quality of ale that was sold. Gender also influenced inheritance customs. Very few peasants could, or did, bequeath their land. Inheritance worked more or less automatically, the land passing on the death of a tenant to his or her rightful heir(s). Primogeniture, a system in which the land was inherited by the eldest son, predominated, though some villages practised ultimogeniture or borough-English, in which land descended to the youngest son. The former ensured that an adult would assume the obligations of the holding while the latter ensured that the last born and least independent would have access to the family's resources. Elsewhere, notably East Anglia and Kent, peasants practised partible inheritance, dividing the property equally among the male children. There were local variations. Villagers in Brigstock, Northamptonshire, for example, left inherited land to the youngest son and any purchased land to the eldest. Some brothers in the village of Redgrave, Suffolk, tried to compensate for the centrifugal force of partible inheritance by holding and working land jointly. Daughters or sisters, however, inherited only if they had no brother to take over the holding and usually divided the tenement equally among themselves. Families also wanted to support non-inheriting children, giving dowries to daughters and land to younger sons whenever possible. Sons could also be provided for by sending them to school or the church. While peasants preferred to pass their holdings on to their children, fertility and economics determined whether they were able to do so. Some died without descendants. Others sold their land and emigrated.

Manorial records reveal an extremely active peasant land market. Family possession was not sacrosanct. When need dictated, peasants sold pieces of their holdings. Indeed, the turnover in East Anglian villages could be astonishing. In Coltishall, Norfolk, 69 per cent of the 900 parcels traded between 1275 and 1349 were less than half an acre. Altogether, it has been estimated that there were some 2,250 transactions involving about 1,150 acres of land between 1275 and 1405. Sales reached an even higher intensity at Redgrave, Suffolk, where villagers engaged in 2,756 transactions between 1260 and 1349 involving a minimum of 1,305 acres.

Such a lively market obviously had profound consequences for families and the community. Several things happened. First, sales deepened inequality among the peasantry. In times of hardship, smallholders parted with portions of their holdings hoping to recover them when conditions improved. Land transactions thus escalated in periods of poor harvests. At Brigstock, for example, early in the century, only about one transaction was recorded in each court session. Yet that climbed to 2.6 during the famine years of 1314–16 and then went up to about 3.4 just before the Black Death arrived. Bruce Campbell's study of the land market in Coltishall similarly found that land transfers were harvest related. The proceeds helped families through bad weather and high prices. Yet when conditions improved, they were forced to repurchase their land in a seller's market, if they could. This market pattern put the poorly endowed even more at the mercy of large holders than they ordinarily were and accentuated disparities in wealth. Smallholders were trapped in a vicious cycle powered by social as well as agricultural conditions. Secondly, only a few families entered the market to enlarge their holdings or provide settlements for their children. Given the expense of buying land, such motives were largely confined to the rich. Very few smallholders could hope to rise in village society by playing the market. Thirdly, not all of the transactions involved strangers. Families used the market for intra-familial transfers as well as outright sales. Retirement or pre-mortem inheritances were worked out through the court, and some families wove elaborate strategies of transfers, sales, and leases in order to keep property among blood kin and in-laws. Finally, the land market contributed to the prosperity of the village by stimulating trade.

Despite sales, residence in most villages was remarkably stable prior to the Black Death. Peasant mobility was a feature of the medieval countryside and some smallholders at any given time emigrated to seek work, land, marriage, or education. In a century and a half beginning in 1311, however, Holywell lost only thirty-eight persons through permanent emigration while 35 per cent of the families maintained continuous residence for three or more generations and another 23 per cent for two to three generations, or up to about eighty years. The preference for inheritance meant that at the core of every village there existed a stable block of families. Since they were usually from the elite, they inherited a hold on power as well as property. The village community and the landlord likewise valued the continuity of possession that helped to stabilize the community and payment of rents. Inheritance gave meaning to community by reproducing the social fabric and property relations generation after generation.

Peasant families thus lived and worked within a matrix of social, economic, and legal customs enforced by the community. Their needs as well as their activities were bound up, and to some degree subordinated to, the work of the village as a whole. The degree of subordination corresponded to the strength of communality. Individual families had to adjust their work to conform to those customs.

Field systems, that is regulations for ploughing, cropping, harvesting, gleaning, fallowing, and pasturing arable fields, are the most familiar examples of communal control. In the common-field system of the mid-lands, with their nucleated villages, expansive open-fields, and strong manorial authority, agricultural practice was clearly directed through community bylaws. The primary concern was the rotation of crops to allow the arable to lie fallow every so often and recoup from cropping. By the early fourteenth century, three-field systems, in which the arable was divided into three fields and crops rotated so that a field lay fallow once every three years, were widespread. In practice, however, rotation could be extremely complicated, based not on fields, but rather on subdivisions of the fields, called furlongs. The point was, how often would a given plot of land be fallowed? In the three-field system it was once in three years, but the term could be reduced to once in four, six, or even eight years for intensive cultivation. In eastern Norfolk, a region of agricultural innovation, some demesne lands lay fallow only once every twelve years and some were never fallowed. Tenants usually held their land in strips scattered throughout the fields and intermingled with those of the other villagers. Communality was forced on them by the very pattern of landholding. Hence, the village tried to certify that neighbours would have free access to their holdings, that they would not take one another's crops, that they would not cart their grain away at night, that they would not pasture their animals on their fallow in the autumn until all the grain had been harvested, and that no one except the very poor would collect the grain that had fallen to the ground during the harvest (gleaning). Neighbourliness was not taken for granted. The rules highlight the points of friction that were inevitable in such a tightly bound agricultural community. They aimed simultaneously at dampening conflict and encouraging productivity.

Another goal was the preservation of village resources. A balanced agricultural ecology was necessary for satisfactory production. Communities thus regulated the use of scarce resources such as woodland, wasteland, or meadows by restricting the cutting of trees or limiting the pasturage of pigs in woods. Pasture itself was essential to raise oxen or horses, as well as market animals such as sheep. The shortage of pasture after 1300 is clearly indicated by the fact that pasture land was often two to three times as valuable as arable in the same village, while meadowland could be worth eight times as much as arable. These figures, however, do not necessarily indicate an agricultural crisis. It has been shown in Norfolk, for example, that highly intensive agriculture could be practised and high productivity achieved even with extremely low arable/animal ratios. Differences in land values could also reflect different marketing strategies. The high cost of animals and the scattering of strips encouraged neighbours to collaborate in ploughing and other work. Very few peasants could afford to own a full plough-team of oxen or horses. Teamwork of various sorts was therefore required to get the fields ploughed and cultivated. The pressure to harvest the grain quickly demanded a similar kind of synergy involving the labour of the entire community.

Every village wanted to foster its survival and the productivity of the fields but the force of communal custom varied from region to region and village to village. It was much less powerful, for example, in Eastern England, East Anglia and Kent, than in the midlands. Tenurial freedom and a highly active land market produced irregular and intensive field systems. Strips were not distributed evenly between fields or sub-fields, so that a common pattern of rotation would not have made any sense. The only discernible common-field element in parts of East Anglia was common pasturing after the harvest. Even in the midlands, communalism was limited and did not stifle individual initiative or obliterate social distinctions. It was only one aspect of the social context in which villagers made economic decisions.

How productive was agriculture? For the middle ages, productivity can be measured only through grain yields, since information about labour is so sketchy. Documents permitting, yields can be calculated either *per seed*, the harvest divided by the amount sown, or *per acre*, the harvest divided by the acreage sown. Around 1300, the author of an agricultural treatise called *Husbandry* reckoned that for every bushel planted wheat ought to yield five bushels, rye seven, barley eight, and oats four. Walter of Henley, another agricultural observer writing around 1286, did not estimate yields, but he did comment that the costs arising from ploughing, sowing, and harvesting were so great that sales of wheat from a three-fold yield would return only enough to break even.

Henley was unduly pessimistic while *Husbandry* was overly optimistic. Actual yields fell between these figures and fluctuated greatly from year to year, region to region, field to field, and perhaps even plot to plot. The yield of wheat per seed usually ranged from 3 to 5 bushels, rye 2 to 4, barley 3 to 5, and oats 2 to 4. At the average rate of sowing of 2½ bushels per acre, wheat might have thus produced between 7½ and 12½ bushels. If wheat were selling at 6s. a quarter (8 bushels, or 9d. a quarter), then the harvest from one acre would be worth between about 5s. 7½d. and 9s. 4½d.; if at 5s., it would be worth only between about 4s. 8d. and 7s. 10d. These are gross returns, before costs such as seed corn have been deducted. The variations even in a calculation as simple as this one demonstrate the uncertainties of medieval agriculture. The farmer's income depended on many factors: the quality of the soil, the amount of grain sown, the weather, the quality of the harvest, and the price of grain, which of course depended ultimately on other factors such as the size of the harvest, the time of year, and the overall demand. In periods of highly changeable weather, harvests, and prices, uncertainty could turn to despair.

Techniques for improving output were known and applied. They fell into three overlapping categories. The first was capital improvement, of which the most common was enclosure. Some lords with sufficient power and wealth could consolidate their arable land, enclose it with hedges or ditches, and take it out of the common-field system. More than half of twenty-two demesnes in the Chiltern Hills, for instance, were completely, and the remainder partially, enclosed. Land in enclosures was far more valuable than land in common fields. From the thirteenth century onward, the Berkeleys of Gloucestershire bought freehold land, consolidated it in the fields with demesne land, and then enclosed it. When Maurice de Berkeley forfeited his estate in 1322 for rebelling against Edward II, he had 325 acres in enclosures ranging in size from 1 to 60 acres. The average value of these enclosed lands was 10½d. an acre and could go as high as 12d. an acre, considerably beyond the 3d. to 4d. an acre recorded for land lying in common in the same villages. Another kind of capital improvement was manuring, that is, improving the quality of the soil by the application of marl (a highly fertile clay soil), dung, sand, or night-soil. Because of the costs of purchasing, digging, or collecting the substance, carting it to the fields, and applying it to the land, manuring was not a practical option for everyone.

Another kind of improvement was simply a change in agricultural practice. Surveyors in 1322 specifically attributed the remarkably high value of land in the Berkeley enclosures to the fact that they were not subject to communal control. That meant that the lord could vary the use of the land, for example, by intensifying the cropping and reducing the fallow time. Lords could similarly increase the amount of seed sown. Although that had the effect of reducing the yield per seed, it did help to choke off weeds and increase the yield per acre. Enclosures also enabled the lord to plough the land frequently, keeping down the weeds. Some lords even went beyond these measures. During the early fourteenth century, Battle abbey created the manor of Marley in Sussex by buying out small freeholders and making small closes. In those closes it practised convertible husbandry by shifting production between pasture and arable in a complex rotation spread over several years. In eastern Norfolk, large acreages of legumes were planted to help maintain the quality of the soil. They also permitted the stall-feeding of livestock. Stall-feeding was important not only because it helped the animals to survive through the winter, but because it facilitated the collection of manure.

Finally, as these practices emphasize, the most important factor in improving agricultural output was manual labour. All of these techniques were labour intensive. The erection of enclosures, manuring, stall-feeding, repeated fallow ploughings, and mundane activities such as sowing and weeding demanded constant work.

English farming down to the Black Death was not stagnant. Yet such improvements, though widely known, were not widely adopted. Indeed, they remained exceptional during the middle ages. Local conditions –

natural, economic, and social – had to be right before they would be tried. In eastern Norfolk, there was a high concentration of fertile, easily worked soil along with a dense population that provided cheap labour and a buoyant demand for grain. Producers had access as well to the voracious London market, which helped to keep prices up and repay investment and labour costs. Communal and seigneurial interference was minimal. This freedom was important because it allowed peasants to use their labour as they wished. Information about agricultural innovations comes from demesnes and little is known about how peasants actually cultivated their plots. Yet East Anglian peasants had to apply similar techniques to their tiny holdings to make them economically viable. With higher yields, they could survive on smaller plots.

Innovations, therefore, would most likely be adopted in two different circumstances. The first was in regions that had good soil, a high degree of peasant freedom, and access to markets. Landlords would be encouraged to improve their demesne yields because rents from free tenants were low while the high population guaranteed low labour costs. These conditions could be found in East Anglia, Kent, the region around the Wash, and the Thames valley. Outside those areas, improvements were isolated in pockets of enclosures created by lords such as Battle abbey or the Berkeley family. They had the authority and resources necessary to create enclosures in the first place, and the wealth to hire sufficient labour to make them fruitful. Most peasants, bound by the needs of the village community and the authority of their landlord, could not find the time or resources to undertake extensive changes. In other words, even in areas conducive to improvement, new agricultural techniques did not result in a breakthrough to a stable, high surplus, market-oriented system of agriculture.

The determining factor was the relationship between rents, wages, and seigneurial income. If they could not obtain through rents the level of income they wanted, landlords tried to increase their demesne profits. That had been the motive behind the adoption of high farming or demesne farming after 1200. Agricultural experimentation was a further step in that direction. It was taken only where control over the peasantry was feeble and/or demesne produce was small; where, in other words, the traditional kinds of extraction did not meet the landlords' needs. Like high farming, moreover, agricultural innovation reached its peak in the first half of the fourteenth century, when high population and prices, combined with low wages, made it economically feasible. Otherwise, landlords were interested in taking a sufficient income with as little trouble to themselves as possible.

That meant collecting rents. Families and villages functioned within a framework of authority erected by lordship. Every peasant in England had a landlord and was obliged to pay some kind of rent. The individual burden, however, varied.

To begin with, the peasant population was divided crudely into two groups: the free and unfree. The line was drawn over access to the common law. The free could avail themselves of the king's writs and royal justice while the unfree, or villeins, were excluded from royal courts and only had recourse to their landlords' courts. From the time of Magna Carta onwards, free rents and obligations had been fixed. If a landlord tried to raise them to meet rising prices, free tenants could drag him to court and have them halted. In contrast, unfree rents rose along with prices after 1200. Furthermore, the quality of rents differed. Free rents were usually in cash or kind, that is in goods, with perhaps some light labour services. The unfree owed labour services in addition to rents, though the amount and kinds of labour were not uniform. By the late thirteenth century, money rent predominated everywhere in England so that on average, unfree tenants paid at least half of their dues in cash. Labour could comprise as little as a quarter or less of their total burden. Nevertheless, it was a significant difference.

Legal theory placed villeins entirely at the will of their lords. They were viewed as a special kind of chattel, subject to the lord's economic needs. They were bound to the soil and had no right to move without the permission of their lord. Their lands and goods were not their own, but belonged rather to their lord. They could not, therefore, bequeath or inherit except with their lord's consent. Free alienation of land was denied them, and they could not acquire free land. A villein had to get his lord's permission to marry off his daughters or to send a son into the church. Permission was likewise necessary to sell livestock or ploughs. On the tenant's death, the family gave up a heriot, the best animal. On inheritance, the new tenant owed an entry fine, which could be adjusted at the lord's will. The law thus gave a landlord broad discretion over the lands, goods, lives, and families of his servile servants.

The division of society into two legally unequal groups was evident at every turn in fourteenth-century England. In 1297, the nobility called on this distinction to protest against Edward I's taxation. They claimed that by taking taxes without their consent, he was disinheriting them and reducing them to villeinage. Their indignation made clear their perception of the differences in status. The bishop of Exeter made the same point in 1337 protesting against royal encroachments on his temporalities. He declared that the bishops of Exeter held those temporalities of the king and his predecessors by homage and that any arbitrary change in the tenure would bring a new servility (*novel servage*) and disinheritance of the church. Others, such as Walter of Henley, urged lords to moderate their treatment of tenants. Piers Plowman echoed this advice, warning the knight not to mistreat his tenants and bondmen lest he place his soul in danger. Seigneurial oppression could thus be a subject of priestly confession. Knowing first hand the effects of tenurial distinctions, villeins embarked on sophisticated and costly legal battles to prove that they were free tenants and roll back increased rents and services. These views are important not because they indicate how lordship was actually exercised, but because they are acknowledgements of the power of landlords over the unfree.

In fact, by the early fourteenth century, landlords did not fully exercise the powers accorded them by legal theory. Villeins bought, sold, and leased land, married free men and women, and took on free holdings. Manorial courts adopted legal actions used in royal courts. Unfree rents and services had stabilized and were no longer climbing as they had during the thirteenth century.

Yet villeinage had not died and landlords had not relinquished authority to village communities. The point for landlords was not to exploit every legal prerogative to the fullest, but rather to emphasize where power lay and use it to gain economic leverage. They did not need and indeed had reasons not to squeeze every last penny from villeins as long as they received sufficient profits. Lords recognized that there were limits to what they could take from tenants before either jeopardizing the peasants' productivity or driving them to rebellion. Lordship was thus contoured according to the abilities of the landlord, the size of the estate, the history of the village, and the customs of the region in which the landlord and tenants lived. It was as varied as the landscape. Lightest in northern and eastern England, the burdens gradually increased into the midlands. The village, moreover, functioned as a unit, oblivious of legal distinctions. Agricultural demands and social forces melded free and unfree into a single society.

Nevertheless, the differences between the free and unfree were important for the lord's revenues. Villeinage gave lordship economic flexibility because lords profited from it in many different ways. Court proceeds, for example, fattened their profits. On two manors belonging to the abbey of Crowland, fines rose 148 per cent between 1302 and 1315, while the abbey of Bury St Edmunds acceded to the conveyancing of unfree land clearly to reap the fines generated by such transactions. In a vigorous land market such as that of East Anglia, even small fines on the huge volume of sales or leases could produce a handsome return. Furthermore, the total burden of villein rents was on average two and a half times greater than that of free rents. Within particular villages, the difference could be even more dramatic. At Thornbury, near the Severn in Gloucestershire, John Pyl, a customary tenant, held a virgate of land (approximately 30 acres) in 1322. Over the year, he owed his lord 50 days of ploughing and 220 days of manual labour, as well as 8s. 4d. in money rent. Altogether, when the labour service was commuted to cash, his obligations came to 33s. or about 13.2d. an acre. Within the same village, a freeman, Robert Geffray, also held a virgate of land but only owed a rent of 7s. 1d. or about 2.8d. an acre, less than a quarter of the burden of his neighbour. The gap between the two widened with the inclusion of irregular levies to which villeins were liable, such as heriots, entry fines, and fees for marriage or livestock sales. Elsewhere, the contrast was not so striking. Just to the north of Thornbury, in Berkeley hundred, the average rent per acre of unfree holdings from 10 to 60 acres hovered between 7.4d. and 7.6d. Free rents ranged from 5.3d. an acre for the larger holdings up to 7d. for smaller ones. Rates for smallholders (those holding less than 10 acres) really jumped: free tenants paid 21.2d. an acre while customary tenants paid only 10.8d. The burden of rent increased appreciably as the size of the holding diminished. Greater profits could also be had from life tenants. Within Berkeley hundred there was a large number of life tenants whose leases came to 12d. and more an acre, close to the rate paid by the Thornbury villein.

Two things stand out. The first is the variability of rents, whether free or unfree. Lordship had to be opportunistic, because, as a second feature of this sample shows, neither free nor unfree rents matched the market value of the land. This is clearly evident in the disparity between rents and life-leases. Leases were attractive precisely because the lord could charge close to the prevailing market rate. Seigneurial extraction stopped short of full economic exploitation. The village land market, life tenures, and leases of unfree land reveal that peasants could expect some return over and above what was taken in rent and what was needed for survival. Thus, a landlord such as the abbot of Tavistock converted some tenancies to leaseholds precisely in order to profit from the high demand for land. In 1339 he hoped to lease 976 acres of arable, 460 acres of pasture, and 418 acres of meadow, which had been worth a mere £2, for £10 a year.

The landlord's takings from hereditary tenants were thus limited, but they were also fixed despite harvest and price fluctuations. For any given acre of tenement, the tenant's profits were variable, not the lord's. This contrast, on top of the sheer weight of rents, services, and fees, must have made lordship hateful for the unfree, even if the rents did not meet the full market value of the land. It helps to explain the antagonism between lords and tenants that lay behind villeins' persistent efforts to win freedom.

The medieval village was thus a complex society, made up of several overlapping spheres of engagement and obligation. It might be best to try and see these through a peasant's eyes, as she made decisions for herself and those close to her. The most immediate sphere was her family – her husband, children, parents, and in-laws. The woman had to obey her husband, work with him when necessary, care for the children, and contribute to the family purse. She could count on certain rights in the land and house when her husband died and would be entitled to land of her own if her parents died without sons. She expected her children to pitch in and help with family work, gradually expanding their responsibilities and chores as they grew older. Her own work brought her into the sphere of the market, which was a matter of buying and selling small commodities and working for extra pennies – grain from the holding; beer she brewed herself; vegetables, fruit, or eggs from the croft; or carding and spinning wool. If she was an heiress or widow, she might lease her land or enter into a contract with her children to guarantee support in her old age in return for the use of her land. Such dealings entered the sphere of lordship. Whether as wife, heiress, or widow, she was a tenant. She had to meet the rents and services to keep her land. It was that simple. Every three weeks or so, the meeting of the manorial court would remind her of her obligations. She paid fees for her lord's permission to marry or remarry, to sell livestock, or to part with her land. She paid fines for breaching his authority, failing to perform her services, or brewing 'small' beer. The lord was an unseen party to virtually every transaction she entered into. His presence was not as much cancerous as arthritic: a throbbing reminder that she did not have complete control of her life and produce. The manorial court, however, also encompassed the sphere of social interaction in the village, regulating daily, private affairs. When she entered court, the peasant was confronted by men who were at once the lord's officials and the village elite, the hierarchy of power that shaped her social life and market activities. She would look to these men to borrow money, to sell land, to hire her children as servants, or to find a pledge for fines.

Our peasant, therefore, had to cope with several interrelated forces which pushed and pulled her in different directions. If we could see her material priorities, the market and lordship probably ranked first. They were so deeply intertwined that they dominated her economic choices and actions. This is not to say that she did not feel a deep loyalty and affection for her family, or a solidarity with the village community. Ephemeral emotions are hard to catch in the crude net of manorial sources. Yet the need to maintain her tenement, coupled with a strong desire to support her family, kept up the pressure to buy and sell. She did not consume as a modern individual does, to satisfy personal desire, but rather to meet objective needs.

The village community was the essential cell in the English medieval economy. The wealth it produced was destined primarily for the peasant family and the lord. Given the structure of these villages and the distribution of their surplus, it can be readily seen how alien or unnatural external demands for a share of the surplus must have seemed to the members of the community, lord and tenant alike. The king had to work hard at justifying the additional expropriation. No one in the village, including the lord, had an obvious economic interest in the intrusion. Of course, only the lords had any say in the matter, and the king had to appeal to other interests they shared to gain taxes. The landlords demonstrated their economic alliance with villagers by continually pointing out the hardships created by taxation, lamenting the poverty they caused, and warning of peasant unrest. There was, of course, a great deal of rhetorical posturing in these protests. But they none the less reveal baronial sensitivity to the economic condition of the peasantry on whom they depended. It made the king's task all the more difficult.

4

MARKETS AND TOWNS

———— • ————

While family and the village community formed the heart of the agrarian economy, trade was its lifeblood. Tenants needed money to pay their rents and buy commodities. Smallholders needed food. Lords wanted to buy luxuries, build churches or castles, and hire servants. In meeting these demands, towns grew and flourished. As centres of trade and authority, they were clearly differentiated from villages and offered opportunities and services that were unavailable in villages. A sophisticated marketing system thus stretched into every corner of the countryside, linking the brisk trade in village grain, goods, and land to market towns and large cities. At the centre stood London. It dwarfed all other towns and during Edward's reign gradually emerged as the political and cultural capital of England as well as its commercial hub. Internal trade, moreover, offered an inviting target to a government bent on tapping every resource in its drive for war as well as to lords hoping to fatten their revenues. This chapter outlines the network of markets and trade before turning to an investigation of towns and urban society.

The growing population and the consequent heating up of the economy over the thirteenth century led to the propagation of markets. Though the overwhelming majority of people lived as farmers, a strong demand for foodstuffs was generated from four sources. The first was the village community. Smallholders who did not have enough land to feed themselves had to buy food. Some peasants planted wheat, because it fetched the highest prices, and sold it to raise money to pay their rents and purchase cheaper grains such as rye, barley, or oats for themselves. There were likewise different grades of bread from the fine simnel or white wheat bread to coarse rye bread. Peasants often had to play on these marginal differences to get them through the year. It should be added that lords were conspicuous as sellers rather than as buyers of grain. Most consumed at least a portion of the produce of their estates and marketed the surplus for profit. Demand for grain came secondly from non-producers in the village or surrounding countryside. Servants, craftsmen, and workers needed to buy food. Towns added to this demand. Despite many rural attributes, English towns survived by importing food from the countryside. Furthermore, though small by continental standards, they were numerous, making the aggregate demand considerable. Finally, some grain was exported overseas.

Landlords took advantage of this demand by establishing markets. By the middle of the thirteenth century, all markets and fairs had to be licensed by the king. Royal supervision was intended to guarantee fair trading, the use of uniform weights and measures, the punishment of offences, and the profits of the market. Markets were held on one or two days a week, and the crown stipulated that neighbouring markets should not be held within two or three days or located within 6⅔ miles of one another. These regulations were often ignored. Densely populated regions like East Anglia or the Lincolnshire coast teemed with markets. The king also chartered fairs. Held once or twice a year for a period of several days or weeks, usually in the summer, fairs attracted a wider array of traders and products than did local markets.

A royal charter did not signal the initiation of trade. Rather, it marked a lord's attempt to capitalize on existing commerce by having it conducted at a fixed time and place under his authority. Lords profited by levying tolls and collecting fines for the enforcement of market regulations. Though new markets merely crowded in on older ones and sapped existing trade, lords continued to establish markets right up to the Black Death. By that time, about 1,200 had been licensed though many unlicensed, informal markets flourished as well. They were sprinkled throughout the countryside, particularly along the coasts, waterways, or main thoroughfares, so that most villagers had a market within easy reach. In Derbyshire, for example, 28 markets altogether conducted 33 days of business each week, while 24 fairs during the summer lasted a total of 120 days. On average, there was a market for every 36 square miles, so that most people lived within about 4.2 miles of a market, compared to 3 and 2.8 miles in Warwickshire and Lincolnshire respectively. There appear to have been regional clusters of markets in Nottinghamshire focused on towns that held Saturday markets. Traders could easily make a circuit of surrounding towns during the weekly markets and converge on Saturday for the most intense and assorted business.

Two overlapping networks developed. The first consisted of non-

specialized markets, dealing primarily in foodstuffs, victualling, small manufactures like cloth, leather, or pottery, and general merchandise like coal,
salt, or fish – goods that were not readily available in every village. They
testify to the vitality of local commerce. Indeed, it has been shown that
market structures deeply affected the patterns of production and accumulation. Smallholders tended to concentrate on goods for survival or purely
infra-village trade, while wealthy peasants could invest in products such as
livestock or malting grains which opened up to them wider economic
possibilities. Professor Hilton has referred to this relationship between villages and towns as 'complementary economies'. Cuxham in Oxfordshire,
for example, obtained hay, livestock, timber, and stone from villages in the
surrounding countryside, though it might also reach further afield, to Spain,
France, or Germany, for iron and millstones. Grain was sold as far away as
London.

The second network consisted of long-distance trade in food, wool,
wine, cloth, and luxuries that earned high returns for both producers and
merchants. Concentrated in towns or fairs, it was dominated by merchants
rather than the chapmen or tradesmen who were familiar figures in villages
and market towns. The networks were interdependent. Petty commodity
trade anchored by local markets fed into regional commerce which in turn
funnelled products from the countryside to towns and from there to
London and overseas.

Specialization in production, moreover, created regional interdepen-
dencies. The north-eastern counties of Cheshire and Lancashire, for
instance, were not well suited for growing wheat and had to import it from
other areas. Conversely, the region specialized in salt, which was sold
all across England, as well as in livestock, dairy products, and leather
goods. Thus, not all trade was localized. As consumers or grain producers,
lords travelled far to find the best markets. The prior of St Augustine's,
Gloucester, sold grain at Cardiff in the early fourteenth century. Durham
priory bought furs in Darlington, spice and wine in Boston, and almonds in
Hartlepool. They paid dearly to ship goods purchased in Boston back to
Durham, about 150 miles by a circuitous land and sea route. Both routes had
their dangers; pirates lurked along the coasts while transportation by road
was slow and expensive. Despite these liabilities, neither house hesitated to
seek out distant markets for their commercial needs.

Markets competed fiercely for trade. In 1330, the town of Dunwich,
located on the coast of Suffolk, petitioned the king and council in parliament for assistance against its neighbour Sir Edmund de Clavering. Clavering was lord of the small port of Walberswick, less than three miles north of
Dunwich, and eager to enlarge his town's business. The citizens of
Dunwich complained that Clavering and his men had forced boats to turn

away from Dunwich and land at Walberswick, killed the keeper of the port, unjustly taxed boats for anchoring in Dunwich Haven, and interfered with the jurisdiction of Dunwich court. They furthermore lamented the encroachment of the market at Blythburgh, just inland from Walberswick, and belonging to another Clavering, Sir John. Earlier, they had condemned the foundation of a market at Southwold, north of Walberswick, which had attracted merchants, trade, and boats that ordinarily would have gone to Dunwich. Their complaints underscore the intensity of competition between small markets in an era when trade was not growing as fast as it once had. Throughout the fourteenth century, Dunwich petitioned against neighbouring markets and fairs. The elements, however, proved to be even greater enemies than rival markets. The harbour silted up, boats were diverted to other ports, and in 1328 a storm destroyed much of the town, forcing it to seek a reduction in the town farm.

These towns can be roughly classified in three categories according to size and function. Small market towns were oriented to the surrounding countryside, thriving on the commerce generated by peasant production and consumption. Most of the inhabitants lived on trade rather than manufacturing or crafts. Winchcombe in Gloucestershire was such a town. In 1381 it had a taxable population of 201 (meaning that the actual population was between 800 and 1,000). Within a five-mile radius, there were thirty-two villages, whose combined taxable population came to 1,418 (5,700–7,100). Winchcombe was a commercial magnet, providing a location for trading and hiring.

Larger markets that linked regions to the country as a whole formed a second type of town. Romford, on the royal manor of Havering, Essex, provides an example. Located on the road between London and Chelmsford, it was the primary market for the immediate region but was also a conduit for sending produce, such as livestock, down to London and bringing in London wealth. The inhabitants, like those at Winchcombe, were clearly townsfolk, devoted to victualling, clothing, trade, and small crafts. An impressive example of this kind of town was King's Lynn, on the coast of Norfolk. It drew grain from nearby villages as well as from distant towns such as Cambridge, Peterborough, Huntingdon, Crowland, and Ely, as much as forty miles away by river or road. The grain was then shipped on, either overseas or to the insatiable London market. Chester, a town of perhaps 4,000, similarly acted as the hub for trade in the north-east. The small town of Dunwich, whose trade the Claverings had so harassed, seems to have been an intermediate port for fish and other commodities. Their petitions mentioned fish, herring, and livestock and bemoaned the loss of business from victualling fishing and cargo boats. Although overshadowed in long-distance trade, the town of Gloucester was none the less an important marketing centre for nearby villages for whom it served as a primary market. Beyond that area, Gloucester merchants met competition from other market towns though they clearly engaged in reciprocal trade with their competitors. Most trade involved grain, bread, and ale, but traders also bought iron, leather, and wool to supply the town's main industries and sources of prosperity. Perhaps the most famous of such market towns was Stratford upon Avon in Warwickshire. Founded by the Bishop of Worcester in 1196 at a favourable location for communication by road or river, the town grew by leaps and bounds over the thirteenth century. Markets, fairs, and courts were added, so that in the early fourteenth century it was a thriving urban community of more than 300 tenants. Oxford market offers a picture of trading in such towns. The town regulated the selling of hogs and pigs, ale, pottery, gloves, furs, cloth, coarse bread, white bread, dried and fresh fish, poultry, leather, cheese, eggs, milk, rushes and brooms, grain, fruit and vegetables, herbs, dishes, thorns and bushes, meat, shoes, bows and arrows, armour, cutlery, saddles and bridles, parchment and books, spices, wine, timber, and wool. Salt, tin, iron, and other products were also commonly traded. The currents of this trade enabled larger towns to live off the countryside, and, indeed, to grow and prosper.

What did these market towns have in common? First, they were favourably located with respect to communications and other markets. Second, they were close to areas of production. The towns' tradesmen and merchants were familiar figures in the countryside. It was vital that they travel to outlying villages to drum up business, and they complained bitterly when-ever unscrupulous lords, bent on controlling the market, prevented them from doing so.

Major centres of population, trade, and government represent the third type of town. What is remarkable in England is how few really large towns there were. It was not at all heavily urbanized. After London, the largest cities were Bristol, Norwich, York, and Lincoln. Some indication of their relative wealth can be gained from tax assessments. Thirty-two towns were assessed at £300 and above in 1334. The assessments certainly underestimate the towns' true wealth, but assuming the underestimation is uniform, they can be used to rank the ten wealthiest towns as in Table 1. As this list indicates, most wealthy towns were either ports or centres of cloth-making. It also demonstrates London's commanding position. Its assessed value was greater than the combined assessments of the next nine towns on the list. Small towns had even lower valuations. King's Lynn was assessed at £500, reflecting its commercial vitality, Stratford at £131, and Winchcombe at £106 10s. Dunwich was assessed at £120, Blythburgh and Walberswick at £110 10s., and Southwold at only £54 2s.

The size of towns is harder to calculate. It is now estimated that at the

Table 1. *Ranking of English towns by tax assessments*

1.	London	£11,000
2.	Bristol	£2,200
3.	York	£1,620
4.	Newcastle upon Tyne	£1,333
5.	Boston	£1,100
6.	Great Yarmouth	£1,000
7.	Lincoln	£1,000
8.	Norwich	£946
9.	Oxford	£914
10.	Shrewsbury	£800

(*Source:* Glasscock, 'England *circa* 1334', 184.)

beginning of the fourteenth century, the population of London may have been as high as 90,000. One estimate has put the population of Norwich at 25,000. York may have had a population of around 20,000, Bristol 10–12,000, Winchester (assessed at about £515) 10–12,000, Lincoln 7,000, and Boston 5,000. These figures are constantly being revised as new research is undertaken. What is clear is that there were very few towns of more than 5,000 inhabitants, and that the majority of townsfolk lived in towns of around 500–1,000.

Many residents were newcomers. Because living conditions in the towns were so atrocious and the death rates so high, towns could not have maintained themselves without a constant injection of new inhabitants to replenish the population. From one-third to one-half of the residents in Lincolnshire towns in 1332, for example, were immigrants. A similar pattern has been found in the West Midlands, where immigration could supply as much as half of the population of growing towns such as Stratford upon Avon, while in smaller market communities the percentage could drop to a fifth or sixth. Immigrants to small towns usually came from the immediate neighbourhood, but those going to larger towns such as Lincoln often travelled more than thirty miles. Immigrants and investors from distant counties such as Yorkshire or Dorset even turned up in the small village-town of Godmanchester in Huntingdonshire. London, of course, attracted people from all over England, though in the fourteenth century most probably travelled from East Anglia, the route followed by much of London's grain. This migration produced a profoundly important change in dialect from a southern, Saxon one to an Anglian or midland dialect. Because of the towering influence of London, and of writers such as Chaucer, this dialect came to dominate spoken and written English.

Market towns were also focal points of authority. When Edward III asked the counties for assistance in 1337, the sheriff of Staffordshire had the matter proclaimed in all of the market vills (*villis mercatoriis*). At the subsequent meeting of the county community merchants approved the tax from thirteen of twenty-six towns in the county. These represented important marketing centres. Nine ranked among the top ten in tax assessments or numbers of taxpayers between 1327 and 1334, though only seven of them were taxed as towns in 1334 when their combined assessment came to £1,140. The incident illustrates the commercial and governmental importance of such towns and the way the crown relied on influential county merchants to win support for its policies.

What were these towns like? In appearance smaller market towns were similar to villages. It was only larger towns, with several thousands of inhabitants, which would have appeared 'urban' to us. Relatively peaceful conditions within England meant that small towns founded in the interior during the twelfth and thirteenth centuries did not need defences, though many were encircled by a ditch to mark them off from the countryside. Ports and large towns such as London, York, Southampton, Norwich, Leicester, and Chester were walled. Growth took place inside, leading to crowded conditions. By 1300, population growth in York had forced construction to spill out into the countryside. The physical characteristics of the city had changed. The bridges, castle, and public buildings were now constructed in stone, as were important ecclesiastical structures. The huge minster towered above the ramshackle homes and shops which were still largely constructed of timber or wattle and daub and still apt to catch fire. Only wealthy burgesses built in stone. The important religious houses in the city had acquired stone walls, to shut out the worldly bustle of the city and preserve the sanctity of their religious life. Communities within communities, they faced inward, away from the town. Outside, the public streets were narrow, crowded, and filthy.

Even large towns had rustic touches. 'The pig was ubiquitous', Maitland long ago intoned. So was pig dung. Large gardens, 'curtilages', or 'crofts' usually stretched out behind the dwellings lining the streets. Burgesses grew fruit and vegetables in them, or raised pigs, chickens, even livestock. The typical house in Southampton had a frontage of about 20 feet along the street, but could stretch back as much as 100 feet. Some yards were larger and could accommodate a brewhouse as well as a garden. Towns were also studded with small orchards. The burgesses of Southampton eagerly secured their grazing rights on Southampton Common in the mid-thirteenth century and thereafter preserved the deed as well as the common as symbols of their liberty and power.

Despite these rural features, towns were clearly distinguishable from villages, characterized by a richness of occupations not found in the countryside. A few townsfolk would be farmers, but they never accounted for more than about 10 per cent of the population. The rest pursued various crafts and trades. The Chester community in the early fifteenth century hosted at least forty-seven different occupations. Victuallers were often paramount – the vintners, bakers, cooks, fishmongers, butchers, brewers, millers, innkeepers and tavern-keepers who catered to the appetites of urban and rustic traders on market days. Among the crafts, cloth-making and leather working were to be found in almost every town, though their importance varied from region to region. Clothiers and tailors were also conspicuous. The urban work force might also include carpenters, coopers, drapers, glovers, masons, potters, saddlers, skinners, tanners, and tylers among others. Producing goods, maintaining the town fabric, serving townsfolk, lords, and villagers, and producing goods for consumption and exchange were the kinds of activities that set town life apart from village life. They constituted the 'social resources' which, Professor Raftis has argued, enabled the small town to become a viable economic enterprise and a critical part of the economy as a whole.

In one crucial respect, these resources had been seriously depleted during the thirteenth century. Cloth-making, a prime source of employment and revenue, had drifted out of many towns into the countryside. One indication of that drift was the relocation of fulling mills, used to make the fabric denser and tighter. By the early fourteenth century, there were only a few fullers to be found in Leicester where a century earlier they had been numerous and prosperous enough to form their own guild and to make an annual payment to the lord of the town. The decline of cloth-making was evident in other large towns. Whereas Lincoln hosted 200 spinners under Henry II, only a tiny fraction of that number could be found in 1321. The weavers had been so weakened by rural competition that they pleaded to have their annual fee to the king reduced.

England faced a powerful Flemish industry that produced and exported massive amounts of cloth. To compete, English merchants needed to lower costs. They found cheaper, unregulated labour outside towns. Despite the flood of Flemish imports, internal demand for cloth was strong enough so that landlords and merchants could hope to profit by setting up their own looms in competition with urban cloth-makers. As a result, the cloth industry in England was not exclusively urban. Small towns and villages in the sheep-raising districts of East Anglia, Lincolnshire, Yorkshire, the Cotswolds, and Wiltshire prospered from this diffusion of manufacturing.

There were exceptions to this trend, most notably York. The Scottish wars probably account for the difference. On the one hand, relentless pillaging unsettled the countryside and drove some cloth-makers to the protection of walled towns. On the other hand, the movement of the English armies and government to York to combat the threat augmented local demand for food and goods. Work was readily found for carpenters, ropers, bowyers, fletchers, and clothiers to outfit and arm the royal troops. Just at this point the presence of textile crafts in York becomes noticeable. By the end of the century, weavers, fullers, dyers, and others engaged in cloth-making were prominent in the city. The weavers' guild revived. In general, the second half of the fourteenth century appears to have been a period of prosperity for York. The cloth industry in Shrewsbury similarly revived in the 1350s and 1360s.

These townsfolk tended to fall into three social groups: merchants, crafts-men, and workers and servants. Like villages, towns were hierarchical with wealth and power concentrated at the top. Merchants or wealthy retailers dominated urban society. They engaged in overseas trade, reigned over the town's internal commerce, and predominated in property-holding. Rental income was never great enough to subsidize, by itself, great mercantile enterprises, but it could be used to underwrite less ambitious enterprises such as crafts or retailing. Property-holding augmented not only the mer-chants' profits, but their authority within the town. Their interests were thus highly diversified. Neighbourliness, office-holding, kinship, status, business partnerships, and royal service bound them into a cohesive, if not always peaceful, elite.

The merchant class of fourteenth-century London was broadly based, numbering around 1,000. They were primarily wholesale traders with diversified interests, including retailing and industry: mercers, grocers, drapers, fishmongers, goldsmiths, skinners, tailors, and vintners. The elite of Southampton, as might be expected for a major port, was composed almost entirely of merchants. In Exeter, merchants who made their wealth in local and overseas trade, above all in wine and cloth, formed the core of the oligarchy. They appeared more often as creditors than as debtors and often acted together in business ventures as well as in civic government. Official duties reinforced private enterprise. Indeed, members of the Exeter elite were much more likely than others to secure profitable contracts from the town for farming the city customs or for building and repairing town structures. They were also likely to serve on royal commissions or as royal officers, illustrating the linkage between local power and royal authority. Even in Godmanchester, the power of the wealthy is striking. They kept a tight grip on offices and sometimes convened the town court in their homes. These men were not powerful merchants. Their prominence was based on local trade and landholding. In other towns, for example in cloth-making regions, wealthy artisans constituted the oligarchy.

Despite their power, English merchant families generally failed to estab-lish dynasties over several generations. In part, this failure was biological. It has been shown for fourteenth-century London, for example, that merchant families failed to reproduce themselves, to have enough children to keep the family going generation after generation. The high rate of immigration to towns argues that such failure must have been common at all levels of urban society. A few families of the Exeter oligarchy persisted for several generations, but most disappeared, largely because of failures of male heirs or businesses. The lack of continuity can also be attributed to the ambitions of some merchant families. Once they had attained a certain degree of wealth, some London merchants bought rural property and adopted the airs of landed gentlemen, moving from town to manor. Early in the century, Colchester merchants invested heavily in land outside the town and seemed closer to the gentry than to the merchant community.

Below the ranks of the wealthy, the towns teemed with men and women practising various crafts. Their lives are less well documented than those of the elite. They engaged directly in manufacturing, employed workers, and trained apprentices. Local retailers also fell into this diverse middle group. Some craftsmen and retailers, willing to risk their earnings in overseas trade, moved up to occupy niches vacated by elite families, just as smallholders could move up in village society by piecing together larger holdings. But upward mobility seems to have been as rare in towns as in villages in the first half of the fourteenth century.

The bulk of the urban population rested at the bottom of the economic scale: apprentices, day-labourers, or servants. Approximately 20 to 30 per cent were described as servants in the poll-taxes of 1377 and 1381. Hired by kin, neighbours, or business acquaintances, servants generally contracted to work for a year at a time and most often found employment with merchants and victuallers. Though not well paid, such work was attractive enough earlier in the century to lure young men and women from overpopulated villages.

Women contributed to urban productivity in many ways. Whether married or unmarried, they were a crucial element of the work force and their role in the economies of small towns seems to have been more pronounced than in those of villages. In Halesowen women made up about 75 per cent of those who illegally entered the town between 1293 and 1349. Once in the town, they engaged in retail trade, brewing, or even weaving, sometimes on their own rather than in association with a man. Single women were prominent in towns such as Battle holding, buying, selling, and leasing urban properties. They often delayed marrying while they worked to accumulate money. Lower down the social ladder, women found work as spinsters, hucksters, or second-hand clothiers. The least fortunate hired out as servants or resorted to begging and prostitution, which were rife in medieval cities. Married women often assisted their husbands in crafts or trade and could have the responsibility for training apprentices. Women's economic importance is obscured by the secondary, dependent position into which the customary conceptions of authority placed them. The documentation that arises out of and mirrors that authority veils their multifarious activities. Their role, moreover, was limited by the urban power structure which only grudgingly admitted women to citizenship in their own right.

Town government was in the hands of wealthy men. As sites moved from mere markets to towns, some gained greater legal definition in the form of royal or seigneurial charters. They became known as boroughs, characterized by the presence of burgage tenure, certain rights, and the lord's acknowledgement of the town's corporate institutions. Burgage tenure was freer than most agricultural tenures, involving only a money rent with the right to bequeath the property, something that was much harder to do under other forms of landholding. Few towns achieved borough status. In Derbyshire, for example, only a handful of the twenty-eight markets became true boroughs. This legal distinction, however, was of only limited importance. Many town-like centres – Westminster is an example – flourished without ever obtaining borough status or burgage tenure. In these small towns government was essentially the manor court. Elsewhere, though the exact titles and offices varied, there was a broad institutional similarity, with power vested in councils, mayors, stewards, chamberlains, and other lesser officials.

Participation was frequently restricted to the freemen or citizens of the town, which meant property-holders, those who had served their apprenticeship, or those who were admitted as citizens by election or by payment of a fine. Citizenship was a civic status and was not universal. It generally excluded women as well as most craftsmen, workers, apprentices, and servants. The bulk of the freemen were merchants. Admission to the 'freedom' or citizenship of the town was therefore a sign at once of social and institutional status. It could also be a source of friction. At Exeter, the elite became more and more selective over the fourteenth century. Beginning in the 1340s when objections to the admission of unfit men to the freedom were aired, the oligarchy gradually choked off traditional avenues of advancement such as patronage, gift, service, and even inheritance. They increasingly preferred election by the citizens as the means of admission, giving the citizens greater control over the composition of the urban government than they had before. Individuals were thus identified according to citizenship as well as occupation. All inhabitants of the town were legally free in terms of the common law, but they were not economically or socially equal.

Urban oligarchies gained greater solidarity and self-consciousness through merchant guilds, which appeared in the twelfth century. By the fourteenth, they combined the functions of conviviality, trade restriction, social welfare, and religion. Membership had been open to all prosperous townsfolk though after 1300 it tended to grow restrictive, sometimes becoming synonymous with citizenship and thus excluding apprentices, workers, and women. Merchants reacted to the fierce competition from Flemish cloth-makers and foreign merchants by tightening their grip on the economic and civic life of the town. In some places, the merchant guild had become identical with town government. In Southampton and Walling-ford, for example, the head of the guild was also the head of the town. The guild could thus become a comprehensive social, economic, and govern-mental entity. It brought together the town's 'best', regulated trade in their interests, and gave them preferential treatment in government. It is little wonder that in the fourteenth century it came under attack.

This period saw the rise of craft guilds or mysteries, bringing together the masters of trades such as weaving or baking. Since merchant guilds no longer readily admitted craftsmen, artisans devised their own organizations for protection. The prime function of craft guilds was economic regulation. They specified the criteria for good craftsmanship and determined who could practise the craft. Some of these groups, notably weavers and dyers who depended heavily on merchants, resented the power of the merchant guild and fought for greater autonomy and self control. That could lead to conflict within the town government. Nevertheless, craft and merchant guilds alike confirmed the power structure of urban society, so that women were admitted only with their husbands and almost never formed guilds of their own.

The corporate urge was not solely economic. Guilds attended to mem-bers' social and religious needs as well, looking after families and sending members into their anticipated after-life with a suitable burial. Parish guilds, whether urban or rural, performed similar functions. They were less restric-tive than the merchant or craft guilds and were often open to women. In some cases, most notably the Corpus Christi guild in London, the organiz-ation aimed at keeping out the wealthy. It was envisioned as the preserve of the middle ranks, of retailers and craftsmen. In London, those groups stood out in their benefactions to parish guilds. The guild of Holy Trinity in London, founded in 1369, grew to around 530 members, including both men and women, clergymen, gentry, merchants, weavers, chandlers, brewers, carpenters, and other artisans. The main purpose of these guilds was the upkeep of the parish church, participation in religious festivals, and the celebration of intercessory masses for the souls of deceased members. It thus extended backward and forward in time, to embrace members living and dead and to ensure that their souls would be remembered in the future. As might be expected of such organizations, their rules stressed proper moral conduct and religious observance. The guilds helped to organize civic processions on the feast days of their patron saints. The most impressive and famous of these processions occurred at the feast of Corpus Christi (on the Thursday after Trinity Sunday, the eighth Sunday after Easter). Despite this primarily religious orientation, these parish guilds, like their economic cousins, came to occupy places of social, economic, and political importance within town or village life.

Lords were also part of town life. Approximately two-thirds of English towns were subject to seigneurial control after 1300. Some market villages had blossomed into real towns, as in the case of Stratford upon Avon, while urban centres gradually developed outside the gates of castles and monasteries. Lords benefited from their power over towns in three ways. First, as lords they extracted a portion of the revenues through rents, tolls, and fines. Not only did landlords collect rents inside towns, but the vitality of urban economies pushed up land values in neighbouring areas. Proximity to a town meant more opportunities to earn money through trade and labour than in the countryside, enabling landlords to charge higher rents. Those obtainable in the region surrounding London are famous, but the same process occurred near provincial towns. The bishop of Worcester was thus able to collect higher rents in villages near market towns such as Bristol or Worcester than in remote locations. Tolls added to their profits. In northeastern England, for example, nearly 200 different tolls were levied on roughly 100 different items in 13 different boroughs. The tolls ranged from a farthing for 1,000 teasels to 6d. for a shipload of goods. At Leicester the earls of Lancaster received income from tallage (a tax), through-toll (levied on the transit of goods through the town), tronage (for weighing goods), tolls on buying and selling goods, pickage (for setting up stalls in the market), stallage (on the stalls themselves), and cannemol (on brewing). They also pocketed the excess proceeds from various funds collected for the upkeep of the town: murage (for the city walls), pavage (roads), and pontage (bridges). All commerce was thus taxed, and usually taxed in several different ways. At every step in the marketing process a lord waited to collect his fees.

This revenue was not great but it augmented manorial income. The earls of Gloucester, for instance, controlled several boroughs scattered throughout England, Wales, and Ireland. Income ranged from about £8 (Bletchingley) to £19 (Tewkesbury) a year, out of a total income of nearly £6,000 in 1314. Leicester was worth about £80 a year in 1375, a mere drop in the bucket compared to the profits from the duke of Lancaster's vast estates. Finally, it is estimated that the bishop of Worcester earned around £30 a year from his urban properties at the end of the thirteenth century, which represented only about 2.5 per cent of the bishop's total revenues at the time. Clearly, noblemen did not get rich as urban entrepreneurs alone.

Secondly, however, lords participated in town life as both consumers and producers, as buyers of luxuries and sellers of agricultural produce. Towns offered their lords specialized services and goods. Battle abbey, for example, depended on its small urban community for trade, carpentry, masonry, law, and even the fabrication of pilgrims' souvenirs. It is estimated that the abbey spent between £600 and £650 a year in the town, underscoring the reciprocal benefits in lord-town relations. Durham priory's dealings with merchants from neighbouring towns give the flavour of relations between lords and retailers. The monks typically bought on credit. They ran up bills for oxen, dried fish, malt, oil, herrings, cloth, lead, salt, and wine. They repaid those debts with 'sales' of cattle, wool, or grain, in which they turned the produce over directly to the creditor. They also assigned appropriated tithes for the repayment of loans.

Finally, towns and markets were essential to the very functioning of agrarian lordship. Markets enabled tenants to earn the money necessary to pay their rents, an important consideration since by 1300 most rents were paid in cash. The bishop of Exeter made this connection between markets and rents in his reply to Edward III's request for a county tax in 1337. The community of Devon urged him to stress that because of poor economic conditions, 'the great men of the county (*majores patriae*) are never, or hardly ever, able to collect their rents or the commoners (*populares*) able to sell their grain . . . ' The thrust is clear: the inability of peasants to get a good price for their grain jeopardized seigneurial revenues.

The fourteenth-century English economy was a complex mesh of villages, markets, and towns. Lordship depended on the smooth circulation of goods and money to remain economically viable. It was not an alien parasite imposed from the outside on an established agrarian economy. The two had matured together. By 1300, many characteristics of the English economy had been determined by this interplay of seigneurial authority and local trade. Peasants' marketing decisions, merchants' trading opportunities, and landlords' estate policies were interwoven.

Yet, in skimming off a portion of the commercial as well as agricultural surplus, lords hobbled development. Merchants and townsfolk, like peasants, chafed at their seigneurial fetters. The most infamous example was the relationship between the king and royal boroughs. Beginning in the twelfth century, royal towns agitated to lighten the burden of lordship, and by 1300 the majority of large boroughs had won charters of liberty which gave them rights of self-government and of appointing officials in return for a single annual payment, the farm of the town. The seigneurial record was not as good. Many towns had achieved only a limited degree of independence. Aware of the encouragement that freedom gave trade, lords offered townsfolk personal freedom and burgage tenure, though they kept hold of the reins of authority by collecting revenues and appointing officials. Friction remained. The monastic boroughs of Cirencester and Abingdon were so distressed about the demands made by their lords for fees and tolls that they dragged them before royal judges in 1319, 1342 (Cirencester), 1363 and 1368 seeking relief and an end to seigneurial intrusion into their affairs.

The causes of this irritation at seigneurial interference stand out in a royal survey of the borough of Leicester conducted in 1322. The lord of the town, Thomas of Lancaster, had been executed for rebelling against Edward II and his lands forfeited to the crown. The townsfolk complained at length about Thomas' actions, claiming that he had perverted the customary relationship between lord and town by introducing extortionate practices. He forced fullers, butchers, brewers, weavers, and sellers of oatmeal, salt, herrings, and fish to pay fines to ply their trades. He tightened up the jurisdiction of his courts and the collection of debts. He took dung from all the streets of the town rather than from the two that had traditionally been his right. It got so bad that his foresters fined anyone buying wood, even from poor women who sold branches door to door.

There is no sign that these particular actions led to violence. In Bury St Edmunds, however, relations between the abbey and the town degenerated into armed riot. In January 1327 some of the leading men of the town seized control of the government with the intention of liberating it from the abbey's grasp. They broke into the abbey and seized the town records, that is, the instruments of the abbey's authority. They then proceeded to govern the town themselves, collect rents and tolls, and conduct courts in their name. Their anger had been aggravated by the abbey's mismanagement. By 1327 it was deeply in debt and discipline among the monks was shockingly lax. They led an easy life while their indebtedness drove them to borrow from the town, a debt that they had not repaid by 1327. Antagonism smouldered for several years, occasionally flaring into violence. Part of the abbey was burned, townsfolk were killed, monks held hostage, and the abbey's agents harassed or killed. The abbey finally attained a £133,000 legal judgement against the conspirators, though in 1331 the abbot agreed to accept 2,000 marks. The episode shows how deep the animosity between lord and town could run.

Conflict, however, was not inevitable. Westminster, for example, never attained any degree of autonomy from its lord, the abbot of Westminster, and never secured any of the privileges of burghal status. Relations between lord and town nevertheless remained cordial throughout the middle ages. Communal independence could progress peacefully. At Leicester, Thomas of Lancaster's harsh lordship seems to have been a temporary digression. The town had developed a limited sense of corporation in the thirteenth century and took further strides toward autonomy in the fourteenth when it pressed for freedom from tolls. Partial success came in 1360 when the earl relinquished his right to tolls from the fair and turned them over to the town. Then, in 1375, Leicester leased its own jurisdiction for £80 a year for ten years from John of Gaunt so that henceforth the community collected tolls, held the courts, appointed officials, and reorganized the town finances. The victory was costly though not bloodstained.

Towns and markets were thus firmly implanted in the social and economic landscape of fourteenth-century England. The penetration of the market and the ubiquity of commerce comes out in Henry of Lancaster's *Livre de seyntz medicines*, a remarkable devotional tract written in 1354. In the course of the work he compares his heart to a market, because the market is held at a place that men from all over can easily reach by the streets of the town. As might be expected from one who was himself the lord of a town – Leicester – Lancaster's metaphor is heavily weighted towards the seigneurial aspect of markets: they are held in one place and merchandise sold only there so that the lord can collect tolls and supervise the use of true weights and measures. Lancaster thus compares the devil to the lord of the market, collecting his customs, prises, and tolls (that is, the soul) in the heart so that he will not lose what is due him and seizing forfeited goods because they had not been properly weighed. At another point he sees the devil as the catchpole, the hard-hearted sergeant of the market eager to snare merchants for the slightest infraction and before whom none may find mercy or grace. This contrasts with the true lord of the market, Jesus, who will pardon their trespasses. Further elaboration of the metaphor brings the bustle of a medieval town to life. Taverns ring the market-place, cooks and innkeepers hawk their wares, patrons eat and drink until they hurt, prostitutes decked out more elegantly on market day than at Easter lure fools with a penny to spend, while merchants seek to buy cheap and sell dear. Though somewhat strained, the metaphor is striking and enlivens a picture from administrative records that is otherwise static and dry. It sounds, in fact, much like Leicester. All the main roads converged in the centre of town at High Cross, where two weekly markets were held and where inns lined the streets.

Commercialization had spread to the point that it earned the condemnation of moralists. In *Piers Plowman* William Langland denounced the corruption brought about by money. Fees and wages were ubiquitous. They could be divided into two classes, those as payments for doing good work and those used to corrupt. Servants, minstrels, royal officers, schoolmasters, priests, merchants, and even beggars sought rewards for their work. 'No man, as I understand it, can live without reward.' In a personification of

Avarice as an apprentice in guile, Langland brought to life the world of petty commerce. Traders used false weights, drapers stretched their cloth, women weavers cheated the spinners, and the ale-wife mixed good ale with bad to cheat extra pennies out of the labourers and low folk at fairs and markets.

England's commercialized agrarian economy was thus powerful, though limited in scope. Grain production was prosperous enough, and demand high enough, to underwrite trade in commodities ranging from simple goods such as brush, nails, and fish to luxuries such as spices, wine, and silk. Everyone, from peasants to lords to merchants, relied on this commercial exchange to satisfy particular deficiencies. Very few, however, depended solely on the market for their survival. Except for the truly landless, the market offered peasants an opportunity to make up what their holdings could not supply or to expand their holdings and gain an added degree of security. For landlords, markets and trade were ancillary to their preoccupation with rents, agricultural production, and patronage. Even within the mercantile community, where market dependence was most obvious and widespread, many invested in property and rents, partly to underwrite commerce but also to escape its uncertainties. An attitude of free-wheeling risk-taking, the compulsion to invest and reinvest profits, was rare in this society. Trade and towns, moreover, were permeated by the seigneurial relations that structured all of medieval society. Lords founded and controlled markets, held urban property, and siphoned off a portion of the commercial revenues. Urban society was hierarchically structured. Oligarchs, like lords, wielded civic and economic power over the lesser townsfolk, through formal and informal institutions such as offices, guilds, the workshop, and family. Towns may have been freer than villages, but freedom was never absolute for medieval people, even in the market-place.

It is striking, none the less, that lords, peasants, merchants, and writers as different as Brinton and Lancaster grasped the importance of markets. Their common interests were made clear whenever the crown interrupted the normal course of trade. It looked to towns and markets for several things. They provided, in the first place, financial resources. The conspicuous role of English merchants in Edward III's regime was not the sign of any forward thinking commercial policy. It reflected their value as royal creditors. Secondly, well-developed commercial networks assisted the logistics of war. The enormous enterprise of collecting, shipping, and dispersing food, goods, and men was made easier by the expertise of seasoned merchants. Thirdly, town elites linked the crown to the urban community. The importance of this linkage was underscored by Edward's reliance on merchant assemblies and individual financiers in formulating and executing his policies. Finally, the marketing network was a tempting target for exploitation. The most notorious form of exploitation was purveyance, the king's prerogative right to purchase foodstuffs for his household or armies. The problem was the meaning of 'purchase'. Chronically short of cash, kings bought on credit. Problems arose because sellers, stuck with receipts in the form of tallies, often had difficulty recovering the purchase price. Purveyance was thus seen as an intolerable intrusion into the market, opposed by merchants, retailers, and producers. The depth of their resentment, similar to that directed against the lords of boroughs, betrays their desire to free trade from arbitrary dues and interference. Commerce in England had grown into a rich prize, and one which lords and the king could not presume to control.

5

OVERSEAS TRADE: WOOL AND TAXES

Imports and exports broadened England's commercial horizons. Wool in particular gave England a major role in international trade and generated handsome profits for producers and merchants alike. By the early fourteenth century, Europe's local economies had intertwined. The precocious urbanization and textile manufacturing of northern Italy and Flanders depended for their prosperity, indeed survival, on regular supplies of raw materials as well as on markets through which finished cloth could be sold. The volume of business transactions had grown enormously.

Yet the importance of the wool trade was not solely economic. The appetites of governments had grown apace. Kings and princes, whose need for funding seemed insatiable, looked to merchants for loans and taxed trade. When they could not gain what they wanted legitimately, they resorted to force or extortion, holding trade hostage to political objectives. Edwardian England resorted to all of these ploys. It offers a good example of how fourteenth-century governments manipulated trade to forward their policies. England's overseas trade will therefore be examined by looking firstly at the wool trade from sheep raising to the export of wool and secondly at the fluctuations of the wool trade with particular emphasis on the crown's manipulation of exports. It underscores the point that after 1300, participation in the wool trade was so universal in English society that heavy-handed tactics by the crown to raise money incited political reaction.

The pattern of England's overseas commerce had been set during the thirteenth century. Essentially, England exported raw materials such as wool, hides, coal, and metals and imported consumer goods such as wine, furs, and spices, along with some manufactured products such as woollen and silk cloth. Most imported luxuries were destined for royal, noble, or gentry households. Non-luxury items such as iron, millstones, grain, and other goods, however, were also imported and found their way into local markets.

But wool was far and away the most valuable part of this trade. Between 1303 and 1311, it is estimated that the annual value of wool exports averaged £334,656, falling only slightly to about £323,500 between 1322 and 1336. The value of other exports did not even come close to these figures. Precise figures are hard to come by because these goods were not taxed as rigorously as wool and customs records provide the only information about export trade. Since Edward I imposed the Ancient Custom of 6s. 8d. (half a mark) per sack in 1275, wool had been continuously subject to customs duties. Tolls on other goods, whether imported or exported, were imposed in the New Custom of 1303, but it applied only to aliens and was suspended between 1311 and 1322. Then, in 1347, because of the rising importance of cloth exports, the government imposed the cloth custom on alien and denizen exporters alike.

It appears from tax accounts that grain, coal, and tin were exported in considerable quantities in the fourteenth century. Grain was shipped to the continent from eastern ports such as Lynn, Hull, Sandwich, and London and may have amounted to 13,000 quarters in the first decade of the century before falling off. Newcastle coal shipments increased in size and value. Between June and September 1349, 22 of 29 ships leaving the port carried coal, but at least 107 shiploads were shipped out in the year beginning in September 1377. The value of exported coal often exceeded that of the imported cargo. Tin production reached a peak of between 1,000,000 and 1,650,000 lbs. in the 1330s before falling precipitously in the decade after the Black Death. Fish, dairy products, iron, and small manufactured goods were also traded overseas.

Among the imports, wine and cloth were paramount. In 1300, England imported around 20,000 tuns of wine a year, representing nearly a fifth of Gascony's exports. Cloth imports were also impressive. During the thirteenth century, Flemish textile manufactures gradually dominated the trade, replacing English cloth at the upper end of the market. Italian woollen and silk textiles were also imported, though not in large amounts. Altogether, approximately 12,000 cloths a year were imported from 1300 to 1310, though the number fell off to just under 10,000 on the eve of the Hundred Years War. By that time, England and Flanders were bound together in a commercial symbiosis. Each needed the other's markets and products. In the first half of the century, Flemish textile manufacturers increasingly concentrated on luxury cloth, abandoning the market in cheaper textiles to local competitors. Because English wool was the finest in

Europe, the Flemings needed it more than ever before, a dependence that benefited English wool producers.

Wool was profitable. It was estimated that 1,000 sheep produced about 50 marks (£33) annually, so that even small flocks were worthwhile. Sheep raising was widespread. England was exporting on average 33,000 sacks of wool in the early 1330s before war broke out. If it took about 260 sheep to produce a single sack, then there were at least 8,580,000 sheep producing for export alone. The size of the domestic market is not known. At that point, however, England was importing nearly 10,000 cloths a year, which represented approximately 1,818 sacks of wool (at about 5.5 Flemish textiles per sack). Now, if this cloth was destined for the upper end of the market, it made up, at the most, only about half of the total market for woollen textiles. English manufacturers, therefore, must have produced at least another 10,000 cloths from 1,818 sacks of wool which would have required another 472,680 sheep. This rough calculation suggests a minimum sheep population of 9 million, though Postan has offered a figure of 15 to 18 million.

Some were herded in very large flocks. The Winchester and St Swithun's flocks, for instance, reached 20,000 in the fourteenth century. Henry de Lacy kept upwards of 13,000 sheep, Canterbury cathedral priory 13,700, Crowland abbey 11,000, the bishopric of Worcester 5,600, and Bolton priory 3,500. In Leicestershire, the abbeys of Leicester, Croxton, and Garendon, as well as the Lord Ferrers of Groby, all had flocks of around 5,000 to 6,000 sheep, based on the amount of wool they were supposed to have sold, while at least nineteen Wiltshire manors had flocks of at least 600.

Huge flocks seize the imagination, but they represented only a fraction of the total number of sheep. Flocks of 5,000 were found only on large estates, and it would have taken 1,800 of them to account for 9 million sheep. There were not that many individuals or institutions with that kind of wealth. Most flocks probably ranged from about 100 to 300 sheep. A. R. Bridbury has hypothesized that large landholders were responsible for only a third of the wool exports in the early fourteenth century and that the remaining two-thirds came from 20,000 producers with average flocks of 260 sheep. Assessments made in Sussex in 1341 show that there were approximately 110,000 sheep in 270 parishes. Twenty parishes had between 1,000 and 2,000 sheep, and three had between 2,000 and 3,000. Assuming, conservatively, that the total number of sheep in these parishes came to around 30,000, then each of the remaining 247 had around 325. Only ten parishes recorded no sheep at all. It has been found that tenant flocks like-wise existed all over Wiltshire, some larger than 1,000. At the very bottom of society, anyone with access to pasture would be inclined to raise even a few sheep and try to cash in on the wool trade. Not surprisingly, however, sheep, like other forms of wealth, were concentrated in the hands of village elites. It has been estimated that in Bedfordshire in 1297, three-quarters of the peasant flocks had ten or fewer sheep and that 10 per cent of the peasantry held 45 per cent of the sheep.

Though most peasants probably had no sheep at all, a sizeable part of the population was involved in sheep raising. Another indication of the extent of the practice is the ease with which flocks were replaced. Sheep were extremely sensitive to outbreaks of disease, called murrains, causing their numbers to oscillate dramatically. The murrain of 1315–17 was catastrophic. Bolton priory's flock fell by two-thirds within a year, Crowland's from 11,000 to 2,000 in 8 years. Disease and marketing decisions caused the number of sheep on the manor of Cuxham in Oxfordshire to move up and down in the early fourteenth century; from 3 to 5 between 1303 and 1310, up to 150 in 1334, down to 92 in 1335, to none in 1336, and back up to 102 in 1337. Similar oscillations have been noted in Wiltshire, Essex, and the Ramsey abbey estate during murrains in 1357 or the late 1360s. The fact that estates made up their losses so quickly argues that there were many middling or small producers with sheep for sale.

Changes in the marketing of wool after 1300 reflect this pattern of dispersed production. In the thirteenth century, production and marketing had been dominated by the great abbeys, particularly the Cistercian houses. They produced the finest wool and marketed it through contracts with first Flemish and then Italian merchants. Sales were often centralized. The abbey and merchant negotiated a price for the wool clip, taking into account local variations in the quality of the wool. Yet national price lists invariably show that Cistercian and Gilbertine wools obtained the highest prices, reflecting not only superior quality but also the care and expense that those houses took in cleaning and packing the wool. The clip was collected and delivered to the merchant at a central location. Along with the estate wool, the abbeys often contracted for the *collecta*, or wool collected from smaller lay and peasant producers. The abbey acted as a middleman. Bolton priory in Yorkshire, for example, sold nearly as much wool from the *collecta* as from its demesne in the late thirteenth century. These estates thus dominated the market as middlemen as well as producers.

They sometimes ran into financial difficulties as a result. They usually contracted for the clip in advance, sometimes several years. The merchant was in effect advancing the abbey a substantial loan on the security of the wool. Problems arose when producers were unable to deliver the contracted amount of wool on time. Debts could mount spectacularly if the clips were smaller than anticipated. Houses were forced to buy wool to make up the deficit or to borrow elsewhere to pay off the loans. For these reasons, the Cistercian order forbade the practice, though the fact that it had to repeat the prohibition several times suggests that it was a dead letter. What is striking in the fourteenth century is the disappearance of these abbeys from the records of the trade. Take Bolton priory, a modest producer compared to the great Cistercian houses. In the 1290s, its sales of demesne wool averaged about £205 a year, while sales of purchased wool averaged £108, for a total sale of £313 a year. For five years in the 1320s, however, its demesne sales dropped to an annual average of only £95 and its purchased wool to a mere £26, for a total annual average of £121. Now, overall, exports of wool were lower in the 1320s than in the 1290s, but not by a significant amount. Prices, in fact, were substantially higher, meaning that Bolton's drop in output was all the greater. Whereas it was accounting for about thirty sacks of purchased wool a year in the 1290s, it was buying only four to five in the 1320s. Another indication of change is found in wool price lists. Thirteenth-century lists testify to the importance of the abbeys. They are organized around the abbeys and the assumption that they were marketing the finest wool. Those drawn up in the fourteenth century are organized by county and had the political purpose of setting minimum prices to ensure that producers did not lose because of Edward's wool schemes. The political bias is important, showing that sales and hence worries about trade had broadened out since the thirteenth century.

Furthermore, during the first decades of the fourteenth century, English merchants gradually took over the lion's share of the market from their Italian rivals. The Italians were also overtaken by German merchants who assumed the position of leading alien exporters. English wool merchants appear to have benefited from several circumstances. Italian companies experienced internal difficulties from the late thirteenth century onward, including a number of bankruptcies. Governmental policies added to their adversity. The New Custom of 1303 increased the duty that aliens paid on a sack of wool by 3s. 4d. Finally, the government fashioned a 'staple' policy that at times gave an advantage to English merchants. A staple was a system of enforced marketing through a particular town or towns. All wool for export had to be brought to the designated location(s) and exported by authorized merchants. The staple eased the government's task of collecting duties, but it could also help Englishmen when other merchants, such as the Italians, were prohibited from purchasing wool directly from producers.

Three other features of the wool trade in this era stand out. The first is the leading role of London. By the 1330s, it accounted for about half of all the wool shipped overseas. Another feature is the growing importance of the northern ports of Boston and Hull and of the merchants associated with them. Close to sources of wool, the ports together accounted for about a third or more of all of the exports. Northern merchants, who had prospered during the Scottish wars, played an important part in this trade. When Edward moved his government north in the 1330s to pursue the Scots, Yorkshire merchants stepped forward to victual and arm his troops and bureaucrats. Then, when Edward conceived his monopoly export scheme in 1336–7, northern merchants were conspicuous in planning and carrying it out. A final feature is that a few ambitious, or perhaps unscrupulous, merchants pulled away from this rising pack of English traders to become merchant capitalists. Melchebourn and Wesenham of Lynn, Chiriton and Malwayn of London, Goldbetter of York are just a few of the names that figure prominently not only in the records of trade and finance, but in the annals of government and politics as well.

The most infamous of these characters was William de la Pole. His notoriety rested on his financial services to the crown, for which he was promoted to banneret in 1338. Whatever his detractors said about him at the time, his accounts make it clear that his success was not solely the product of favouritism and underhand dealings. They reveal a shrewd business mind. Careful accounting and the hiring of good personnel helped him enormously. His wealth allowed him to practise economies of scale – paying high wages, buying wool in bulk, renting large warehouses, and so forth – that were out of the reach of lesser merchants.

Though conducted on a grander scale, his business practices were not all that different from those of other merchants. He handled, for example, a wide variety of items rather than specializing in a single product, dealing in metal, grain, wine, and salt as well as wool. In addition, he loaned money, made profits on currency exchange, owned urban and rural property, and was a shipowner. Such diversification is likewise evident among the merchants who did business with Durham priory in the early fourteenth century. Wool was only one, though the most lucrative, of their trading interests. They also bought and sold grain, malt, wine, fish, spices, and cloth. Their focus was primarily regional, but the wool trade connected them to international networks. Their activities mirrored those of de la Pole on a smaller scale. Thus, like the pattern of trade in England as a whole, the merchant community can be divided into two overlapping groups. The first, and most numerous, were those men dealing in market towns with lords and villages, acting as intermediaries between the local economy and the world of exports and imports. The second were the de la Poles, Conduits, Melchebourns and others whose horizons were broader but whose activities were similar.

Both were essential in marketing wool. The first step was collecting wool from the producers. An army of small tradesmen, chapmen, and woolmongers bought the wool of hundreds of village flocks. Some was gobbled up by agents of the greater merchants or by landowners acting as middlemen, but in the fourteenth century local trade does not seem to have been highly centralized. This wool was then funnelled to major ports such as London, Boston, Hull, Southampton, or Lynn where it had to be stored before being shipped abroad. Merchants usually consigned their cargoes to several ships in order to reduce risks. The hazards of seafaring mounted after 1336 because of the war with France and periodic squabbles with the Flemings. Piracy, whether sanctioned by governments or carried out on private initiative, was rife. Once the wool reached port overseas it had to be stored again before it was sold. The enterprise cost about £1 to £2 per sack, narrowing the merchant's profit to around £1 to £3 a sack, depending on the quality of the wool.

Quality varied greatly. Differences are visible in price lists drawn up in 1337 (the 'Nottingham prices'), 1343, and 1357. In the first, wool from Herefordshire, Shropshire, and Lincolnshire ranked at the top. That order reappeared in the 1357 list, indicating that these counties produced the highest-quality wool. At the opposite end of the price spectrum, East Anglian wool was almost always ranked at the bottom along with wool from Devon and Cornwall. The differences in value could reach as high as £5 a sack.

J. H. Munro has pointed out two remarkable changes in these valuations from the thirteenth to the fourteenth centuries: the apparent fall in the quality of Yorkshire wool and the disappearance of Welsh wool from the lists. The Cistercians were the source of both. Munro therefore attributes the decline in value to managerial changes on the Cistercian estates. They decentralized sheep raising as they leased out their demesnes. Peasants became responsible for wool production and were unable to produce as fine a quality of wool as their Cistercian predecessors. Although this argument seems to antedate the process of demesne leasing and to underestimate the ability of peasant producers, it has the virtue of uncovering and addressing a significant change in wool production.

Three things should be noted in regard to profits from the wool trade. First, they trickled down throughout all ranks of society. Second, profit margins were thin. While a few nobles and merchant capitalists enjoyed spectacular profits, most participants made much less. Producers' costs are difficult to estimate but they varied according to the care lavished on sheep. At Bolton priory in the 1290s, costs for the raising and shearing of sheep ran between £9 and £16 a year. Wool sales averaged £313 a year, so that the costs represented about 3 to 5 per cent of the income. At Bibury on the bishop of Worcester's estate sales of wool in 1383–4 came to about £14 while the costs were estimated at £6, or 42 per cent of the total. At Hampton Lucy they came closer to 55 per cent. Yet income and expenses could swing wildly, as on the manor of Beddingham, Sussex, where costs ranged from

£4 to nearly £16 between 1354 and 1367 and wool sales from about £6 to £42. Third, because revenues were uncertain and spread over such a wide field of producers and dealers, any governmental policy affecting profits, such as wool taxes, embargoes, or privileges, would have significant political repercussions. Merchants could not afford to absorb additional costs imposed by taxes. They had to pass them on, either to the producers or to the buyers. But producers were likewise loath to trim their profit margins. Take, for example, the wool from Bibury. The sale in 1383 represented about 1½ sacks. At that time, the duty on wool was about 50s. a sack, so that the total duty on the Bibury wool would have been 75s., or 27 per cent of the total sale price. The combined weight of the costs of producing the wool and the customs would have accounted for nearly 70 per cent of the sale price. Of course, the sale price might already reflect the merchant's effort to pass the cost of the duty on to the producer. In either case, it is abundantly clear that encumbrances on the wool trade had profound implications.

Fluctuations in the volume and value of the wool trade, moreover, reverberated throughout society. Between 1300 and 1337, exports underwent two changes, evident in Figure 1. The century opened with a tremendous boom in exports. They topped 46,000 sacks in 1304–5 and averaged nearly

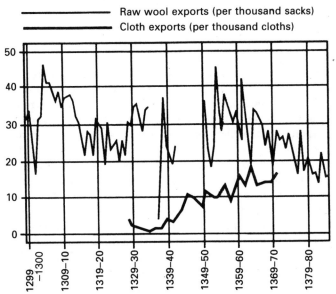

Figure 1. Raw wool and cloth exports in England, 1300–1380 (E. M. Carus-Wilson and Olive Coleman, *England's export trade, 1275–1547* (Oxford, 1963):122, 138).

38,000 sacks a year between 1311 and 1313. The continental appetite for wool must have been ferocious, for despite the high volume of trade, prices did not slump dramatically. The boom, however, collapsed after 1313 because relations between England and Flanders deteriorated. Competition between English and Flemish merchants had been flaring into acts of violence against rivals on land and at sea. In 1313, Edward II established the staple on French territory at St Omer, not with a view to depriving Flanders of wool, but rather to providing neutral ground for trade where English merchants would not be harassed. War between France and Flanders worsened problems. The French demanded that the English live up to their treaty obligations and support them against the Flemish rebels while the Flemings resented England's refusal to support them. The war quickly ended but unstable relations lasted until England and Flanders sealed a truce in 1323. Exports, however, only improved slightly because the city of Bruges revolted against the count of Flanders in 1323 and did not quiet down until 1326. Trade was also upset by the dreadful sheep murrain of 1315–17. Wool exports plummeted to around 27,000 sacks a year between 1313 and 1323 then slipped even further to just under 24,000 sacks a year between 1323 and 1329. The only consolation for producers was that prices rose to the highest level in fifty years, as the supply of wool to Flemish looms was choked off. With the end of the civil war in Flanders in the 1330s, English wool exports stabilized at around 33,000 sacks a year. Yet, from the lofty heights achieved in the 1320s, prices fell to the lowest point in memory.

The experience of the first generation of the fourteenth century confirmed that great profits could be made in the wool trade, but that it was highly sensitive to political and economic shocks. The lessons of boom and bust were apparent between 1314 and 1323. From a high of 32,514 sacks in 1314–15, exports the following year plunged by 11,663 sacks, or more than 4 million pounds. This 36 per cent fall was followed by a rise of more than 7,000 sacks in 1316–17. Exports were slightly lower in 1317–18, only to fall by nearly 6,000 sacks to 21,641 in 1318–19. They reversed themselves the next year, shooting up by 9,901 sacks, or 42 per cent of the 1318–19 total. Performance was slightly down to 29,869 sacks in 1320–1, but then experienced a plunge exceeding 11,000 sacks in 1321–2. That fall was made up and surpassed when exports climbed to 30,069 sacks in 1322–3. Though these oscillations were probably exaggerated by the exchequer's method of recording export duties, they emphasize the uncertainties of the trade in these years when political dislocation was at its greatest. It is not hard to imagine the relief shared by merchants and producers alike when the wool trade along with relations between England and Flanders stabilized over the next five years.

Relief, however, was only temporary. Edward III had his eye on wool, convinced that he could obtain higher revenues than usual by manipulating the wool supply and raising duties. He needed cash for war and wool would underwrite his military ambitions. As a result, between 1336 and 1353 governmental interference was responsible for most of the fluctuations in the wool trade.

Edward had two objectives, financial and diplomatic. Wool was the single most valuable product in England and merchants had the largest cash resources of any group. Edward wanted them both as a reservoir of credit on which he could draw at will. He used his prerogative power to stop overseas trade and convince merchants to help him. On the diplomatic front, he brandished wool as a weapon to try to bully Flanders into allying with him against France. He threatened to move the staple, either to punish the Flemings or to reward others. What he did not consider was that the king of France could respond with inducements or restrictions of his own. He, too, could lavish favours on the count of Flanders. He, too, could harass shipping in the channel or even attack English ports, driving up the dangers and costs of the trade.

When Edward stepped into the wool trade in 1336, therefore, he was overly optimistic. Blind to the dangers and wildly hopeful of the benefits, he embarked on a policy that produced little profit for anyone. For nearly twenty years, the wool trade was a captive of royal policy. Exports fluctuated widely and the uncertainties of the 1320s returned.

The policy was set up in a series of three meetings between the king and merchants in 1336 which led to an increase in customs. In August, Edward declared an embargo on the export of wool intending to coerce the merchants into agreeing to an increased levy, called a subsidy, and Flanders into siding with him. The effect, however, was to create a glut of wool and low prices in England and in Flanders scarcity and high prices – a situation highly favourable to merchants. They subsequently agreed to the increased duties in the third meeting with Edward on 23 September. That meeting also produced a price list known as the 'Nottingham prices'. These were probably *maximum* prices that producers were allowed to charge so that merchants would be guaranteed a profit despite the rise in customs rates. In subsequent plans, the list served as *minimum* prices to reassure producers that they would not suffer from the king's schemes.

In 1337 the government took a more active role. In a meeting with Edward on 26 July, the merchants agreed to create a royal monopoly. They loaned Edward £200,000 and pledged to pay him half of the profit on 30,000 sacks of wool. In return, they received a monopoly; only those merchants agreeing to the terms of the bargain would be permitted to export wool. Most other exports were banned. The monopolists were promised

that their loan would be repaid with a farm of the customs, which were
raised to 40s. a sack. The wool was to be sent to Dordrecht in three shipments and the king to be paid in three instalments. Altogether about 250
merchants participated in the monopoly, 50 of whom were members of the
English Wool Company. The company was led by a small core of capitalists
such as Reginald Conduit and William de la Pole. The latter, in fact, was
only the third largest dealer in the scheme, responsible for exporting 383
sacks or 139,412 pounds of wool. Participants outside this circle exported
on average 40 sacks of wool apiece. Even this sum represented the clip from
more than 10,000 sheep and must have been collected from between ten
and twenty villages if taken from the flocks of peasants and gentry. Collecting this wool must have consumed the energies of most local tradesmen. In
the 1350s, for example, at least thirty merchants from the city of York were
engaged in buying up wool in the North and East Riding of Yorkshire,
demonstrating once again the importance of small producers and local markets in the fourteenth-century English economy, even in a large-scale business such as the wool trade.

The shipments, however, were slow and the proceeds less than anticipated. The government stepped in, seized the wool, amounting to about
11,500 sacks, and put it up for sale itself. Merchants were given receipts or
bonds (the so-called 'Dordrecht Bonds') for their wool. They could either
redeem them directly at the exchequer or use them to ship wool duty free.
Since the government was so short of money, redemption was problematic
at best. The original scheme thus collapsed and the collection of wool was
halted.

Nevertheless, the crown pursued the plan in 1338–9, this time with parliamentary consent. The parliament meeting on 3 February authorized the
collection of the remaining 20,000 sacks as purveyance. Producers received
royal bonds that promised payment for the wool out of tax proceeds. Under
this plan, the king acted as a monopolist, collecting and selling the wool
himself. He tried to profit directly, rather than indirectly. Producers, however, were wary of governmental promises for repayment, so that little wool
was collected. In July 1338, therefore, a great council ordered the collection
of taxes in wool. Taxpayers were charged with wool in proportion to their
assessment for the fifteenth, the standard tax. This effort likewise proved disappointing. Proceeds were meagre and because the king had assigned so
many of them to creditors to repay loans, virtually nothing came to the
government. In December, Edward turned back to the merchants for
additional loans, to be repaid out of customs.

In 1340, as the government sank deeper into financial ruin, it hoped again
that wool would pull it out. Edward got the merchants to agree to a total
duty of £4 per sack of wool for exports by Englishmen while aliens paid

£5 3s. 4d. a sack, but parliament forced him to back down in return for a grant of taxes for two years. In July, parliament agreed to a new loan of 20,000 sacks of wool, which the government would pay for out of the tax proceeds. All other buying and selling of wool was prohibited. This was the least successful of all of the wool schemes. The government changed tack in April 1341. Parliament consented to a tax of 30,000 sacks of wool to replace the second year of the tax. Each county was assessed for a certain amount of wool. Though the assessment proved to be more than twice the value of a fifteenth, this plan proved moderately successful. The crown used the wool it collected to repay creditors and even gave some to military commanders for the payment of wages.

The government, however, abandoned this project in 1342–3 and then vacillated for nearly a decade over its wool policy. At first, Edward opened trade and tried to profit only through customs. Merchants as well as the house of commons attacked the plan. Merchants were upset at the fact that the holders of the 'Dordrecht Bonds' would be able to export free of customs. They felt bond-holders should pay half the rate. Commons were displeased at the raising of customs rates without parliamentary consent. They voiced the anxieties of the producers who feared that merchants would pass the cost of the new customs on to them in the form of lower prices. To alleviate their fears, Edward had stipulated the 'Nottingham prices' as the price floor, but in 1343 consented to a new price list that averaged about 32 per cent higher than the 1337 prices. Commons concurred in a subsidy of 40s. a sack. For the next decade, the customs were in the hands of a series of companies of English merchants. These companies farmed the customs but also made their resources available to the crown through loans. In 1347, Edward levied a new loan of 20,000 sacks, but it turned out to be a tax. It was collected on the basis of the 1341 levy with little likelihood of repayment. Individuals were supposed to be able to pay in cash or wool, though they were given little choice in the matter. Finally, in 1353 a new scheme was introduced. Natives were barred from the export trade, home staples were established, and Edward took over the collection of customs directly.

For seventeen years, the wool trade had been at the mercy of war and royal finances. When it was allowed to operate freely, the market fluctuated widely. At other times it dried up altogether. The fortunes of merchants and producers were rendered uncertain. Profits hung on the whim of policy, putting a premium on royal privilege. Merchants in the king's favour could count on some form of repayment for their loans and might hope to make up some of their losses. Yet such privileges only diminished others' hopes. Antagonisms sprang up between those with access to the king and those left outside. The import trade likewise suffered, running at only one-half to two-thirds of its previous levels. Fighting in Gascony, for example, disrupted wine production and trade. Naval action and piracy posed additional threats. Yet, despite the disruption, imports still outran exports because of the woes of the wool trade.

The measures introduced in 1353, along with other factors, finally stabilized the wool trade. The European economy recovered quickly after the first onslaught of the plague in 1348–9. While the population decline caused overall demand for cloth to contract, the frightening mortality also left many survivors wealthier than before, keeping up the demand for high-quality, durable cloth. There was a sudden jump in the consumption of luxuries. Both Flanders and Florence, moreover, were free of conflict for the time being. Wool exports returned to a robust average of 33,000 sacks a year between 1353 and 1362. There was, in addition, a surge in cloth exports, from about 2,222 cloths a year between 1351–5 to 8,700 between 1355–62. Cloth imports dropped correspondingly, producing a positive trade balance. Wool prices, however, remained low throughout the 1340s and 1350s in contrast to grain prices which shot up. Contemporaries blamed the price collapse on the ban on denizen trade. This is unlikely. Wool taxes were the real culprit. In the 1350s, the wool subsidy stood at 50s. per sack. Since wool prices were low in Flanders, reflecting the drop in production after the Black Death, merchants probably passed the costs of taxation on to producers by demanding lower prices. The cash returns per fleece on the bishop of Winchester's estate, for example, reached their lowest point in the century. Parliament, moreover, failed in 1353 and 1357 to impose minimum prices.

Wool prices did not rise again until the 1360s. Initially, a severe sheep murrain slashed supply, creating intense competition for wool, forcing up the price, and shifting the burden of taxes from producers to manufacturers. An increase in currency maintained the high prices. The return per fleece jumped up and the Winchester flock expanded to 35,000 in 1369, as the greater availability of pasture after the plague made sheep raising even more attractive.

During the 1370s, however, a long term weakening of demand set in, as production in Flanders tapered off in the wake of population loss. Wool exports declined, a slide that lasted until the end of the century. The falling off of trade also resulted from the establishment of the staple at Calais in 1363. The experiment with home staples ended in 1357 when the government located the staple at Bruges. It was shifted to Calais in order to provide the town with a secure income. Calais had been a drain on royal finances, and the crown hoped to make it less financially dependent. The government of the town and staple was entrusted to a consortium of twenty-six English merchants. Alien merchants were at a disadvantage and exports fell to an average of only 28,000 sacks a year under the Calais staple. The glory days of the wool trade had passed. Removal of the staple from Calais, bans on denizen exports, and other changes in royal policy did not help. Wool exports dropped even further to 20,000 sacks a year between 1376 and 1380. Cloth exports made up some of the loss. The revival of the cloth industry is one of the most significant, but also most obscure, stories of fourteenth-century England. The actual size of the domestic market is not known because it remained untaxed until 1353 and even after a tax was introduced, evasion was so common that the internal trade remains shadowy. Other evidence, however, shows a reviving industry. Cloth *imports* began to slacken prior to the Black Death and disappeared in the 1370s, while cloth *exports* expanded enough to justify an export duty in 1347. At that point, only a few thousand cloths a year were exported, but they climbed to around 15,000 by the end of Edward's reign. That number represented only slightly more than 3,400 sacks of wool, so that exports of cloth did not quite offset the erosion in wool exports. Yet cloth was of higher value than wool. Every region of Europe had its own textiles for ordinary use. The export industry was geared to the upper end of the market, to elite households. David Nicholas has shown that by 1371 Flemish merchants were willing to risk large fines to smuggle English cloth into Flanders, which had banned English imports. Some cloths were of ordinary quality, but others were exceptionally fine, capable of fetching prices high enough to encourage the evasion of strict import regulations. High-quality English cloth was exported to Castile as early as the late thirteenth century, though most exports to that country in the fourteenth were of inexpensive cloth. England was competing successfully in a restricted market and had become a net exporter of cloth as well as the prime supplier for the home market. This remarkable turnround occurred in the space of a few generations.

The reasons for the recovery are far from certain. Several forces were at work. The most noticeable, though probably least effective, was governmental. Manufacturers' laments reached sympathetic ears on the king's council, and from 1326 onwards, the crown tried periodically to boost domestic production with protectionist legislation. A statute in March 1337 did several things. It banned the export of English wool and the import of foreign cloth, prohibited the wearing of foreign cloth, declared that only those with £100 or more in annual income could wear furs, and encouraged the immigration of foreign cloth workers by offering them various privileges. The measures were largely diplomatic in intent. Edward hoped to frighten the Flemings as well as to lay the groundwork for his grandiose scheme of a royal wool monopoly. Chroniclers were generally contemptuous of the statute, declaring that it was ineffectual because no one paid any attention to it. Only Geoffrey le Baker held a contrary opinion. He said that notwithstanding the fact that the statute *at first* seemed unfruitful, cloth-making increased more than twentyfold in the years that followed. Baker was blinded by hindsight. The ban on exports and imports lasted only a short time and the legislation had no teeth to it. It is less indicative of the effectiveness of governmental action, than of the government's awareness of the workings of the wool and cloth trade. A second force was social. Some Flemings did emigrate to England and brought with them their cloth-making skills. Their numbers and impact, however, were not as great as has sometimes been portrayed.

If social and governmental forces do not explain the increase in English cloth-making, can technical ones do so? Over the thirteenth and fourteenth centuries, there was a dramatic increase in the number of fulling mills located along rural streams. They were partly responsible for the flight of cloth-making from some towns. Fulling was a process of pounding woollen cloth in water to make the weave denser and tighter. It was originally done by foot. The fulling mill did the same job with wooden paddles. It needed, however, a stream to power the mechanism. Hence, it is argued, production moved to the countryside as weavers located near the new technology. Yet, fulling did not constitute a large percentage of the cost of cloth, and the savings achieved were not all that significant. At the same time, the costs of erecting a mill were substantial, and could only be borne by a wealthy lord or merchant. There was no reason, moreover, why mills could not be located in towns. It is better to see the advent of rural fulling mills, therefore, as part of an overall pattern of competition within the native cloth industry among rivals jostling for a share of the market, than as spearheading a new expansiveness.

Market forces may have been the most influential in reviving the textile industry. The fact that the Flemish export industry began to concentrate almost exclusively on finer quality cloths (broadcloth) in the first half of the fourteenth century probably encouraged the expansion of English crude or medium grade cloth (worsteds, kerseys, etc.) at lower prices. Competition from the Flemings forced English manufacturers to lower their costs as much as possible. The depression in wool prices between the 1340s and 1360s must have further encouraged domestic production.

These elements may help explain how English cloth gradually recaptured the domestic market, but they do not explain the growth of exports. Openings for English cloth were made by difficulties within the Flemish industry caused by war, taxation, civil strife, and increased competition. High taxes and a shortage of wool in the 1370s significantly raised the costs of Flemish producers, giving a slight edge to the English. Thus, medium quality English cloths appeared in greater numbers in markets such as Castile, where they could undercut Flemish cloth yet were sufficiently superior to local production to make them attractive to the elite. Disruption in older cloth-making centres also opened the door to competitors. Throughout these years, for example, the Flemish industry was periodically convulsed either by war or by conflict within the towns. In Ypres, production fell from over 90,000 cloths a year in the first decade of the century to around 40,000 in the 1350s. It rebounded to over 50,000 cloths during the 1360s and 1370s, but the shortfall was significant. English cloth was taking up some of this slack, and cloth from Brabant also made significant inroads into overseas markets. In addition, Hanseatic merchants took a greater interest in cloth exports. They turned from the wool trade, in which they were at a disadvantage, to the cloth trade, where they could supplant Flemish cloth with English. Their exports jumped from an average of about 400 cloths a year between 1358 and 1363 to nearly 2,300 in 1364. Simultaneously, English cloth appeared in greater numbers in the Castilian market and other locations in Europe. English cloth-making thus did not need to create a new market or expand existing markets. Instead it took over economic niches left vacant by the dislocations of war and disease.

It is thus essential to view English commerce, and indeed English economic development generally, in the context of the European economy as a whole. There were limits to the achievements of English merchants. J. L. Bolton has described the English economy in the early fourteenth century as 'quasi-colonial'. He is referring to the English production of a raw material (wool) for a foreign industry (Flanders) and the control exerted over English trade and finance by foreigners (Flemings and Italians). English merchants and cloth-makers gained a greater share of the export market, took over from the Italians as major lenders to the crown, and broadened the range of English exports. Yet, English overseas trade was still subject to foreign control. Nicholas' study of the seizure of English goods at Bruges in 1371 shows how Italian and Flemish merchants continued to exert a powerful influence on English trade. The Italians supplied Flemish merchants with English wool through the staple at Calais while simultaneously exporting wool directly from England to the Mediterranean. The Flemings acted as the chief middlemen for England's import trade. Bruges was just one of several entrepôts where English merchants contacted exporters and arranged for the transfer of goods. Flemings were supposed to be the middlemen for all such trade. The most prominent agents were innkeepers, who added warehouses to their victualling trade. Goods were thus supposed to have been shipped to Bruges, warehoused, brokered by Flemings, and then shipped out again. Despite such regulations, the English did have direct contact with Castilian, German, or Italian merchants, though Bruges retailers still benefited from the side-effects of trade. Furthermore, goods were usually shipped in Flemish boats because the English merchant marine was underdeveloped. Nicholas estimates that 470 to 475 ships a year travelled between Bruges and London alone and that imports from Bruges may have amounted to 31,000 tons a year. That represents substantial earnings for Flemish brokers, merchants, and shipowners. The terms of trade were also favourable to the Flemish. Wool was still England's most important export commodity. English cloth was not yet exported on any considerable scale and the Flemings were highly protective of their industry. Besides wool and cloth, England exported cheese, hides, and other commodities to Flanders. Imports on the other hand included herrings, tallow, soap, olive oil, almonds, ash, flax, spices, and materials for textile production such as alum, wood, iron, and madder. Whether by weight or value, these imports were far more important than England's exports to Flanders. This pattern of English trade dependency on the Low Countries would last into the sixteenth century.

It already had a profound impact on the English economic landscape. Flemish competition had forced English textile manufacturing out of the cities in search of cheaper labour and supplies. In contrast, Flemish production was concentrated in a few large centres such as Ghent, Bruges, and Ypres, to the detriment, though not impoverishment, of the countryside. Flemish towns represented the outer ring of concentric arenas of trade centring on the English village. Dense urbanization was possible in Flanders in part because of the ready availability of English raw materials, control of the wool trade by a handful of mercantile companies, and the existence of an English market for the finished product. Cloth production remained in the cities, where Flemish merchants dominated not only the marketing of the product, but the supply of raw materials. English towns did not have to grow that large. Cloth production was decentralized, and most towns were centres for local, small commodity trade or way stations in international commerce. What was needed was not a number of great urban concentrations but rather a series of smaller market centres that were close to production. When the textile industry revived in the early fourteenth century, it was already located in the countryside and did not result in greater urbanization. Towns facilitated the growth of industry, just as they had the wool trade, not as centres of production but as market outlets.

Edward III tried hard to exploit this interdependency between England and Flanders for his own purposes. The wool trade was an inviting target in the 1330s. Active, profitable, and geographically concentrated, it appeared to be ripe for exploitation. Edward's calculations, however, were faulty. The margin of profit was not wide enough to bear the burdens that he wanted to impose. He miscalculated politically as well as economically. Flanders needed English wool and English markets, but the English were just as dependent on the Flemings. Disrupting the wool trade might bring diplomatic benefits but it certainly brought economic problems. It also caused trouble at home. Edward's consultations with merchants were crucial to winning support for his schemes. What he apparently did not foresee, however, was the profound impact the policy would have on producers and their reaction against it when it proved financially harmful. A broad segment of English society looked to wool for profits. When Edward's projects jeopardized those revenues, producers dragged their feet or protested through parliament. The policy ultimately foundered because economic and political considerations were inextricably bound together.

6

ECONOMIC CHANGE

———— • ————

England in 1300 was prosperous. Yet over the next seventy-five years a series of profound shocks jolted the country. Famine, deflation, inflation, and disease rocked the foundations of English life. The crises reverberated up and down the social ladder. The effects were not the same at every rung and spelled hardship for some, prosperity for others. When the period was over, changes had been set in motion that would profoundly alter England's economy and society.

The intensity of these shifts can be shown most graphically and simply by the rise and fall of grain prices, illustrated in Figure 2. Since the vast majority of the population was engaged in the production of grain, everyone felt the movements, which affected income as well as expenditure. After a steady rise during the thirteenth century, prices remained stable for over a decade from 1290. This was the peak of the medieval economy with a high population, moderate wages, and healthy trade. After 1307, however, uncertainty set in. Sharp inflation began in 1307 and lasted until 1330, reaching its highest level between 1315 and 1321. There followed an equally significant period of deflation from about 1330 to 1345. Prices fell steadily before bottoming out in 1340. By 1345 they were well on their way toward recovery and, indeed, were heading for yet another remarkable inflation that peaked in 1370. The final period began in 1370 when prices once again fell, reaching the levels of 1290–1307 in 1380.

The changes were determined by a host of factors. The quality of harvests, the time of year, the population, the market, and the supply of money worked to push grain prices up or pull them down. Weather was a constant, though usually temporary, danger. Worse, it was unpredictable. Chron-

iclers looked upon nature with wonder, misgiving, and respect as a force
that was far beyond their control. *The Brut* linked a fall in prices in 1337 to
the appearance of a comet in June and July. John of Reading noted that a
solar eclipse in May 1361 was followed by drought and that a rare astro-
logical conjunction of Mars, Saturn, and Jupiter in 1365 resulted in heavy
rains, pestilence, and other disasters. Adam Murimuth told how in the
autumn of 1345 the rains were so heavy that grain could not be harvested
and stored. Many, even in the valleys and most fertile places, perished.
People put their experience into verse: 'If it rains at the feast of Processus
and Martinian (2 July) then it shall rain excessively and suffocate the grain.
If the translation of St Martin (4 July) gives rain, then it customarily contin-
ues for forty days.' People were apprehensive about weather precisely
because harvests were so vulnerable, prices so sensitive, and so many lived
poised on the brink of hunger or even starvation. Chroniclers noted harsh
conditions in 1337–9, 1345, 1347, 1352, 1353–4, 1361, 1362, 1363, and
1365. At those times, weather seemed the sole culprit for people's misery.

Despite the intimate relationship between harvests and the cost of grain,
however, identical harvests did not always yield the same prices. Other
forces intervened to exacerbate or ameliorate local conditions. Changes in
the supply and value of money, for example, fuelled the volatility of price
movements in these years. The size of the population determined the
demand for grain and the supply of agricultural labour, so that demographic
change had a fundamental impact on the economy. Though it is hard to be
precise about population levels, some general conclusions can be drawn.

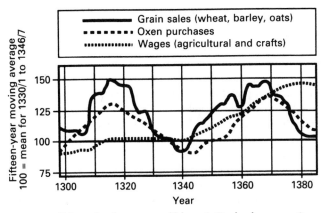

Figure 2.   Prices of grain, oxen, and labour in England, 1300–1380
(D. L. Farmer. 'Crop yields, prices and wages in medieval England', *SMRH*, new
series 6 (1983): 142).

The number of English men and women rose throughout the thirteenth century and may have crested in the early fourteenth when there are indications that people were straining the available supplies of food. Drops in harvest levels produced jumps in mortality, chiefly among smallholders and cottagers. M. M. Postan argued that the population at least levelled off and probably began to decline somewhat. Other researchers have argued that the demand for land stayed high and wages low in many parts of England, indicating that there might not have been much change. It is hard to be conclusive. It is known, however, that an exogenous, biological force, plague, caused a sudden drop in the population through repeated visitations from 1348 through the 1370s. The effects of that reversal were immediate and long-lasting.

Put in this way, people's lives appear to have been at the mercy of impersonal forces. At this historical distance, it is difficult to see personal choices but it is important to keep in mind that lords and peasants made individual decisions about consumption and production based on desire, whim, and fancy as well as need, and that the cumulative weight of those decisions pushed the economy in different directions. People were not merely reactive pawns. The economic context in which they made their choices is laid out in four sections. The first charts the period from 1300 to 1348, the next two deal with the plague and its consequences, and the last considers the economic consequences of war. Altogether, they reveal an era of startling economic contrasts, embodying both difficulties and opportunities and underscoring the vulnerability of the peasant budget to changes in weather, money, and population.

AGRARIAN AND MONETARY CRISES, 1307–1348

There was no single cause for the ailments that afflicted England during the first generation of the fourteenth century. The crisis was a series of short-term problems which began as inflation heated up around 1307. Only changes in the money supply could have produced such rapid inflation. The population was not rising fast enough, if at all, to drive up demand, while a healthy grain supply should have held down costs. Except for two years, 1308 and 1310, wheat harvests were above average between 1305 and 1314. Barley yields were lower than average in 1305, 1306, 1307, and 1314, but otherwise performed well. Only oats were consistently disappointing.

The initial cause of the inflation had to be monetary. Because England mined little silver, it could augment its stock of currency only through a favourable balance of trade or through plunder and ransoms. If the value of exports exceeded that of imports, then silver flowed into England, though it flowed out just as easily if the relationship were reversed. Since the reign of Edward I, moreover, the crown had imposed strict controls on the export of bullion, specie, or plate, on the circulation of foreign coins, and on the import of counterfeit or poor-quality coinage. Combined with the boom in wool exports, these measures produced a positive balance of payments and a net flow of silver into the country at the beginning of the century. More money was minted than ever before and less was exported. But the boom had an adverse side. The greater amount of silver in circulation caused a rise in prices. Thus, despite abundant supplies, the cost of grain and other goods stayed high.

Inflation was intensified by famine and cattle murrain between 1315 and 1321. Heavy rains and freezing weather caused disastrously low harvests in 1315 and 1316. Thefts of foodstuffs increased. Deaths among poor small-holders surged, partly because the famine was accompanied by a typhoid epidemic. At Halesowen and in three Essex communities the population declined as much as 15 per cent, though other villages suffered smaller losses. The harvest of 1317 was only slightly better and real relief did not come until 1318. Conditions improved for a few years, but there was another poor harvest in 1321 when wet, freezing weather returned. Custodians of the forfeited lands of the Contrariants in 1321–2 in Gloucestershire and Herefordshire reported over and over again that the continuing snow and frost destroyed gardens and reduced the proceeds from arable, pasture, and meadow. In the meantime, a cattle murrain had devastated herds through-out England, driving the price of oxen to new heights. Custodians declared that they were unable to lease some forfeited pasture land because the inhabitants had no animals. The loss of oxen and the excessive price of replacing them simply complicated the difficult task of cultivation and magnified the hardships of the poor.

Political disaster heightened the problems. Edward II's humiliating defeat by the Scots at Bannockburn in 1314 left the Scots free to plunder northern England. According to the *Chronicle of Lanercost*, in 1315–16 they invaded Northumberland, Westmoreland, Cumberland, and Durham; burned the town of Hartlepool; besieged Carlisle, Berwick, and Richmond Castle; and everywhere burned the crops and buildings of the districts through which they passed. Local inhabitants were reduced to buying off the raiders; Cumberland paid 600 marks in tribute.

While the north was exceptionally hard hit, all across England manorial court rolls bear witness to the difficulties facing the peasantry. Not only do they record an increase in heriots and entry fines as holdings turned over on the death of tenants, they also show a startling increase in land transfers. These are the signs of smallholders struggling to make ends meet by selling off some of their capital. Four manors of the abbey of St Albans, three in Hertfordshire and one in Cambridgeshire, offer clear indications of the trend. On average, the Hertfordshire court rolls record roughly twenty-two transactions a year for the years 1307–15, the Cambridgeshire court rolls a brisker fifty-six, and all four about seventy-eight land transactions a year. Between 1315 and 1317, these averages leapt to 84, 90, and 174 respectively. Although the rate of transactions afterward subsided, it stayed at a level higher than before the famine. The same trend is evident on the estates of Titchfield abbey in Hampshire: 12.4 transactions per year from 1297 to 1307, 25.5 in the following decade, and 20.4 from 1317 to 1327. The land market at Coltishall displays the same crisis symptoms. Peasants responded to the harvest failures and high prices by selling portions of their holdings. They also migrated. Emigration from the village of Broughton steadily mounted as conditions worsened, seriously depleting the population.

Conditions improved slightly in 1322, though there were still difficulties. The Coltishall records show another poor harvest in 1330–1, sending prices and land transactions upward. Drought conditions seem to have prevailed over the eastern part of the country, affecting Kent as well as Norfolk. Murrain struck cattle and sheep once again in 1334. Estate owners found it hard to lease pasture land because tenants had lost their animals.

Then deflation struck. Grain prices had peaked in 1315–16 and fell steadily after 1322. Good harvests between 1325 and 1327 and in the early 1330s helped bring prices down. Yet the primary cause of deflation was monetary. The coinage in circulation may have dropped from a high of more than £1 million in 1311 to around £500,000 in the 1340s. The output of the royal mints dwindled to almost nothing by 1337. The money supply was ordinarily depleted by wastage (the normal wear and tear on the coinage) and hoarding (a customary means of saving). But during the 1330s an unfavourable balance of trade drained off additional silver. The commons decried the shortage of money in the realm in 1337 and asked the king to take measures to rectify the situation. Unfortunately, beginning in 1336, his wool schemes slashed exports while imports held steady. Because of the imbalance, currency streamed out of the country. Differences in exchange rates added to the problem. Throughout the early fourteenth century, the value of gold in England was marginally higher than it was on the continent, tempting Italian and Flemish bankers, who controlled large volumes of specie, to sell gold in England for silver. As a result, silver shifted overseas while English stocks of gold mounted. Gold, however, was not useful for ordinary transactions, and day-to-day business was further starved of money.

Edward III's bid for the French throne contributed to the outflow of silver after 1337. He spent lavishly to secure allies and support his army in Flanders. Initial payments to his nine leading partners in 1337 alone came to about £124,000. Though he did not export huge quantities of bullion, relying instead on Italian, Flemish, and English creditors, he spent more than

£400,000 overseas by 1341. Furthermore, the taxation needed to pay off these loans and meet Edward's expenses took cash away from buyers, hurting demand, and from producers, who were already hurt by low prices. Prices fell to levels that had not been seen since the 1260s. The chronicler Adam Murimuth put his finger on the problem when he declared that low prices were the result of a shortage of money rather than an abundance of grain. Despite harsh conditions from 1337 to 1339, prices continued to edge downward. Indeed, though the harvest of 1339 was the worst in years, with yields comparable to those of 1315, prices did not rise. A popular song complained that there was such a shortage of money and so many people were destitute that there were few buyers at market, even though men had cloth, wheat, pigs, or sheep to sell. Political and monetary forces had thrown the market off balance, setting deflation in motion.

The government grew alarmed. Threats of rebellion were heard. The scarcity of money and consequent low prices hurt individuals' ability to pay their taxes just when the government needed tax receipts the most. Something had to be done.

Monetary policy was dominated by two ideas. The first was the conservation of currency. Medieval rulers made profits on their mints, taking fees, or a seigniorage, for the minting, which could be increased by lowering the silver content of the coins. England did not frequently adjust the quality of its currency for profit, unlike the French monarchy which relied heavily on debasement to raise revenues in the 1300s. England's monarchs proceeded cautiously, partly because of parliamentary opposition to debasement. This conservatism also arose out of the second idea, the importance of acquiring bullion. Bullionist ideology stated that the health of a country was measured in its stocks of currency. Like most other medieval governments, therefore, England's encouraged measures that led to the acquisition of specie. In 1328, even before the bite of deflation had been felt, for example, the government ordered Thomas Cary to find John le Rous and Master William de Dalby and bring them before the king, because he had heard that they made silver through alchemy.

The experiment must have failed, for in 1335 Edward III debased the coinage for the first time since the re-coinages of 1279 and 1299. He wanted to raise money, but he may have also acted out of concern over the falling stock of silver in circulation. The debasement was a mild 4 per cent from the 1279 standard, but deficits and deflation pushed Edward further in the same direction. He debased the coinage again in 1344, 1345, 1346, and 1351, by which time debasement totalled 19 per cent. Parliament howled in protest. Edward promised not to do it again, and, indeed, no further debasement was attempted in the next sixty years.

In the meantime, Edward had introduced a new gold coinage. Foreign

gold coins circulated in large numbers in the 1330s and early 1340s, largely
Florentine 'florins' and French 'ecus'. They were not legal tender but were
used to hoard wealth, to pay foreign debts, or to offer security for loans. Parliament proposed in 1339 that these coins be accepted as legal tender, that
is, that all but small merchants be compelled to accept them as well as sterling
in transactions of more than 40s. The proposal was explicitly tied to the
shortage of money and was envisaged as a means of increasing the money
supply. Edward did not respond. In 1343 he decided to mint his own gold
coins. His first attempt, with the 'leopards', was not a resounding success,
but subsequent mintings of the 'nobles' proved very successful. Unfortunately, the new coins were valued too highly *vis-à-vis* continental coinage
so that England continued to attract gold at the expense of silver. The situation was not really rectified until 1351 when the 'nobles' were debased.
Thus, in the short run, gold coinage did not change the flow of bullion and
did not solve the deflationary woes.

The government also looked to the wool trade to improve the situation.
In 1339, parliament proposed that merchants exporting wool be required to
bring back 40s. of bullion per sack. They were to deliver this plate to the
exchanges where it would be minted. In 1340, the government required
merchants to deposit plate of a certain value which they could redeem by
showing a receipt that bullion had been turned in to the mint. The government also required deposits for the payment of the wool subsidy. Thus,
merchants had to find money for deposits as well as for paying customs. Cash
payments could come to 73s. 4d. per sack before the wool could be shipped,
a prohibitive amount for many. Such regulations were as chilling to trade as
Edward's fanciful monopolies, but they may have succeeded in their professed aim. The output of royal mints jumped in 1343. The willingness of
English merchants that year to accept Edward's offer to manage the customs
in return for 10,000 marks a year can only be explained as an effort to get out
from under the deposit scheme. It put them in a position to arrange a way
for paying customs and deposits that was not financially crippling. In any
case, once they took over the customs, the records cease and the security
deposits disappear from view.

In 1343, after calling on the expert advice of merchants and goldsmiths,
parliament prohibited the export of English money and the import of poor
and counterfeit coins. To enforce the measure, the government appointed
searchers who would receive a third of the imported and exported money
they discovered. Parliament also decreed that if the Flemings improved the
quality of their coinage, it would be accepted in England as legal tender, to
help stem the outward flow of silver.

Finally, because money was so scarce, the government in 1340 adopted
the novel expedient of levying taxes in kind. Taxpayers had to produce a

ninth of their harvest, as well as the ninth lamb and ninth fleece. Though called a ninth because it was levied after tithes had been deducted, the tax was simply a tithe, a tenth. The produce was to be sold at fixed prices and the proceeds paid to the crown. It provides a good indication of how serious the money supply problem had become.

Chroniclers, poems, and parliamentary protests all remark on the hardship caused by the shortage of money. While direct testimony of its impact on the peasantry is harder to come by, some insight into the fate of villagers can be gleaned from the assessments for the ninth in 1341, the inquisitions of the ninth (*nonarum inquisitiones*). Local juries from the north of England, Shropshire, Sussex, Bedfordshire, Buckinghamshire, Cambridgeshire, and Hertfordshire all told of land going out of cultivation since 1291. For example, 4,870 acres were idle in Cambridgeshire, 5,539 in Buckinghamshire. Two-fifths of the parishes of Bedfordshire reported lower values for grain, wool, and lambs than in 1291. Fifty Shropshire parishes reported land lying uncultivated. Jurors blamed the losses on soil exhaustion, flooding, bad weather, fears about invasion, murrain, and even rabbits. Yet one explanation crops up over and over again – peasant poverty. The combination of deflation, rents, and taxation aggravated the ordinary difficulties of the peasantry. Incomes fell with prices but rents stayed the same, so that they gobbled up a larger share of the budget than in times of normal prices. Rents had to be paid, whatever the economic conditions. Just at this point, when deflation was most severe, Edward geared up for war with France and heaped one demand after another on communities: lay subsidies, clerical taxes, wool subsidies, taxes in wool, purveyance, and military service (see Table 4, p. 184). The loss of wool profits, hard enough for large producers, might have been catastrophic for smaller ones who desperately needed that supplementary cash to meet their obligations. After deducting rents and taxes, there would have been little left from a peasant's greatly depreciated income. To make matters worse, wages, too, seem to have dipped slightly in these years.

Some peasants gave up their holdings and others sold portions to raise cash. The number of land transactions per manorial court at Coltishall in Norfolk suddenly jumped in the years around 1340, reaching its highest level in the period between 1280 and 1420. While it is true that a run of good harvests in the 1330s helped the peasantry, it has to be measured against prices, rents, and taxes. Peasant producers lived in a delicate economic equilibrium. Excessively low as well as excessively high prices threatened to upset that balance. The swing from one to the other within a single generation must have placed an unprecedented strain on most peasant budgets. Little wonder, then, that jurors often laid the blame for uncultivated land at the feet of poverty and taxation. As has been seen, John de Grandisson, the bishop of Exeter, similarly linked weather, rents, and taxes in trying to decline Edward's request for a county tax in 1337. Townsfolk faced similar problems. In the early fourteenth century, town populations appear robust and their economies, thanks to buoyant overseas and internal trade, prosperous. The rent receipts of Canterbury cathedral priory (Christ Church) in Canterbury, for example, show no marked weakening. The pattern, however, was not uniform. Rent movements in Oxford suggest that receipts reached a peak in the 1260s, after which landlords found it difficult to collect customary rents. They were forced to negotiate slightly lower rents or suffer arrears in payments. There were not many vacancies, but there may have been a slight tapering off in demand for urban property, indicating a stagnation or decline in the population of some towns.

The international fair also faced problems in the early fourteenth century. Fairs in England, like the great fairs of Champagne and Flanders, had attracted merchants and wares from all over Europe by offering a centralized facility for trade, exchange, and credit. After 1300, however, war disrupted commerce on the continent while changing trade patterns, the rise of banking, and the development of centralized mercantile houses deprived fairs of the very reason for their existence. In England, the experience of the great fair of St Giles at Winchester typifies the consequences. From the late thirteenth century, French and European merchants gradually stopped visiting the fair. London merchants and other traders took their place, but soon they, too, stopped attending. The fair thus lost its international and interregional characteristics and became important only as a centre for local commerce.

In general, however, the late 1340s seem to have been a period of recovery. The tremendous price swings smoothed out giving peasants a chance to recoup financially. Harvests were good, and prices rebounded from their nadir in 1340. In some areas population decline was arrested or even reversed. Records from Halesowen and Coltishall, for instance, indicate rising populations to 1348. The number of marriages each year at Halesowen also seems to have been on the upswing before the Black Death, demonstrating that villagers were sufficiently prosperous and optimistic to start new families. Elsewhere, however, the downward trend in population continued after the 1315 famine. Some Essex communities and Broughton in Northamptonshire showed signs of decline. It is difficult to be certain from a few, isolated examples, but in some areas, at least, the thesis that the population could not have continued to grow and was in fact declining does not hold true. The balance of harvests, prices, and rents produced a temporary return to the kinds of conditions that prevailed at the beginning of the century.

THE BLACK DEATH, 1348–1375

The advent of the 'Great Pestilence', as contemporaries called it, or Black Death, as it came to be known in the sixteenth century, was momentous. The epidemic arrived in England in 1348 and struck again in 1361–2, 1368–9, and 1374–5, killing a substantial portion of the population and triggering massive social and economic changes. For the moment, it is important to examine the spread of the pestilence and the resulting mortality.

In that year [1348] and the following year there was a general mortality of men throughout the world . . . Then the dreadful pestilence penetrated through the coastal regions from Southampton and came to Bristol, and almost the whole strength of the town perished, as if overcome by sudden death; for few there were who kept their beds for more than two or three days, or even half a day. Then this cruel death spread everywhere, following the course of the sun. At Leicester, in the small parish of St Leonard's there perished more than 380 people, in the parish of Holy Cross, 400, in the parish of St Margaret's, Leicester, 700; and so in every parish a great multitude . . . After the pestilence many buildings both great and small in all cities, towns, and boroughs fell into total ruin for lack of inhabitants; similarly many small villages and hamlets became desolate and no houses were left in them, for all those who had dwelt in them were dead, and it seemed likely that many such little villages would never again be inhabited.

Henry Knighton's chronicle, from which this is extracted, is the most complete contemporary account of the epidemic. It reveals not only the virulence of the plague but the horror it aroused in the population.

The exact nature of the epidemic is open to question, though the historical consensus is that it was bubonic plague. It did not display all the characteristics of outbreaks of plague recorded in the modern world and there are serious doubts whether the rat population and dispersed human population of medieval England could account for such a high death rate. That rate, however, seems to be consistent with better documented outbreaks of the disease in other eras and places. While the exact mechanism of destruction is still a puzzle, it seems that the general cause was probably plague.

As Knighton notes, it struck the south of England first and probably arrived by ship. The standard account is as follows. Plague was enzootic, residing in the rat population of Central or East Asia until it burst out in general pandemics. The disease is actually a bacillus that ordinarily survives in rats or rodents. As the bacilli multiply in the diseased rat, they are taken up by fleas that live on the rats. If the rat dies, then the fleas will look for a new host, including humans. When the infected flea bites its victims, it regurgitates some of the bacilli into the blood, infecting its host. In humans, this produces bubonic plague, so called because the disease results in a swelling of the lymphatic glands, a bubo, nearest the bite, in the neck, armpits, or groin. Mortality ranges from 60 to 85 per cent. There is another variety, pneumonic plague, which is even more virulent than ordinary plague because it forms a kind of pneumonia in which the bacilli can be spread directly from human to human. Death is virtually certain and the disease is highly contagious. Finally there is septicaemic plague in which the blood is so quickly diseased that there is no time for the formation of buboes.

Both rats and fleas are highly mobile. Once the pandemic started, it marched relentlessly across the Middle East and Europe. Under the right conditions, fleas could survive without hosts and it was no problem for them to hitch a ride on merchandise travelling either by cart or ship. After arriving in southern England, the plague moved across the British Isles, infecting the northern Isles of Scotland and Ireland by 1349. By the beginning of 1351, the threat had subsided for the time being.

Because the fleas are most active in warmer weather, the incidence of bubonic plague climbed during the summer months and subsided during the winter. Pneumonic plague, however, because it was associated with pneumonia, rose during the cooler months. This variation may account for the pattern discovered in the hundred of Farnham in Surrey. The death rate there rose noticeably not in the summer of 1348, but during the fall and winter. Deaths declined after December but then rose once again in June 1349 and stayed high during the summer.

It thus seems possible that the 'Great Pestilence' involved both bubonic and pneumonic plague and that England became an enzootic area itself, in which a portion of the rat or small animal population remained infected. There were further outbreaks of plague from the fourteenth into the seventeenth century. The first in 1348–50 was the most virulent and widespread, but plague none the less became for a while a regular feature of the English environment. It is also likely that diseases other than plague played a role in the population loss. As has been seen, typhoid was instrumental in the deaths during the famine of 1315–21 and local outbreaks of plague, influenza, typhoid, and other diseases were common in the fifteenth century.

The second pestilence, as chroniclers termed it, broke out in 1361–2. *The anonimalle chronicle* of St Mary's abbey in York stated simply that in 1361 'there was the second pestilence in England which was called the "mortality of infants", and in which many people and a great number of children died'. Knighton similarly commented that the plague struck both young and old, but mostly youth and infants. Demographic trends derived from the Halesowen court rolls seem to bear out this depiction of heavy child deaths. John of Reading said the pestilence affected men above all.

Reading, moreover, commented on what he saw as moral collapse among the survivors. Although many men died, it was the womanly life that was most grievously pained. 'For shameless widows, the love of their former husbands forgotten, flinging themselves at strange men and even more at cousins, begat false heirs conceived in adultery. But in many places it was said that brothers took their sisters for wives. Afterwards many of whatever status, grade, or order, paying no heed to sin, had no concern for any lapse of flesh: fornication, incest, or adulterous games.' Despite the misogyny of a clerical observer, the passage is an interesting indication of contemporary attitudes. Gone is the horror of widespread death, replaced by a concern for order and morality. Reading attributes to women the desire to procreate, not merely for sexual pleasure, but to have heirs. Yet women perverted those drives because they failed to observe social norms. The children are not true heirs because the marriages are not valid, but made within the church's prohibited degrees (cousins and brothers) and against society's standards (strangers). Another chronicler underlined the latter point, emphasizing that women took as husbands men who were unsuitable because they were social inferiors or idiots. The passage thus says more about conceptions of social order than about actual practice. Nevertheless, data from the manor of Halesowen show that the number of marriages did indeed increase in the wake of a high number of deaths in 1348–50 and 1361–2.

The plagues of 1369 and 1375 carried off additional victims. *The anonimalle chronicle* said that the 'fourth pestilence', that of 1374–5, started in towns in the south and was especially severe in London. Death rates also climbed noticeably at Halesowen. Other minor outbreaks of plague were described by John of Reading in 1365 and by *The anonimalle chronicle* in 1378. A change in the pattern of death among tenants-in-chief, as recorded in the inquisitions post-mortem, also suggest that the plague may have become endemic after 1348. Before then, most deaths occurred during the winter, but afterwards the summer saw the greatest number of deaths, even in years when there was no major outbreak of plague. This pattern is consistent with the epidemiology of bubonic plague. England may have been assaulted by plague not only on the four major occasions, but on a recurring basis. What was the cumulative effect?

In trying to estimate the overall population loss, it is important to keep two things in kind. The first is that the plague did not have the same effect everywhere. The second is that there were no censuses or complete population listings. Changes must therefore be teased out of incomplete and disparate sources. One such source is the record of institutions of priests which shows that there was a significant increase in vacant parish livings during the plague years. In the diocese of Lichfield, for example, 184 of 459 (40 per cent) benefices opened up in 1349, meaning that most of those parish priests had died. In other dioceses, the percentage of vacancies ranged from 40 to 45. These figures are in line with the mortality recorded in monastic houses.

Inquisitions post-mortem provide similar information. On the death of a landholder who held land directly of the king (a tenant-in-chief), royal officials took temporary custody of the property, held an inquest to determine who the heir was and the value of the property, and then delivered the lands to the heir or guardian depending on the findings of the inquest. The inquisitions record that only 27 per cent of those holding lands in 1348–9 died of the plague. They generally deal with men and women of the knightly rank or higher who could take some measures to avoid the plague.

Manorial sources such as court rolls and rentals provide important information about the deaths of tenants. The problem with this material is the myopia of seigneurial documentation. Lords were concerned about their *tenantry*, about those who were directly responsible for paying rents, performing services, and attending courts. Families, sub-tenants, lodgers, or servants were not their primary interest and tended to escape notice. Hidden from historical view, those classes of people can only be brought to light through painstaking family reconstitution. Thus, information about mortality derived from manorial documents generally refers to the tenantry, not to the general population.

Manorial records none the less depict a bleak world in 1348–9. Forty per cent of the tenants at Halesowen died, 60 per cent at Coltishall, 65 per cent at Waltham, and two-thirds at Cuxham. Information from Glastonbury abbey lands suggests losses ranging from 33 to 69 per cent with an average of 55 per cent. An array of sources from the diocese of Worcester gives a broad view of the mortality. Forty-four per cent of the tenantry died in the plague while approximately one-third of the livings fell vacant. In 1360, the tax liability of Worcestershire had to be reduced by more than £55 or 11 per cent of the 1334 total because of the decline in the population. Income from recognitions (payments made by the unfree tenantry to a new lord whenever there was a change in lordship) dropped from over £40 to £1 8s. 8d. in 1349. With the elevation of a new bishop in 1353, officials could collect only £3. Nevertheless, even in this case, losses varied greatly from manor to manor and village to village. Thus, the impact of the plague was severe but uneven. A comparison of the bishoprics of Worcester and Lichfield displays the same characteristics. The loss of tenants was much heavier on the former than the latter while losses were made up faster at Lichfield.

Since these were tenants, each death created a vacancy. The rate at which landlords were able to fill those vacancies tells something about the population as a whole. At Halesowen, 82 per cent of the vacancies were filled within a year. At Waltham, all were filled. Similarly at St Albans, where most vacancies were filled by heirs of the deceased. Elsewhere, recovery was slower. At Cuxham three years after the outbreak, 69 per cent of the unfree holdings were still vacant and were only filled up by 1355 through migration. On Battle abbey's manor of Alciston, 22 per cent of the holdings still lacked tenants in 1352. The abbey absorbed some of them into the demesne and tried to lease the remainder. In the diocese of Worcester, recovery took another turn. The bishop had trouble finding occupants for small holdings because survivors preferred to move up the economic ladder and take large, vacant tenements. The death rate in the general population could not have been much different from that among the tenantry. It is astonishing, therefore, that despite so many deaths, so many vacancies were filled so quickly. These figures suggest that parts of the countryside were crammed with people, eager to step into niches as soon as they emptied.

Given crowded and unsanitary conditions, it seems that the death rate in towns might have been higher than in the countryside. It was said that 7,000 died in Norwich, perhaps half the population. Knighton comments that both Bristol and Leicester suffered heavily, and mortality in Oxford and Canterbury was quite high. Rent receipts dropped off precipitously and landlords had some difficulty finding tenants in the first few years after the Black Death.

Overall, it seems likely that mortality in England reached 35 to 45 per cent in 1348–50. A huge 'surplus' population meant that in many areas landlords did not have to worry about holdings standing vacant for long. Marriages, to judge by the Halesowen material, may have risen markedly in the aftermath, helping the recovery. The data indicate that England's population had certainly grown to the point of diminishing returns by 1348. The smallholders, cottagers, and landless boarders who crowded into villages increased food production only marginally. Their numbers meant that even a sharp rise in the death rate did not immediately upset the pattern of occupation and lordship on most manors.

Subsequent visitations of the plague, however, crippled the ability of the population to recover and landlords to find tenants. By 1361, surplus numbers no longer existed. As a result, new vacancies were not automatically filled. At Halesowen losses amounted to 14 per cent in 1361, 16 per cent in 1369, and 12 per cent in 1375. If it was true that in 1361 the death rate was particularly heavy among children, then the chances for replacing the lost population were dramatically reduced. Localized visitations added to the mortality. In all, this disastrous generation may have seen a drop in the population of nearly 50 per cent.

THE EFFECTS OF POPULATION LOSS, 1348–1377

The dramatic fall in population resounded throughout the economy, affecting wages, prices, and agricultural production. It marked a significant turning point, even though there were a number of forces at work besides population. Wages rose as the supply of labour plummeted. Knighton observed that livestock wandered the fields because there was no one to watch over them. He went on to explain that 'the following autumn no one could get a reaper for less than 8d. with food, a mower for less than 12d. with food. For this reason many crops perished in the fields for lack of harvesters.'

The data bear out Knighton's assertion. Demands for higher wages came immediately on the heels of the plague and continued until the end of the century. Wages differed according to the local labour supply and the bargaining abilities of workers, so that the rate of change was not uniform. The wages of agricultural workers rose faster than others. Between the 1340s and 1350s, harvesters' wages went up an average of 23 per cent, mowers' 28 per cent, and threshers' 12 per cent. The average for all workers was 18 per cent. On the bishop of Worcester's manor of Hampton Lucy, the loss of population caused a dramatic increase. In 1357, when the statutory wage rate for reaping was 3d. a day, employers in the region were paying 6d. Reapers received 6½d. a day in 1372. Labour costs at Hampton worked out to about 12½d. an acre. Elsewhere, the accepted rate was 8d., though 10d. an acre was not unheard of. Harvest wages were vulnerable because of the urgency of getting the crops in. Other labourers did not fare quite so well, and indeed, the wages of skilled craftsmen lagged behind those of agricultural workers, at least initially.

Prices, too, changed. Knighton, once again, makes a good starting-point. He remarked that prices went down during the pestilence: 'there was a great cheapness of all things for fear of death, for very few took any account of riches or of possessions of any kind'. The cost of livestock plummeted. By the following winter, conditions had changed: 'all necessities became so dear that what in former days had cost a penny now sold for 4d. or 5d.'. The inflation may not have been quite as steep as he implies, but prices did rise steadily from before the Black Death to 1370.

The house of commons found the situation alarming and in 1363 proposed a number of remedies. The price rise was arresting that year because poor harvests in 1362–3 followed four good ones, which had sent prices down for the first time in over a decade. In response, the commons asked for a ceiling on prices for fowl and a ban on exports of food, though grain exports had already been prohibited in 1360. They denounced the engrossment of grain and victuals by grocers because they thought it inflated prices.

They also believed that inflation was caused by people wearing apparel and eating foods beyond their station and wanted measures to guarantee that individuals would consume only goods appropriate to their rank. The commons thus saw inflation as the product of presumption, privilege, and dearth caused by hoarding or exporting. In 1363, the king responded to their complaints by setting prices for fowl, breaking the monopoly of guilds, and regulating dress and eating. The following year, however, the commons relented and asked that the measures be dropped and free trade restored. Edward assented.

Other forces sent prices upward despite the apparent decline in demand brought about by widespread mortality. In part, the rise occurred because of bad harvests resulting from poor weather in the 1350s and 1360s. Furthermore, as in the earlier cycle of inflation and deflation, monetary factors played a prominent role. With the drop in population, the per capita supply of money increased. A favourable balance of trade fuelled inflation. High exports of wool and the beginnings of cloth exports during the 1350s allowed for a partial recovery of the wealth that had drained overseas at the beginning of the Hundred Years War. The introduction of gold coinage and debasement helped to boost the supply of silver. Since gold was useful for large transactions, the amount of silver available for petty commerce increased. The debasement of 1351 further boosted the currency in circulation. John of Reading and Geoffrey le Baker both claimed that it led to higher prices. Reading carped that it also produced higher wages so that labourers worked less and worse. Monetary factors thus helped to increase the money supply at a time when the number of people using it had declined substantially. It is little wonder that prices rose.

Changes in consumption may have also played a role. With more money in fewer hands, higher income from wages, and lower rents than before the Black Death, many peasants found themselves in a position to purchase goods they could not previously have afforded. Others might simply have improved their diet. At Colchester, ale drinking increased and there was a shift away from inferior oat to barley malt, necessitating an increase in barley production. All across Europe there are signs that the demand for luxuries and manufactured goods at least remained stable and may even have increased despite the drop in population. If the social conservatism of the commons is anything to go by, the 1360s were characterized by frenzied social climbing. The sumptuary legislation of 1363 complained that the lower orders were able to ape the higher by purchasing finer clothing and food. Towns seem to have benefited from this changing pattern of demand. All were hard hit by the plague, but many of them, York for example, remained fairly prosperous into the 1370s. Plague did not kill the desire for luxuries or simple commodities and may have in fact stimulated the market.

The second great inflation of the fourteenth century was therefore not as difficult for the peasantry as the first. For one thing, it was not associated with famine. For another, changes in the supply of labour and money meant that there were greater opportunities for making money. Finally, peasants had greater access to land in an era when the profits from grain were higher than ever. As the population went down, opportunities for acquiring land rose.

The drop in population led to a decline in rents. Knighton commented that:

All the magnates of the realm, and lesser lords too, who had tenants, remitted the payment of the rents lest the tenants should go away, because of the scarcity of servants and the dearness of things – some half their rents, some more, some less, some for two years, some for three, some for one, according as they could come to arrangements with them. Similarly, those who had let lands by days' work of a whole year, as is usual with bondmen, had to waive and remit such works, and either pardon them entirely or accept them on easier terms, at a small rent, lest their houses should be irreparably ruined and the land remain uncultivated.

The point is that population decline forced landlords to bargain with tenants over rents, shifting the balance of power in lord/tenant relations. If tenants did not get what they wanted, they migrated in search of land with fewer obligations. Many left villages and moved to towns, occupying places left empty by the plague. As a result, some villages disappeared altogether, though this was not common before the last quarter of the century. Desertion was generally related to the burden of lordship. Wherever rents and services were onerous, tenants were apt to leave. This is precisely what happened at Hatton, part of the manor of Hampton Lucy in Warwickshire. Though prosperous, the village had a high percentage of servile tenants with heavy dues. Between 1370 and 1385, most packed up and left, leaving a deserted village that the bishop was hard-pressed to maintain.

Despite these changes, agriculture did not change drastically right away. Some land went out of production. The cultivated acreage on Battle abbey's manor of Marley fell from 404 at the beginning of the century to 141 by the end of the 1350s. In contrast, less than a fifth of the arable on the extensive Winchester and Westminster estates went out of production between 1350 and 1380. Peasant production may have declined even less because of an infusion of women workers. Their agricultural labour had largely been seasonal, but at the end of the fourteenth century, there are indications that the number of women working at agricultural jobs all year round rose.

The quality of cultivation might have changed more than the extent. Less intensive cropping than before the plague has been discovered in Norfolk, the Chilterns, and Essex. Rotation schemes seem to have relaxed, allowing land to lie fallow longer. Arable did not go out of cultivation altogether; the cycles of planting and fallow simply stretched out. There may also have been a shift away from wheat in favour of barley and oats. Evidence compiled by D. L. Farmer comparing yields on the Winchester and Westminster estates during the fourteenth century seems to confirm this trend. It shows that there was a modest improvement in yields of all grains between the first and second quarters of the century (1300–1325–1350). Demand was high and there was little change in the overall size of the population despite the famine years, which may have impressed upon farmers the need for intensive cropping. Between the second and third quarters (1325–1350–1375), however, there was a pronounced decline in yields except for oats. This fall would be consistent with a relaxation in the agricultural regime. Pressure on the food supply was not as great as it had been before the Black Death so that farmers opted for less intensive cultivation. The slight increase in oat yields might have been due to the lack of interest shown in wheat coupled with increases in livestock herds, which would have propped up the demand for oats. Thus, English farmers could have cultivated roughly the same acreage as before the Black Death though much less intensively.

In many ways, therefore, the fundamentals of English social and economic life had not altered beyond recognition as a result of the dramatic loss of life between 1348 and 1378. Yet changes accelerated during the 1370s and on into the next century as the effects of population loss on villages, landlords, and trade deepened. At the end of Edward's reign, it was apparent to all that their world was heading in a different direction from the one they had known.

THE COSTS OF WAR

Another force in the economic life of England in Edward's reign was war. The precise nature of its impact, however, is highly speculative because of the absence of hard economic data. Two positions are usually taken up, due perhaps as much to temperament as to evidence. On the one hand there is the optimistic view that war sparked economic activity and brought windfall profits through spoils and ransoms. On the other, there is the pessimistic view that war added to the burdens of an overtaxed peasantry, disrupted economic activity, and in general funnelled resources from the 'productive' to the 'non-productive' sectors of the economy. On balance, what evidence there is seems to tip the scale toward the latter view.

To begin with, war upset international trade. Edward's foolhardy wool schemes were calamitous for producers and traders alike. No one escaped unscathed. Fighting, moreover, disrupted wine production in Gascony while war and piracy in the English channel further disrupted trade. Fluctuations in imports along with purveyance and the closing of markets likewise took a heavy toll of business.

Towns suffered as well. Great Yarmouth endured a period of severe losses in trade and shipping while community as well as individual fortunes in Southampton declined. Towns also paid for defence and fortifications. Coastal towns, for example, were required to outfit ships for the king's navy. The crown was supposed to repay these expenses, but the burgesses of Newcastle upon Tyne had to pay more than £50 out of their own pockets for keeping three ships at sea in 1337. Finally, the northern border and the southern coast were vulnerable to attack. Repeated raids by the Scots effectively destroyed Berwick upon Tweed as a market. Ports such as Winchelsea, Rye, and Hastings were subject to destructive and costly attacks by the French after war broke out. A raid on Southampton in October 1338, for example, caused destruction that took years and considerable sums to repair. Town issues fell to just under £17 for the year following the raid. They gradually crept up to £19 in 1339–40 and then leapt to nearly £66 in 1341–2. That recovery is symptomatic of the resilience of the economy, but it was not enough. The citizens lamented throughout the 1340s that they could not raise the town's farm of £200. The exchequer halved it in 1342, but Southampton still could not meet all its obligations. By 1345, it had run up a debt of over £1,800 at the exchequer. By contrast, a few towns profited from wartime conditions. York, for example, did extremely well in these years. The presence of the government for long periods in the 1330s stimulated the local economy.

Furthermore, although, as Bridbury has observed, a suffering government is not necessarily the sign of a faltering economy, the two were linked. Edward's government staggered financially during the 1330s and 1340s and again in the 1370s. Despite taking more than £400,000 in various levies between 1337 and 1340, the government still fell deeply into debt. Royal policies ruined the wool trade and hastened the flight of silver from the realm, worsening the deflationary tendencies in these years.

The individual burden of taxes varied greatly. Among the wealthy it was very light. At Christ Church, Canterbury, the percentage of receipts eaten up by taxes ranged from 8.63 (1292–1307), to 4.4 (1308–15), to 5 (1320–37); at Bolton priory, from 4.4, to 3, to 1.9; and at Cuxham manor from 5 to 8 (1336–1368), leaping to 15 per cent in 1354–5 when income fell. Mavis Mate has concluded that taxation did not force a dramatic change in Christ Church's standard of living, though coupled with high expenditure and economic problems in the 1330s it created problems for the priory. The impact on the peasantry could be quite serious. The government extracted far less than either church or landlords, and the weight of taxes was far lighter than that of rents. Marjorie McIntosh, in fact, found that the tenants of

Havering were greatly under-taxed and that many who should have paid escaped altogether. A crude comparison of taxes and rents can be made for Cuxham. In 1334, its tax liability was £2 15s. 4d., while in 1332–3, the unfree tenants owed £5 12s. ½d. in labour services alone, outstripping taxes more than 2 to 1. The disparity was even greater because the demesne owed 32s. or nearly 60 per cent of the tax.

Taxes *by themselves* were not onerous, but placed on top of other dues they could easily strain a peasant budget. Maddicott's argument that royal exactions created individual hardship and weakened the economy seems convincing. The accumulation of demands – taxes, military service, purveyance, and fines – simply increased the outflow of cash. Furthermore, the closure of markets, prohibitions on exporting grains, delays in making payments, and rampant corruption obstructed local exchange already crippled by deflation. Jurors in the inquisitions for the ninth thus claimed that some peasants deserted their lands because of taxation. Since the land market was finely tuned to market conditions and peasants readily sold land to raise cash, it is not hard to imagine that some, already hard-pressed to pay rents, found the additional expenses too great and sold out. After 1334, when the minimum rate for taxation was dropped and taxes were apportioned by the community, the burden of taxes was borne by a far wider portion of the population than it had been before. Between 1327 and 1338, the number of those on the tax rolls in Kent increased by 6,000 in a period when population growth was negligible. As for indirect taxes, it has been argued that European customers helped to pay for England's wars because merchants passed the costs of increased customs primarily on to Flemish manufacturers who boosted the price of textiles. The English were immune from such increases because they were producing their own cloth. Certainly, export duties were reflected in textile prices. Yet low wool prices in the 1350s and the clamouring in the house of commons for minimum price schedules surely indicate that merchants were able to transfer some of their costs back to producers.

The costs and benefits of war fell unequally. The nobility supported war, at least until 1372 or so. Whether or not they in fact profited, they must have assumed they would. Peasants, however, had little reason to serve in the army. Overseas service was unknown and dangerous, payment was uncertain, and leaving one's tenement, no matter how small, was risky. Despite the existence of an enormous pool of under-endowed tenants throughout the 1360s, the crown had difficulty enforcing military obligations. There is some evidence of social advancement through war, which will be examined in Chapter 8, while the economic fall-out from equipping and victualling armies enriched some local tradesmen. Individuals profited, but there is no sign of general advancement.

As difficult as the war may have been for some, it could not begin to match the calamities or structural changes brought about by inflation, deflation, and the Black Death. The contrasting fates of Colchester and Great Yarmouth after 1348 show that war could cause more disruption than plague in certain circumstances. Yet, the short-term dislocations of royal policy did not touch the deeper structures of society and economy. Remarkably, however, between 1327 and 1377 breathtaking change occurred on both levels simultaneously. Not only did squalls race across the economic and political surface but deeper demographic and social currents shifted and flowed in different directions. Problems and uncertainties on one level were magnified by those on the other, challenging landlords as well as peasants.

7

THE LANDLORDS' RESPONSE

Rapidly changing conditions caught lords as well as peasants in their current and forced them to reconsider the management of land and tenants. Although they did not respond uniformly, lords gradually abandoned the direct management of their estates in favour of less risky methods. All the while, they increased the pressure on the peasantry to make up some of their losses, until peasant resentment exploded in the English Rising of 1381.

To understand the landlords' response to changing economic conditions, it is important to have a clear picture of their powers and resources. They controlled the two critical components of an agrarian economy, land and labour, through property rights, legal authority, and economic monopolies. Proprietary authority guaranteed them land to work or lease. Jurisdiction enforced the payment of rents, the performance of services, and the regulation of the lord's tenements. Monopolies such as markets or mills not only produced a small income but supplied necessary services.

These powers were organized with tenants and land into estates, which might consist of lands in a single region or be spread across several counties. Estates sometimes included woods, chases, parks, or warrens, where lords hunted with their friends, as well as castles or residences. Markets, fairs, and towns were integral elements of an estate's resources. The basic sub-unit of the estate was the manor. Though there was no such thing as a 'typical' manor, virtually all had three essential components: demesne land held directly by the lord, tenant land held by hereditary free or unfree tenants for rents and/or services, and a court. Manors also contained pasture, meadow, woodland, or scrub. Proportions varied. A manor could have primarily demesne land with only a few tenants, a large number of tenants with no demesne at all, predominantly arable land, or mostly pasture, woodland, and meadow with only a little arable. Sometimes manor and village were coterminous. Other villages were divided between two or more lords so the village functioned as an agricultural unit, though the villagers belonged to different manors.

Two manors, located near Cirencester, Gloucestershire, illustrate the diversity. When they were surveyed in 1327, both were in the hands of Edmund earl of Kent. Lechlade, the larger of the two, had a house, barn, oxhouse, and dovecote. It contained 304 acres of demesne arable, worth over £5 a year, and a staggering 595 acres of demesne meadow worth £44 a year. There was pasture for 27 oxen, 17 cows, 40 young steers, and 300 sheep. Four free tenants, one of whom had 16 sub-tenants of his own, owed about £2 rent. Eight men and women had life tenancies that paid 117s. 10d. while 52 customary tenants, including a smith, owed about £26 rent. Rents from the town of Lechlade exceeded £14 and the manorial court produced £8 10s. a year. Altogether the manor was valued at £101 11s. 9½d. Barnsley, in contrast, was worth only £16 7s. 2d. a year. It had domestic and farm buildings, 192 acres of demesne arable, and only 13 acres of meadow. A park and pasture were worth 40s. a year. Ten free tenants paid rents totalling 52s. 7d. and 36 customary tenants paid nearly £6.

Manorial differences also show up regionally. Leicestershire, for example, was characterized by small demesne lands and fragmented lordship. Of 134 villages surveyed in 1279, 37 had only one lord, 34 had two lords, and 63 had two or more lords. Most demesnes, 65 per cent, were smaller than 150 acres and a mere 15 per cent exceeded 250 acres. Indeed, 40 per cent of the villagers lived on manors with no demesne at all. A sample of lands in Gloucestershire forfeited by rebels in 1322 was very similar. Of sixty-nine holdings taken into custody, only twenty-one had demesne and tenant land exceeding 500 acres but they averaged 1,562 acres apiece and comprised about 84 per cent of the sample acreage. They clearly overshadowed the smallholdings, which had only 128 acres on average. Small demesnes comprised about 72 acres compared to 158 acres for larger ones. Extensive demesne lands, averaging 426 acres, were found on the fourteen largest manors. The distribution of free and unfree land followed these differences in size. Free tenants held nearly 40 per cent of the land and the unfree about 31 per cent, though on large manors the unfree held about 34 per cent compared to 14 per cent on small manors. Smallholdings thus tended to have a high percentage of demesne but few villeins.

Estates, too, differed. Some were quite extensive, as some examples from the early fourteenth century demonstrate. The earl of Lancaster's mammoth estate sprawled across northern England and produced over £11,000 a year. The earl of Gloucester's was worth about £6,000 a year from manors, hundreds, towns, rents, and tenements in eighteen counties, as well as from lordships in Wales and Ireland. The archbishop of Canterbury had more than forty manors and towns spread out over six counties, more than 7,000 acres of arable, and a total value of about £2,600. The bishop of Worcester's estate was not quite so valuable. It produced around £1,200 and consisted of 7,000 acres of arable, 800 of meadow, 350 of pasture, and about 200 of waste, of which 21 per cent was held in demesne, 61 per cent by unfree tenants, and 18 per cent by freemen. Knightly estates were smaller and more localized than noble ones. Two Sussex families illustrate the point. The Etchinghams held six manors in Sussex, three in Kent, and one in Buckinghamshire, while the Sackvilles held four in Sussex, one in Suffolk, one in Essex, and one in Oxford, altogether worth around £200 a year in the 1370s. Similar patterns emerge in Bedfordshire, where the Braybroke family held lands in six villages plus five holdings in Northamptonshire and Leicestershire. Of forty-eight knights and esquires in Gloucestershire in 1316, about 25 per cent held only one manor, 66 per cent held three or more, 20 per cent held five or more, and 58 per cent held one or more outside of Gloucestershire.

Estates also changed over time. Lay estates were particularly fluid, as marriage, inheritance, family gifts, and politics added or broke off assets. Ecclesiastical estates, which were not subject to the same forces, changed slowly. Lords, however, disliked the diminution of lordship caused by gifts of land to the church and secured the statute of mortmain (*de viris religiosis*) in 1279 which prohibited religious houses from acquiring land. In practice, the crown assumed the right to license acquisitions so that religious grants did not halt altogether.

Professor Holmes has remarked that during the fourteenth century, barring misfortunes, great lay estates tended to grow larger. Much depended on inheritance. If there were no heirs, the estate reverted, or escheated, to the lord. Estates descended by primogeniture to the eldest male heir, who in most cases was the eldest son. Women inherited only if there was no male heir, and heiresses divided the estate equally among themselves if there were more than one. That happened to the estate of the earls of Gloucester after Gilbert de Clare died at Bannockburn in 1314 leaving three sisters as his heirs.

Family sentiment complicated the running of an estate. Like peasant households, noble families were strongly nuclear in orientation and affection. The endowments that landowners made for prayers for the dead show that they were attached primarily to their wives or husbands, children, and parents. Aunts, uncles, and cousins were left to fend for themselves. Wives often focused their concern on their children and their own parents, rather than on their in-laws.

Families were torn. They wanted to consolidate their wealth as well as provide all their children with a reasonable livelihood. As a compromise, most practised a modified form of primogeniture in which the largest share of the estate went to the eldest son but gifts were made to other family members. The most significant deduction was the endowment of daughters or sisters with marriage portions or dowries. No woman could marry without a dowry, and dowries were traditionally given in land. Landholders similarly gave land to younger, non-inheriting sons or brothers. Widows and widowers were also provided for. When a man died leaving a widow, she was entitled to one-third of his property as her dower to hold for her lifetime. She could not permanently alienate her dower land, but it was none the less lost to the heir until she died. Widowers similarly had a right to curtesy, the use of their wives' property for their lives if they had had a child. Taken together, these practices amounted to a powerful tradition of family support.

In addition, all landholders were tenants, not owners, and tenancy imposed restrictions on their use of land. They could not, for example, bequeath land. They had no way of compelling their heirs, after they had died, to support other children or augment their widows' dower or repay their debts out of the issues of their estates. They could not prevent an heir from inheriting except by granting the estate to someone else. If they died leaving a male heir under twenty-one or a female heir under fifteen, their lands fell into the custody, or wardship, of the landlord, or landlords, until the heir came of age. Some landlords, notably the king, also acquired the right to marry minors to whomever they pleased. Tenants-in-chief were even more restricted than other tenants; they could not alienate – that is, give, sell, or lease – land without the king's permission. Most other freemen enjoyed freedom of alienation. Though not as restrictive as unfree tenure, free tenure did limit the tenant's freedom to use the holding.

From the mid-thirteenth century, lawyers fashioned legal devices to get around some of these restrictions, give tenants greater discretion over their holdings, and limit the damage of family grants. To lessen the dissipation of property, for example, families began giving leases, life grants, or annual rents to younger sons and cash dowries to women. The most potent instrument was a grant and regrant with conditions. A landholder granted property to someone else, called a feoffee. The feoffee immediately regranted the land to the original holder, stipulating certain conditions under which the property would be held. For example, in a jointure, lands were regranted jointly to a husband and wife. Each had equal title so that the survivor would have full possession for the rest of his or her life. Or land could be entailed. The regrant settled land jointly on a husband and wife for their lives on condition that after their deaths the land would descend only to their children or only to a male. Reversions and remainders could be established. The regrant could stipulate that if the couple died without male descendants, the land would revert to the original donor's heirs or remain to another person altogether. Landholders spun complicated conditions to cover every eventuality. One example illustrates the process and one reason for its popularity. In 1314, Edmund Deincurt was troubled. His grandson had just died so that his heir-apparent was his great-granddaughter Isabella. Fearing that when she inherited, his surname and arms would be lost to memory, he received the king's permission to grant and regrant his lands. Edmund disinherited Isabella by granting his lands to a feoffee and receiving them back for life with an entail which stipulated that on Edmund's death his lands would go to Isabella's uncle William and the heirs of his body, or, if William or his descendants died without heirs, to William's brother John and the heirs of John's body. In another settlement, Edmund left more than 300 acres to his grandson's widow for her life and then to Isabella and her heirs. The whole undertaking guaranteed that the bulk of the Deincurt property would descend through males though it left a small provision for the women. Landholders also used these devices to make life grants for children and to avoid feudal wardship.

Lawyers achieved the same goals through enfeoffments to use. In this device, a landholder transferred title to several persons jointly, called feoffees. They then gave the original donor the use of, but not title to, the lands for his life. They retained title. Before he died, he wrote out instructions to them, his 'last will', detailing what he wanted done with the lands after his death. For practical purposes, this was a method of bequeathing land. Records are sketchy, but a study of the gentry in Berkshire has shown that enfeoffments to use were not employed widely before the end of the century and that when they were, they were primarily intended to keep the estate intact.

Despite these precautions, families fell into debt, estates were fragmented, and lands drifted out of the male line. The flux of property enabled some families to enrich themselves further. Growth and failure were complementary processes, as the history of the Percy estate illustrates. The Percies were a baronial family with extensive holdings in Yorkshire, Lincolnshire, and Sussex. Their estate grew in two spurts, at the beginning and end of the century. In 1309–10, Henry Percy purchased the barony of Alnwick in Northumberland along with lands in Scotland from the bishop of Durham, who had acquired them from the Vescy family. Percy's son augmented these holdings by preying on another Northumberland landholder, John de Clavering, who had fallen deeply into debt. Seeking a remedy, John granted the bulk of his estate, whose value surpassed £700 a year, to Edward II, stipulating that it would stay with the crown if John died without male heirs. In return, he received some lands from the king for life, though he still had to sell off other lands to raise money. When Edward III came to the throne, he gave Percy, a staunch supporter, 1,000 marks a year for life in return for his service. Shortly thereafter, Edward assigned Percy the reversionary interest in Clavering's estate in place of the annuity. When John died in 1332 leaving only daughters, the property passed to the Percies. Between 1375 and 1379, the Percies acquired the reversion of half of the estate of Gilbert de Umfraville, the last earl of Angus. Henry de Percy, grandson of the earlier one, married Gilbert's widow, Matilda, daughter and heir of Thomas de Lucy and a granddaughter and co-heir of Thomas de Multon. Through her, the barony of Cockermouth in Cumberland along with lands in Northumberland passed to the Percies. In the meantime, the family had been purchasing property in Lincolnshire and elsewhere.

Growth occurred at the expense of other families. The fragmentation of the Vescy, Clavering, Umfraville, and Lucy estates enabled the Percies' estate to grow. The families either disappeared or descended into social insignificance while the Percies steadily enlarged their holdings through purchase, favouritism, and the good fortune of having a healthy run of male heirs. Therefore, if there was a tendency in the fourteenth century for some estates to grow, as the Percy, Neville, Mortimer, Arundel, Lancaster, and Stafford estates did, it could only happen because others declined.

The income derived from these estates can be divided into sales, rents, and the perquisites of lordship. The Percy manor of Petworth in Sussex is illustrative. In 1352–3 the reeve accounted for a total receipt of £157 8s. 2d. (excluding arrears from the previous year). Of that, £66 8s. 9d. or 42 per cent came from sales of grain, livestock, wool, dairy products, and other goods. Free and unfree rents, the commutation of labour services, and various leases produced another £79 5s. 1d. or 50 per cent. Court fines, tolls, and miscellaneous items brought in £11 14s. 4d. or 7 per cent of the total. While the sale of produce was lucrative, it was clearly overshadowed by the profits from lordship. The balance varied. Around 1300, 63 per cent of the archbishop of Canterbury's estate revenue arose from agricultural production. On Battle abbey's much smaller estate, 25 per cent of the income in 1346–7 came from rents, 66 per cent from 'sales' of produce, and 6 per cent from other sources. (Grain 'sales' were often fictional, to account for the delivery of grain from manors to the household. In 1351–2, for example, 37 per cent of Battle abbey's 'sales' receipts were actually grain deliveries to the abbey.) Bolton priory in the north of England earned its highest revenues between 1303 and 1315 when rents made up 35 per cent, grain sales 17 per cent, wool 23 per cent, livestock, wood, and meadow 14 per cent, and miscellaneous sources 11 per cent of its income.

Managerial choices hinged on the demesne land: how could it be used most profitably? Lords could elect to take either direct or indirect profits. That is, they could either cultivate the demesne at their expense and collect receipts by selling the produce or they could lease it to someone else for a cash payment, called a 'farm'. Indeed, they leased (or, in medieval terminology, 'farmed') entire manors. Rents from hereditary peasant tenants were always an important part of the lord's income. The choice was whether to increase that proportion by leasing the demesne or to engage in agricultural production and marketing.

The trend in the thirteenth century had been toward the direct cultivation of demesnes or, confusingly, 'high farming'. High farming, however, had never been complete and did not exclude leasing altogether. The earl of Lancaster's demesne lands in Leicestershire, for example, were at farm (leased) in 1314. In two villages, villein tenants held the demesne under a scheme of sharecropping. Canterbury cathedral priory (Christ Church) began cultivating its demesnes only after 1270, with mixed results. Bolton priory committed itself to high farming around 1295. Durham priory cultivated only eight of its twenty-two manors in the early fourteenth century while five others alternated between leases and direct management. The Percy family similarly mixed techniques. It cultivated its Yorkshire and Sussex manors directly, but leased out demesnes closer to the turbulent Scottish border. Finally, there is little evidence of high farming on large estates in Cheshire and Lancashire where the greater lords had been leasing their demesnes to the local gentry since the thirteenth century.

Four considerations weighed heavily in deciding how to manage the estate. The first was its size and composition. The direct management of manors located far from the centre of the estate could be expensive. Widely scattered holdings posed great difficulties for small lords. Management costs were the same as on a large estate, but they ate up a greater percentage of the output. Similarly, lords with few villein tenants tended to rely more heavily on demesne production than those with large rental incomes.

A second consideration was consumption. Large households, notably monasteries, required huge quantities of food and drink. Most lords tried to satisfy these needs out of their own estates. They distinguished between 'income' manors which provided cash and 'home' manors which were located near the centre of the estate and were used to stock their households. Benedictine monasteries developed a sophisticated system of management geared toward supporting the community. The purpose of demesne cultivation at Durham priory was thus consumption, not profit, and sales of surplus grain were used to defray management costs. Changes in consumption could herald changes in management. When Christ Church switched from beer to wine in the late thirteenth century, for example, the consequences rippled throughout the estate. Less barley was needed, so less was planted, and some arable was converted to pasture. On large estates, pastoral husbandry was not simply a handmaiden to arable. The consumption or sale of animals and their products (wool, dairy products, etc.) determined the allocation of estate resources. This role is most conspicuous for sheep, yet similar incentives were at work for horse and cattle raising.

As this last example makes clear, landlords had their eyes on a third factor, the market. To be responsive to market forces, they had to be flexible in the use of their resources. Christ Church was finely attuned to the markets for grain, livestock, wool, and dairy products and tried to shift production in step with price changes to get the most out of its sales.

Finally, lords had to consider costs. Demesnes were profitable only if well run. Yet supervising villein services, collecting rents, marketing grain and livestock, overseeing reeves and bailiffs, and auditing accounts were time-consuming and expensive tasks. Even then, as the well-managed Battle abbey estate demonstrates, the lord could not prevent all losses. As it had evolved since 1200, direct management consisted of three components. At the bottom, the manorial staff included the reeve and *famuli*. The reeve was the foreman of the manor, drawn from the ranks of the unfree. He collected rents, supervised work on the demesne, and accounted for manorial receipts and expenses. As Chaucer portrayed him, he was a figure at once of cunning and dread. No lord could outwit him. Clever reeves indeed found a multitude of ways to pilfer from their lords. On the other hand, they could strike terror into the hearts of villagers, for they were the lord's representative, a role they likewise turned to profit. The *famuli* were dependent farm workers, ploughmen, swineherds, dairymaids, and so forth. They formed the core of the demesne workforce and worked year round for food and board. Additional workers were hired for specialized tasks such as threshing.

Between the manor and the lord's household there were bailiffs. Manors were often grouped into territorial units called bailiwicks, with a bailiff assigned to each. Riding from manor to manor, he watched the demesnes and reeves and held the manorial courts every three weeks or so. At the top there were estate stewards, auditors, and receivers. Over the fourteenth century, management became more centralized and authority concentrated in fewer hands than it had been a century earlier. The estate steward emerged as the pre-eminent official. Receivers collected the revenues and auditors scrutinized carefully the manorial and household accounts. These men formed the core of the lord's council which not only handled policy making and administration, but also took a hand in important legal issues. The numbers of intermediate personnel declined. On the bishop of Worcester's estate, the bailiffs' duties were reduced to holding courts while central officers took over the management of manors.

Each layer was intended to supervise the one below, to prevent cheating, and promote the best use of assets. Estate treatises, written at the end of the thirteenth century to instruct landlords how to manage their estates, focused on the problems of supervision. One version of *Seneschaucy* recommended weighing the relative costs and profits of direct cultivation and leasing, as well as changing bailiffs, to get the best return. High farming clearly involved considerable expenses.

Despite these costs and uncertainties, most landlords before 1350 directly cultivated at least some of their demesne land. Conditions were propitious. High population kept up the demand for land, boosted grain prices, and held down wages. It gave lords with large numbers of villeins the luxury of reckoning whether it was more profitable to apply villein labour to their demesne or to commute their services, hire workers, and pocket the difference. The existence of a large pool of expert administrators, knowledgeable in accounting and law, also encouraged the spread of direct management. Their expertise is reflected in the treatises on estate management, law, and accounting that circulated in growing numbers from the end of the thirteenth century onward. In most cases, they, not the lord, decided whether to work or lease the demesne.

Inflation and deflation, famine and plague, war and taxation challenged the wisdom of high farming. Yet, because conditions changed so rapidly, it was difficult to determine the most profitable course. Lords began to move away from direct cultivation, but the movement was halting and did not gather momentum until the very end of Edward's reign.

It seems safe to conclude that from about 1290 onward estate profits stagnated or grew only slowly. High prices boosted revenues, but they also increased costs. Ramsey abbey's ordinary expenses rose dramatically, eating up an ever greater proportion of its income. Rents were not rising, rent rolls were no longer lengthening, and profit margins were shrinking. Famine and inflation between 1315 and 1321 only worsened the situation. Deflation in the 1330s brought a different set of problems. Lords saw returns from grain sales plummet just as the wool trade collapsed. In addition, war and plundering in the north, purveyances, high taxation, the collection of debts to the crown, and political forfeitures complicated the task of managing estates. These were not easy years, and landlords had to summon all the administrative manoeuvrability they could to steer a profitable course.

Some resorted to leasing. Hit by problems such as short episcopacies, vacancies, and high indebtedness, the bishop of Worcester began leasing lands of marginal value around 1299 and did so increasingly after 1311 when conditions were at their worst. The profitability of Bolton priory's manors was diminished by Scottish raids and inflation. It began leasing in 1314 when its own calculations clearly showed that high farming was producing no profits and perhaps losses. Ramsey abbey leased some demesne land, and the abbot complained in 1319 of economic hardship. Landlords of smaller estates may also have backed away from high farming. One investigation of the gentry in Gloucestershire found that on three manors unfree labour services had been entirely commuted to cash payments between 1300 and 1348.

By and large, however, it does not appear that these transient crises prompted widespread changes in management. The population recovered from famine, demand for land was robust, and rents and entry fines stayed high. By the late 1340s, most landlords of large estates had weathered the crises. There is evidence from Canterbury Cathedral priory and Ramsey abbey, for example, that landlords enjoyed a period of prosperity comparable to the boom at the beginning of the century. The manor of Langenhoe, Essex, displays similar signs, in rising grain production and sales. For landlords, economic conditions seemed propitious.

Any such optimism was abruptly shaken by the advent of the Black Death in 1348. Initially, the pestilence did not cause a revolution in estate management. Manorial records picture reeves, bailiffs, and stewards soldiering on as though oblivious to the horror around them. The sudden windfall of heriots and entry fines from survivors actually meant that manorial income jumped. Administrators were severely tested none the less. They scrambled to find tenants, buyers, and labour. Since the plague arrived so late in 1348, there was little difficulty harvesting that year's crops, but problems appeared the following year. And, as the plague receded, conditions returned to near normal.

A. R. Bridbury has termed the 1350s and 1360s the 'Indian summer' of high farming. Several things induced most landlords to continue direct cultivation, though on a reduced scale. To begin with, even though between 35 to 45 per cent of the population died in 1348–9, the huge surplus population meant that survivors quickly filled most vacancies. Most landlords did not suffer a catastrophic drop in rents. Rental income was not quite as strong in the 1350s as it had been before 1348, and 'decayed rents' from unfilled tenancies were recorded into the 1360s. But rents had not yet eroded enough to cause widespread alarm.

Inflation similarly heartened landlords. Canterbury priory leased some demesne land right after the Black Death but took it back under direct management in the late 1350s, hoping to profit from the surge in prices. Evidence of profitable demesnes abounds. The accounts of Petworth manor, for example, show it operating in 1352 much as it had five years earlier. The manor of Beddingham produced wheat for consumption as well as for sale up to the 1370s. Because of high grain prices, its income, like that from Canterbury priory's Essex holdings, surpassed levels attained in the early years of the century. Conditions near towns could be very good.

Colchester, for instance, experienced population growth and commercial prosperity. Its resurgence increased the demand for foodstuffs and strongly influenced the policies of landlords in the surrounding countryside. Livestock profits were likewise healthy. As has been seen, wool exports were strong. Although prices were not high, stable government policies ensured stable returns. Other livestock prices rose through the 1360s, pushed up by the persistence of high farming, which required some investment in animals, and, most importantly, by the increased money supply. The rise in fact lagged just behind the rise in grain prices, but then continued after grain prices began to fall in 1370. Peasants may have used the increased money at their disposal to buy meat and dairy products, propping up the demand for animals. Considerations such as these induced Canterbury priory to shift some of its arable to pasture and build up its herds and flocks.

Another way to increase revenues was to buy land. The tendency for large lay estates to grow meant that some incomes grew as well. The Black Death stimulated the process by bringing land on to the market. Some lords purchased land during the 1350s and 1360s when it was abundant and cheap in order to lease it. Others lost out. In Lincolnshire, absentee aristocrats gradually bought out and replaced older gentry families. Ecclesiastical lords, discouraged from large-scale acquisitions, could not participate in this market and had to make do with essentially fixed assets. The consolidation of wealth in a few great lay estates helps to explain why the higher nobility was able to indulge in conspicuous consumption toward the end of the century. Under these circumstances, there was no reason for landlords to abandon a system of management that had served them well for several generations.

Yet, despite these rosy hues, there were some troubling portents. Demesne production fell off, or ceased altogether, leading to a new emphasis on rents. The demesne sown on Battle abbey's most profitable manor fell to only 141 acres at the end of the 1350s. Rising wages forced reductions on the Worcester and Canterbury priory demesnes. Worcester began concentrating on rental income in the 1360s. It permanently commuted services and replaced tallage and miscellaneous dues with fixed payments. Manorial revenue on the bishop of Coventry's estate dropped 56 per cent between 1307–8 and 1358–60. Some unfree tenements remained vacant for a decade or longer because the bishop could not find anyone willing to occupy them for the services they had previously rendered. Elsewhere on the estate, the bishop attracted new tenants by releasing them from heavy customary obligations and lowering rents. The vacancy rate was lower but so was his income. Demesne cultivation fell because the bishop could no longer count on services or rental income to subsidize his agricultural costs. Durham priory aimed in the 1360s at reducing its dependence on an uncertain market and meeting its need for grain by switching from growing grain to purchasing it from its tenants. It even replaced some cash rents with payments in grain, a perfectly rational option, given the priory's grain consumption.

Profitability, moreover, required stringent management. Take Battle abbey. At a time when wheat was very expensive, its profits were higher than ever. But they were achieved only through drastic measures. The abbey held expenses down so that the per acre cost of cultivation rose by only 1s. and was even cut at one point by 1s. from an average of 3s. an acre earlier in the century. Higher wages forced it to reduce the amount of labour it employed. The *famuli* were trimmed. Gifts and payments of food were eliminated. The wages of Durham's manorial serjeants doubled from 10s. a year to £1. Though it reduced the *famuli* from sixteen to nine, the cost rose from £3 8s. a year to nearly £6. *Piers Plowman* sneered that those who had no means of support other than their hands would complain if they were not highly paid or if they had to eat day-old vegetables or thin ale or bacon. Workers wanted, and by implication could afford, fresh food, drink, and meat. Further, high wages pushed up all other expenses such as maintenance, construction, and reclamation. To be profitable, estates needed expert administrators who could manage them as austerely as possible with a bare minimum of labour.

Similar stories of the struggle to cut expenses and maintain profits can be told for estates around the country. Durham priory began economies even before the Black Death, trimming expenditures by half to around £100 a year. Administrators for the duchy of Cornwall adopted far-sighted measures that stemmed severe losses after the plague. They lowered rents and fines to reflect the new structure of demand for land. Because agriculture was practised alongside tin production, demand in Cornwall did not decline as much as in purely agricultural regions. Canterbury priory raked in high revenues precisely because it exploited every possible source of income – livestock, tile-making, quarrying, and rentals of ploughs, fulling mills, and other equipment. Lords none the less faced a nagging problem of indebtedness. Canterbury priory fell into debt because its income, healthy as it was, could not keep pace with rising expenses. To repay loans, it leased portions of its demesne to its creditors. Durham, Ramsey, and Battle similarly faced rising debts. As Mavis Mate has concluded: 'estate management was not an easy task in the second half of the fourteenth century'.

While there was no general stampede to lease demesnes, there was a steady movement in that direction. In 1363, the common petition lamented that because of the plague lands and tenements were wasted and destroyed and unfree tenants could not be found as before. It therefore asked the king to relax the requirement on tenants-in-chief for permission to alienate lands so that they might profit by leasing them. The lords of Winchester and

Westminster took roughly 20 per cent of their demesne arable out of cultivation between 1350 and 1380. At Hanbury, Worcestershire, where the villein tenantry plunged from sixty-one in 1299 to four in 1349, the bishop of Worcester found it impossible to keep up demesne production, especially in the face of resistance to services. Not surprisingly, by 1378 all the demesne had been leased, though elsewhere on the estate leasing was not widespread before 1400. The lords of Canterbury, Battle, and Durham all leased portions of their demesnes in the 1350s. The movement, however, was slow and not completed until after the turn of the century.

Demographic trends were working against landlords. Though the number of deaths was lower in each succeeding bout of pestilence than in the first, the cumulative toll mounted, shrinking the tenantry and demand for land. Wages were rising and inflation drove up other expenses. Inflation also increased receipts, but the change was only temporary. Is it any wonder that landlords wavered in the management of their demesnes? High farming continued, but its confidence was gone.

Blaming high wages for their troubles, landlords clamped down on workers with all their public and private power. Even before the Black Death had subsided, the king's council acted to lower wages with the ordinance of labourers on 18 June 1349. Parliament did not meet because of the plague, but when it assembled again in February 1351 it swiftly enacted the statute of labourers to supplement the ordinance. These acts tried to roll back wages to pre-plague levels and guarantee a full supply of labour at reasonable rates. They provided the first comprehensive control of wages and prices for the entire kingdom.

The ordinance aimed at fulfilling these goals in several provisions. The first ordered all able-bodied men and women – free or villein, under sixty, and without enough land to support themselves – to serve whoever offered them work at wages no higher than in 1346–7. Landlords had precedence hiring their tenants, as long as they did not take more work than necessary. The second provision ordered that any worker who was hired by contract and left work without permission be imprisoned. The third prohibited anyone from giving or demanding wages higher than those in 1346–7. The fourth similarly forbade artisans and craftsmen to charge excessively for their goods or labour, while the fifth ordered innkeepers and others not to charge exorbitant prices for victuals. Finally, the ordinance prohibited giving alms to anyone who could work to discourage them from idleness, sin, or crime.

Knighton complained that workers ignored the ordinance:

Meanwhile the king sent into each shire a message that reapers and other labourers should not take more than they had been wont to do under threat of penalties . . . The workmen were, however, so arrogant and obstinate that they did not heed the king's mandate, but if anyone wanted to have them he had to give them what they asked; so he either had to satisfy the arrogant and greedy wishes of the workers or lose his fruit and crops.

Motivated by the same hostility toward workers' arrogance, parliament supplemented the ordinance by setting terms for agricultural work and fixing wages. According to the statute of labourers, all workers had to swear before lords and town officials to uphold the legislation and not to leave service before their term expired. The ordinance left most of the enforcement up to sheriffs and other royal officials. The statute gave precise instructions. It assigned a panel of justices in each county to hear indictments of workers and to determine penalties. Initially, the justices were also keepers of the peace. Between 1352 and 1359, however, the government issued separate commissions for labour and peace, but afterward reverted to the original scheme. Henceforth, control over wages and prices was fully in the hands of the justices of the peace.

Enforcement rested on the county and local communities. At the county level, justices heard indictments from hundred juries and constables four times a year, in quarter sessions, and pronounced sentences of fines, stocks, or imprisonment. If the defendant challenged the indictment, a jury was summoned to testify. The justices also heard a few private suits against labourers. The most common punishment was a fine in the form of taking from the worker the excess wages he or she had received above the legal limit. Since the justices' wages were paid out of the labourers' penalties, they had an incentive to levy fines. The justices were drawn from the ranks of the county elite. A few noblemen were appointed to each commission to give it weight and lawyers were added for their expertise, but the majority of the 671 men appointed between 1349 and 1359 were knights, esquires, and wealthy freeholders. Enforcement clearly lay in the hands of the landlord class.

Constables, stewards, and bailiffs played an equivalent role within villages and towns. They took oaths from workers to obey the ordinance, inquired into violations, and delivered the names of offenders to the justices. At this level, legislation dovetailed with local regulations. Villages had long sought to guarantee an adequate supply of labour at critical times, such as harvest. Parliamentary legislation broadened labour control and placed workers firmly under the authority of village officials. It thereby acknowledged the interlocking nature of central and local authority and the crown's dependence on community leaders to enforce its will.

Another aspect of enforcement was the application of workers' fines to tax relief. Parliament consented to three years of taxes in 1348 and 1352 (see Table 4, p. 184). In 1349, the council decreed that excess wages be used to reduce each county's tax liability. Bertha Putnam estimated that between 1352 and 1354 as much as £10,000 was collected in fines, of which just over £7,747 was used as tax relief. Since taxes amounted to £114,767, fines made up less than 7 per cent of the total. In a few counties, however, fines represented from a third to a half of the burden, and in a few local districts they accounted for nearly all of the tax. Essex fines, for example, topped £675 in 1352, more than half of its tax quota of £1,234 15s. 7¼d. The effect of this policy was to shift the burden of taxation away from employers and the wealthy onto the shoulders of workers. It also acted as an inducement to justices, leading to a greater regularity of sessions and a more thorough enforcement of the legislation than when fines went directly to the crown.

The plan, however, was fraught with problems. It involved coordinating several sets of officials and offered opportunities for embezzlement, especially by tax collectors. The government, moreover, had difficulty in collecting arrears. By 1362 it gave up. The entire process was turned over to the justices of the peace and excess wages were used for the communities.

Despite these problems, the legislation was welcomed by two groups. It should be recalled that wealthy peasants needed wage labourers to work their holdings. Before 1348 village elites used the manorial court, bylaws, and office-holding to control village labour. National legislation flowed into and supplemented this stream of customary law rather than washing it away. It specifically strengthened the hand of employers in contract disputes. Any employer bringing a successful suit against a servant received the fine as well as the enforcement of the contract. Employees who sued employers got no such benefit. The penalty was offered to encourage private litigation. While it was not particularly effective on the national level, the number of labour cases in some manorial courts increased dramatically from the mid-fourteenth century onward. The voice of these local elites may be heard in a parliamentary petition of 1368 from those who lived by the cultivation of land or trade and who had neither lordships nor villeins to work for them. They urged that justices of the peace be given the power to hear and determine cases at the suit of private parties and that those found guilty of charging high wages be forced to restore double what they had taken. The crown reaffirmed the justices' role in enforcement, but did not grant the double penalty. However, employers in some areas, Havering is one, simply ignored the legislation and managed very well by paying high wages on short-term agreements. Similarly, though borough courts were largely responsible for enforcement, those in Colchester do not show a radical increase in labour litigation.

The primary beneficiaries were the landlords. They wanted to regain the upper hand in dealing with the peasantry. Rising wages had taken a

substantial bite out of their profits. Competition for scarce labour, moreover, threatened to put landlords at one another's throats. Fixing wages and
controlling workers' mobility were means of eliminating workers' leverage
and reducing conflict between employers. By giving landlords the first call
on their tenants' labour, the ordinance may have induced some landlords to
continue the direct cultivation of their demesnes. Finally, the very groups
who benefited most from the legislation were given responsibility for
enforcing it.

The ordinance and statute of labourers thus strengthened the social hierarchy in village and nation. But was it effective? The volume of fines indicates that for several years it was vigorously enforced. It must, at the very
least, have had a chilling effect on workers' demands. Bertha Putnam's
hypothesis, that the legislation kept wages from rising to levels they would
have reached had it not been put into effect, seems plausible.

Legislation was only one prop in the maintenance of high farming. Landlords also flexed their seigneurial authority. They countered tenant independence by energetically levying chevage (permission to leave the manor),
merchet, heriots, entry fines, and all of the other perquisites of lordship from
their unfree tenants. Fines increased, in some cases nearly doubling.
Though, overall, court proceeds were not great, their increase while the
number of tenants fell meant that those caught in their lords' legal nets
shouldered a heavier burden than ever before.

The enforcement of labour services had mixed success. Canterbury
cathedral priory compelled its villeins to perform their services into the
1370s, though stiff peasant resistance forced it to give ground and make
some temporary concessions. The bishop of Worcester and abbot of
Ramsey were not as effective and had to commute services for cash rents.
In 1351, the duke of Lancaster drew up a covenant with four of his
Lancashire villages in which he commuted unfree services and dues for a
cash rent, but retained rights to heriots and fines for the alienation of land.
Elsewhere, lords used contracts to create a kind of 'second serfdom'. In any
kind of agreement between a lord and tenant, for employment or permission to leave the manor, the lord could insert a conditional clause in
which the tenant bound him- or herself to certain obligations.

In the long run, the struggle to retain labour services was fruitless, but in
the short run it helped buoy demesne production. Professor Holmes discovered that seigneurial incomes dropped only about 10 per cent between
the 1340s and 1370s. Two forces aided lords: Inflation pushed demesne
revenues higher than ever before despite a cutback in production. Private
and public power kept wages lower than they would have been and
increased income from courts. The Indian summer of high farming was
therefore largely the product of inflation and increasing exploitation.

Class tension heightened as a result. Peasant resistance had flared up from time to time throughout the middle ages. In the second half of the 1370s it seems to have become endemic. In 1376, the commons sent an angry petition to the king complaining that peasants refused to obey the labour legislation, left employers if they felt their wages too low, and took to the roads in quest of better wages or alms. They played lords off against one another to get the best deal for themselves and generally behaved maliciously and arrogantly. The petition demonstrates the weakness of legislation as a weapon against economic forces. It also reveals the frustration of landlords and employers as they tried to keep the peasantry in check. They were unsuccessful in the long run precisely because peasants increasingly resisted those demands. One way in which they did so was to take their landlords to court claiming that they were tenants of the 'ancient demesne'. Tenants of the king's lands, or lands that had formerly been part of his demesne, enjoyed a privileged status. Their rents could not be raised. In 1376–7, there was a sudden upsurge in claims by villeins in several counties that their lords had unjustly increased their rents and services. The swell alarmed the commons who drew up another petition, revealing their alarm and anxiety. They decried the legal process and called for royal help against rebellious villeins who banded together to resist demands for service and threatened to kill their lords. Pressured by the relentless assertion of lordship, peasants formulated ideals of ancient rights and liberties to protect themselves and halt seigneurial demands. Their drive for self-protection gained coordination and aggressiveness, until it erupted in the English Rising of 1381.

Social relations did not suddenly change nor did lordship or high farming suddenly collapse after the Black Death. Change was piecemeal. Nevertheless, the gathering momentum of demographic, monetary, and social forces during the 1350s and 1360s spelled an end to the economic regime which had prevailed over the preceding century. This became evident to all in the late 1370s when economic conditions as well as the peasantry turned against landlords.

PART III

GOVERNMENT AND COMMUNITIES

Monarchs never rule by themselves. They depend on agents to carry out their will. A crucial feature of medieval government was that the king's representatives were drawn from the ranks of social elites. Landlords served as royal officers, participated in decision making, and fought in the king's armies. They exercised private authority through manorial courts and public jurisdiction through franchises. Despite this overlapping of public and private power, England had produced a remarkably effective government by 1300.

The landed hierarchy on which administration depended clarified itself into distinct ranks during Edward's reign. The development of the house of lords in parliament provided the basis for identifying the nobility. Individually summoned rather than elected, the peers or peerage as they came to be known were differentiated from the knights and squires who made up the gentry. Peerage simultaneously symbolized social exclusiveness and defined a constitutional role. The clergy were likewise ranked hierarchically, with the higher members – archbishops, bishops, and some abbots – comparable to peers. And these noble grades took greater pains than they had before to define the boundaries between themselves and those below.

Government service corresponded to one's place in the echelon. Magnates, whether lay or ecclesiastic, generally occupied the highest positions as peers, councillors, military captains, and ministers. They played out their roles on a national stage, with the court as their focal point. County administration was the gentry's arena. During Edward's reign they tightened their grip on local offices and significantly expanded their authority through the creation of the justices of the peace, which combined administrative and judicial powers in one office and gave the gentry a primary role in the enforcement of social as well as criminal legislation. Thus, economic uncertainty did not cause landholders to shrink from service. On the contrary, they used public offices to bolster their private authority over local communities.

Edward's plans for military conquest in France and Scotland depended on the leadership of the nobility and gentry. Only they could sanction the massive marshalling of resources that war demanded. Only they could lead the armies. Only they could manage the logistics of raising men, food, and taxes and keeping order in the counties. In turn, Edward's wars gave knights an outlet for their chivalric enthusiasm and an opportunity to plunder. Each of these elements helped the landed elite maintain its equilibrium in a period of economic change.

8

NOBILITY AND GENTRY

Contemporary thought ranked society in orders or grades, setting those of high degree apart from those of low. In the concept of the three orders the knights and church were supported by the work of the peasantry while they provided protection and prayers. In the image of the mystical body social, the head and right arm were the king, princes, prelates, and knights. Most, if not all, of the nobility equated *gentil* with noble; *gentilesse* separated the *gentils* from the *churls*. Because of the central position the nobility occupied in society as well as in Edward's schemes, it is necessary to understand who constituted this governing elite and the forces that worked to bring it together or pull it apart.

What constituted nobility or *gentilesse*? Henry of Lancaster, clearly the noblest of men, provided one answer: 'It seems to me that for one who ought by right to judge the gentility of a person, it would be useful to know three things before he was entitled to be held as gentle. The first is to know if his father was gentle. The second, if his mother was a gentlewoman as well. And the third is to know if he holds himself in words and deeds as gentle and a friend of the company of gentlemen. And he who does not mimic his father brings great shame on his mother. If he is thus by his mother, father, and himself gentle, then he ought to be called and held gentle.'

Lancaster emphasizes two factors, birth and behaviour. A third, wealth, was probably too obvious to be mentioned. Nobility was a quality, not simply the arithmetic of inheritance, though wealth was necessary to maintain one's estate. Actions revealed one's true status, and one's peers judged whether one was truly noble. In Chaucer's view, in the 'Wife of Bath's

Tale', reputation formed the basis of a radical critique of nobility. The nobility saw it differently. They rejected some outsiders as unworthy of high rank but accepted others. Ralph de Monthermer, Piers Gaveston, and the Despensers were all reproached because they had been elevated beyond their true status, while Edward III's favourites were accepted without murmur. Uneasiness over royal promotions shows that there were no fixed criteria in England by which nobility could be determined.

After the Black Death, however, many feared that economic mobility was blurring the line between gentility and peasantry. As early as 1336, parliament set guidelines for the proper use of the symbols of nobility, declaring that only the royal family, prelates, earls, barons, knights, and ladies with at least £100 annual income could wear fur. In 1363, parliament passed the first sumptuary legislation, attempting to regulate diet and clothing according to a precise scale of wealth and function. In crude terms, it allowed those with £100 or more to eat and dress more luxuriously than craftsmen, servants, grooms, yeomen, and ploughmen. The fear was that 'the outrageous and excessive apparel of various people contrary to their estate and degree' would bring impoverishment and confuse status. Henry of Knighton stated the message plainly, declaring that by imitating wealthy fashion, the lower orders obscured distinctions between rich and poor. A profound change in apparel occurred in the 1340s, in which the traditional medieval costume gave way to ornate clothing. Moralists denounced the new fashions for being excessive and effeminate, but they were the most obvious way the wealthy could display their superior status and distance themselves from their inferiors.

While contemporaries recognized a nobility, they were troubled by its divisiveness. William Marshal on his deathbed in 1219 lamented because the English were of so many different minds and so envious of one another. *The Brut* concluded that the ferocity of the battle of Boroughbridge in 1322 was due to the fact that 'the great lords of England were not all of one nation, but were mixed with other peoples'. Thomas Gray picked up this theme and explained in his *Scalacronica* that the upheavals of Edward II's time were 'characteristic of a medley of different races. Wherefore some people are of the opinion that the diversity of spirit among the English is the cause of their revolutions.' Higden, in his popular *Polychronicon*, likewise alluded to the mixed nature of the English people and to legends of their contentiousness. He echoed the *Vita Edwardi II* when it deplored reckless ambition: 'the squire strains and strives to outdo the knight, the knight the baron, the baron the earl, the earl the king'. Higden brought the observation up to date by saying that men of one order tried to represent themselves as belonging to another, thereby confounding the hierarchy.

This restlessness was evident in the use of titles. The most important were earl, baron, banneret, knight, and esquire. By the fourteenth century, earl had become purely honorific. Baron no longer implied any exact function and was seldom applied individually. A number of men held lands of the king *by barony*. While they had no special privileges, holding by barony came to be associated with the right to be summoned to parliament. A banneret was an exalted knight, entitled to carry a square banner as opposed to a knightly pennant. Knights were, of course, medieval warriors, while esquires had originated as their assistants. Both derived prestige from their civil duties as officials and jurors.

Many who had sufficient wealth refused to become knights. Titles were hereditary, but as early as the twelfth century modest landholders balked at spending the money necessary to equip themselves or to perform the civil and military duties of knighthood. For this reason, the crown had instituted compulsory knighthood in the thirteenth century, demanding that anyone with lands of a certain value take up knightly arms and serve as knights. Until Edward's reign the policy had only limited success and the number of actual knights shrank. As a result, after 1300 many who did not want to become knights, yet still wanted an honorific title, called themselves esquires, raising the status of the title. Englishmen, therefore, could choose whether or not to take up titles, though at the highest ranks they never refused the honour.

During Edward III's reign, titles did not change, but the elite gradually recombined into four informal ranks. The nobility and gentry split apart and each divided into two groups: higher and lower. The parliamentary peerage formed the nobility, split between the titled aristocracy and the barons and bannerets. Within the gentry, wealthy knights and esquires were distinguished from those whose horizons did not extend much beyond the parish. Status was crudely associated with the sphere of one's influence, whether the parish (esquires), the county (knights), or the country as a whole (peers). The sense of order and precedence was deeply ingrained. A parliamentary tract from Edward II's reign explained the seating arrangements in parliament saying that 'such a division [was] habitually observed among the grades and their respective places, so that no one sits except among his peers'. New signs of status thus supplemented older ones to form a system which would last through the Tudor–Stuart era.

The creation of the parliamentary peerage was the most significant step in this process. Although Magna Carta referred to 'peers', the term was not widely used until Edward II's reign, when his baronial opponents called themselves 'peers of the realm'. Under Edward III it became commonplace in official documents such as Edward II's 'abdication' or the process against Mortimer in 1330. According to these sources, the peers of the realm were the bishops, earls, barons, and other major landholders. They advised the king, assented to legislation, and rendered judgements. The peers were the 'natural advisors', on whom kings had customarily relied for counsel and consent. This advisory emphasis recalled polemical works such as *The song of Lewes* which asserted that counsel was the prerogative of the baronage. Being a peer meant belonging to a group that had historically surrounded the king. History, power, and privilege thus bestowed honour and amplified social status.

Political arguments in 1341 provided further definition. The exclusive right of the peers to provide royal counsel formed an important strand in archbishop Stratford's protest letter to Edward and likewise underlay the earl of Surrey's declaration that 'those who should be the chief men (*principals*) are shut out, and other unworthy persons are here in Parliament who ought not to be at such a council, but only peers of the land (*peres de la tere*), who can aid and maintain you, sire king, in our great need'. The passage contains a strong element of social exclusiveness; mere officials (*gentz de mester*) are unworthy to sit in the highest council. A parliamentary petition argued that royal administrators should account for their conduct in office before the peers in parliament. Finally, in the first statute of 1341, parliament adumbrated the idea that peers should be judged only by their peers. Though Edward later declared the statute invalid, the principle seems to have been followed.

Several key attributes of the peerage had thus appeared by the middle of Edward III's reign. It formed the king's council in parliament, or house of lords as it came to be known. It enjoyed certain privileges. Peers were summoned individually to parliament, not elected. They were tried by one another, not in common law courts. Other developments gave the peerage greater coherence and identity. As parliament met more frequently, summonses became less arbitrary. The crown settled on a list of peers which did not change much, except in periods of political unease, such as 1309–14, 1327, 1336–41, and 1371. Edward III occasionally added a few new peers to show favour, as in 1348 when he summoned four distinguished soldiers who had served him in France in 1345–7. The practice of summoning peers' heirs gave the peerage definition and exclusivity. An individual summons to parliament, like many other privileges, evolved into an hereditary right and the peerage became an hereditary caste.

Institutional development had social significance. G. O. Sayles has pointed out that the bishop of Exeter could state as a matter of fact in 1337 that the 'substance of the nature of the crown is principally in the person of the king as head and in the peers of the realm as limbs', echoing the *Vita Edwardi II* which observed that the barons were the 'chief constituent of monarchy, and without them the king cannot attempt or accomplish anything of importance'. In 1343, the commons asked Edward not to overturn statutes as he had in 1341 'for the state of your crown and the salvation of

Table 2. *Creations and restorations 1300–1377*

Date	Title	Name	Royal family	Age	Death	Heir	Notes
1308	Cornwall	Piers Gaveston		23	1312	forfeited	executed
1312	Norfolk	Thomas Brotherton	x	12	1338	daughter	
1321	Kent	Edmund of Woodstock	x	20	1330	forfeited	executed
1322	Carlisle	Andrew Harcla			1323	forfeited	executed
1322	Winchester	Hugh Despenser Sr		61	1326	forfeited	executed
1326	Lancaster (R)	Henry of Lancaster		45	1345	son and heir	
1326	Hereford (R)	John de Bohun		20	1336	brother and heir	
1328	March	Roger de Mortimer		40	1330	forfeited	executed
1328	Cornwall	John of Eltham	x	12	1336	died 'sine prole'	died in war
1330	Kent (R)	Edmund	x	4	1331	brother and heir	
1333	Chester	Prince Edward	x	3	1376	son and heir	
1335	Devon	Hugh Courtenay		60	1340	son and heir	
1337	Duke of Cornwall	Prince Edward					
1337	Salisbury	William de Montagu		35	1344	son and heir	
1337	Huntingdon	William de Clinton		31	1354	died 'sine prole'	
1337	Suffolk	Robert de Ufford		39	1369	son and heir	
1337	Northampton	William de Bohun		25	1360	son and heir	
1337	Derby	Henry of Grosmont		37	1361	daughter	
1337	Gloucester	Hugh d'Audeley		48	1347	daughter	
1340	Cambridge	William of Juliers		41	1361	lapsed	
1342	Ulster	Lionel of Antwerp	x	4	1368	daughter	by marriage
1343	Prince of Wales	Prince Edward	x	13			
1351	Richmond	John of Gaunt	x	11	1399	son and heir	
1351	Stafford	Ralph de Stafford		50	1372	son and heir	
1351	Duke of Lancaster	Henry of Grosmont		51			
1354	March (R)	Roger de Mortimer		26	1360	son and heir	
1362	Cambridge	Edmund of Langeley	x	20	1402	son and heir	
1362	Duke of Clarence	Lionel of Antwerp	x	24			
1362	Duke of Lancaster	John of Gaunt	x	22			
1366	Bedford	Ingelram de Coucy		26	1377	married to Isabella	resigned

R = Restoration
(*Sources:* Given-Wilson, *English nobility*; *Handbook of British chronology*; *Dictionary of national biography*; Cockayne, *Complete peerage*).

your subjects, the peers of the land and the commons'. The peerage had become a social rank.

Under Edward III, the peers were drawn from 60–70 families. Numbers fluctuated as some died out and others were summoned. At the pinnacle stood the titled aristocracy of earls and, later, dukes, who held at least £1,000 worth of lands. Edward significantly increased their numbers. Between 1300 and 1336, the average number of earls active in any one year was eight but jumped to thirteen between 1337 and 1380. 1337 marked the turning point. As can be seen in Table 2, Edward elevated six men to earldoms and named his eldest son duke of Cornwall, the first time the title was used in England. It was an unprecedented display of honour and generosity.

It was also costly. Only Grosmont and Audeley already had extensive holdings. Edward promised three of the others 1,000 marks and the poorest, Bohun, £1,000 a year until he found them lands befitting their new rank. Endowing these men was a politically sensitive task. Not only did Edward lack resources of his own but he was about to embark on a war that would eat up whatever surplus was available. Furthermore, the creation and endowment of new earls over the past generation had been a political disaster. Edward II's elevation of Gaveston, Harcla, and Despenser Senior had been unpopular, and all three had been executed. Closer to home, *The Brut* declared that Roger de Mortimer's elevation to the new earldom of March in 1328 was 'against the will of all the barons of England and to the prejudice of the king and his crown'. Mortimer was condemned in 1330 precisely for his acquisition of royal property to the disinheritance of Edward and the crown. Seen against this background, Edward's move in 1337 was risky.

Edward may have understood this. He made the elevations in parliament. His charters conferring the dignities dwell on the importance of honourable titles to the strength of the kingdom, bemoan their diminution resulting from the division of inheritances among women, laud the achievements of the recipients, and stress the participation of parliament. They are positively ornate in comparison with similar grants by other kings. Edward exercised care in doling out wealth to his new earls. Promises of lands that were due to revert to the crown on the death of the holders (called reversions), grants of forfeited property, and profitable marriages, rather than crown lands, formed the bulk of the endowments. He stipulated that the lands would revert to the crown if the holders died without male heirs. Only one chronicler condemned the expenditure. Others seem to have regarded the creations as worthy of note, not censure. Even Stratford in 1341 declared that they were to the king's interest and honour.

Edward demonstrated tact in another way. Determined to heal the political divisiveness of his father's reign, he restored to honour some of those who had been disgraced. Hugh d'Audley is one example. The Despenser family is another. Though he held Caerphilly castle against Isabella's army in 1326, Hugh, son of the notorious younger Despenser, received an annuity of 200 marks in 1331 and in 1337 recovered many of his father's lands. A year later Edward summoned him to parliament, placing him in the peerage. His marriage in 1341 to the daughter of William de Montagu, one of Edward's favourites and the new earl of Salisbury, signalled his social rehabilitation. More astonishing is the Mortimers' quick recovery. Roger's son Edmund died the year after Roger's execution leaving an infant son Roger. Edward treated the boy well. He restored some of his Welsh lands in 1342 and the following year gave him Wigmore, the head of the family estate. Roger won Edward's admiration by distinguishing himself in tournaments and battle. Roger was knighted by the Black Prince in 1346, recovered the rest of his family lands after valiant service at Crécy, and was included among the first Knights of the Garter. Edward reversed the sentence against the first earl of March in 1354 and then summoned his grandson to parliament as the second earl of March in 1355. His restoration was complete. It was complete in the eyes of his peers as well. Like Despenser, he married a Montagu, taking William's granddaughter Philippa as a wife.

These restorations and creations underscored three points. First, they depended on royal favour. A kingdom might be strengthened 'where many nobles of lofty status and eminence are at hand', to quote from Edward's charters, but in England those heights could only be scaled with the king's help. Second, these nobles formed the core of that group 'by whose certain counsels and aid our realm can be directed and in adversities sustained'. Edward thus endorsed and strengthened the concept of a peerage. Finally, the emphasis on titles confirmed the stratification of the peerage.

Edward, moreover, placed his own family at the forefront of the titled nobility, creating an elite within an elite. Edward was blessed, as contemporaries saw it, with a large brood of five sons and four daughters as seen in Figure 3. Before 1337, he made only three family endowments. That year, he bestowed the duchy of Cornwall on his eldest son Edward and gave the duchy palatinate status, differentiating the duke from mere earls. Of the nine titles awarded after 1337, Edward gave only three to men outside his family. The elevation of three of his sons in 1362 illustrates his change of policy. John of Reading noted that the creations came on the last day of parliament, which was also Edward III's fiftieth birthday, his jubilee. To celebrate, he pardoned criminals, recalled exiles, and honoured his sons. According to the parliament roll, the chancellor told the lords and commons that Edward had spoken with several lords about how God had done well for him in many ways, notably in begetting sons who were now of full age. Therefore, he wished to increase their names in honour.

Once he had honoured them, however, Edward needed to endow them. The lion's share of wealth had gone to prince Edward, leaving little for the others. Gaunt obtained the earldom of Richmond and the honour of Hertford, Langeley received lands in Yorkshire and Lincolnshire, and Isabella acquired manors scattered around the country, but Edward did not make any other grants of English lands to his family between 1337 and the 1370s. Marriage was the most expedient means of finding endowments and it served to anchor Edward's relations with the nobility. Edward, for example, arranged three important matches in 1358–9. His daughter Margaret married John Hastings earl of Pembroke, his granddaughter

Philippa married Edmund de Mortimer, son of the second earl of March, and John of Gaunt married Blanche of Lancaster who would eventually bring him the huge Lancastrian inheritance. These marriages not only provided his children with wealth, but they also united the royal family with noble families wielding power in the sensitive regions of Ireland and the marches of Wales and Scotland. Edward looked abroad to find wealthy partners for Isabella, Edmund, and Mary as well as to advance his diplomatic schemes. Prince Edward, however, benefited the most by receiving the duchy of Aquitaine. Edward thus knitted his children into the social order through titles and marriage, strengthening the camaraderie between crown and nobility that enabled Edward to achieve such glory.

Beneath the titled nobility, the peerage was made up of barons. It is difficult to be more precise. Tenure by barony did not guarantee the holder a summons to parliament nor did all those summoned hold baronies. There was a tendency to include among the peers those who acquired baronial lands by marriage or inheritance, but it was not a rule. The king promoted some bannerets for their personal or military service. The bannerets seem to have formed the lower echelon of the nobility. Probably £250 worth of lands was the minimum necessary for a peer. Once the peerage became hereditary, with new additions made only at the king's will, it became self-defining.

Clergymen were also part of the peerage. Church personnel were ranked hierarchically according to office-holding from the minor orders through the parish clergy, to deans, priors, abbots, bishops, and archbishops. The bishops and two archbishops were routinely summoned to parliament from Edward I's reign onward. Some, but not all, heads of religious houses likewise received summonses, the number varying from roughly 20 to 100. The development of a fixed list began around 1324 and reached fulfilment in 1364 when 27 were summoned to parliament and thenceforth ranked among the peers.

As the nation was coming to be led by a peerage, so knightly peers governed the counties, consulting as intermediaries between the community and the king. This was the highest rank of the gentry. A meeting between Edward's emissaries and the community of Staffordshire on 9 September 1337 to discuss his request for aid had to be postponed because the greater men and most peers (*maiores et plures pares*) could not get there on time. Who were these county peers? The return indicated knights, lords of vills, and town merchants. The meeting was led by the bishop of Coventry and Lichfield, Ralph Basset of Drayton, a peer, and Roger de Swynnerton, soon to become a peer. Philip de Somerville, a knight, was their spokesman. He had served as a keeper of the peace, knight of the shire, and collector of men and taxes in Staffordshire. In Devon, the bishop of Exeter, the knights, stewards, and bailiffs of hundreds and liberties discussed the issue in full county court. A similar group, consisting of the bishop of Ely's steward, two coroners, eight knights, and representatives of five other knightly land-holders, assembled in October·1338 to elect a sheriff for Cambridgeshire. Marriage reinforced associations among office-holders. Somerville's wife, for example, was the daughter of another Staffordshire knight, Sir Thomas de Pipe. One of his daughters and co-heirs similarly married a local knight and member of parliament, Sir John Stafford. His granddaughter continued the tradition by marrying Sir Richard Stafford. Kinship, office-holding, and participation in national affairs thus solidified the county elite.

Given-Wilson has estimated that there were roughly 50 to 70 such men per county, or about 2,300 to 2,500 throughout England. Most were knights or esquires whose incomes ranged from £40 to £250 a year. The higher ranks merged into the peerage. Philip de Somerville, for example,

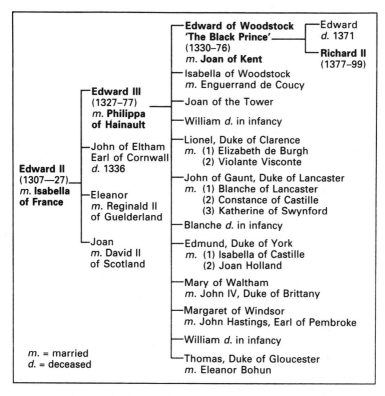

Figure 3. The royal family (*Handbook of British Chronology*, 3rd edn, 39–40).

was a younger son who acquired his Staffordshire estate partly as a gift from his eldest brother and partly in marriage. In 1337 he inherited the entire family estate with manors in seven counties, though he never advanced beyond knighthood.

Edward's military and chivalric policies seem to have sparked a revival of knighthood. R. H. Hilton has shown that the assessment for the 1337 tax divided 104 members of the Staffordshire gentry into six grades of wealth. Only 35 styled themselves knights. During the 1340s, however, 60 or so became knights and 90 fought overseas. Edward issued orders compelling those with £40 of land or more to become knights on seven different occasions, usually in conjunction with a military campaign. The returns indicate that most became knights, though knights 'of force', as they were called in the Robin Hood ballads, were socially distinct from hereditary knights. After Edward's reign the numbers of knights fell once again.

A wide gulf, economic and social, separated the higher and lower gentry. Given-Wilson has estimated that there were some 9,000–10,000 'parish gentry' whose influence did not extend much beyond their villages or hundreds. Their service was highly localized and limited to lesser offices such as hundred juries. At the lower end, they merged with the elite of the village peasantry and might compete with them for land and markets.

The urban oligarchies must not be forgotten. Their specialized economic interests tended to separate them from the gentry and peerage, and throughout the century landlords betrayed a social bias against merchants. One line was drawn at marriage, always a sensitive test of social acceptability. Sylvia Thrupp showed that only the very wealthiest of London merchant families married into landed society and the same appears to have been true in provincial towns such as Exeter and Chester. There was certainly no sense of a caste system that prohibited intermarriage, yet such matches were exceptional.

Such prejudice did not prevent merchants from participating in government and politics. On the contrary, their activity mushroomed under Edward III. Pressured by wartime finances and debts, Edward repeatedly consulted merchants on taxes and financial policy in council and special assemblies. Merchants such as William de la Pole, Reginald Conduit, and William de Melchebourn were prominent purveying victuals, collecting customs, and executing Edward's preposterous wool schemes. In Staffordshire in 1337 they were consulted as leading members of the community, though they, like the clerics, met separately to determine the rate of tax on themselves. Merchants and gentry served together on royal commissions and acted in concert on matters of mutual concern. Some Exeter merchants, for example, served in the earl of Devon's affinity, while gentry sometimes acted as executors or sureties for merchants.

It has been argued that English towns differed from continental ones in that English merchants failed to build family dynasties, preferring instead to use their earnings to buy land and merge into the gentry. In fact, there is not much evidence for this gentrification in the fourteenth century. The rise of the de la Pole family from Hull, beginning with William's profitable service to Edward III, is remarkable but also unique. London merchants, for example, bought land, particularly in the 'home' counties around the city, but Thrupp estimated that between only 5 and 10 per cent of the merchant class had sufficient wealth to become gentry and that their numbers hardly made a ripple in local society. Nor has a sustained movement out of the towns been found in York, Chester, Nantwich, or Exeter. For the latter, it has been suggested that mortality was much more effective than gentrification in checking the rise of merchant dynasties. At York, the mercantile oligarchy bought rural property as a short-term investment, to be resold, borrowed against, or leased rather than as the foundation of a life as one of the gentry. This attitude may have changed after the Black Death. The availability of land coupled with a per capita increase in the money supply may have enabled merchants to buy up additional property. A greater number of merchants than in the past, for example, seem to have become office-holders in Gloucestershire, changing the composition of the county elite.

In the other direction, gentry often held some urban property, especially if they were lords of boroughs. The forfeiture of the Contrariants' properties in 1322 brought to light the fact that local gentry such as the Berkeleys of Gloucestershire or de la Beches of Wiltshire possessed London establishments, as did greater lords such as Lancaster, Badlesmere, and Bohun. Their presence became conspicuous as the century wore on and frequent parliamentary meetings brought them to Westminster more often than before. But the gentry and nobility did not become urban residents. They might sojourn in towns, but they did not live there. They remained a rural class with only a little civic refinement.

Gentrification is a reminder that there was some social mobility though it was not easy. It is least visible where the gentry and peasantry merged and money and patience were necessary to escape humble origins. The upward climb of Richard Young's family in Berkshire, charted by Eleanor Searle, is one example. Although a villein, he was wealthy enough to marry his daughters and granddaughters well and to send a younger son to school. The latter became an estate steward while a grandson became a priest. Movement in the higher ranks may have been no less difficult, though it was easier to move upward from a solid landed base than it was to acquire a foothold. It may be recalled from the last chapter that the wealth of the Percies, who began as barons, rose steadily over the fourteenth century.

Several features of their story deserve attention for the light they shed on social mobility. First, marriage was one of the surest ways to advance. Through dowries and women's inheritance, families could acquire new property, as Percy did in marrying the Lucy heiress. Royal favour was a second path to wealth and status. The Percies' support for Isabella in 1326 resulted in the annuity that in turn led to the acquisition of the Clavering inheritance. Henry Percy's elevation to the earldom of Northumberland in 1377 acknowledged several generations of loyalty. Other families, such as the Scropes of Bolton and Masham, ascended to the peerage because of their service to Edward III, while Roger de Beauchamp, Guy Brian, Reginald de Cobham, Oliver Ingham, and Walter Manny were promoted for their military achievements.

War, therefore, represented an upward path, though its precise effect is controversial. For one thing, it produced scores of new knights. As well as creating six earls in 1337, Edward knighted twenty-four men. Mass knightings became a prominent feature of his campaigns. In 1345–6, for example, the earl of Derby supposedly made forty Englishmen and Gascons knights while Edward knighted his eldest son and many others on landing in Normandy. Prince Edward in turn knighted many of his followers. Service brought rewards. The careers of two Cheshire knights, Hugh Calveley and Robert Knolles, are instructive. They began campaigning in the 1340s, commanded companies at Poitiers in 1356, plundered as freebooters in the 1360s, and resumed military command in the 1370s, when Knolles was paid 8s. a day, far above the 2s. that knights ordinarily received. Heroic reputations brought them to the attention of others. Knolles joined John of Gaunt's retinue while Calveley received 200 marks a year from the Black Prince.

Plunder, spoils, and ransoms presented other opportunities. Whatever high-minded goals kings might have had, soldiers often looked on war as an enterprise. Edward III shrewdly appealed to this attitude to garner support. When his navy came into sight of the huge French fleet before Sluys, he boosted morale by saying that those who fought well would have not only God's blessing but whatever they were able to lay their hands on as well. Even humble soldiers won spoils. Murimuth vividly described how the English chased the French fugitives after Crécy, cut down their captives, despoiled the fallen, and cast lots to divide the spoils. 'The English were truly transformed from paupers to rich men, now dancing, now rejoicing.' Victory also brought ransoms. Those ultimately negotiated for king John of France and David II of Scotland together came to nearly £567,000. Even though they produced less than half of what was anticipated, they greatly boosted Edward's financial position in the 1360s. David's actual captor, John Coupland, did not receive any of the ransom; he got a £500 annuity from Edward instead. Walter Manny and Thomas Holland raised £8,000 and 20,000 marks respectively by selling other prisoners to the king. Edward's wars also helped to elevate merchants, who not only profited from financing the government and provisioning the armies but were brought into royal counsel to an unusual degree.

K. B. McFarlane was right to be impressed by the wealth generated by war. He was also correct in pointing out that the English had far more opportunities than the French to profit from the war. But it is doubtful that this advantage resulted in widespread advancement. War produced rewards, not a social revolution. In the first place, the captains, who were already wealthy, did much better than their followers. Secondly, most probably squandered their spoils quickly. Those who did not could take advantage of the decreasing value of land after 1348 to expand their holdings. Knolles, for example, probably began as a bowman, gained more than 100,000 crowns during the 1360s (according to Froissart), and ended up with property in London, Kent, Norfolk, and Wiltshire.

Several forces acted to give this acutely rank-conscious and acquisitive nobility some cohesiveness. Chivalry was one such force. Maurice Keen has called it a fusion of 'martial, aristocratic, and Christian elements'. A true knight was supposed to possess prowess, liberality, courtesy, and virtue. Men tried to live up to those ideals. The Black Prince's biographer, Chandos Herald, ranked him with three of the greatest worthies, King Arthur, Julius Caesar, and Charlemagne, and intoned that he never 'thought of anything but loyalty, noble deeds, valour and goodness, . . . was endowed with prowess, [and] . . . wished all his life to maintain justice and right'. He was a model for all knights. The treatment of king John after his capture at Poitiers – the Black Prince humbly serving him at dinner; a progress across southern England; a parade through London in the company of the Black Prince, mayor, and bishop; and his luxurious imprisonment in the Savoy palace – underscored the courtesy and liberality of his English captors. Between campaigns, knights flocked to tournaments, where they could display and sharpen their skills. At least fifty-five were held in England between 1327 and 1357. These were structured yet dangerous combats in which participants were divided into teams competing for honour and prizes and which might or might not include jousts. Some knights pursued chivalric glory and Christian values by crusading in Prussia, Spain, or the eastern Mediterranean. All delighted in the mirror of heroism held up by romances and chroniclers.

But there were contradictions. The highly sophisticated ideals of chivalry clashed with the realities of war. Courtesy did not inhibit pillaging; knights did not shrink from personal gain through plunder. The Black Prince sacked Limoges and massacred most of its inhabitants when it betrayed him and went over to the French. Medieval laws of war may have exonerated him, but there is none the less a discordance between such actions and Chandos Herald's portrait. Furthermore, feats of arms were dangerous and injuries were common at tournaments. Military commanders were often reluctant to fight because of the risks involved and preferred the *chevauchée*, a raid for plunder and spoils. Great set battles such as Crécy, Poitiers, or Nàjera were the exception.

Socially, chivalry was important not because it was prescriptive, because it laid out a code of conduct which men were expected to follow strictly, but because it helped to bring the nobility together and set it apart from the rest of society. Chivalry created a noble fellowship and a litmus test of honour. Edward III understood this and used chivalry to glorify himself and his war, inspire knights and magnates, and bind them to him. He avidly encouraged tournaments and often participated himself in the company of his sons. He inspired comparisons with Arthurian legend. The foundation of the Order of the Garter around 1348, the establishment of the College of St George at Windsor, and the annual tournaments held on the feast of St George (23 April) every year thereafter set a model for chivalric practice. The twenty-six founder members did not include all of Edward's favourites, but nearly all had seen action at Crécy. The traditional story – in which Edward at a ball celebrating the fall of Calais picked up the countess of Salisbury's garter, tied it around his knee, and silenced a group of snickering knights with the retort 'Honi soit qui mal y pense' (He ought to be ashamed who thinks ill of it) – is apocryphal. The motto was more likely a defiant assertion of Edward's right to the throne of France which he probably used during the Crécy campaign. By adopting the motto, the order became a living memorial to Edward's achievement.

Another social force that helped give the nobility cohesion was the retinue or affinity. Contemporaries thought of elite society as organized into groupings of knights and noblemen around individual lords. The view is apparent in an impressively wide array of sources, such as military records, chronicles, inquests, and even the Robin Hood ballads.

Barons, knights, and esquires stood at the centre of the retinue. They provided a base upon which the lord could build a military company for war. Surrounding them was a larger group of lawyers, stewards, and bailiffs, which administered the lord's estate, household, and legal affairs. Lords called on their retainers, as well as friends and family, to witness charters, help in the arrangement of marriages, and act as feoffees in land settlements. On the outer fringes, a crowd of menials waited to serve the lord's personal needs. The retinue was thus hierarchically structured. Each retainer received livery and fees, whose quality and amount corresponded to his status. Fees were annual cash payments, annuities. Knights received about £20 or more and officials 5 marks or more a year, while lesser servants were paid a daily wage. Livery consisted of robes fashioned in the lord's distinctive cloth. Bishop Grosseteste in the thirteenth century advised the countess of Lincoln to 'order your knights and your gentlemen who wear your livery that they ought to put on that same livery every day, and especially at your table and in your presence to uphold your honour'. Livery displayed the retinue's allegiance and projected an image of collective power on the lord's behalf.

Retainers were hired by contracts, called indentures, which specified the terms of service and reward. Earlier historians dubbed this system 'bastard feudalism' because they saw contracts and money as a corruption of feudalism, but recent work has emphasized instead the underlying similarities between the two forms of lordship. Both sought to establish lifelong associations and emphasized reciprocity between lord and retainer. Contracts were advantageous because their terms could be adjusted to cover any circumstances, cash payments unlike grants of land did not deplete the lord's capital resources, and they could be easily suspended if the retainer failed to live up to the bargain. Traditional feudalism, moreover, did not disappear with the advent of contracts, and lords drew many of their retainers from the ranks of their feudal tenantry.

Retinues varied in composition and size. In 1384–5, for example, the earl of Devon had 135 retainers: 8 knights, 41 esquires, 14 lawyers, 8 clergy, and 62 lesser servants. Under Edward II, the core of Thomas of Lancaster's retinue consisted of about 55 knights while the earl of Pembroke retained 40 to 50 knights. Beyond that core, the retinue could swell enormously. Thomas de Berkeley, a Gloucestershire baron, retained 12 knights, but when squires and household staff were added, the total retinue numbered around 300. Edward III's wars stimulated retaining. Between 1369–75, when John of Gaunt assumed the country's military leadership, his permanent retinue exceeded 220, including 2 earls, 4 lords, 2 bannerets, and 124 knights. Others were taken on for specific campaigns. At least 538 men served Henry of Grosmont during his lifetime, but only 46 knights received land or annuities. Not everyone served for life. The retinue expanded, contracted, and changed composition in step with the lord's activities.

Retinues had a political dimension. Justices and other officials accepted robes and fees from lords. Both William Bereford and Henry le Scrope, chief justices of the two highest courts, were receiving Lancaster's robes and furs in 1318–19. Not only did lords retain justices, but their men became sheriffs, justices of the peace, or knights of the shire. They gave the lord influence and leverage. Indeed, the increasing power of the county gentry made them ideal candidates for recruitment into the affinities of magnates seeking to exert their influence in a particular region. Most lords thus tended to build up their local, rather than national, power by seducing the gentry with livery and fees. The earls of Devon, for example, drew their top men from the territory in and around their estate in Devonshire. Retinues certainly expanded and increased their power during the fourteenth century, but local interests and international war, not politics, stimulated growth.

Retaining, however, was costly. The bill for Thomas of Lancaster's retinue came to between £1,500 and £2,000 a year. The Black Prince spent £1,537 on annuities in 1369. But annuities were not all. In 1357, he gave out land, offices, pardons, exemptions, timber, pasture, and other favours to his followers. Fees might come to around 10 per cent of the lord's income, and other rewards could push the total up to 30 or 40 per cent.

The affinity was strengthened by social intercourse. Retainers' families, for example, often intermarried, creating what M. Cherry has called an 'affinity within an affinity'. Marriage knit retainers and other gentry families into a loose fabric of kinship, strengthening ties between the affinity and local society. Retainers also performed mutual services for one another as witnesses, sureties, attorneys, or feoffees. The affinity, in other words, did not consist merely of vertical ties between lord and follower, but of lateral ties between the followers themselves, creating a cohesive, though flexible, social unit.

The lord's household deserves special attention. Every lord, whether lay or ecclesiastic, gentry or noble, had a household organization, varying in size according to the lord's wealth and power. It consisted of the officials, servants, friends, and family who were in attendance on the lord. Many of his retainers or estate administrators, for example, were linked to him only by contracts and were not usually in his presence. But his daily life teemed with servants ranging from humble household boys, pages, and grooms to cooks, ushers, and yeomen up to the officials who ran the household and estate. The majority were wealthy freemen or lesser gentry from the estate or district for whom household service offered advancement. Some families maintained a tradition of faithful service over several generations. The lord's immediate nuclear family was part of his household, but distant kin, such as aunts, uncles, cousins, or grandparents, did not usually reside there. In contrast, the household often included the children of other lords, sometimes referred to as henchmen. Noble children typically resided in other households, served in ceremonial posts, and received part of their training there.

During the fourteenth century, households changed in three ways. First, instead of travelling constantly with the lord, they settled in one place which served as the head of the estate and the lord, too, tended to travel less. Second, they grew larger. At the beginning of the century, noble households averaged around fifty people but by the end of Edward III's reign they averaged closer to ninety. Gentry households approximately doubled in size from about twenty to forty. Third, they were better organized. Because documentation before 1300 is so scanty, it is hard to tell precisely when this trend started. Stricter accounting and organization became necessary as the household and its expenses grew. John of Gaunt spent £5,525 of his £10,000 income in 1376–7 on his household, and that proportion, 50 to 60 per cent, is probably representative. The bulk of that money, one-half to two-thirds, went on food and drink with the remainder on clothing, maintenance, and construction.

The household and the retinue were cohesive forces, organizing lords, gentry, and servants into stable affiliation. They maintained the lord's dominance while providing security and support for his followers. Communality was reinforced by fighting in tournaments, dining in the household, or worshipping in the lord's chapel. The practice of sending children to serve other lords cemented relations between households. The king, too, benefited since this organization provided a platform for recruiting armies. Though the retinue and household thus helped to unify the elite, they could be divisive as well. Competition for influence, retainers, or offices might set lords and affinities at odds or even erupt into violence. The temptation to abuse the enormous power that lay in the hands of retainers who served in private and/or public offices was often too great to resist.

The landed elite was also integrated through family, marriage, and kinship. These elements may be appreciated best through the experience of noblewomen. The retinue was a male domain; not only was the personnel overwhelmingly male, women did not participate directly in warfare, administration, or politics. They were spectators. That role can be seen in the New Year festivities at King Arthur's court depicted in the opening of *Sir Gawain and the Green Knight*. Though set in the past, it mirrors the bustle of a fourteenth-century hall. Arthur's knights join in tournaments, jousting, dancing, and feasting. Arthur announces that he will not eat until he has heard a tale of chivalric deeds or witnessed a challenge to knightly combat. Ladies are present, the most beautiful in the world, but other than Queen Guinevere, they are not identified. Just so, Queen Philippa and many other noble ladies attended a tournament at Cheapside in 1331. Adorned in red velvet and hoods, they walked behind the knights and before the squires and minstrels in the procession that opened the ceremonies and later caused considerable anxiety when their viewing stand collapsed, though no one was hurt. In these public settings, women were always present but never central to the proceedings.

Their world was the household. They were expected to stand in for their husbands when they were absent and make sure everything functioned properly. Their leadership blossomed in widowhood, when a woman emerged fully independent and responsible for the first time in her life.

Widows had a right to a third of their husband's estates, while the growing practice of settling lands in jointure and the right of female inheritance often potentially gave them control over sizeable holdings. Noblewomen could indeed be powerful. Elizabeth de Burgh, one of the Clare heiresses, was married and widowed three times between 1308 and 1322. She accumulated a huge estate which she controlled until her death in 1360. Her retinue and household were as noble as any in the kingdom, consisting of 15 knights, 93 esquires, 39 clerks, 49 administrators, 51 lesser officials, and 12 pages.

Because dowries, dowers, and inheritance gave women access to such large fortunes, their marriages had to be carefully supervised. Delicate negotiations surrounded each match. Documents for marriages between the earl of Arundel's daughter Joan and the earl of Northampton's son and heir Humphrey, and between Arundel's son and heir Richard and Northampton's daughter Elizabeth, drawn up between July and September 1359, stipulated the settlement and inheritance of property, papal dispensations, and royal licences. The seriousness of the event is evident in the stipulation of penalties of up to £6,000 for failure to carry out the agreement. With so much at stake, it is not surprising that the families worried about mésalliances or disparagement, marrying below one's rank. *Winner and Waster* and Thomas of Erceldoune's prophecy even saw marriages of ignoble lads to ladies as omens of impending disaster.

Bonds of marriage and kinship criss-crossed the elite providing connections and potential alliances. John of Gaunt's marriage to the daughter and heiress of Henry of Grosmont, for example, linked him to some of the most powerful families in England: the Percies, the earl of Suffolk, the earl of Arundel, and through him to the earl of Northampton. Marriage at this level was an occasion of great significance. Little wonder, therefore, that Edward III travelled to Hereford in the summer of 1328 to be present at the marriages of two of Roger de Mortimer's daughters, Agnes and Beatrice. Agnes married Lawrence de Hastings, the eventual earl of Pembroke, while Beatrice married Edward, son of Thomas de Brotherton, the king's uncle. A tournament was held to celebrate the event.

As a class, the landed elite existed in a state of tension. Some forces pulled individuals together while equally strong motivations drove them into competition. Agreement was never universal or lasting. The kinds of difficulties the elite faced can be seen in two further areas, economic interests and privilege. Everyone in the elite shared similar economic interests. They depended on the control of the peasantry for rents and labour and on markets for income. Hence, everyone generally agreed on the need for law and order and low taxation to maintain the prosperity of their estates. Beyond that, agreement broke down. Some, for example, benefited from war and high taxes. They shifted the tax burden to others and profited from military contracts, plunder, and patronage. Others at lower levels of the gentry suffered from taxation and purveyance. Retinues gave lords prestige and retainers security. Outsiders, however, viewed those perquisites jealously and resented the high-handed tactics of overbearing neighbours.

Privilege was similarly a hallmark of status, bestowing authority, honour, and income. Every lord wanted to maintain his or her 'liberties'. Yet, privilege also aroused resentment. It is most evident between the gentry and the higher nobility. The commons presented a number of petitions that complained about the privileges of the few. In 1343 they protested that bailiffs of liberties demanded too much from the people and asked that lords' stewards should not be made justices of the peace. In 1352 they condemned immunities from taxation and called for the greater lords to pay a fairer share of the taxes, contrasting the position of lords (*seignurs*) and gentry (*mesnes gentz*). In 1368, the communities of Surrey and Sussex pointed out that franchises had reduced the sheriff's income and made it hard to pay the county farm.

Despite their shared privileges and interests, the elite was not inherently unified. The king could not take their solidarity for granted. Leadership, therefore, was not simply a matter of offering them a war to fight. He had to shape them into a cohesive whole. It made Edward III's task all the harder and his achievement all the more remarkable.

9

THE CHURCH AND CLERGY

The church formed a distinct entity within English society, marked off by its liberties and functions. It was at once a community of believers ministered to by the clergy and an institution with its own laws and property staffed by the clergy. After 1300, people increasingly referred to it as the 'church of England', not to claim independence from Rome but rather to express adherence to their own traditions. National identity, however, did not give it autonomy. The clergy had to function in accord with English law and social norms and faced continual demands for money and service from the papacy, crown, and nobility.

The English church in Edward's reign faced a fundamental dilemma. On the one hand, the forces of reform and education drove the church forward, with impressive results. Schools and universities flourished and, indeed, developed a distinctive intellectual tradition which influenced scholars throughout Europe. A cadre of well-trained clerical administrators emerged from these schools and dominated ecclesiastical and royal administration. Significant strides were taken toward improving the quality of the parochial clergy, on whom depended the church's mission. A new spirituality emerged within the church and among the laity, fostering a unique tradition of English devotion and mysticism. On the other hand, the clergy was necessarily entangled in worldly affairs, which distracted them from their calling and gave rise to criticism from within and without the church. Most clergy depended on clientage and patronage for advancement so that their loyalty was pulled in several directions at once. To many, these ties did not preclude learning and spirituality, though critics questioned that assumption. They took aim at the church's shortcomings, denouncing its wealth and worldly ties which they believed were incompatible with its primary duty of moral improvement and salvation. War and taxation, moreover, strained relations between Edward, the papacy, and the clergy. The clash of these contradictory forces reverberated throughout the English church and helped ignite a movement for spiritual reform which would have profound consequences for church and society in the last quarter of the century.

In keeping with the themes of this book, this chapter largely focuses on the role of the clergy in church and state, its connections with the laity, and the effects of those roles on the quality of the clergy. The critical link between the church hierarchy and the body of believers was the parochial clergy. For the vast majority of the population the parish church was the centre of religious life and a source of instruction, aid, and contact with a wider world. The parish priest, often assisted by a chaplain, met the laity's needs by ministering the sacraments such as mass on feast days and baptisms, confessions, and burials through the villagers' life cycles. He offered religious instruction and preached the importance of moral improvement. He blessed the crops and conducted religious rituals and processions on the feast days which dotted the Christian calendar. His work followed the rhythm of the agricultural year binding religion and work, clergy and laity through belief and ceremony.

There were approximately 9,500 parishes scattered across England. In some large parishes, chapels of ease were established for the convenience of those parishioners living far from the parish church. The manors or households of the wealthy had their own chapels and formed separate units of religious practice. Thousands of chantries and guild chapels were sprinkled across the landscape. Founded by laymen to say mass for their souls and the souls of their family or friends, these chapels occasionally performed services for local inhabitants.

The parish priest was the focus of the church's ambitious programme to raise the moral and spiritual level of Christendom. It needed priests capable not only of instructing the population properly but of serving as moral examples. Unfortunately, the parochial clergy did not always live up to the ideal. The decrees of the Fourth Lateran council in 1215 acknowledged this failing and called for strict supervision of the parish clergy by their superiors, opportunities to study, a programme of education, and an end to immorality. They sought to narrow the huge gulf that yawned between the remarkable achievements of monastic and university thinkers and the parochial clergy. It was an enormous task.

In fourteenth-century England, this programme bore fruit in several ways. In the first place, there was a renewed emphasis on clerical training. Educational opportunities in the middle ages were much more restricted than in modern times. Women and villeins, for example, were excluded, though the latter could attend school with their lord's permission. Nevertheless, a greater number of students in each diocese was taking advantage of educational opportunities than a century earlier. The numbers of pupils and students actually increased throughout the fourteenth century, despite plague and war. Education was largely carried out under clerical supervision. The church did not set a curriculum, but most teachers were priests and students were tonsured. Schooling usually began at the age of seven with the rudiments of Latin pronunciation and reading taught by a parish priest or chaplain through singing (plainchant) and learning the psalms. It continued with Latin grammar taught in secondary (or grammar) schools, which could be found in most large towns. Most students stopped there, having acquired just enough training for ecclesiastical or secular service. Some went on to either Oxford or Cambridge, the two English universities, where it could take up to twenty years or more to complete one's education. An equivalent education could be acquired outside the universities. The mendicant orders, the Franciscans and Dominicans, had extensive and well-organized schools. Early in the century, bishops revived their cathedral schools by appointing university graduates as chancellors. They encouraged theological and pastoral education in the cathedral chapter and provided preferment for graduates. The households of university-trained bishops became important centres of learning and scholarship.

Opportunities for secular training likewise abounded. Schools for letter writing, conveyancing, drafting wills, auditing accounts, and holding courts, as well as vocabulary and grammar, had probably existed at Oxford since the mid-thirteenth century, though they came to prominence a century later in Thomas Sampson's teaching. The period around 1300 saw the rise of sophisticated legal training centred primarily in London around the royal courts. Instruction was based on writs, year-book reports, and lectures. This sophisticated system, encompassing more than just apprenticeship in the courts, reflects the general surge in professional education.

Against this background, the English church redoubled its efforts to improve the quality of the parochial clergy. The number of university-trained priests rose. Manuals for parish priests, such as that of William of Pagula, provided guidelines about what parishioners should know (the 14 articles of faith, the 10 commandments, the 7 virtues, the 7 vices, the 7 sacraments, and so forth), instructed priests how to conduct confessions twice a year, and brought out fine points of Christian doctrine. They emphasized the ideal qualities of the priesthood and advised priests how to behave. Their goal was to produce a clergy which could exemplify Christian qualities, indeed represent Christ to their parishioners, while instructing them about their Christian duties and leading them to spiritual understanding. If, for the church, priests were the link between the institution and the people, for the parishioners, they were the link between this world and the next, controlling the path to salvation. Thus, the church's pastoral mission required attention to instruction and the sacraments, one leading to moral conduct, the other to the absolution of sin.

At the same time, the laity deepened its involvement in parish affairs. To fulfil their obligations of maintaining the church fabric and its fixtures and to give them a louder voice in the church for which they were responsible, parishioners created vestries and church wardens. The practice of collective responsibility, coupled with stronger religious instruction than in the past, may have prompted the laity to cultivate supplementary forms of religious devotion. Chantries and religious guilds, for example, flourished in the second half of the century and provide evidence of an intense lay involvement in religious life.

The most spectacular evidence of this trend is *Le livre de seyntz medicines* written by Henry of Grosmont, the first duke of Lancaster. A renowned warrior, skilled diplomat, and trusted official, Henry devoted considerable attention and resources to spiritual matters. He was a benefactor of religious institutions in Lancaster and Leicester, founded chantries, and established a college of secular canons at Leicester with a dean, 29 clerics, 100 poor, and 10 female attendants. Though Lancaster's foundation was especially handsome, this kind of foundation was a common form of religious expression. His *Livre* was not. It is a confession in the form of an elaborate allegory. He suffers from seven perilous wounds in his ears, eyes, nose, mouth, hands, feet, and heart through which the seven deadly sins, like enemies breaching a castle, have entered his body (soul). His heart, moreover, he compares to the sea, a fox's hole, and a market-place to show its wickedness. Like a sick man, therefore, he seeks a physician, in this case Jesus. The remedies, too, are allegorical. To take but one example, he compares his sinfulness to poisoning and spins out an allegory based on antidotes to venom. The medicines to cast out the venomous sin are saintly sermons, good lessons, and true examples received through his ears from good men and good books. This passage highlights the church's programme of instruction in the fourteenth century, which was clearly successful if it could prompt a layman to reflect on his condition in the manner of *Le livre de seyntz medicines*.

The book can be seen as part of a broader movement towards an individual, Christo-centric devotion which produced the great English mystics and mystical literature of the late middle ages. They too were products of the ecclesiastical emphasis on education, confession, and devotion. The author of the *Cloud of Unknowing*, Richard Rolle (d. 1349), Walter of Hilton (d. 1396), and Julian of Norwich (d. 1413), are the outstanding examples of this movement. It stressed individual devotion leading to direct communion with God, but without breaking with the church's basic practices and principles. Nor was it open to everyone. The writers conscientiously limited their advice to a favoured few.

Mystical literature, a devout laity, vigorous teaching, and instructional manuals are all signs of a vital, flourishing religion. How far those elements penetrated into the local population, or how much the typical parishioner understood or benefited from them, is less clear. What is known is that despite these achievements, the English church came under attack for failing to do more.

Paradoxically, the church's very success in training the clergy created difficulties. School-trained clergy were desperately needed within the halls of royal and ecclesiastical administration, so that at any given time, a portion of the clergy was employed in work that took them far from their religious vocation. As a huge organization, the church itself required many administrators. The clergy were divided into two main groups, secular and regular. The former included the archbishops, bishops, archdeacons, deans, and parochial clergy whose primary responsibilities were to instruct the laity, minister the sacraments, and supervise the clergy. The latter included the monastic and mendicant orders: the abbots, monks, and friars whose responsibilities lay in devotion, learning, and instruction. The houses of each order were grouped into chapters which convened every so often to deliberate matters concerning the order. Each house had its own estate and household which it managed itself. Relations between these elements were not always harmonious. Since their arrival in England in the first half of the thirteenth century, for example, the mendicants had been deeply mistrusted by secular and regular clergy alike, because they tended to trespass on functions and rights claimed by older offices and orders. Whether schooling, preaching, or burials, this encroachment siphoned revenues away from the established clergy. Moreover, the friars, who theoretically lived on alms and did not own property, claimed to be the true heirs of the apostolic church and denounced the wealth of the 'possessioners', those clergy possessing land. Other jurisdictional squabbles erupted between the regular and secular clergy. The bishop of Norwich, for instance, was mired in an acrimonious debate with the abbot of Bury St Edmunds from 1345 onward over the abbot's claim to be exempt from the bishop's supervision. The church can thus be seen as a huge corporation subdivided into more or less independent units of authority.

Archbishops and bishops exercised the greatest authority and had the most elaborate administrative machinery at their disposal. England was divided into two metropolitan provinces, Canterbury and York, and into seventeen English and four Welsh dioceses by 1300. Within his diocese, the bishop had charge over the cathedral chapter, any monastic houses not exempt from his authority, the beneficed and unbeneficed clergy (parish priests and chaplains), and his own officials. He was responsible for conferring orders, examining and instituting new clergy, blessing new abbots and priors, and consecrating church buildings. Four times a year he ordained new priests. He held a consistory court once a month which was staffed by the bishop's officials and lawyers and had jurisdiction over the diocesan clergy and the morals, wills, and marriages of the laity. The bishop was supposed to visit the parishes and religious houses once every three years to investigate the clergy's performance. Most bishops, in fact, accomplished it only once during their episcopacy because it was such an enormous task. They also held synods once or twice a year which promulgated legislation and discussed matters of concern to the diocesan clergy. It is hardly surprising that bishops' registers, records of episcopal work, swell enormously during the fourteenth century.

Each diocese, moreover, was divided into two or more archdeaconries; the huge bishopric of Lincoln had eight, York had five, London four, and so on. The archdeacon was appointed by the bishop and called the 'bishop's eyes', because he carried out most of the bishop's duties under his authority. Much hated by villagers for bringing men and women before the church courts, he represented the backbone of the diocesan administration. Archdeacons also held deanery chapters for the parish clergy once a month. The archdeaconries were further divided into deaneries served by rural deans.

The work of the diocese was thus enormously burdensome. It demanded not only time on the bishop's part, but the assistance of an army of reliable personnel. If the bishop can be likened to a monarch in his diocese, then this personnel constituted his bureaucracy, managing lands, collecting revenues, writing letters, directing personnel, holding courts, charging fines, recording decisions, and reprimanding and encouraging clergy and laity alike. Most of the administrators were drawn from the ranks of the beneficed clergy within the diocese, not imported from outside, and most were appointed by the bishop himself. Thus, simply managing the affairs of the church drained some talent away from the parishes. Others served the papacy. Justice, finance, and diplomacy on an international scale demanded highly competent personnel and the pope drew on the clergy throughout Europe to fill his posts.

The demand for administrators was equally voracious outside the church. Until lay literacy became general, the crown had to rely on clerics to perform many government chores. For example, 11 of 17 chancellors, 14 of 21 treasurers, and 14 ex-keepers of the privy seal in the fourteenth century were bishops. In the case of the privy seal, service in the office provided a stepping-stone to the episcopacy. In the case of the chancellor and treasurer, appointments worked the other way around, so that the king drew on the experience of the episcopacy in filling these offices. There was a noticeable lay element at the top of the royal administration during Edward III's reign, but it did not reverse the clerical dominance. Further down the ranks virtually all of the offices were staffed by clerics. The chancery, for instance, had 12 clerks of the first grade, 12 of the second, 24 cursitors, and a host of minor officials who were also often clergymen. The nobility and gentry likewise called on the clergy's expertise, as feoffees, witnesses, executors, lawyers, and household officers. Many of these men were in minor orders and were hardly distinguishable from laymen. Yet the very skills that the clergy acquired to fulfil their clerical duties made them attractive administrators and drew them away from religious affairs.

Besides having trained personnel, the church also had vast resources with which to reward them. Much of its wealth was organized into benefices or livings. Each office had two aspects, the duties that the incumbent was supposed to perform and the revenues attached to it, the living. Offices can be roughly classified into those with cure of souls and those without. The ministering of sacraments, the cure of souls, was left to those in higher orders, bishops, priests, and deacons. A number of offices did not require that (they were without cure of souls, *sine cura*) and could be filled by those in minor orders. Benefices ranged from parishes, to diocesan offices such as dean, archdeacon, or treasurer, to prebends, offices within the cathedral chapter. Parish livings were made up of tithes, land, and oblations, or gifts to the priest for various services. Tithes were levies for the support of the priest of one-tenth of the parish grain harvest (great tithes) and of other products such as animals and fruit (small tithes). Parishes varied greatly in value. In Cleveland, Yorkshire, they averaged about £22 a year and in Warwickshire about £10, while Cheshire parishes ranged from nearly 200 marks to only 5. Snitterfield parish in Warwickshire, for example, was valued at more than £17 in 1330, not a princely sum, but a comfortable living. Of this, 16 marks came from the tithe of corn, nearly £3 from land, and £2 6s. 9d. from tithes of wool, lambs, milk, calves, chickens, bees and honey, geese, eggs, pigeons, pigs, flax, hemp, and apples.

The problem facing a clergyman was getting appointed to a benefice. When a vacancy appeared, the person controlling the appointment named a candidate, so that a clergyman had somehow to bring himself to the attention of the patron. From the outset, therefore, clerical careers at every level depended on patronage. A complicating factor was that the power of appointment was not vested in a single authority. It was dispersed among several, each of which jealously guarded its rights. To begin with, bishops held the power of appointment over many offices and parishes in their dioceses. Over time, many religious houses had appropriated parish tithes, giving them the right to appoint a vicar who performed the duties of the parish priest in return for an annual stipend. (In unappropriated parishes, the priest was called a rector.) Although the regular clergy made up only 25 per cent of the Cheshire clergy in 1379, about 50 per cent of the parishes were in their hands, compared to 45 per cent in Cleveland. These appropriations did not mean that they controlled the wealthiest parishes. In Warwickshire, the average value of appropriated churches came to only £4 5s.

The king, nobility, and gentry similarly held advowsons, or the right to appoint a parish priest. In Cleveland, lay patrons controlled 31 per cent of the parishes, which tended to be among the richest. Two-thirds averaged more than £40 a year, compared to an overall average of £22. The king's patronage expanded enormously whenever a bishopric or abbey fell vacant or a tenant-in-chief came into wardship, because while the estates were in his custody, he could make any ecclesiastical appointments which opened up and which the landlord, bishop, or abbot was entitled to make. Furthermore, the crown maintained rights of appointment to some fifteen freechapels – collegiate churches which were free from episcopal supervision and to which the king collated deans and/or canons. Edward III used these exclusively to support his officials.

The importance of these patrons to a clergyman can be illustrated in the successful career of Adam de Harvington. An administrator of outstanding ability, he worked extensively inside and outside the church. He was procurator for Worcester cathedral priory and the bishop of Hereford in parliament in 1307, a canon in Hereford cathedral, vicar-general and attorney for Adam de Orleton when Orleton was bishop of Hereford, and vicar-general of the diocese of Worcester after Orleton was translated to the bishopric in 1327. He served on innumerable judicial and administrative commissions for the crown during the 1330s. At the same time, he rose in the ranks at Westminster. He started out as chamberlain of the exchequer (1305), moving on to become keeper of the writs and rolls of king's bench (1314), chief clerk of the common pleas (1314–22), an assize justice (1327–30), chief baron of the Dublin exchequer (1323–5), and finally chancellor of the exchequer at Westminster (1327–30). His skills and connections made him indispensable to lay and ecclesiastical patrons and he reaped substantial rewards. Worcester priory granted him a lifetime annuity of 5 marks in 1316. He was appointed to parish livings by John de Hastings, the bishop of Hereford, the bishop of Worcester, the prior of Great Malvern, and the king. He was named to prebends by Guy de Beauchamp, earl of Warwick, and the king. The pope referred to Adam as John de Hastings' clerk in a dispensation that John obtained for Adam in 1310 to hold two churches at once. Adam also obtained manors from the king, Guy de Beauchamp, Roger de Mortimer, the abbot of Bordesley, and the abbot of Bruern. The abbot of Pershore granted him an advowson for life. His strongest ties outside church and government were to the Beauchamp family, acting as their attorney and as one of Guy's executors. On his death in 1345, Adam used his wealth to establish a chantry of two secular priests in the abbey church at Pershore, where he was buried, to pray for his soul, Guy's soul, and for the good of Guy's son Thomas and Thomas's wife, Katherine.

Most clerics did not enjoy Adam's influence and so did not gain as handsomely. But though exceptional, his rewards show how widely clergymen cast their nets fishing for preferment. Everything hinged on making the proper connections. Once established, individuals could move up and even raise their family's status. Archbishop Melton of York, for example, was from a modest freeholding family that rose to gentry status only after he had become archbishop and made considerable wealth through moneylending.

Administrators also received pensions and corrodies at the king's behest. Pensions were annual cash payments made to royal clerks until they were appointed to a benefice; a corrody was annual support in food, clothing, and money to any retired official, clerk or otherwise, and might include children or servants. By Edward I's reign, the crown had established the custom of naming a royal clerk to receive a pension of 40s. or more from houses founded by the crown whenever a new abbot or prior was elected. About 106 of the 452 monastic houses whose founders are known were of royal foundation. Requests for corrodies were also linked to the right of patronage, but they soon expanded beyond that limit. Edward II submitted roughly 420 requests to more than 200 houses. Once a house gave in to a request and assigned a corrody, the crown assumed that a right had been established and put forward a new candidate when the previous one died. If houses resisted, the king would apply additional pressure. Some houses supported several candidates. Early in the century, Glastonbury paid out four pensions and six corrodies to royal candidates at a cost of more than £40 a year. In 1327 Battle abbey claimed that it was paying out 70 marks a year to royal servants. The crown clearly hoped to shift some of the burden of official salaries from the exchequer to monastic houses.

The pope, too, wanted to tap the wealth of the English church and asserted a right of appointment called papal provisions. From the midthirteenth century, the papacy had claimed the right to present its own candidates in certain circumstances, such as when an incumbent who had been appointed by the pope died and vacated a benefice or when an incumbent died while at the Holy See. The Avignon popes reaffirmed and clarified these claims, substantially broadening their rights in the process. They affected all offices from bishoprics down to prebends, superseding the rights of local patrons. As a result, the numbers of provisions increased dramatically. Between 1305 and 1342 there were a total of 929 provisions to English benefices, at the rate of approximately 25 a year. Yet during the next 4 pontificates that covered the remaining 35 years of Edward III's reign, there were a maximum of 4,655 provisions, or 133 a year.

Despite fears that English parishes would be filled with ignorant foreigners, few outsiders were in fact appointed. In the middle of Edward III's reign (1342–52), the ratio of Englishmen to foreigners provided to prebends was 5 to 1 and to lesser benefices 20 to 1. Papal provisions had a much greater impact on the composition of cathedral chapters, where the proportion of aliens could range from 1 in 6 to as high as 75 per cent. Furthermore, because those who held the right of presentation often challenged papal provisions, only about 50 per cent of those provided actually obtained the benefices they had been promised. A foreign presence was conspicuous in only one respect: cardinals. Between 1305 and 1334, 29 cardinals were given 103 benefices, of which 39 were parishes. Between 1349 and 1378, 38 cardinals held 128 benefices, of which only 14 were parishes. English suspicions could only have been deepened by the fact that between 1310 and 1368 there was no English cardinal at Avignon, while there were 112 Frenchmen and 14 Italians. To most English people, it would have looked as though their enemies dominated the papal curia and were using papal provisions to gain a foothold in England.

Papal provisions thus sparked vehement protests. English clergy and laity alike saw them as unwarranted intrusions on their rights, and their anger is evident in Adam of Murimuth's chronicle. Adam had been a royal envoy (proctor) at the papal curia, but he regarded the papacy and papal provisions with contempt. He reported, for example, that the prior and convent of Norwich elected William Bateman bishop in 1344 but that William preferred to have the office by papal provision. He was then in service at Avignon, and had the pope send him to England where he received the temporalities of the see from Edward. He then rushed back to Avignon to be consecrated. The pope granted him a procuration, that is a reimbursement for his travel expenses of 4 florins (11s.) a day before and 8 florins (22s.) a day after he was consecrated. The archbishop and dean of St Paul's in London were directed to raise the money through a tax of ½d. in the mark. Though only a rate of about .3 per cent, Murimuth lamented that the tax advanced the bishop-elect's profits rather than the good of the parishes and that thus England was always burdened. Furthermore, the bishop procured that the pope would give the deanery of Lincoln, vacated by his elevation to Norwich, to John Offord, keeper of the privy seal and archdeacon of Ely, and then give the archdeaconry to a cardinal. 'And thus the benefices of this realm are always transferred to aliens.'

In practice, many shared in the patronage arising from papal provisions. The crown, for example, not only protected its own rights, it reached an accommodation with the papacy that expanded its opportunities for appointments. Indeed, Thomas Bradwardine, who himself gained from the system, was supposed to have remarked that Edward's influence had grown so great that if he asked the pope to make a jackass bishop, he would not be refused. This cosy relationship is visible between the lines of Murimuth's account. The crown and papacy both benefited from Bateman's elevation, since Edward's official Offord got a plum position. Most provisions in England were made at someone's request. Universities tried to take advantage by submitting lists of graduates to the papacy for consideration. Furthermore, the papacy granted others the faculty of exercising provisions on their own behalf. Archbishop Walter Reynolds, for example, advanced twenty-two members of his household in this way and vigorously defended the appointments whenever a patron resisted. The rapid expansion of papal provisions in the middle decades of the fourteenth century thus happened because kings, archbishops, bishops, and universities had a stake in their success. Papal provisions potentially increased their patronage and made appointments secure by giving them papal sanction. They did not preclude, moreover, the advancement of some of the most talented men of the time, such as Bradwardine, Bury, FitzRalph, or Grandisson, each of whom received benefices through papal provision. The real losers were local patrons who saw not only their rights trampled on, but competitors reaping the bounty.

Another problem was the distribution of rewards. As Harvington's career demonstrates, some clergy held more than one office. Canon law had tried to restrict pluralism, as it was called, particularly when it involved benefices with the cure of souls. Pluralism could lead to absenteeism, since a priest could not be in two parishes at once. Absenteeism also occurred when an incumbent received permission to attend university or worked in ecclesiastical or royal government. The absentee cleric collected the fruits of the office and hired a substitute at a lower salary to perform the duties.

These practices sparked controversy within the church, which had long legislated against pluralism. Boniface VIII (1294–1303) began the practice of taking back benefices held in plurality, not with the intention of ending pluralism but rather gaining control over it by licensing it. In the bull *Execrabilis* in 1317, John XXII suspended all previous papal dispensations for plurality and ordered those holding more than one benefice with cure of souls to vacate all but one. The vacated benefices were then to be available for papal provisions. In England, approximately 200 benefices were given up as a result of the legislation, though by no means all were filled by papal provision. Urban V (1362–70) took up the attack in the bulls *Horribilis* (1362) and *Consueta* (1366), which resumed the practice of recalling pluralities.

Some of the harshest words against these practices flowed from Thomas Brinton's sermons. He condemned the clergy, saying that while in modest livings they attended to their duties diligently, but when exalted by fat benefices and many livings they grew worldly and neglected their spiritual calling. Benefices were heaped on the unworthy. Those too young or too ignorant to be priests, to whom one would not risk the care of a thousand fruit trees, were given the care of a thousand souls. Brinton consistently decried worldly ambition and temptation, scorning priests who attended more to vain honours, riches, and pleasures than to the honour of God and the cure of souls. Secular writers such as Gower, Langland, and Chaucer picked up these themes and denounced the worldliness and covetousness of some clergy.

Returns for southern England made in 1366 for Urban V's resumptions reveal that roughly 550 clerks held more than one benefice. The highest rate of pluralism was found in the diocese of London, where 169 benefices were held in plurality. The next highest was Lincoln with 72, while Rochester and Llandaff in Wales ranked at the bottom with 5 apiece. Not all pluralists were alike. A few fit the picture painted by critics. Twenty-four highly privileged clergy received incomes of £100 or more and held altogether 9 archdeaconries, 5 dignities, 23 rectories, and 85 prebends. The wealthiest of all was Edward III's minister, William of Wykeham. He earned £873 6s. 8d. from 11 prebends and 2 benefices with cure of souls. Most of the privileged pluralists lived in London, where they were close to government and many were related to nobility or officials in royal or ecclesiastical government. Yet these men were exceptional and most pluralists gained just enough to make a modest living.

Furthermore, the majority of parochial clergy were resident and fulfilled their clerical responsibilities. In Cheshire, for example, 75–80 per cent were resident in 1379, while in Cleveland only 13 to 14 per cent received licences to be non-resident in the 1370s (though licences are not a completely accurate record of absenteeism). Brinton was right. It was the privileged pluralist with lucrative offices and powerful ecclesiastical, royal, or baronial patrons who tended not to reside in the parish. The less wealthy the incumbent or parish, the more likely the priest was to be resident. Thus 100 of the 131 graduates whose livings amounted to only £30 were resident. One hundred pluralists did not even have any offices with cure of souls. Of the 450 who did, at least 245 were resident and most of those were not well off.

Not all churchmen condemned pluralism. It was vigorously defended by Robert Burnell in 1279 and again by Roger Otery, a notable pluralist, in 1366. They made several important, though self-serving, points, arguing that pluralism was essential for the administration of both church and state, that pluralists acted as mediators between the two, that pluralism rewarded good men who were able to do more for the church than a number of mediocrities were, and that disturbing a custom that had been in place for a long time would only anger a highly influential group of clerics. Furthermore, pluralism and non-residence helped to promote the education of the clergy and hence raise the quality of the church as a whole. Boniface VIII's legislation *Cum ex eo* in 1298 allowed non-residence for those who wanted to study at university and opened up opportunities for large numbers of clergymen.

The problem facing the clergy was simple: the church had great wealth and a growing number of highly qualified personnel, but it lacked a system of allocating its resources to individuals on the basis of merit and did not have sole control over those resources. In the absence of a meritocratic system of distribution, most clergy were forced to engage in a quest for patrons. The households of the king, pope, bishop, abbot, or nobleman were the loci of preferment and the first post in a clerical career. Deeply embedded in the culture of its time, the medieval church could not escape clientage and patronage. Only those within the mendicant or religious orders, supported by their houses, could afford to ignore them. Critics attacked church patronage from two angles. The first was jurisdictional, the complaint being that papal provisions and church liberties deprived laymen and other churchmen of their own rights and property. The other was pastoral. Patronage, wealth, pluralism, and non-residence diverted the clergy from their pastoral mission. How could men so absorbed in worldly affairs properly attend to instruction and the sacraments? For some, there was a fundamental contradiction between the spiritual and worldly church.

Any judgement about these practices depends on an assessment of the clergy. What kind of men were promoted? To take at face value the opinions of either moralists or apologists would distort the picture. Here, two groups are considered, the bishops, for whom information is plentiful, and the parish clergy, for whom information is much scarcer.

The effects of the compromise over papal provisions were most evident in episcopal appointments. Bishops were supposed to be elected by their cathedral chapters, but the election of John Trilleck to Hereford in 1344 was the last time an English bishop was freely elected. Elections were still conducted but, as the case of William Bateman illustrates, everyone realized that there was no hope of installation without a papal provision. Most candidates advanced through royal nomination, and were often brought to the king's attention by relatives, officials, churchmen, or courtiers. Edward used the compromise to create a subservient episcopacy. He wanted bishops who could perform well as diplomats or administrators and it was widely understood that loyalty earned advancement. Once in office, few bishops wished or dared to oppose Edward. The souring of relations between the church of England and the papacy abetted the close relationship between the crown and episcopacy. Many clerics, as echoed in the chronicles of Murimuth and Knighton, viewed the papacy as a greater threat to the independence of the church than the monarchy.

The most notable feature of Edward's episcopal appointments was the high proportion of university graduates. Edward I appointed only two scholars in his later years and Edward II placed even greater emphasis than his father on civil servants. Edward III abruptly changed course. Roughly 85 per cent of his appointees had some university training and a few, such as FitzRalph, Bradwardine, Grandisson, Courtenay, and Bury, were outstanding scholars or patrons of scholarship. Service, moreover, was not necessarily a hindrance to further study. Bradwardine, FitzRalph, and Buckingham wrote important works as bishops and Bury boasted that he used office-holding to collect books. Since universities did not have salaried positions, there was no such thing as a university career. To support themselves, scholars, as did all other clergymen, had to scramble for patronage. A scholastic reputation could be advantageous because scholars occupied posts throughout royal and ecclesiastical administration and, in turn, opened doors for others in the universities.

Richard de Bury exemplifies this kind of administrator/scholar. Though he did not have a distinguished university career, it was good enough to earn him a post as prince Edward's tutor in 1322. He gained handsomely after Edward assumed personal control of the government in 1330. He received numerous prebends, acted as the king's secretary, and in 1333 became bishop of Durham. He went on to serve as chancellor, treasurer, and royal envoy. His personal household numbered at least twenty clerks and thirty-six squires and included at one time or another scholars such as Bradwardine, Holcot, and FitzRalph. It was said that Bury conducted disputations at the dinner table except when hindered by the presence of noblemen. Discussions continued on after the meals and the atmosphere was sufficiently stimulating to prompt these scholars to pursue their studies and writing after leaving Oxford. Presence in Bury's household was also a step toward royal preferment because of his close connections with Edward. Of course, not all scholars did so well. John Wycliff is one example of a university man who did not attain a bishopric though he did find patronage in Lancaster's household.

Edward's bishops had two other notable characteristics. One was their training in law, reflecting a shift in interest in the universities, where graduates in law outnumbered those in other fields. A second was their military activity. This was the age of the warrior bishop. Edward III enlisted the episcopate in the war effort early on, asking bishops to disseminate information, conduct prayers and processions, and inculcate support for the war in the population. He also asked for practical assistance. He gave the task of defending the southern coastline to the archbishop of Canterbury, the bishops of Winchester and Chichester, and the abbot of Battle. Others engaged in combat. John de Kirkby, bishop of Carlisle, fought against the Scots in the 1330s and 1340s and was actually unhorsed in combat in 1345. The archbishops of York were also in the fray. William Melton fought against the Scots in 1319 and William de la Zouche commanded the victorious English forces at Neville's Cross in 1346. Bishop Northburgh of London accompanied the army on the Crécy campaign in 1346, as did Thomas Hatfield, bishop of Durham, who was also in Scotland in 1356. Whatever their other qualifications and services, Edward expected his bishops to play a leading role commensurate with their status as peers of the realm.

Episcopal appointments in the first half of Edward's reign illustrate these trends. In the thirteen years between 1327 and 1340, there were eighteen openings in fifteen of the seventeen bishoprics in England. Seventeen different men were promoted. Of these, a number were prominent civil servants: Richard de Bury, Thomas Charleton, John, Ralph, and Robert Stratford, Robert Wyvill, and William de la Zouche. Five (Antony Bek II, Thomas Bek II, Thomas Charleton, John de Grandisson, and Simon de Montagu) were aristocrats but all five were highly educated. Montagu clearly owed his promotion to his kinship with Edward's favourite William de Montagu; the Beks to their kinship with Antony Bek; and Ralph and Robert Stratford to their kinship with John. In three notorious cases, Bath and Wells in 1329, Norwich in 1337, and York in 1340, Edward failed to get his candidate placed, though two of the successful candidates (Shrewsbury and de la Zouche) did not give him trouble. Several (Antony Bek II, Thomas Bek II, and Grandisson) had been active in papal administration. And nearly all of them had at least some university training.

In the following decade, Edward seems to have concentrated on rewarding his servants. After his turbulent relations with John Stratford, he may also have wanted a compliant episcopate. Ten men received positions in eight bishoprics. Six of these had served the crown in important departments or as envoys prior to their elevation. William Bateman rose through papal service while John Gynwell rose through his connections with Henry Grosmont. Though the cohort was notable because of the presence of prominent civil servants such as William de Edington, Thomas Hatfield, Simon Islip, John Offord, and John de Thoresby, it was also marked by the high educational standards of the reign, most notably in the person of Thomas Bradwardine, another bishop who had served in the royal administration.

Edward's appointees exhibited not only steadfast loyalty to the crown, but the greater professionalism and educational opportunities that characterized fourteenth-century England. While, on the one hand, the episcopacy failed to maintain the tradition of staunch defiance of royal power and defence of the church's liberties that stretched back to Anselm, on the other it recognized the common interests that bound church and monarchy and worked to promote good men. Looking at the totality of their careers – education, royal and ecclesiastical service, and pastoral performance – one can only be struck by the diligence and excellence of Edward's bishops. They were the bearers of the ideal of civic responsibility and learning in the feudal state.

There was also improvement among the parish priests, though at a much slower pace. Studies of Cheshire, Yorkshire, and Warwickshire show that the parochial clergy were primarily local men from wealthy peasant or burgess families. One historian has concluded that the costs of entering the church were not terribly great, so that it offered a relatively easy path to social mobility. Villeins usually had to pay a fine for their lord's permission to send sons into the church; primary and grammar school education could be costly, but not much was required; and university training was available at a very high cost, though the ambitious could easily find patrons to subsidize it. The grandson of the prosperous villein Richard Young who became a priest, cited in the previous chapter, may have been fairly typical. A few came from the local gentry; younger sons and cousins looking for a stake denied them by the practice of primogeniture. These men tended to do better than others because their kin controlled wealthy appointments giving them a head start in the race for connections. Roughly three-quarters of the clergy of gentry stock received their livings from the hands of lay patrons.

Not everyone was successful. Many were ordained but only a few got benefices. An ordinand was supposed to have title, means of support, but the support could be quite nominal and did not mean an actual appointment to a living. In early fourteenth-century Yorkshire, the unbeneficed clergy, those without a living, outnumbered the beneficed by four to one. This ratio was not simply the product of high population, since almost the same proportions are found in Cheshire after the Black Death. There were openings for these men as chaplains serving parish priests, in chapels of ease, or in chantries. They could hope to move up the ladder, but the existence of such a large body of hopefuls made it difficult.

As a whole, the parochial clergy was probably better educated than at any previous time. A study of Warwickshire thus concluded that about 10 per cent of the local priests had university degrees. In Yorkshire, 22 per cent of the unappropriated rectories but only 11 per cent of the vicarages were held by graduates. The latter were less attractive to graduates because canon law stipulated that the vicar had to be resident. Theoretically, then, graduates were attracted to rectories because the possibility of non-residence gave them greater scope to realize their ambitions. There may have been a tendency toward absenteeism among university graduates, but not all of them hungered for worldly glories. William of Pagula is a good example of a graduate using his university training for pastoral purposes. As did many others, he used the provisions of *Cum ex eo* to go to university. He received a doctorate in 1321 but returned to his parish, which by the way was a vicarage, and held only the one living until he died in 1334. After his training and while in his parish, he wrote several treatises. One was a vehement denunciation of the practice of royal purveyance written in the form of advice to the young Edward III, *De speculo regis Edwardi III*. Its underlying theme was the injustice of taking subjects' property without due payment or taking something for a lower price than the seller wished to get for it. Another treatise, the *Oculus sacerdotis*, was perhaps the most influential manual for parish priests in the fourteenth century. It was familiar not only among the higher, well-educated clergy, but among the parochial clergy as well. Its three parts on confessions, the instruction of parishioners, and the sacraments, offered straightforward and useful advice. Not all graduates were as conscientious. Yet, Pagula's career demonstrates one powerful current in the fourteenth-century English church directed towards educating and improving the parochial clergy. Another current of moral laxity and worldly preoccuptions was revealed in visitations and generated criticism after mid-century. Parochial clergy were sometimes ill-trained, absorbed in gambling, money-lending, fine clothes, or mistresses.

It was this element of the church, along with the baronial prelates such as Wykeham, that caught the critics' attention. Despite impressive achievements in logic, science, and theology at the universities, a corps of well-trained thinkers and officials capable of guiding government inside and outside the church, and sensitivity to the needs of parishioners and parish priests, the church came under increasing attack from Edward's reign onward. The ubiquity of patronage, the channelling of rewards to a handful of well-connected clergy, and the demands of service were all condemned. In part, the church was the victim of high expectations engendered by its own achievements, as many have argued. It was also a product of its time and society. Clientage was virtually unavoidable. Indeed, only those free of patronage were able to concentrate exclusively on spiritual or pastoral concerns. Such freedom may be one explanation why the thrust for reform in the last quarter of the century would come from among the mendicant orders, the Carthusians, and poor parish priests.

IO

LAW AND ORDER
IN LOCAL COMMUNITIES

———— • ————

Secular government faced the same problem as the church: how to get its subjects to live by its rules. Royal administration was hierarchically organized, from the village to the king, with sophisticated systems of accounting, adjudication, and communication. But for all its expertise, it had trouble collecting taxes and raising troops, catching criminals and executing judgements, and even getting its officials to perform their duties properly and impartially. The crown, moreover, did not have a monopoly on governing institutions at the local level. Ordinary individuals found themselves in overlapping, sometimes complementary, sometimes competing jurisdictions. The crown was only one authority in their lives; landlords, church, and community likewise commanded respect.

Four trends are discernible in fourteenth-century local government. One was the increasing activity of royal administrators because of war, crime, and a proliferation of legislation. A second trend was an effort by local elites to exert even greater control over local government than they already had, by determining appointments and the terms and duties of office-holding. More than ever before, to govern effectively the crown had to work through influential leaders, notably at the county level. Tout pointed out that the crown had a central bureaucracy but not a local one. It deputized elites in villages, towns, and counties to look after its interests and enforce its laws and commands. Since these agents were recruited from the very communities which they governed, they maintained a double allegiance that sometimes compromised their effectiveness. This problem was part of the third trend: corruption. The crown battled against greed and retaining to maintain an impartial administration.

Finally, like all other medieval governments, the English crown made landlords, church, and communities partners in governing by giving them liberties or franchises. Liberties represented an immunity from royal administration since the liberty holder's officials, not the king's, carried out royal orders. Yet liberties also entailed responsibility. The crown asserted and had succeeded in enforcing the principle that liberties could only be retained if they were properly exercised. Abuse or non-use led to revocation.

There were many kinds of liberties. One of the most common was the private hundred, in which the landlord exercised hundredal jurisdiction including the supervision of weights and measures, beer and ale as well as the punishment of petty crimes. A more impressive franchise was the 'return of writs' because the holder's appointee executed all royal commands within the liberty, that is the territory covered by the franchise. Thus, a private official took the place of the sheriff for the tenants. At the very top were liberties that turned virtually all of the functions of government over to private administration, such as collecting royal debts and dues and hearing all pleas, thus placing royal justice in the hands of private judges. These powers were normally reserved to the palatinate franchises of Durham and Chester, though others, such as the bishop of Ely or the abbot of Battle, exercised similar authority over smaller territories. Edward III extended palatinate rights to the duchy of Cornwall in 1337 and to the duchy of Lancaster in 1351 and again in 1369.

Through franchises, 'public' and 'private' authority flowed together in a peculiarly medieval manner that makes the distinction almost meaningless. Governmental institutions in medieval England did not function solely in the interests of the 'state', but were also used by landlords to rule the peasantry.

The village represented the basic level of governance. For most people, the manorial court was the primary jurisdiction and the lord's officials the paramount authority. Chaucer's reeve, for example, was feared more than the plague by those beneath him. Church officials were equally dreaded, though less conspicuous. Responsible for supervising churches, priests, and parishioners, archdeacons and rural deans were hated for their hypocritical, corrupt meddling in villagers' lives, as Chaucer's *Friar's tale* reveals. Royal authority was felt through the village constables and the tithings. One or more constables were elected by the village and were responsible for keeping order. They watched suspicious persons, organized the pursuit of wrongdoers whenever the hue and cry was raised, arrested criminals, and seized felons' chattels. They may also have been responsible for keeping arms and armour for use when the local levies were summoned.

Policing was also done through the frankpledge system. All male villagers twelve years old and over were supposed to be enrolled in groups of ten called tithings, though in practice tithings were usually limited to the poor and unfree. They were collectively responsible for one another's actions and swore to report crimes or face a fine levied on the tithing as a whole. The hundred bailiff conducted a 'view of frankpledge' village by village to ensure that the tithings were properly maintained and crimes reported. Hundreds were ancient administrative units embracing a number of villages and townships and serving as critical points of contact between crown and subjects. Each had a court which adjudicated petty disputes and brawls, though its peacekeeping functions faded during the fourteenth century. The bailiff was kept busy executing judgements and royal mandates, making summonses and arrests, and assembling juries. Two constables of the peace supervised military and police matters and organized the local defence. Hundred juries, made up of leading villagers from around the hundred, made criminal indictments (or 'presentments') and answered royal inquiries about the performance of officials and the exercise of crown rights. Twice a year, the sheriff conducted a 'tourn' in which he toured the county and stopped at each hundred in the king's hands to receive indictments, check on the tithings, and adjudicate minor issues.

By 1300, more than half of all the hundreds had been granted out as liberties. Only 11½ of 38 hundreds in Wiltshire remained in the king's hands. In the others, private lords exercised hundredal jurisdiction and held the view of frankpledge. Private hundred courts came to be known as courts leet. The jurisdiction could be held over a hundred as a whole, or simply attached to a manor and exercised over one's tenants within the hundred.

Town government embraced many of these functions. York can serve as an example. Its government was essentially an amateur oligarchy dominated by the leading citizens, called aldermen. From among this group a mayor was elected annually. The position was prestigious though onerous. The aldermen formed a city council which was subordinate to the mayor and probably functioned as an executive body. An assembly of the commonality of the town convened to deliberate on matters such as taxation which touched the entire citizenry. There were also three bailiffs who collected revenues and supervised the market, three chamberlains who were in charge of city finances, a city clerk, coroners, bridgemasters, keepers of weights and measures, gate keepers, constables, and parish clerks. Three major courts – the bailiffs' held three days a week for debts, trespasses, and accounts, the mayor's held every Monday for various pleas, and criminal courts for assaults and disruptions – kept order and settled disputes in the city. In return for a fixed farm of £160 a year, York gained freedom from the local sheriff and some royal courts, the right to collect exchequer debts, and jurisdiction over all pleas arising in the city.

Within towns, lords exercised liberties that sometimes brought them into conflict with other citizens. In York, for example, the archbishop, St Leonard's hospital, and St Mary's abbey all held liberties. Citizens resented these pockets of exemption because they barred the exercise of urban jurisdiction within those areas as well as any contribution to the city's farm and taxes. Early in the fourteenth century, citizens attacked the liberty of St Leonard's, threatened the abbey with attack, and cut off food supplies in 1343 and 1350. A compromise was reached in 1354 which extended the city's jurisdiction over the abbey's liberty but protected the abbot and monks.

The most important administrative unit was the county or shire. Three officials served as the guardians of royal interests in the county. Sheriffs were the king's general agents. They collected customary revenues, fines, and rents, executed writs, impanelled juries, guarded prisoners, conducted tourns twice a year, and presided over the county court. Coroners worked closely with the sheriff. They held inquests upon dead bodies to determine whether they had died by murder, suicide, or accident; received abjurations of the realm by criminals in sanctuary; heard appeals and confessions of outlaws; conducted outlawries in the county court; and 'kept' the crown pleas – pleas of great importance such as burglary, arson, or homicide – by recording them as they came up in the presentations of the hundreds or in the county court and then reporting on them to royal justices. The escheators were responsible for safeguarding the king's feudal and regalian rights. They took custody of the lands of deceased tenants-in-chief, held inquests to determine who the heirs were and if they were of age, took custody of ecclesiastical lands during vacancies, seized lands for various reasons, and held a variety of ad hoc inquests into matters relating to the king's feudal prerogative. Each of these officers had a suite of subordinates and clerks to help him do the work.

The county court, held once every three or four weeks, was a bustling congregation of about 150 people. Indictments and appeals were heard, outlawries pronounced, and juries sworn in. The court had cognizance of pleas involving less than 40s. Anything above that went to the central courts, though many suits that started in the county court were transferred to the central courts through special writs. But the court was also an occasion for reading statutes, ordinances, and proclamations handed down by the king, council, or parliament. It played a very important role in moulding popular support for Edward's wars. Newsletters reporting on the progress of campaigns were read out, while requests for men and supplies were put forth. The two parliamentary representatives from each county, the knights of the shire, were chosen in the county court and transmitted the opinions of the community back to parliament. Thus, communication flowed the other way as well, in streams of petitions to king, council, and parliament.

There existed a separate administration for the king's forests. They were not simply natural features but territories under special forest law, outside common law. They had their own set of officials and their own courts. Forests were a constant source of friction between the king and the general population, which continually pressed on its borders seeking arable land at the expense of the king's hunting preserves.

Alongside these fixed offices, there existed a much more flexible system of government by commission, in which the crown appointed officials to perform a specific task at a specific time. Many functions did not yet require a permanent bureaucracy. Because taxes were approved and levied on an ad hoc basis, for example, assessors and collectors were newly appointed each time parliament consented to a tax. After 1334, when the returns from parliamentary taxes were fixed, approximately three of the gentry per county were assigned to collect the assigned quotas from towns and villages. Sub-collectors in each community were responsible for apportioning the quota and collecting it from the inhabitants. In contrast, because customs were routinely collected with only occasional interruptions, customs officers became permanent fixtures in major towns.

The crown similarly raised its military forces by special commissions. According to the statute of Winchester (1285), all males between fifteen and sixty had to prepare for war by maintaining armaments proportional to their wealth. Those with lands worth less than £2 a year were required to have scythes, battle axes, knives, or other small weapons, while those with more than £15 a year were to maintain a hauberk, an iron helmet, a sword, a knife, and a horse. Anyone who could afford it should at least have bows and arrows. The entire country was supposed to be in arms. Hundred constables originally had responsibility for 'viewing' the arms, making sure that the population was properly armed, but it was later given to the justices of the peace. Concerned that hockey, football, handball, cockfighting and other frivolous amusements were distracting men from archery, Edward ordered in the 1360s that on holidays men should practise archery and desist from worthless games. Edward wanted even more. He increased the required armament and asked those liable for service to find the required men rather than serve themselves. In 1346, the high-water mark of these demands, he stipulated among other things that anyone with 10 marks had to find a hobelar, that is a man with a horse, armed with a sword, knife, and lance, and wearing a small helmet, armoured collar, padded jacket, and iron gauntlets. The hobelars were an essential part of Edward's new armies, but the obligations went way beyond those established by the statute of Winchester. A storm of protest forced him to add that the demands would not set a precedent.

Whenever the king needed an army, he issued commissions of array, charged with gathering a specified number of footmen and archers from each county. The commissioners travelled from hundred to hundred selecting men brought forth by the constables and organizing them into vintenaries (groups of twenty), centenaries, and millenaries. They then led the troops to muster. Troops were generally paid from the time they left the county border, though the crown would have liked to begin paying them only at the muster.

Armies had to be fed, so the crown commissioned purveyors to collect quotas of grain, livestock, and other supplies. Because the crown was chronically short of cash, purveyors often failed to pay for the goods and issued receipts or debentures that were often hard to redeem. Fierce protests against purveyance and the corruption of purveyors as revealed in inquests such as those held in 1340–1 fuelled parliamentary protests. The crown backed away from an assertion of its right to compulsory purchases in favour of gathering supplies through contracts with merchants. Nevertheless, direct purveyances for the household continued and sparked complaints throughout Edward's reign.

Ad hoc commissions thus greatly magnified contact between the crown and its subjects. Purveyors and their deputies, arrayers, constables, and their local subordinates, tax collectors, sub-collectors, and customs officials, escheators and sub-escheators, coroners, and sheriffs, under sheriffs, and sheriffs' clerks amounted to a considerable force, even if some men played several roles.

Despite increasing numbers of officials, the crown had difficulty performing its primary service to its subjects, keeping law and order. Whether or not the crime rate was actually going up during the fourteenth century, as some have argued, England was a violent place. Larceny, burglary, and robbery constituted nearly three-quarters of all the felony indictments between 1300 and 1340, while homicides accounted for 18 per cent. Keeping in mind that crime statistics are not strictly comparable because of changes in both the definition and the reporting of crime, in the United States today homicide represents less than 1 per cent of all crimes and in England less than .1 per cent. The homicide rate in medieval towns significantly exceeded that of modern American cities, in Oxford perhaps by as much as four to six times. Even in villages, where the rate was lower, violence was still common. It was overwhelmingly male and usually occurred in sudden outbursts. Inquests in the 1320s and 1330s revealed an infestation of 'common malefactors', petty ruffians who disrupted markets and fairs with assaults, thefts, and extortion.

Crime occurred among all social ranks. If Oxford was typical, homicide was a phenomenon of the lower orders, though rivalries led to affrays among town oligarchs from York to Southampton as well. Village elites turned to crime for personal gain or as an instrument of social power while gentry and magnate leaders likewise used it to further their aims. As at all times, the motives for crime were complex, though special circumstances stimulated the incidence of crime in medieval England. One study has thus affirmed that movements in grain prices affected the crime rate. During the disastrous harvests in the early years of the century, for example, crime surged as individuals scrambled to find sustenance. It subsequently levelled off when prices declined and conditions became more tolerable than they had been. At the opposite end of society, heavily armed retinues and a culture that ennobled warfare were powerful inducements to crime.

War aggravated the problem. The unsettled political conditions of the 1320s encouraged lawlessness, sometimes under the banner of one of the contending factions. Crime was rife in the north where raiding by the Scots had destroyed law and order. War with France introduced new problems. The commons on several occasions voiced their fear that the king's absence overseas would embolden criminals. Another problem was returning soldiers. Edward followed earlier precedents and offered pardons to criminals if they joined his army, though the exact numbers who did are not known. In France they and their army comrades grew accustomed to plundering, pillaging, and living off the land. To the horror of the commons, many returned to England after demobilization and pursued the same activities, sometimes forming companies much like those roaming France. Edward promised in 1328 to limit pardons but did not follow his promise through, for statutes in 1330, 1336, and 1340 called for the enforcement of the measure. The commons in 1347, 1350, and again in 1353 pleaded with Edward to cut back on his pardons because they emboldened criminals and increased crime.

Some of the blame for disorder must be borne by the wealthy and those charged with maintaining order. Corruption was rampant among local officials who frequently used their official authority for private gain. The crown as well as its subjects suffered. The lesson is clearest among the crown's financial agents. Prior to 1334, taxes involved a dual process of assessment and collection, each of which opened the door to bribery and corruption. Customs, similarly, involved several steps, such as weighing, assessing, and collecting, that invited fraud. For revenue collection to be successful, the crown needed to supervise officials closely to prevent cheating but also to help them resist outside inducements and pressures. In both respects the government failed and lost income. Meanwhile its subjects had to bear the costs of extortion and bribes. Juries in 1341 complained that tax collectors demanded fees for carrying out their duties or bribes to evade the tax; wool collectors used false scales, collected more than was required, and kept the excess; sheriffs and coroners refused to perform their duties unless they received bribes; and purveyors extorted money not to collect goods, collected more than they were ordered, or failed to make any form of restitution. Corruption was thus a hidden tax on the population, siphoning money away from subjects into the pockets of officials and increasing the overall burden of government.

Another problem was maintenance, or conspiracy. An ordinance in 1305 defined conspiracy as individuals binding themselves by oath to support one another in false suits, or individuals retaining men by fees and robes to assist their criminal activities, or seigneurial officials using their authority to maintain others in quarrels or pleas that did not touch themselves or their lords. In other words, it denounced the use of retinues to exert pressure on the legal process. Lordship and gift-giving exacerbated corruption. Officials often accepted fees and robes and sometimes took on retainers of their own. These issues came up in Edward III's first parliament, producing a statute that prohibited his officials and great men of the realm from maintaining others in their suits. A 1330 statute broadened the adjudication of maintenance while an agreement in parliament the following year ordered magnates to refrain from retaining criminals and to assist royal officials in executing their judgements and duties. These measures proved insufficient. The commons complained about the problem in 1336, 1340, 1343, 1347, and again in 1348 as part of their concern for law and order. It should be noted that the commons did not denounce retaining per se, as it would later in the century; it concentrated on the perversion of retaining to forward illegal activities.

Behind these pronouncements lay private petitions bemoaning the harm caused by maintenance. Sir John de Berkeley lamented in 1330–1 that Sir Thomas de Berkeley, keeper of the peace in Gloucestershire, unjustly seized his plough-teams and would not give them up. John alleged that the sheriff and bailiffs could not help him because they were in Thomas' retinue, receiving his fees and robes. To make matters worse, Roger de Mortimer supposedly aided (maintained) Thomas by securing him a new franchise of the return of writs. Not long after, a group of petitioners complained that the keeper of Gloucester castle, Thomas de Bradeston, and his wife prevented justice being done to their valet, who was accused of several murders including that of his wife. They asserted that Thomas was so powerful and stood in such favour with the king that he acted with impunity, oppressing all over whom he ruled. There was no quarrel in the county in which he did not side with the malefactors. Good men were thus rebuked and the bad honoured.

Edward addressed the problem of retaining in the ordinance for justices in 1346. He issued it just as he was departing for a campaign in France with the intention of easing fears about his absence from the kingdom. It stresses the ideal of impartiality by repeating the stock formula that justice be made available to rich and poor alike. It forbade maintenance and ordered magnates to oust any maintainers from their retinues. Royal justices should never deviate from the path of justice and should not accept fees, robes, or gifts, except food or drink, from anyone other than the king. Henceforth they had to swear an oath with these provisos. Edward also promised his judges higher wages in the hope of immunizing them against the temptations of bribery, retaining, and gift-giving. How effective the ordinance was is another matter. Justices Willoughby in 1341 and Thorp in 1351 were convicted of accepting bribes.

The confluence of retaining and crime is also evident in the activities of professional, or habitual, criminal gangs, a problem that seems to have grown worse after 1300. The criminal rampages of Henry de Leybourn, Gilbert de Middleton, John le Boteler of Llantwit, Malcolm Musard, and the Folville and Coterel gangs have been chronicled many times. The latter grew so bold as to seize justice Willoughby and hold him for a ransom of 1,300 marks. John Molyns' career nicely summarizes the problems. On one level, he was a respected member of gentry society. He was a retainer of Edward III's favourite, William Montagu, and served Edward in the 1330s as a soldier, keeper of the peace, keeper of the king's hawks, custodian of royal lands, and as an envoy. He advanced both materially and socially, acquiring lands worth more than £800 and rising from valet to banneret by 1340.

A darker picture came to light during the inquests of 1341. It turned out that in 1326 he had his wife's uncle and son murdered in order to acquire a manor. He subsequently relied on his friendship with a royal justice, John Inge, to wriggle out of any convictions in that and several other cases. In 1336 he hired himself out to Canterbury cathedral priory to intimidate the priory's unfree tenants who were claiming to be free and organizing themselves against their lord. Molyns broke into the houses of the ringleaders and carted them off to prison in the priory where conditions were so miserable that two died. The tenants submitted to the prior's demands. In 1340, Molyns' men attacked the sheriff of Buckinghamshire, tore up the local village, and rode across the county assaulting the sheriff's tenants. Molyns later stole twenty-four sacks of wool which the sheriff had collected for the king. The inquests revealed that he had also committed a number of petty crimes. Murder, harassment, maintenance, and theft – these were the staple ventures of criminal gangs.

Molyns did not answer the charges and went into hiding. He received a full pardon in 1345, recovered some of his lands, and once again led a respectable life. He served in the Crécy campaign, entered the peerage when Edward summoned him to parliament in 1347, returned as a keeper of the peace, and became steward of Queen Philippa's household. He went back to his old ways, however, and in 1357 was charged with various felonies. This time he was convicted and imprisoned, though he tried to save himself by claiming benefit of clergy. He died in prison in 1362. The story is unusual in two respects. First, Molyns attained high social standing. Criminal gangs were usually made up of younger sons or lower gentry. Second, he was convicted. Most of the infamous leaders of criminal gangs such as the Folvilles and Coterels escaped punishment, because of either a failure to convict them or royal pardons. Not even a third of all of those indicted for felonies down to 1340 were ever convicted. In fact, of 1,513 individuals accused of crimes in Lincolnshire in 1328, the government managed to bring only 514, one-third, to trial, though 60 per cent of those were convicted. The failure to arrest and convict must have been powerful disincentives to those responsible for apprehending criminals. On top of that, how could the government keep order when its own members flouted the law?

The problem became so troubling that Edward initiated several experiments in law enforcement between 1327 and 1350. In 1328, 'desiring that the peace of his land and his laws and statutes . . . may be kept in all points', he issued the statute of Northampton which ordered sweeping criminal inquests. They were insufficient, however, and in 1331 Edward offered additional measures. A year later, Geoffrey le Scrope, the chief justice of the king's bench, told parliament that criminals formed great companies; destroyed the king's liege subjects, churchmen, and justices; seized some and held them for outrageous ransoms; put some to death; robbed others; and committed many other evils and felonies in contempt of the king, to the breaking of his peace, and the destruction of his people. In the ordinance of Nottingham in 1336, Edward with parliament's consent created a system of informers and ordered the arrest of criminals and maintainers. These measures did not solve the problem and in 1339 and again in 1343 Edward asked parliament what to do to keep the peace. There was obviously no ready solution and the feverish legislation betrays the government's confusion.

There were basically three ways the crown could deal with lawlessness. It could encourage self-policing by local communities. It could dispatch panels of judges and magnates to local communities with powers of investigation and judgement. Or it could give local elites responsibility for policing and justice. Edward tried all three, but what is notable is the gradual triumph of the third option as the prime method of law enforcement, embodied in the justices of the peace.

Self-policing had been one of the goals of the statute of Winchester (1285). Not only was every man to be armed, but villages and their officials were to keep an eye on strangers and suspicious persons, uncover crime, and keep the peace. Individuals, moreover, could lodge appeals of felony against criminals who had harmed them or their kin. Appeals declined during the fourteenth century, but the ideal of self-help was carried forward in writs of trespass. A trespass was a non-felonious wrong, that is, a petty theft, assault, or damage that did not have to be heard by royal justices and was punished by a fine rather than by death as in a felony. While the crown jealously protected its right to judge serious crimes and had inhibited local juries from hearing felonies, trespasses were often adjudicated in manorial, hundred, or county courts. The crown also offered litigants a writ of trespass which brought minor wrongs, in which it was alleged that the king's peace had been broken, before royal justices. It proved to be very popular, even among the lower orders. In Lincolnshire, the number of trespass suits soared after 1300, and over 80 per cent were initiated by villagers.

The government also used judicial commissions, on the model of the eyre, to combat disorder. Through the thirteenth century, the eyre brought comprehensive justice to the counties. Teams of judges heard civil and criminal pleas, supervised franchises, entertained complaints against local officials, and inquired into 143 separate issues. But the eyre died out. After 1294, it was used primarily to assert control over franchises, and then only on a limited basis. The government's profound uneasiness over lawlessness, however, prompted it to revive the eyre for law enforcement in 1329. In a speech at the opening of the eyre in Northampton, Geoffrey le Scrope reported that earlier attempts at fighting crime had failed and that the king and council had therefore gone back to the proven methods of the eyre. It was a reasonable decision. No other court offered as thorough an approach to justice. The eyre conducted a searching inquest of local officials who were partly responsible for the disorder, and it was headed by experts. Unfortunately, it was cumbersome and the results were disappointing. The government halted the experiment after 1330 and never again used the eyre for law enforcement.

In the meantime, new judicial commissions appeared. Groups of justices were periodically sent to try criminals who had been arrested and placed in the county gaols. These commissions of gaol delivery were eventually absorbed by the local assize justices, so that during the fourteenth century, the 'assizes' became the usual forum for trying felonies. Panels of justices assigned to hear and determine complaints lodged by private parties, called commissions of oyer and terminer, appeared in the 1270s. They became enormously popular among the gentry, and flourished during the 1320s. In 1305, Edward I established a more powerful investigative device than oyer and terminer in the commissions of trailbaston. They empowered justices to inquire into all kinds of felonies and trespasses, but were principally concerned with the perversion of justice through conspiracy or main-tenance. The country was divided into five circuits and trailbaston com-missions were issued periodically thereafter. The broad inquisitions set in motion by the statute of Northampton in 1328, by Edward III in 1340–1, and by parliament in 1343 were based on the the model of the trailbaston commissions. Finally, during Edward II's reign, the court of king's bench became more involved in criminal justice than it had been in his father's reign. While it was sitting at York in 1318, it took the first step by delivering the gaol there and hearing a larger number of trespass cases. It took another step in 1323 when Edward II ordered it to travel around the country and hear felony and trespass indictments, much like a trailbaston commission. Then, in the 1350s, it was used as an eyre to investigate an array of issues.

The most serious drawback to these panels was that they aroused the dis-trust of local communities. To begin with, they were often extortionate. The crown wanted to keep order but it did not overlook an opportunity to raise money from fines on offenders and officials alike. This dual motive is apparent in the Cheshire eyre of 1353. Having heard innumerable com-plaints about lawlessness in the county, the Prince of Wales ordered an eyre. Yet, just as it began, a delegation from the county community offered the Prince 5,000 marks to end it. The Prince took the money, suspended the eyre, but then ordered his justices to sit as a trailbaston commission, only slightly less onerous than the eyre. It heard over 130 cases and resulted in the replacement of virtually all of the county administrators. The chronicler Henry Knighton, perhaps echoing the sentiments of the county, con-demned the trickery and claimed that the justices levied fines beyond num-ber and seized countless lands and holdings. The Prince was none the less sincere in his judicial aims. He concluded the proceedings in Cheshire with a general legislative session that heard complaints and petitions and rectified certain problems. He acted as the king often did; he saw no incompatibility with using justice to repress crime and raise money. Justice Shareshull used the king's bench in this way for the king in the 1350s and conducted eyres for the Prince in his dominions in 1347, 1348, and 1362.

Judicial commissions also posed a threat to the local elites. They directed much of their attention, after all, to the activities of officials. Their disci-plinary power was demonstrated by the Despensers' use of the eyre in 1321 to punish London for its support of Thomas of Lancaster. It conducted a searching inquest into the city's liberties that resulted not only in fines but in an erosion of its independence. The inquests in 1341, which heard com-plaints about franchisal and ecclesiastical as well as royal officials, likewise prompted complaints. The house of commons protested that under the statute of Northampton persons other than criminals had been attached and asked that the statute be voided. They grumbled that the 1341 inquest had not been affirmed by parliament as it should have been, that fines levied on convicted officials were greater than their crimes, and that sheriffs had been burdened with unreasonable work. It is telling that they not only called for a repeal of the commission and a redress of its excesses, but asked that future inquiries be assigned to local men who were familiar with the conduct and condition of local officers. In 1344 they condemned the inquests set in motion the preceding year in the same terms and again used the opportunity to press for commissions of local men. They returned to the attack in 1348, 1355, and 1356, denouncing eyres, forest inquests, trailbaston hearings, and general inquiries. The commons took up the issue in another form in 1376, when it complained about unjust influence exercised over the appointment of justices of the peace and asked that they be nominated by the lords and knights of the counties in parliament. Finally, the local antipathy toward central justices and officials came out in the grudging admiration displayed by some for the kidnappers of Sir Richard de Willoughby. He was disliked because he was one of the trailbaston judges while Knighton labelled his chief kidnapper 'a fierce, daring, and impudent man'.

As the commons' protests demonstrate, the county communities were pushing another agenda besides their annoyance at the financial burdens of the inquests. They wanted complete responsibility for law enforcement – arrest, indictment, judgement, supervision of local officers, and control of maintenance – placed in the hands of the justices of the peace. The crown, however, balked at giving local officials judicial powers, the right to hear and determine cases.

Keepers of the peace first appeared in the thirteenth century. After 1300, they became a regular part of the administration, primarily responsible for enforcing Magna Carta and the statute of Winchester (1285). The mounting clamour over lawlessness forced the government to take additional action. But what action? The crown wavered. Keepers were appointed with sweeping authority in 1327, but the following year in the statute of Northampton the government tried trailbaston commissions instead. Under pressure from the county communities, the next year it gave keepers judicial competence, but immediately reversed itself and appointed an eyre. Judicial authority was likewise bestowed and rescinded in 1332. Then in 1338, new commissions were issued in association with the Walton Ordinances. Edward was just embarking on his wars. Against a background of financial shortage, apprehension over law and order during the king's absence, and the desire to placate the local gentry whose participation was crucial to the war effort, the government gave broad powers to the keepers, who were now called justices. It also conceded the right to choose them in the county courts with final approval by the king and council. The experiment, however, ended with the general inquests of 1341, which returned to the use of centralized commissions and stripped keepers of the power to determine.

The final shifts in policy occurred after 1348. As has been seen, the Black Death prompted the passage of the ordinance and statute of labourers. Initially, the government gave responsibility for enforcement to the keepers of the peace, but then revoked it between 1352 and 1359. After 1359, it was permanently in the hands of the peace commissions. In the meantime, the crown had conceded the right to judge in 1350, and it was only taken back for a short period in 1364–8. During the 1350s, however, real control lay in the hands of royal justices and sergeants who were appointed to the commissions. In 1359, their numbers were reduced so that local men recovered power. Two years later, the keepers were officially styled justices and their powers were summarized in a statute of 1368. The establishment of justices of the peace thus took a tortuous path, and they did not become a significant presence in the counties until the 1370s.

It is important to be precise about who benefited from this development. The 'community' in this case was not egalitarian, embracing rich and poor alike. It was limited to the wealthy and powerful. The creation of the justices of the peace helped to solidify their control over the peasantry. The economic context in which this transformation occurred is significant. Violent swings in prices, which were especially harmful to peasants and holders of small estates, coupled with rising governmental demands caused an upsurge in crime among distraught peasants and lesser gentry and younger sons trying to establish themselves. Local elites wanted the power to keep these groups in line. This power was particularly welcome in the wake of the Black Death when demographic change slowly eroded the props of manorial authority. The expanding scope of the justices' authority, with responsibility for wages and prices, played into their hands, giving them a means of shoring up their power.

The central government was right to be wary of entrusting so much to local officials. Inquests held in Lincolnshire in 1328, in Northamptonshire in 1329–30, and throughout the country in 1341 underscored the problem of corruption within local administration. The careers of the Coterel and Folville gangs show that criminals were often aided by local functionaries, either royal or private. Many officers, whether through maintenance, corruption, or outright crime, easily crossed the line between legal and illegal actions. A study of the commissions of oyer and terminer has demonstrated that they were frequently initiated simply to harass opponents rather than to repress crime. The county gentry, therefore, viewed local law and order as their exclusive preserve and resented any intrusion of royal justices that questioned or undermined their power. It was up to them to judge who was a criminal, not the crown. It is unlikely that law enforcement dramatically improved once the keepers were transformed into justices. But it ceased to be a *political* issue.

For the peasantry, local commissions were no better than central. They complained bitterly about both. Protest poems from the early fourteenth century lament the venality of all royal officials, whether sheriffs, trailbaston judges, bailiffs, or commissioners of array, tax, and purveyance. They do not distinguish between local and central officers as the commons were wont to do. Their attacks on bribery, corruption, and maintenance bristle with contempt for unjust officials and link up with similar assaults in *Piers Plowman* and sermons by Brinton and others. The poems were informed by the ideal of impartial justice for rich and poor alike which appeared in the ordinance for justices and elsewhere. But they pointedly bemoan the failure of the ideal.

There were thus three levels to the problem of law enforcement. There was the 'real' problem of lawlessness as experienced by villagers and townsfolk. At the opposite extreme there was the crown's dilemma about how to fulfil its responsibility for keeping order. And in between there was local power, whether exercised through offices or retaining. Everything the crown did had to be mediated through county, town, and village elites. That is precisely where much of the problem lay.

This discussion raises an important question: to what extent were administrative territories social communities? Administrative development produced a patchwork of jurisdictions that were sometimes exclusive but most often overlapped with others – village, township, manor, parish, borough, hundred, liberty, deanery, archdeanery, county, diocese, estate. These were not necessarily social units. They did not limit or define social intercourse or, by themselves, create a common identity. Yet a rough correspondence evolved between hierarchies of authority and social communities. At the base of the pyramid, village communities comprised peasant social organization. Hundreds were the domains of petty knights and non-armigerous freemen who would later be given the name 'gentlemen'. The county was the realm of knights and bannerets.

The county's inchoate social identity was strengthened by Edward III's policies. He conferred with local assemblies about war and taxation; ordered sheriffs to read out ordinances, statutes, and newsletters to county courts; and asked bishops to conduct public prayers and processions for deliverance from the Black Death, victory in France, and thanksgiving for the capture of king John of France. Edward's direct requests to the counties for taxes in 1337, 1360, and again in 1371 helped bind communities. The commons in 1339 declared that they had to consult with their communities before consenting to a tax. The system of fixed taxation introduced in 1334 meant that county representatives apportioned the burden among the hundreds and towns. The justices of labourers and tax collectors similarly conferred with county representatives on how to apportion the tax relief from fines for excess wages in 1352. Frequent meetings of parliament early in Edward's reign impelled the counties to meet regularly to select representatives, to discuss the issues raised in parliament, and to draft petitions to the king and council. Frequent military campaigns meant that local gentry repeatedly came out to serve as commissioners of array to raise and lead the county forces.

As they conferred so often on so many different matters, the gentry developed a proprietary attitude toward local offices. It is most evident in the negotiations over the justices of the peace but can be seen in other issues as well. There was a perennial demand, for example, that major officers should hold sufficient land in the county they served. The restriction meant that offices would only be filled from the ranks of the county elite, though the king for his part wanted to be able to recover debts. Legislation in 1311 (the Ordinances), 1316, 1322, 1326, 1328, and 1340 formulated the provision for sheriffs, and it was applied to escheators and coroners in 1340. Parliament established an explicit qualification of £20 of land for escheators in 1362 and 1368, and it was adopted for sheriffs in 1371.

County communities also wanted to choose their own officers. The power of appointment seesawed back and forth between central ministers and the localities, though the record of the counties in actually electing officials was not good. The *Articuli Super Cartas* (1370) and the Walton Ordinances (1338) gave counties the right to appoint sheriffs, but it was not exercised widely. The election of Warin de Bassingburn as sheriff of Cambridgeshire in 1338 and 1339 was conducted by the greater landholders of the county under the supervision of the two coroners, though at least ten men dissented. Otherwise, the counties petitioned the crown for the right to name keepers of the peace throughout the first half of the century. In at least three of the five parliaments between 1349 and 1359, the commons likewise asked the king for the right to appoint justices of the peace and labourers. Parliament kept the issue alive through the 1370s, though the king never fully conceded the right of election.

Finally, the counties urged shorter terms for most officers. A one-year term for sheriffs was the subject of petitions down to 1371 and seems to have been achieved in Gloucestershire at least. Similar petitions in 1372, 1377, and 1378 to change escheators annually met with refusal. Other issues, such as the payment of wages or prohibitions on stewards serving as sheriffs or sheriffs as members of parliament came up from time to time as well.

The power that the gentry wielded within county administration can be illustrated by the Cobham family in Kent. By 1300 it had a long tradition of service. Henry de Cobham (d. 1339) was appointed constable of Rochester castle for life in 1304 and served as keeper of Guernsey and Jersey, Dover castle, the Cinque Ports, Tonbridge castle, the forfeited lands of the Templars and the Contrariants in Kent, and the bishopric of Worcester. He was sheriff (1315), a commissioner of array (1324–5), a tax collector (1310), a justice (1310, 1314, 1317, 1321–3), a commissioner of oyer and terminer (1302, 1309–12, 1316, 1318, 1321, 1323–6), a knight of the shire (1311), and a keeper of the peace (1315, 1318, 1320). His son John (d. 1355) took up where he left off, becoming keeper of Rochester and serving prominently on commissions of peace, oyer and terminer, and array. They both served the crown loyally in administration and war and were rewarded by individual summonses to parliament, raising them to the peerage. Edward III made John a banneret in 1354 and gave him an annuity of 100 marks. The family's social climb was marked by John's marriage to a daughter of the earl of Devon in 1332. Two cousins, Stephen de Cobham of Rundale and Reginald de Cobham of Sterborough, likewise had distinguished careers as royal commissioners in Kent and elsewhere, performed their military service, and were elevated to the house of lords.

Like any community, however, the county was riven by competition. Individuals or cliques could upset the terms of competition by monopolizing authority or marshalling outside powers. For this reason, there was an increasing wariness of retaining. Early in the century, it was denounced only in terms of maintenance. Later, it came under attack because it was seen as upsetting the local balance of power. The change reflects the change in retaining, noted earlier, in which magnates made a concerted effort to gain the gentry's allegiance. Retainers, puffed up by their lofty connections, sometimes bullied their neighbours, inciting resentment and resistance. The county gentry did not abhor retaining itself, and many eagerly accepted fees, but they feared that it could unsettle local power networks. Clientage and its problems had been around for centuries; what was new was that there was a great deal at stake in the county.

Edward III's reign marked a profound, though not revolutionary, change in the nature of English government. The demise of the eyres and the creation of the justices of the peace shifted emphasis away from appointed crown agents to commissions of local elites working in the name of the crown. Henceforth crime and the enforcement of all new legislation were largely turned over to the justices of the peace. The government still kept tabs on local officials through special inquests, but the triumph of the justices of the peace, along with the control exercised by the gentry over sheriffs, escheators, coroners, and parliamentary representatives, signalled greater autonomy for county elites. They had matured to the point at which they expected to have full responsibility for the affairs of their community and resisted unwelcome intrusions.

II

ADMINISTRATION AND FINANCE

For the central government, Edward III's reign was a period of professionalization and definition rather than innovation. What stood out most was the unusually close rapport between Edward and his ministers. Except for tensions in 1340–1, 1371, and 1376–7, Edward could count on their unqualified support in executing his programmes. This story will be told here through the different functions of government: administration, justice, military organization, and finance. If the last two take up a disproportionate share of space, it is because they dominated governmental work in these years of war and conquest.

Edward was fortunate because the government he inherited was small and personal. No office was immune from his intervention, and ministers served at his pleasure. While he pursued the Scots in the 1330s, the chancery, exchequer, and common bench packed up and moved to York to be near him. Nevertheless, most business was conducted routinely, without his personal participation. Government, moreover, was becoming sedentary. The process of implanting offices at Westminster began long before Edward came to the throne, and he carried it further. After the government returned to Westminster in 1338, for example, it never again strayed for long. London and Westminster gradually became a capital. Meetings of parliament contributed to the development. Of twenty-four councils and parliaments summoned in the first decade of the reign, only a third were held at Westminster. Over the next fifty years another fifty-one were summoned, but only three were held outside Westminster or London. The great wardrobe was housed in London and the exchequer had its own building next to the royal palace in Westminster. In the 1340s, the council gained a foothold when the star chamber was erected next to the exchequer. Government was acquiring a physical identity.

The royal household still travelled with the king, combining domestic and public functions. It included offices and servants such as the wardrobe and chamber, the steward, the chamberlain, the keeper of the wardrobe, the controller, the cofferer, the almoner, knights, clerks, chaplains, ushers, butlers, tailors, physicians, buyers, carters, and a horde of menials. This crowd served the king, though some also had a hand in national affairs. The state offices – the exchequer, chancery, central courts, and later the privy seal, headed by the treasurer, chancellor, chief justices, and keeper of the privy seal – administered the kingdom's finances, justice, and clerical needs. The distinction between 'state' and 'household' was unknown to contemporaries, and, in fact, functions and personnel overlapped. Because administration was not tightly compartmentalized, the king had great flexibility in choosing the instruments of his will.

Problems, of course, cropped up. Getting an accurate reading of income and expenditure proved exceptionally difficult. Personal animosities and jealousies led to antagonisms. Edward's ambitions produced tension. While administrators scrambled to catch up with his demands, he grew impatient. Those demands, in turn, sparked opposition, which was expressed in measures designed not only to lessen his demands but to restrict his choice of ministers and use of offices as well. It used to be argued that kings preferred to use their household offices precisely because they had greater control over them than over state offices, which were supposedly susceptible to baronial influence. There is, however, no evidence of any serious erosion of the king's control over his ministers and departments. The entire administration, whether chancery or wardrobe, exchequer or chamber, was equally subject to his will. Convenience, not politics, explains the king's decision to use one department rather than another. It was easier in wartime, for instance, to rely on the household offices close at hand instead of those lodged at Westminster.

Shared responsibility between mobile and stationary offices and the hardening of bureaucratic routines amplified the problems of governmental communication, whether between the king and his ministers, central and local offices, or king and subjects. The chancery, at the centre of the administration, was the king's original secretariat. It drafted and dispatched royal writs (letters of command), which coordinated the activities of local and central government, set the machinery of justice in motion, gave instructions, and authorized royal gifts. With limited literacy, seals, not signatures, authenticated documents so that the writs and charters drawn up in chancery were sealed with the great seal. By the end of the fourteenth century, this work demanded the presence of just under 100 clerks and menials. Chancellors, arguably the king's most powerful ministers, were traditionally prominent clerics, though on two occasions, 1340–5 and 1371–7, Edward appointed laymen to the post.

Since the chancery was one of the first offices to settle more or less permanently at Westminster, communicating the king's will to chancery became problematic. It routinely issued thousands of writs, chiefly judicial ones, without direct royal authorization. Others, however, were issued on his command to put his policies into effect. During the thirteenth century, the privy seal became an instrument for authenticating the king's personal commands. Lodged in the wardrobe, it developed into a household secretariat. Through privy seal warrants, the king instructed the chancery to draft formal documents which would be issued under the great seal. Early in Edward III's reign, the privy seal travelled with the king as it always had. Yet after the siege of Calais in 1347, it too remained at Westminster for prolonged periods, where it came to be associated with the council, authenticating its pronouncements. Nevertheless, the privy seal was still used to voice the king's personal wishes, above all in matters of patronage or expenditure, and sometimes travelled with the household for short periods. There is abundant evidence of close co-operation between Edward, the privy seal, chancery, and council, especially in the middle decades of Edward's reign, when there were two successive chancellors, John Offord and John Thoresby, who had been keepers of the privy seal.

Of course, the separation between the king and privy seal simply repeated the communication problem. Another seal, the secret or signet seal, had to be used to authenticate the king's personal will. Located at first in the chamber and drawing on the expertise of the chamber clerks, it gradually matured into a distinct office. By Richard II's reign, it was controlled by the king's secretary.

The chancery was also developing into a powerful court. The well-spring of its jurisdiction was the petition. Petitions seeking remedies for all sorts of problems poured into the government from every corner of the realm. The king and council handled some, but sent others to the chancellor. The judicial work of the chancery and council often overlapped and became indistinguishable. Many individuals, beset by administrative errors or incompetence, petitioned the chancellor directly, since he was in charge of the administration and issued judicial writs. The chancellor might conclude that the matter could be resolved through the ordinary machinery of the common law and issue an appropriate writ, or might himself hear the arguments in chancery. By the middle of Edward III's reign, the chancery was offering common law as well as administrative remedies. Edward strengthened this trend by appointing chancellors with legal expertise, such as Parving, Offord, Thoresby, Thorp, and Knyvet. They were judicially more active than their predecessors, intervening in court cases, bringing cases from the common law courts into chancery, and establishing debt litigation in chancery. These changes exemplify the nature of governmental development under Edward. Instead of creating new offices, existing ones were adapted to new purposes and officials applied their skills to new tasks. Medieval administration tended to be conservative, but not inflexible.

The field of law and justice displayed similar characteristics. Originally, there had been little distinction between the two great courts of the common law, common pleas and king's bench, in terms of their business. Both heard criminal and civil pleas, though the common bench was regarded as the proper place to initiate cases involving disputes between subjects over land or debts in which the king was not involved. In 1332, approximately 6,000 cases were recorded in the common bench in one term. Of these, 1,550 were actions of account, 1,500 debt or detinue, 500 trespass, and 820 involved land or lordship in some way. As has been seen, Edward III steered king's bench toward criminal jurisdiction, giving it a particular identity. Another ancient common law court was located in the exchequer, though by the fourteenth century its competence was limited in two respects: first, it was theoretically open only to royal officials and secondly it dealt only with financial disputes. There was also the court of the verge presided over by the steward of the household. It tried cases involving members of the household, trespasses or contempt against the purveyors of the household, and any violation of the king's peace within the verge, that is a radius of twelve miles around the king. Above these courts stood the council, parliament, and king, supervising the entire legal system.

Important judicial refinements occurred during the 1350s. One was the expansion of the chancery's judicial business. Another was the establishment of conciliar courts. The council had long been involved in judicial work, whether in parliament, in conjunction with the chancery, or on its own. Its legal specialization increased with the introduction of three new courts. The court of chivalry adjudicated military issues, admiralty handled mercantile law, and the exchequer chamber oversaw the court of the exchequer. Finally, steps were taken to speed up litigation. Getting a defedant into court was one of the most difficult and annoying aspects of medieval justice. The conciliar courts began to summon defendants directly, and after 1353, added a new clause, called *sub poena* (under pain), that threatened them with weighty fines if they failed to appear. This device proved so effective that it was applied to administrative as well as judicial writs.

The impetus for judicial improvement came from two sources. One was the crown. King and ministers alike had an obvious interest in strengthening the crown's judicial power. The steps taken from the 1330s onward to sharpen the jurisdiction of the chancery, conciliar courts, and king's bench appear to have been the result of executive policy. That impression is reinforced by parliamentary legislation in the 1350s, perhaps drawn up by chief justice William Shareshull, which refined judicial procedure. The king's subjects were likewise concerned about judicial procedure. Fear of crime, for example, was strong enough to prompt changes in law enforcement. But apprehension was only one dimension of popular interest. Courts were essential to resolving disputes and protecting property and family interests. It has been estimated that cases in the common pleas involved more than 15,000 people a year. Additional people were brought into the process as jurors. There was some social bias in participation. In Sussex, it has been found that the gentry were more often plaintiffs than defendants and that they pleaded more often against men of lower than equal or higher rank. Nevertheless, law and justice were inextricably woven into the fabric of daily life. Litigation, moreover, usually aimed at producing a compromise between disputants, so that it was purposefully slow, allowing tempers to cool and opening up opportunities for agreement. Though cases were not always settled peacefully, the fact that the rate of violence associated with litigation was fairly low indicates the population's respect for judicial remedies. Commitment to the judicial system deepened with the invention of devices for the settlement of property and with the assumption of judicial powers by the keepers of the peace. Edward was therefore not acting solely in his own interest when he introduced legal and judicial changes; he was acting within a social environment that highly valued litigation and judicial compromise.

Like justice, war concerned the entire nation. Because of Edward's ambitions, military organization obviously received considerable attention and affected a large portion of the population. Edward mustered impressive forces: 15,000 against Scotland in 1335, nearly 5,000 and 12,000 against France in 1338 and 1340, 13,500 for a proposed expedition in 1341, 32,000 for the siege of Calais in 1347, and almost 12,000 against France in 1359.

Aside from a small contingent of household knights, the king did not have a permanent fighting force. Armies had to be summoned and organized anew for each campaign. During the thirteenth century, it became virtually impossible to compel tenants-in-chief to perform their feudal service, landholders to become knights, or communities to provide infantry free of charge. Pay became the only sure way of raising troops. Edward I took the most important steps in this direction, and Edward III's measures largely built on those initiatives. During the Scottish wars in the 1330s, Edward introduced an important change in tactics by using mounted, lightly armoured foot soldiers (hobelars) and archers working together in disciplined formation, who were better armed and better paid than traditional infantry. Pay followed social rank. Earls received 8s. a day, bannerets 4s., knights 2s. or 3s., squires and men-at-arms 1s., mounted hobelars 6d., and infantry between 2d. and 4d. a day. Foot archers received 2d. a day while mounted archers were paid double that, and their respective wages rose to 3d. and 6d. a day during Edward's reign.

Edward employed three methods of raising troops. He obtained the chivalric core of his armies, the knights, by requesting their service. He issued the last feudal summons until the end of the century in 1327, a disappointing measure that prompted him to abandon feudal compulsion altogether. Thereafter he asked earls, bannerets, and knights to serve for pay along with their retinues of knights and squires. He used commissions of array to raise infantry and archers, the county levies. Finally, he contracted with noblemen to raise companies.

Until the 1360s, Edward largely relied on the voluntary leadership of chivalric forces in conjunction with paid levies. He contracted for some infantry and archers, but levied troops outnumbered contracted, sometimes by as much as eleven to one. For his first campaign in France in 1338, there is only meagre evidence of contracting. Thereafter, contracts were used more often than before, but levies still predominated, about five to two. Contracts were only widely used when the king and his household did not accompany the army. The wardrobe usually served as the army's war treasury and organizational hub. When it was not present to account for the army's pay, the government used contracts to simplify the problems of accounting and maintain control over employment.

From the 1360s onward, the character of the war and the nature of the armies changed. *Chevauchées* were small, aristocratically dominated forces and were entirely contractual in nature. Even in the last great force that Edward accompanied overseas in 1359–60, contracted forces outnumbered levies by about three to two. Captains, such as John of Gaunt or Robert Knolles, contracted with the crown to supply a force of specified size and composition. The contract spelled out the period of service, rates of pay, the regard or bonus for contracting, the compensation for the loss of horses, and the division of spoils. Captains then subcontracted with other lords to raise a portion of their force. The Black Prince, for instance, contracted with his retainer, Sir Ralph Mobberley, in 1355 to produce an esquire and thirty-two mounted archers for service overseas. The group Ralph gathered was composed of kinsmen, tenants, and neighbours from the immediate vicinity of his estate in Cheshire. They were of roughly equivalent status and well accustomed to working together on local commissions and as sureties and witnesses for one another. Social networking eased the task of contracting.

Later in the reign, as the pool of experienced soldiers seeking employment and adventure expanded, it became possible to rely less on affinities or neighbourhoods to recruit armies than it had been in the earlier stages of the war. In some cases subcontracting became highly professional and individuated. Contractors and subcontractors sought out former soldiers, younger sons, and lesser gentry who gravitated toward London where they could easily be enlisted into service. For them, war was almost purely an economic proposition, and the destructiveness of English raids in France in these years can be traced to the acquisitiveness of the English forces.

Contracting also affected the household contingent, an essential part of the king's military organization since the twelfth century. The number of household knights fluctuated according to the king's military activity. When Edward went on campaigns in 1340, 1347, and 1359, for example, they numbered 62, 80, and 47, dropping off to only 19 in the peaceful years of 1353–4. After 1360, however, they disappeared as Edward stopped campaigning in person and contract forces predominated. Their place was taken by chamber knights who first appeared in 1320 and were retained for domestic rather than military business.

The process of raising, equipping, and deploying armies was a monumental task to which the government had to devote its entire energy. Everyone in the country was swept up one way or another. And Edward did it over and over again, cogent testimony to the efficiency of his administration.

It demonstrates as well a remarkable ability to raise money. Through war and peace, finance was the most critical issue Edward faced. Historians usually divide royal finance into two convenient categories: ordinary and extraordinary. Ordinary expenses were those incurred in the day-to-day running of the government, and ordinary revenues were those that the crown collected as a matter of course through its authority as a feudal lord, landowner, and ruler. Extraordinary expenses arose through war and were met by exceptional revenues such as taxation. This categorization makes a messy situation deceptively neat. The English government did not compile a budget. Each office kept its own accounts which were never systematically summarized in a national balance-sheet. Summaries of income and expenditure were attempted at various times, but they contained a large element of uncertainty. Officials knew the government's financial health within crude limits, but they could not measure it accurately. Historians are likewise at the mercy of what often appear to be chaotic accounting procedures.

The exchequer was the single most important office of receipt, expenditure, and accounting, though other departments including the wardrobe, great wardrobe, privy wardrobe, and chamber played a significant role in finances. The lower exchequer received payments from all kinds of officials including sheriffs, customs officers, and tax collectors. The upper exchequer handled accounting and auditing. In a court-like setting, the barons of the exchequer compared the expected and actual receipts of each accountee and demanded explanations for all expenses. Edward III confirmed the exchequer's dominance. The same co-operation that was evident between the chancery and household under the leadership of the chancellor was visible in relations between the exchequer and household under the firm hand of the treasurer, the second most powerful minister. In the 1340s, particularly during William Edington's tenure as treasurer (1344–56), the exchequer implemented procedures that gave it a better sense of the flow of money into, out of, and within the government. The wardrobe's importance lay in its mobility and proximity to the king. Ordinarily, it handled daily household expenditures along with the great wardrobe and privy wardrobe. During military campaigns, it served as a war treasury and its income and expenditure swelled accordingly. Problems arose because it tended to spend money faster than it received it. The wardrobe was supposed to obtain the bulk of its funds from the exchequer, but it often increased its revenues by borrowing. It issued tallies or debentures to creditors who took them to the exchequer for redemption. This system created havoc for exchequer officials and took fiscal control out of their hands. Furthermore, when the government was insolvent, redemption could be difficult. The wardrobe played fast and loose with its finances from the 1290s through the 1340s, igniting protests and attempts to bring it under stricter exchequer supervision. Reformers wanted to lessen governmental demands and assure accountability while the king wanted greater financial stability and a rational approach to household finance. The effort bore fruit; between 1347 and 1359, 94 per cent of the wardrobe's funds flowed from the exchequer, though it fell to 75 per cent between 1360 and 1377. Even though some exchequer receipts were merely accounting devices and the wardrobe still borrowed when it needed to, the exchequer kept better track of wardrobe expenditure than it had in the earlier period.

The chamber was the king's personal finance office. It received some funds from the exchequer but obtained others from miscellaneous sources. For a short time after the Contrariants' rebellion in 1321–2, it managed some of the forfeited lands, and between 1333 and 1356, it handled various crown lands. The chamber's wealth shot up in the 1360s when it received huge sums from the ransom of French prisoners such as king John. This money was entirely at Edward's disposal. He used the chamber revenues for personal expenses but could also deploy them for national purposes, as in the late 1360s when he used his fortune to help finance the renewed military effort in France.

Thus, each household office was responsible for a particular area of spending under the overall coordination of the exchequer. Yet those areas were not constitutionally defined. The flexibility apparent in administration and justice was an equally important feature of royal finance. The king valued the wardrobe and chamber because he could conveniently use them for whatever project lay at hand. There was nothing underhand about this reliance on household offices. He was not trying to avoid constitutional propriety; he was trying to get things done as he saw fit.

The outstanding feature of royal finances throughout these years was that the ordinary revenues were just barely sufficient to meet the ordinary expenses. War, therefore, created financial tension because of its crushing costs. Edward's financial position is illustrated in an estimate of expenditures drawn up in 1363–4. The figures can be categorized as shown in Table 3 (all figures are rounded from the original).

Household and military expenditure were the most important items. In 1363–4, a modest campaign in Ireland, garrisoning castles, paying back wages, and keeping up forces in Gascony, came to about 27 per cent of the budget. The royal household and family accounted for 34 per cent. Household personnel fluctuated between 350 and 700, achieving their highest numbers in wartime, e.g. 701 in 1338–9, 579 in 1359–60, but only 338 in 1376–7. Expenditure on the household rose and fell accordingly. Between 1328 and 1332 it averaged around £17,700 a year, rising to £30,000 during the next six years, when war in Scotland became a major preoccupation. Similarly, for six years after 1347 wardrobe receipts, a good indication of its spending, averaged £18,390 a year, though over the next five years it leapt to £48,892, largely because of the 1356 campaign. Between 1360 and 1376, expenditure averaged about £21,000 a year. Edward's personal extravagance in the early 1360s caused the expenses of the great wardrobe, not included in the wardrobe average, to shoot up from around £5,000 a year in 1360 to nearly £12,000 in 1365–6. It is also reflected in the 15 per cent of the 1363–4 budget that went to pay the costs of his building programme. He cut back sharply, however, when war threatened once again at the end of the decade. Outside the household, the most important expenses were simply the day-to-day costs of government, including payments to officials, allies, and favourites.

War added a huge burden. In the fruitless campaign in Flanders between 1338 and 1340, for example, the wardrobe paid out £337,104 altogether, of which £134,275 went to wages, shipping, household fees and robes, and the restoration of lost horses. Even these sums grossly underestimate total expenditure. Between 1369 and 1375, war cost an average of £96,000 a year for a total of £671,900.

How could the government meet these expenses? Its ordinary income was frail. It has been calculated that in 1342–3, the exchequer received £19,326 from sheriffs, escheators, the operation of the chancery (the hanaper), the mints, rents, fines, and vacancies of one kind or another.

Table 3. *Estimate of royal expenditure, 1363–4*

Royal household and family	£34,305
Building	£15,380
Fees and annuities	£9,895
Jewels and lands purchased	£5,623
Messengers and other expenses	£3,530
Alms	£573
Miscellaneous	£3,605
Sub-total	£72,911
Garrisons	£3,890
Gascony	£2,452
Ireland	£14,734
War wages, victuals, etc.	£6,310
Sub-total	£27,386
TOTAL	£100,297

(*Source:* Tout and Broome, 'A national balance sheet'. The actual total given was £100,298 3s. 9d.)

Twenty years later, receipts from the same sources slumped to £14,014. The government could also count on customs revenue. In Edward's first decade, it averaged about £13,000 a year. For 1363–4, the exchequer estimated that it came to £38,206, of which £6,933 (18 per cent) was assigned in advance to various recipients, giving a cash receipt of £31,273.

The exchequer, in fact, projected a staggering deficit of £64,768 for that year. The situation was not that calamitous, partly because Edward used the income from ransoms to pay some of his expenses and partly because the estimate for customs was too low. It actually averaged £48,250 in these years. The government may have exaggerated the deficit as a political ploy to convince the commons to consent to taxation even though there was no major military campaign under way. Yet the fear of shortfall was probably real. Exchequer officials had struggled valiantly to bring the wardrobe accounts up to date, pay off debts, and tidy up after the financial mess of Edward's early campaigns. Furthermore, faulty estimates probably reflect genuine uncertainty about the reality of royal finances. As long as the pattern of fragmented accounting persisted, and individual officers wielded control over some income and spending, the government would have only a hazy notion of its total income and expenditure. These estimates demonstrate a worthy attempt to grasp the whole, even if they fell short.

The deficits raise an intriguing puzzle. Why had revenues failed to keep pace with peacetime expenditures? Since the mid-thirteenth century, finance had become a contentious political issue largely because kings continually fell into debt, whether because of excessive spending or war. Their requests for taxation were met by demands that the king live less extravagantly – the beginning of the idea that he should 'live on his own', pay his own way. Indeed, why could he not? Over that period, lay and ecclesiastic landholders had undertaken high farming and steadily increased their income. It was not a smooth process, entirely free of indebtedness and failure, but it contrasts starkly with the management of the king's estate.

The crown treated its resources differently from other lords. Like any great landlord, the king derived income from land, tenants, and seigneurial rights, to which he added profits from the operations of government such as fees and fines. The crown saw these resources primarily as opportunities for patronage and family support, to be managed with the least trouble and expense. Thus, after the lands of the Contrariants were forfeited in 1322, bringing a huge windfall, Edward II gave most of them away rather than keep them and enlarge his estate. Experiments with stricter management of wardships, undertaken by Edward I and Edward III, ended after a short time. And the chamber lands were broken up in 1356. The government undertook periodic measures to extract greater returns from its demesnes and tenants, but it never persisted in the effort. Entrenched interests, whether among officials, tenants, or favourites, worked against reform and a more profitable management of the king's estate.

Barring such reforms, the government consistently tried to extract greater revenues from its operations. During the 1340s and 1350s, for example, it aggressively pursued every financial advantage. Chief Justices Thorp and Shareshull increased dramatically the number of fines in king's bench. The chancery increased the fees for writs, raising the proceeds of the hanaper. The coinage reforms in the decade after 1343 not only improved England's currency but reaped profits from minting. The exchequer put additional pressure on debtors and officials, demanding timely payments. Yet, compared to the effort involved, the gains were temporary, inconsistent, and meagre. They are a measure of the government's desperation.

The insufficiency of ordinary revenues forced kings to raise money through direct and indirect taxation and loans, though each presented political difficulties. Two direct forms of taxation, parliamentary and clerical subsidies, required the consent of those taxed. Tradition had created a political logic which distinguished the king's property from that of his subjects. The king could do as he liked with the income that belonged to him and should live, as much as possible, on that income alone. He could ask his subjects for assistance, but he could not appropriate their lands or income without their consent or due process. Traditionally, the king requested a tax only for the good of the entire community, when it was threatened with an emergency that he could not repel by himself. Subjects were expected to contribute to the defence of their community. Because taxes had thus to be negotiated, they offered subjects an opportunity to air grievances. The primary form of indirect taxation, customs, was initially free of these pitfalls, though as rates increased, parliament insisted that its consent be obtained for them as well. The crown could negotiate loans at will, if it could find lenders, but indebtedness and repayment could get tangled up in politics. Purveyance and wardrobe indebtedness thus became public issues because when the government failed to repay loans it was essentially appropriating the creditors' money or goods without their consent or due process. Furthermore, the crown often repaid loans out of customs or subsidies, raising the question of who was actually benefiting from the tax granted by subjects. Taxation was tempting but potentially contentious.

The format and procedures of lay subsidies were well established by 1300. They were levied on *goods*, not land, and were calculated as a fraction of assessed wealth, such as a tenth, fifteenth, or twentieth, with a separate rate, usually a tenth, for towns. Only goods over and above subsistence needs were taken into account, and the poor, those assessed below a certain amount (10s. rural and 6s. urban), were exempt. It was thus a tax on surplus wealth. Once consent was given, the king commissioned teams to assess and collect the tax.

After years of disappointing results, the system was abruptly changed in 1334. Tax officers had been prone to corruption and produced unrealistically low assessments and receipts. When a fifteenth and tenth was granted in 1334, assessment was dropped in favour of a quota system. The total receipt was set at that of the fifteenth and tenth of 1332: £37,429 18s. ½d. This sum was then apportioned between the counties and each community's share was set in negotiations between the chief taxers and the community. From then on, down to the sixteenth century, whenever parliament granted a tax, it was collected in this manner and supposed to return the same amount. It was not free of problems. The quota system eliminated the poverty exemption so that an effort was made to shift part of the burden to lesser taxpayers. Since the yield was fixed, when the population dropped after the Black Death, the per capita rate rose, prompting some communities to petition for relief. The crown, for instance, remitted 10 per cent of Worcestershire's tax in 1349. Finally, the system increased the burden on the countryside, for towns were now taxed at a lower rate than formerly.

The crown continued to experiment after 1334. Between 1337 and 1344 it placed the tax proceeds from northern counties under the authority of a commission with responsibility for defending the border against the Scots. In 1340, deflation forced a tax in goods, the ninth, though it failed miserably.

Then there were Edward's futile experiments with wool, described in Chapter 5. Edward also tried on several occasions to raise money from the counties. His request in 1337 met with mixed results. He used the threat of a French invasion to pry a tenth and fifteenth out of the counties in 1360. Since it was not a proper parliamentary tax, it was of only limited value. Local representatives insisted that it be stored locally, that only half be collected until the French made their intentions clear, and that the receipts be used exclusively for local defence. With so many conditions, the measure could never replace parliamentary consent, as Edward realized. In 1371, he tried a different approach. He asked parliament for £100,000, half from the laity and half from the clergy. Parliament suggested that the lay tax be collected at a fixed, and fairly light, rate of 22s. 3d. per parish, assuming that there were 45,000 parishes. When the government recalculated the figure at 8,600, the rate per parish jumped to 116s., so that it tried to shift some of the weight from poorer to richer parishes. Since the lay quota was more than £12,000 above the rate for a tenth and fifteenth, most taxpayers paid more than in the past. Nevertheless, the tax was a success. £91,703 was eventually paid, 92 per cent of what was asked. In 1377, parliament tried a poll-tax, levied at the rate of 4d. per person.

The crown also collected taxes from the clergy. After 1297, when the issue had been hotly contested, the clergy reluctantly assented to taxes through convocation. The tax was always a tenth, based on the assessments of each church made in 1291. By Edward's reign, the yield was about £18,300. As Table 4 indicates, Edward did not hesitate to ask the clergy to support his war effort.

Table 4 also shows the vital importance of the subsidy on wool. Edward I raised howls of protest when he levied the 'maltot', a subsidy over and above the 'great and ancient custom' of 6s. 8d. per sack. Edward III tried again, with more success than his grandfather. Initially he bargained with assemblies of merchants over the rate of the subsidy, but parliament demanded a voice as the effects of the subsidy on producers became apparent. Edward sought parliamentary agreement in 1340, 1343, and 1348. When parliament renewed the 1348 grant in 1351, he promised that in the future only parliament would have the power of consent, though he went back on his word in 1353. After 1356, consent was consistently in parliament's hands, though the victory did not hamper the levying of wool subsidies through the 1360s.

The government vacillated over the method of collection. Until the Ordainers expelled the Frescobaldi in 1311, Italian merchants had farmed royal customs in return for a fixed annual sum. After that, customs were in English hands, but, like taxes, were plagued by corruption. In 1331, the government reformed the customs service and increased its supervision by officials. Yet Edward abandoned the reforms when he began manipulating the wool trade in 1336. A new system of farming, by companies of English merchants, was introduced in 1343. The government tried reform once again in 1353 with much greater success than it had had in the past. Direct collection of customs, a new staple policy, and improved weighing, policing, and accounting boosted receipts. The crown had learned a valuable lesson: to be profitable for king, merchants, and producers alike, the wool trade needed a stable environment with a moderate and predictable level of taxation and without unnecessary government interference. Annual revenues from customs averaged £87,500 in the decade after 1353. Though yields declined somewhat, the government reaped an average of £48,250 a year between 1362 and 1368 and £53,200 a year down to 1381. In the latter period, wool subsidies accounted for 54 per cent of the total tax revenues of £689,000. Because of customs and the income from the ransoms of the kings of France and Scotland, Edward did not have to ask parliament for a tax between 1357 and 1371.

England achieved financial equilibrium only after years of insolvency and crisis brought on by heavy expenditure and borrowing. Loans were a necessary way of raising money, but they clearly introduced problems. The low yield and inefficient collection of taxes forced kings to borrow to meet the pressing demands of war. Loans were the only way of raising money quickly, a crucial consideration in the 1330s and 1340s when royal finances were heavily strained. Edward thus greatly expanded the credit system, which had developed from Edward I's reign onward, to undertake war with France. What he did not see, or chose to ignore, was that periods of heavy loans are inevitably followed by periods of financial stringency caused by demands for repayment.

From 1290 to the 1340s, the crown relied primarily on Italian merchants and bankers for funds. In the long run, the Italians suffered from this cosy relationship. Of the £400,000 or more that Edward III raised before 1340, half came from Englishmen, the rest from Italians. Yet these sources of credit dried up as Edward drained the financial markets. Shortly thereafter, in fact, the Peruzzi (1343) and Bardi (1346) went bankrupt because of their English loans, and they brought down yet another Florentine banking house, the Acciaiuoli. Edward looked for other creditors. Hanseatic merchants offered some help, but after receiving the customs revenues between 1340 and 1343, they were still owed £11,000. The repercussions of Edward's enterprise rippled throughout Europe.

In the 1340s, therefore, Edward turned to English lenders on a large scale. He had tapped English sources before. For the Stanhope Park campaign in 1327, for example, Archbishop Melton of York advanced Edward 800 marks, which were not repaid until 1333. Altogether, Edward obtained

Table 4. *Taxes levied under Edward III*

Year	Lay taxes	Term	Clerical	Term	Wool	Notes
1327	1/20	1 yr	1/10	1 yr	—	
1328	—				—	
1329	—		—		—	
1330	—		—		—	
1331	—		—		—	
1332	1/10 & 1/15	1 yr	—		6s. 8d.	
1333	—		—		—	
1334	1/10 & 1/15	1 yr	1/10	1 yr	—	
1335	—		1/10		—	
1336	1/10 & 1/15	1 yr	1/10	1 yr	20s.	
1337	1/10 & 1/15	3 yrs	1/10	3 yrs		30,000 sacks
1338	"		"		40s.	
1339	"		"		"	
1340	1/9	2 yrs	1/10	2 yrs	"	
1341	"		"		"	Tax paid in wool
1342	—		—		"	
1343	—		—		"	
1344	1/10 & 1/15	2 yrs	1/10	3 yrs	"	
1345	"		"		"	
1346	1/10 & 1/15	2 yrs	"		"	aid – knighting Edw's eldest son
1347	"		1/10	2 yrs	"	20,000 sacks
1348	1/10 & 1/15	3 yrs	"		"	
1349	"		—		"	
1350	"		—		"	
1351	1/10 & 1/15	3 yrs	1/10	2 yrs	"	
1352	"		"		"	
1353	"		—		50s.	
1354	—		—		"	
1355	—		—		"	
1356	—		1/10	1 yr	"	
1357	1/10 & 1/15	1 yr	—		"	
1358	—		—		"	
1359	—		—		"	
1360	1/10 & 1/15	1 yr*	1/10	1 yr	52s.	*levied by co.
1361	—		—		50s.	
1362	—		—		20s.	
1363	—		—		"	
1364	—		—		"	
1365	—		—		40s.	
1366	—		—		"	

Table 4. (*cont.*)

Year	Lay taxes	Term	Clerical	Term	Wool	Notes
1367	—		—		"	
1368	—		—		30s.	
1369	—		—		53s. 4d.	
1370	—		⅒	3 yrs	"	
1371	£50,000		(£50,000)		"	by parish
1372	—		"		"	
1373	⅒ & 1/15	1 yr	⅒	1 yr	"	
1374	⅒ & 1/15	2 yrs	—		"	
1375	"		—		"	
1376	—		—		"	
1377	4d. per person	1 yr	—		"	poll-tax

(Sources: Stubbs, *Constitutional history*, 2: 395 nn.–400 nn., 411 nn.–425 nn., 433 nn., 445 nn.; *Second report of the deputy keeper*, Appendix 2, pp. 143–71; Weske, *Convocation*, Appendix A, pp. 245–59; Harriss, *King, parliament and public finance*, passim; Lloyd, *English wool trade*, passim; Ormrod, 'Edward III's government', pp. 151, 152, 156.)

more than £3,000 from Melton in the 1330s, representing about 14 per cent of Melton's loans. But Edward repaid only about a third of his debt. Heavy English involvement really began in 1338–9 when William de la Pole raised at least £111,000 for the crown, which he made up by borrowing from other merchants. This sum can be compared with the nearly £126,000 that the Bardi and Peruzzi obtained for Edward in roughly two years beginning in 1338. English credit was similarly conspicuous during the Calais campaign. Chiriton and company, farmers of the customs, raised about £126,000 for the crown between 1346 and 1349. During the 1350s, Edward had to devote a portion of his tax proceeds to pay off his debts from the 1340s. The bulk of the triennial tax levied in 1348, some £150,000, went toward repaying old loans. There is nothing surprising about this. Peace always ushers in a period when governments have to account for the costs of war. Edward still borrowed, though on a vastly reduced scale and largely from lesser merchants.

Edward's various financial schemes in these years brought the English merchant community into the limelight. None did so well or suffered so much as William de la Pole. A wool merchant from Hull, he entered the arena of high finance in the 1320s in company with his brother Richard. William lent Edward increasingly larger sums through the 1330s and was responsible for organizing the 'Wool Company' in 1337 which carried out the doomed programme to monopolize the wool trade for the crown. Edward in turn showered rewards on Pole and in 1338 made him a banneret. Meanwhile, Pole had built up his power and wealth within Hull and became influential within the royal administration as well, becoming second baron of the exchequer in 1339. His career trajectory was similar to that of one of his merchant colleagues, John de Pulteney. A Londoner, Pulteney served on various royal commissions and as mayor of London in the 1330s. In 1337, he was one of those knighted in the general dispensation of honours that marked Edward's preparations to embark on war. He received a grant to help bear the costs of knighthood though he was a wealthy landowner in his own right outside London. He also became one of Pole's financial backers. Both, however, suffered Edward's wrath in 1341 when he vented his frustrations on those who had managed his affairs at home. Pole and Pulteney were imprisoned at Devizes and Somerton respectively and stripped of their gifts. A parliamentary petition demanded an audit of the accounts of all of those responsible for receiving wool and monies. Edward heartily concurred. In a lengthy trial in the exchequer, Pole was accused of fraud and smuggling in carrying out Edward's 1337 wool monopoly scheme. Though Pole recovered and continued to serve the crown in the 1340s he never again reached the same heights. He was instrumental in setting up the system of customs farming by English merchants after 1343, but in 1353, when the government turned against the privileged merchants and financiers, he was once again brought to trial. The action aimed at forcing Pole to give up the last claims to lands given him by Edward, and when he did so in 1354, he was pardoned. All of those financiers, whether English or Italian, who had stepped forward to implement Edward's policies in the 1330s ended up bankrupt. It had been a unique period of opportunity and danger.

When war resumed in 1369, the government was in a better financial position than it had been in the 1330s because of the income from ransoms and customs. Nevertheless, the collection of revenues was still slow, so that Edward once again searched for creditors. Between 1369 and 1375, he borrowed about £150,000, a trifle compared to the 1340s. The source of loans, moreover, changed significantly. Most came from landowners, such as Richard fitz Alan, the earl of Arundel, a trend that began with Edward's campaign of 1359–60. English merchants shied away from lending to the crown after observing the fate of Pole and others who had suffered financially and legally at the hands of the government.

The financial history of Edward's reign can thus be summarized in crude terms. The late 1330s and early 1340s saw financial chaos as Edward spent lavishly and borrowed profligately for war in Scotland and France. The insufficiency of the king's ordinary revenues became all too apparent.

Beginning in 1336 taxes of one kind or another were levied every year except one for the next eighteen years (see Table 4). A period of retrenchment followed in the 1350s and 1360s when peace allowed taxation to abate. The government snatched at every penny and put its finances on a firmer footing. Financial problems only began to loom once again in the final years of the reign.

Figures tell one story, personalities another. Edward was extremely fortunate in being served by a succession of capable ministers throughout his government. Clerks such as Burghersh, Bury, Cusance, Edington, Kilsby, Offord, Stratford, Thoresby, and Wykeham, and laymen such as Parving, Saddington, Shareshull, and Thorp occupied a succession of important posts and forged a tradition of competent service. They provided continuity of leadership between state and household offices, helping to reduce inter-office rivalries. Of course, administrative harmony broke down at times, most notably in 1340–1 when Stratford and Kilsby were at one another's throats. Furthermore, tension between lay and clerical ministers emerged in the crises of 1341 and 1371. Laymen played a more conspicuous part in the higher administration than ever before, even occupying the chancellorship for a time after each crisis. For the most part, however, Edward's ministers got along well with one another and created a unified government.

They shared two important characteristics. One was inventiveness, a necessary quality given Edward's financial problems. Offord and Thoresby in the chancery, Edington in the exchequer, and Thorp and Shareshull in the courts promoted reform in their spheres of government. A second quality was loyalty to Edward. The quarrel between Edward and Stratford was the only violent rift. That was quickly patched up, though Stratford never again occupied a high position. Others, such as Thorp or Wykeham, fell because of corruption or politics. They did not, however, fall from Edward's grace.

Corruption raises the issue of how contemporaries evaluated the conduct of high officials. John of Reading's *Chronicle* praised William of Edington calling him a 'friend of the community' who throughout his tenure performed his duties such that royal power did not oppress the populace with extortions and payments. Through his diligence and prudence, he was useful to king and kingdom alike. Reading thus used the common good to measure Edington's performance, though others were not so laudatory. Edington may have been among that cadre of schoolmen who were so busy in administration in the fourteenth century. There is evidence that he was at Oxford, but if so, his life was soon swallowed up in government. Like Adam de Harvington, he was an associate of Orleton and received his first preferment at the bishop's hands. Once introduced into the court, he served as a tax collector and quickly moved on to become treasurer (1346–56) and chancellor (1356–63). He held a number of prebends before he was elevated to the bishopric of Winchester by papal provision at Edward's request in 1346. He thus exemplified not only the conscientiousness that Edward deeply valued but the kind of clerical administrator who kept government running smoothly.

Yet Thomas Brinton set a much higher standard of conduct. He said counsellors should be flowing with truth and wisdom, free of vices, endowed with virtues, blessed with morals, matured by age, boiling for the common good, and so firm in their deeds that they do not forgo counselling truth for hate, fear, love, or desire for their own gain. Those things destroy the king and kingdom. Accordingly, he condemned ministers who followed the bad example of their lords and worked not for the common good but for their own or their lords', whose only interest was profit and oppression. It would have been hard for even the best of officials to live up to such ideals.

To some extent, they conflicted with the values of Edward's 'court'. The fourteenth-century court had not attained the formality that it would all over Europe in the next century. In peacetime, Edward's life was divided between the private world of his chamber, the public arena of the great hall, and the administrative centre of the council. Public ceremony was also crucial in shaping a political culture around the king. Edward took every opportunity to display the sumptuousness and power of his court. Christenings, marriages, and even churchings were turned into celebrations as festive as those accompanying parliaments, tournaments, hunts, and pilgrimages. Edward and his followers were highly visible. He took a small part of his household to tour holy places in England after the campaign in 1333, after a stormy channel crossing ten years later, and before departing on campaign in 1355 and 1359. Elaborate games were sometimes held at Christmas, replete with costumes and head-dresses for everyone. Chivalric display reached its apogee with the creation of the Order of the Garter after 1347.

This public display was not theatre because no sharp distinction was drawn between participants and spectators. The entire court took part in tournaments, worship, and feasting. These public ceremonies disseminated and solidified Edward's values and ideals. They reinforced ties between himself, the nobility, and officialdom. The court thus forged a solidarity at the national level not unlike that created in the county communities. Court and government, ceremony and administration were equally geared to the same ends – the pursuit of war.

These aims likewise coloured the cultural achievements of the court. Edward had a large library of devotional works and romances which resonated with the chivalric tones of the court. Though Edward did not consciously create a 'court style' of architecture, the buildings that unequivocally bore his stamp reflected his personal tastes: Windsor, private residences surrounding London (Eltham, Sheen, King's Langley, Hadleigh, Moor End, and Westminster), and, above all, St George's Chapel at Windsor to honour the Order of the Garter.

Edward's courtiers energetically patronized scholarship and learning. We have already seen how Lancaster wrote a devotional tract and Bury encouraged scholarship. Similarly, Wykeham, who was in charge of the remodelling at Windsor, established a college at Winchester and New College at Oxford and saw that they were constructed in the same style as Windsor. An earlier treasurer, Walter de Stapledon, founded Exeter College, Oxford, while a chancery clerk, Adam de Brome, founded Oriel College. John Winwick, a privy seal clerk, left money to found a college of civil law, and Robert de Stratford became chancellor of Oxford. Edington bestowed his wealth on the cathedral at Winchester and on rebuilding the parish church in his native village of Edington, Wiltshire. He also established a college at Edington which became a house of Austin friars. These civil servants may not have lived up to the standards of a Brinton, but they displayed impressive achievements inside and outside the government. The rise of men such as Bury, Edington, and Wykeham from humble beginnings through civil service to the heights of government and learning clearly indicates the maturity and professionalism of the royal administration. Despite their secular service, moreover, they did not altogether neglect their religious ideals.

Unity of personnel underscored a unity of purpose. This solidarity achieved at court was crucial because the scale of Edward's demands was novel and controversial. To carry them out required not only steadfastness and administrative efficiency, but political skill. That skill was tested in the realm of counsel, where Edward's policies had to be negotiated over and over again.

PART IV

POLITICS

·

While the king set policy, the prelates, peers, and gentry who executed it worried how his policies would affect their lordships, liberties, and wealth. The political problem facing any king was to get the elite to line up behind him. As G. L. Harriss has concluded, Edward III's great achievement was transforming his personal quarrel into a national enterprise.

What did a medieval king want to do? He had obligations to his people, as outlined in his coronation oath, but he also had his own interests. The line between personal and public, however, was indistinct, a matter for debate. Law enforcement is a straightforward example of public interest. Edward seems to have been genuinely concerned about curbing crime, but baffled about how to do it. The controversy which swirled around the justices of the peace shows another side of his domestic policy: his determination to keep his prerogative and instruments of rule intact. Whether it was a question of the power wielded by local officials, the appointment and dismissal of royal officers, or the control of ecclesiastical patronage, Edward would not tolerate any diminution of his authority. That determination offers a key to understanding Edward's 'foreign' policy as well. He would not suffer any loss of lordship over Scotland, Wales, or Ireland or any loss of territory in France. Reducing the threat from Scotland was certainly in the public interest, though it could have been achieved peacefully through diplomacy. His policy toward France was more debatable. Was protecting Gascony or claiming the French throne in the interests of his English subjects? Finally, Edward seemed to spoil for a fight. His glorification of chivalry in tournaments and the Order of the Garter mirrored his pursuit of war. In Scotland in 1332 he rejected peace in favour of supporting the disinherited and

191

asserting his lordship. In France, he went to war despite overwhelming odds against the project. He prepared for war despite a truce in 1341 and refused peaceful settlements during the 1350s. At the end of his reign he was still hankering after impossible glory. He was single-minded in his pursuit of policies that were not obviously a national necessity. He had to make them so.

The interests of the prelates, magnates, and gentry were grounded in property and lordship, liberties and office-holding, and law and order. They had an obvious stake in economic matters that affected their well-being such as the money supply, trade fluctuations, wages, unruly tenants, and, of course, taxation. They worried about crime and were eager to preserve their grip on law enforcement. Office-holding was of primary importance in maintaining control over their communities and keeping their economic leverage intact. Furthermore, they were ambivalent toward patronage and privileges; they wanted them but were fearful that they could lead to rivalry. Their expectations of government were conservative. They wanted it to protect their property and settle their disputes. They expected a role in it, whether at the level of policy making or enforcement. And they did not want it to be legally or economically intrusive. Finally, they too loved tournaments, hunts, and chivalry. Some ventured forth on crusades and most could be induced to fight the king's wars, if he convinced them that war was in their interest.

The ideal for reconciling these policies, interests, and expectations was counsel and consent. Archbishop Stratford expressed it forcefully in his protest letter to Edward III in 1341. He contrasted the effects of good and bad counsel, beginning with the biblical exemplars of Solomon and Rehoboam. He compared Rehoboam's unwillingness to be guided by wise and mature counsellors to Edward II's disastrous reign, when evil counsel led him to trample on his subjects' rights. It was a warning to Edward, who until then had been guided by the advice of the prelates, peers, the great and wise men of the land 'so that, by means of your good counsel, with the help of your people, and the grace which God has given you, you have had victory against your enemies of Scotland, France, and all parts'. Proper counsel produced the common good, bad led to oppression.

Edward was keenly sensitive to the need for consultation. He took every opportunity to meet with prelates, magnates, gentry, merchants, or communities to get their consent to his enterprises. He was an adroit negotiator and disagreements passed quickly. In contrast, therefore, to the previous century, political bargaining occurred in parliament and council rather than in stormy confrontations between the king and barons. As a result, they became much better defined during the fifty years of his rule, and the commons became an influential force in government and politics.

12

NEGOTIATING CONSENT: COUNCIL AND PARLIAMENT

———— • ————

In practice, counsel and consent took three forms. First, the king routinely sounded his officials in the council. Secondly, he assembled particular groups, such as the magnates, merchants, clergy, or local communities, to consult on specific issues. But, building on Edward I's precedents, it had come to be established under Edward II that parliament was the proper forum for discussing issues affecting the kingdom as a whole. A good example occurred in 1332 when Edward III was dithering over Scotland. He summoned a council to deliberate his options, but the council advised that 'the business was so weighty that it was necessary to summon parliament, so that our lord the king by common assent could ordain what would be for the honour of himself and the salvation of his people'. The maturation of parliament did not diminish royal authority; it buttressed it. Edward wove parliament into every aspect of administration, justice, and politics, but the council remained the centre of decision making and power. Edward's reign thus saw the mutual nourishment of kingship and counsel, enabling an unprecedented mobilization of support and resources.

The difficulty in studying the council and parliament is that procedures and functions grew slowly out of earlier precedents. No acts announced unequivocal changes. Neither kept a complete record of its business. Since there are no signposts clearly marking the stages of development, historians must generalize within broad limits.

We can begin with the council. Its work covered policy, war, justice, administration, and diplomacy. While most of its energy was absorbed in the ordinary business of advising the king and directing departments and officers, it occupied an increasingly larger place in royal justice. As the council's legal work and expertise increased, specialized conciliar courts sprouted up, and it began employing the highly effective procedure of writs *sub poena* after 1353. Under Edward III, meetings were held more regularly than in the past, the privy seal was used to authenticate its communications, and the star chamber became its permanent home after mid-century.

The pool of potential councillors was large, but only a few attended consistently. The trend, as in many other areas of government, was towards a smaller, professional body. Its basic elements were administrative and magnate. The chancellor and treasurer, heading the greatest departments of chancery and exchequer respectively, were the most important members and attended most often. They were joined by the chief justices of common pleas and the king's bench. The steward of the household attended on occasion. By 1376, the keeper of the privy seal was considered an ordinary member. Lesser clerks from household or chancery sometimes joined their superiors. A good example of a lower official wielding disproportionate influence in the council was William de Kilsby, who aroused Stratford's wrath in 1341. A chamber clerk, he acted as receiver of the chamber between 1335 and 1338 and gained even greater influence when Edward entrusted him with both the privy seal and great seal in 1338. Edward brought Kilsby with him when he stormed back to England in December 1340, but the magnates objected to his presence among the peers in 1341 and he was removed from parliament.

Magnates, knights, and foreigners sat alongside this administrative element. Archbishops, bishops, earls, and barons were frequently summoned to council meetings, though they attended irregularly. Many were associated with the government in some way. In keeping with his military aims, Edward III expanded the role of knights, while almost all of his councillors saw military action at one time or another. He named two knights, Robert Bouchier and Robert Parving, chancellor and treasurer in 1341, and appointed others, such as Guy Brian, Bartholomew Burghersh, and Walter de Manny, to the council. Council work could be onerous. According to Burghersh's accounts for his wages from 1351 to 1356, he spent an average of 177 days a year on council business, presumably staying in London most of the time. He served in various administrative positions as well. He was handsomely paid at 20s. a day, but it can be seen why many magnates were reluctant to attend the council. Edward also summoned foreigners, though parliament distrusted men such as Master Raymond Pelegrin who had been sworn to the council. Some councillors were specifically appointed or retained to serve. Robin Forest in 1338, William Bateman bishop of Norwich in 1352, and William de Burton in 1360, were among several to whom Edward granted annuities in return for their council service. For the most part, the king chose his own councillors, though parliament in 1331 appointed Stephen Gravesend, bishop of London, to stay close to Edward and counsel him with the aid of the chancellor, treasurer, and others. Special councils were occasionally appointed. Because Edward was a minor when he came to the throne, a regency council was named to direct policy and dispel fears that arose out of Edward II's reliance on 'evil' counsellors. Henry of Lancaster was the chief guardian, but the council included the archbishops of Canterbury and York, the bishops of Winchester and Hereford, the king's two uncles (the earls of Norfolk and Kent), the earl of Surrey, and four barons, Thomas Wake, Henry Percy, Oliver de Ingham, and John de Ross. It was essentially a baronial council, designed to strengthen the new government. Edward appointed regency councils of a similar kind when he campaigned abroad, while a smaller group of counsellors, predominantly household personnel, accompanied him. He placed his son Edward, only eight years old, at the head of the regency council in 1338 and again in 1341; his son Lionel, then seven, in 1345; and Prince Edward's son Richard, aged five, in 1372. The administrators and magnates appointed with them performed the real work. Stratford, for example, was the effective force on the council while Edward was in Flanders after 1338.

Another variation was the 'great', or enlarged, council. Until around mid-century, great councils and parliaments were not technically defined and so overlapped in composition and function. Summoned by special writs, both debated issues such as diplomacy, taxation, or law which could not be decided by the ordinary council. They could, however, be distinguished in certain ways. Great councils sometimes included representatives and their number and type varied. In contrast, parliament's composition had become fixed early in the century and always included representatives. Furthermore, though great councils heard petitions, they did not have the apparatus that parliament had for dealing with them. Parliament was also more suitable for petitions because it had greater judicial authority than great councils. This difference was made clear in the deliberations about the staple in 1353. The great council approved certain measures, but the representatives asked that they be recited in the next parliament and placed on the parliament's roll because ordinances made in council were not of record as they would be in parliament. In the next parliament, the commons accordingly put the matter before the king and lords who unanimously assented, stressing that it could only be changed in parliament. After that date, elected representatives were no longer summoned to great councils, though they continued to be held throughout the later middle ages.

In contrast to great councils, the work of the 'secret' or 'privy' council was kept secret. Secrecy was particularly important in diplomacy, and many of the councils that chroniclers called secret dealt with French, Scottish, or papal relations. When Edward asked parliament what to do about France in 1331, the lords concluded that 'it would not at all be good if the manner of this consultation were too public, rather it should be held secret' (*q'il ne serroit mie bien que la manere de cele Trete feust trop publie, einz tenu secre*). At times, Edward summoned particular groups for their advice or consent. One example, cited several times now, was his effort to elicit a tax from the counties in 1337 and again in 1361. Hoping similarly to garner support for his Scottish campaign of 1337, he assembled magnates and others to discuss raising troops. Beginning in 1336, moreover, Edward met regularly with merchants to discuss finances and get their consent to staples, wool subsidies, monopolies, and loans. The policy, however, faltered in 1343. The merchant community itself was divided while parliament began to take a keener interest in issues of trade and customs. Edward met separately with merchants in 1345 and 1347, but in 1348 they had been absorbed into commons. The policy revived briefly in 1352–3 when Edward wanted to formulate a new staple system, but it had no future.

Important issues between the king and his subjects were debated in parliament. Under Edward II, the magnates had used parliament to restrain the king, as can be seen in the Ordinances. They decreed that the king needed parliamentary consent to wage war, appoint royal ministers, or make royal grants. Parliament was to be used to settle legal disputes and entertain complaints against royal officials. Edward II, however, overturned the Ordinances after his victory over the Contrariants in 1322. The statute of York enunciated a different view of parliament in which 'things which are to be established for the estate of our lord the king and of his heirs and for the estate of the realm and of the people shall be treated, agreed and established in parliaments by our lord the king and by the assent of the prelates, earls and barons and the commonalty of the realm as has been accustomed formerly'.

The meaning of this last clause has been intensely debated, yet parliamentary relations under Edward III came closer to the statute's vision of parliament as the common ground between the king, lords, and commons, than they had under his father. Debate over crime, war, and, of course, taxes intensified, and parliament encapsulated the political culture of Edward's reign. Frequent meetings necessitated by soaring demands strengthened its self-confidence and identity. As can be seen in Table 5, parliament met often under Edward II, mostly because of political turmoil, while regular meetings of parliament and council helped Edward III gear up for war in the first two decades of his reign. In the last three, parliament met less than once a year, though sessions tended to last longer, especially at the very end of the reign. Altogether, parliament became a regular feature of government.

It was composed of three groups. The first comprised the king's coun-

Table 5. *Length of parliaments*

Decade	Parliaments	Councils	Average length of parliament
1307–1326	24	7	—
1327–1336	16	9	19 days[1]
1337–1346	11	12	22 days
1347–1356	6	3	18 days
1357–1366	8	3	24 days[2]
1366–1377	7	1	24 days[3]

[1] If the first parliament of the reign, lasting nearly 9 weeks, is excluded, meetings averaged only 16 days during the first decade.

[2] Includes only 7 parliaments for which the terminating date is known.

[3] Does not include the 'Good Parliament' which lasted 64 days.

The numbers are all taken from the *Handbook of British chronology*. For the purposes of averaging the length of parliaments, the opening and closing dates were counted as were any intervening Sundays and feast days.

cillors. The chancellor, treasurer, chief justices, serjeants-at-law, administrators, and household officers were summoned separately. A second group, the lay and ecclesiastic peers, likewise received individual summonses. The representatives, or the commons, included 74 knights of the shire elected in 37 English counties (Wales was excluded), citizens and burgesses chosen from various boroughs, and the lower clergy. The choice of towns to be represented was left up to the sheriff, so that the numbers fluctuated greatly, averaging about 75 in Edward's reign. They sent about 160 representatives to parliament altogether. Until 1340, the king made a special effort to get clerical representatives in parliament, placing responsibility for their attendance on the bishops' shoulders. The deans, archdeacons, a proctor from each chapter, and two proctors for the parish clergy were supposed to attend from each diocese. After 1340, the king did not enforce the provision, but the majority of dioceses sent representatives to most parliaments. Parliament, therefore, was broadly representative of every element in the kingdom, with the obvious exception of the peasantry. In 1332, the total number attending came to about 514.

The council formed the ancient core of parliament. In a sense, the lords and commons were summoned to advise the king and council. That relationship reversed during Edward's reign. Thirty-three councillors were summoned to parliament in 1305. By the 1330s, their numbers had shrunk to about ten, and by 1350 had declined to a few justices and lawyers. Thus, by the time Richard II was crowned, councillors came to parliament to offer advice to the lords and commons, who now formed the core elements of parliament. Parliament had acquired an institutional identity distinct from the council.

Relations between the lords and commons likewise changed. Their standing differed, as the *Modus tenendi parliamentum* (The manner of parliament) implied. Probably composed in the 1320s, the *Modus* was the only treatise on parliament written in the middle ages, but it was controversial. While it purported to be a factual description, it was in fact the author's vision of parliament. It argued that because lords were summoned individually, they spoke only for themselves and their unfree tenants, especially on taxation. The commons, however, spoke for their communities and, since Edward I's reign, had been summoned with *plena potestas*, the power of binding their communities to their decisions. The *Modus* thus asserts that 'it must be understood that two knights who come to parliament for the shire, have a greater voice in granting and denying [taxes] than the greatest earl'. Though somewhat inflammatory, the statement captures an essential difference between the lords and commons.

In the thirteenth century, the magnates had been the spokesmen for the 'community of the realm', counselling the king, legislating, and protesting at royal abuses. Michael Prestwich has argued, however, that as parliament took definite shape, the commons took over their role as spokesmen while the magnates occupied the privileged position of peers. By the 1320s, the *Modus* dared to assert that the commons was a crucial partner in the community, and the statute of York seemed to endorse that view. But the real turning-point came with the deposition of Edward II and Edward III's first parliament. To legitimize their actions, the rebels wanted the participation of as inclusive a group as possible so that the deposition was carried out by 'the common counsel and assent of prelates, earls, barons, and other nobles, and all the community of the realm'. That the latter clearly referred to the commons was made clear in the common petition put forth in parliament that year. After 1327, petitions and frequent elections solidified their position as representatives of the community of the realm.

The political transformation went hand in hand with social change. As has been seen, the peerage and county gentry became clearly identifiable as social groups. Just as the institutional development of the peerage exalted the status of the nobility, so the political identity of the commons added a new dimension to the gentry's prestige. They valued parliamentary service and re-election was common: in three-fifths of Edward III's parliaments, previously elected members outnumbered first-timers. A few were elected over and over again, such as Simon de Heselarton who represented Yorkshire in six parliaments between 1362 and 1372. In contrast, lords attended sporadically and many parliaments had to be delayed until enough peers showed up. High wages were one attraction – knights officially received 4s.

a day – but parliamentary service also buttressed the gentry's authority in the county. County communities, moreover, valued the direct voice in national affairs that parliament gave them and complained vociferously whenever elections were disrupted.

The majority of the knights of the shire came from the landholding stratum just beneath the nobility. They were not always knights; only twenty-four of thirty-seven new members from Bedfordshire under Edward III had been knighted, for example, and some came from humble backgrounds. But most represented the county elite. John Chaumont was such a man. Knighted around 1346, he represented Yorkshire in three parliaments between 1360 and 1363. He held a manor and lands in five Yorkshire vills as well as a manor in Lincolnshire. Besides serving in parliament, he was active in the county in the 1350s and 1360s collecting taxes and sitting as a justice of labourers, peace, and oyer and terminer. In 1367–8 he was sheriff of Yorkshire. Knights of the shire were typically experienced county officers, though a few outsiders were elected. John Curtis, for example, represented Bedfordshire in 1368, but was a prominent wool merchant who had only moved into the county in 1352 on purchasing a local manor. He was summoned to a council of merchants in 1356, served in the staples at Westminster and Calais, and other than his stint as knight of the shire did not partake in county office-holding. Thomas de Ingelby, who represented Yorkshire in 1348, likewise came out of a different background. A lawyer who rose to prominence in the judiciary, he combined careers in the county and Westminster, serving as justice and commissioner locally while rising to become justice of the king's bench in 1361. Along the way, he amassed a large Yorkshire estate.

Borough representatives were from the equivalent stratum of urban society, what might be termed the merchant peerage. They were the aldermen or mayors who governed the towns as much as the knights led the county communities. William de la Pole, for example, represented Hull in 1332, 1334, 1336, and 1338 as he rose to prominence in the town and nation. The system of election varied, but most burgesses were selected by their peers. In King's Lynn, a jury of twelve named the representatives. To compile the jury, the mayor chose four men, those four chose four, and those eight chose another four. Half of the twelve had to be from the governing board of twenty-four and the other half from the common council of twenty-seven. The complicated procedure was no doubt intended to achieve a degree of consensus within the narrow elite that ran the town. Those selected were charged with representing the town in parliament and putting forth petitions on behalf of the community and individuals. The town sent letters on important issues to its representatives during parliament and expected them to report orally to the community in the guildhall on their return. Interest in parliament was thus strong and towns valued the right of representation. Lynn paid its members 3s. 4d. for their work, well above the standard rate of 2s. a day.

Most of the commons were thus closely attracted to the communities from which they were drawn and to which they were answerable. In 1339 they refused to grant a tax until they had consulted with their communities. In 1344, 1348, 1352, and 1373, they pressured Edward to publish tax grants as statutes and to stress the necessity for the grants, hoping thereby to justify their consent to their constituents and let the king take the heat for raising taxes. Political scruples, however, did not prevent them from indulging in the lawlessness that plagued gentry society. James de Stafford of Sandon, who represented Staffordshire in 1328, and his younger brother John, who was elected in 1339 and 1340, can serve as examples. Both were embroiled with the Ipstone and Swynnerton families between 1318 and 1328 and were implicated in the murders of Alexander de Swynnerton and John de Pichford. Despite being imprisoned for the latter murder and forfeiting lands for supporting the Contrariants in 1322, they were prominent in county affairs as tax collectors, justices, and commissioners. They also fought in Scotland and France. They may have been in the retinues of Roger de Mortimer of Wigmore and Ralph Basset of Drayton and were closely tied to Ralph, earl of Stafford, whose sister Mary James married and whose daughter Margaret John married, making them in-laws as well as brothers. They quarrelled, however, because their grandfather preferred John to James and so gave John the bulk of the patrimony. John was commissioned to arrest his elder brother in 1334 but was himself committed to prison in 1336 for his feuding. John also helped his father-in-law abduct Margaret, daughter and heir of Hugh d'Audeley. Such activities, unfortunately, were not uncommon in the parliamentary ranks. Political refinement, as yet, was rudimentary and did not always inhibit gentry from taking direct action when they feared their interests were jeopardized.

Parliaments followed a standard routine. In the initial meeting, held in the 'painted chamber' of Westminster palace, all of the members heard the government's 'charge' or announcement of the reason for summoning parliament, delivered by the chancellor or a chief justice. Lords and commons then met apart to discuss the issues; the lords sat in the 'white chamber' in the palace, while the commons occupied the painted chamber, though later they met nearby in the chapter house of Westminster abbey. The two groups often had to confer on difficult points and selected committees for conferences or 'intercommunings'. By the 1370s, it was customary for the commons to call for intercommuning and to nominate the lords with whom they would meet. They also consulted experts. The king charged the prelates, lords, and commons in 1343 with advising him about reforming the currency. They were to meet jointly and separately with merchants, moneyers, and goldsmiths to come up with a reply. Committees of the commons similarly came before the king and lords to answer various points. Sometime during Edward's reign, the commons developed the practice of selecting one man to speak on their behalf in these meetings. The first speaker of the commons known by name is Peter de la Mare, chosen in the Good Parliament.

Parliamentary infrastructure was simple, but it had to be erected with each new parliament. Receivers and triers of petitions and a clerk of the parliament were appointed. Down to 1339, records were compiled haphazardly, consisting largely of petitions. After 1339, the clerk compiled a roll for each parliament, recording the charge, the answers of the lords and commons, and the common petition with the king's replies. Unfortunately, there are no records of discussions among the council, lords, or commons, except for detailed chronicle accounts of the Good Parliament.

Fixed records, officers, and procedures strengthened parliament's institutional identity. It was further reinforced by a sense of precedent, which parliament used to put forward its claims or challenge the king's demands. In 1341, for instance, the commons claimed that before then, inquests into official misconduct as well as into the articles of the general eyre had not been issued without parliament's assent. The lords made a similar plea on behalf of trial by peers. Though their historical vision was somewhat clouded, they clearly believed in parliament as a part of government with distinct powers. The tradition became so firmly embedded that seven times between 1258 and 1377, the magnates or commons asked that parliament be held at least annually, as in 1330 when a statute was enacted to the effect that 'parliament shall be held once every year, or more often if needed'. In 1258 and 1376, the demand was politically motivated, to put pressure on the king, while in 1327 and 1362 it aimed at redressing grievances against royal ministers. The most important reason for annual parliaments, however, was to ensure that individuals would receive timely justice. Because parliament handled so much judicial business, if it did not meet regularly, cases jammed up causing hardship to litigants. The problem eased later in the century as the council took on an increasing share of the judicial burden. In practice, during the seventy years between 1307 and 1377, there were only nineteen in which no parliament was held (fourteen under Edward III), and there were only three occasions when no parliaments were held in two or more consecutive years.

Parliamentary business can be grouped into five major categories: counsel, justice, petitions, legislation, and taxation. The king often asked parliament for advice. John Knyvet, for example, charged parliament in 1373 to 'consider the perils and damages that could happen to the realm and all of the people [by a French invasion] and agree to advise on this matter and give such counsel and advice (*conseil et avys*) that work for the salvation of the king, the realm and all of you'. In this and many other cases, the call for advice was merely rhetorical, a veiled plea for taxation. Nevertheless, by repeatedly framing the issue in this manner, Edward created a sense of partnership between himself and parliament.

Justice formed a crucial part of parliamentary business. The king's council in parliament dealt with knotty legal issues such as cases in which justices could not reach decisions, pleas that could not be settled without the king, delays in procedure, and abuses by royal ministers. State trials, such as Roger Mortimer's in 1330 or Justice Thorp's in 1351, were conducted in parliament. The Good Parliament took a step in another direction when it initiated impeachment proceedings against royal officers. By that time, however, the council handled most of the judicial work, though parliament remained in theory at the head of royal justice. Parliament had too many other things to do.

One of them was hearing petitions, which were of two kinds. The earliest were singular petitions, sent to the king and council in parliament 'to get the law altered in favour of the petitioners', in the words of J. G. Edwards. Receivers and triers took the petitions and determined who should pass judgement on them. They sent those involving simple issues to the appropriate office or court, while difficult petitions went directly to the king and council. They involved all kinds of issues, whether property or family disputes, administrative complaints, requests for favours, or pleas for pardons. By 1327, petitions against royal officials had become a characteristic feature of petitioning, partially filling the gap left by the demise of the eyres as a check on the administration. After 1332, however, singular petitions were no longer automatically recorded on the parliamentary roll and their numbers declined. The common petition came to prominence. In Edward II's reign, the commons occasionally drafted lists of grievances similar to those fashioned by baronial reformers. The procedure came of age in Edward III's first parliament, when the commons presented a petition of forty-one items on behalf of the 'commonalty'. Thereafter, the presentation of and king's answers to the common petition formed a crucial part of parliament's work. It was known as a common petition because the items touched on issues of widespread concern, not because it was composed by the commons as a whole. Members could put forward any item they wanted, and the privilege was abused. In 1372, the commons demanded that lawyers not be elected to parliament, because they had been offering petitions that were in their clients' rather than the common interest.

Common petitions were the inspiration for much of the legislation under Edward III. Whereas before, laws were handed down by the king and council, most were now created at a lower level out of parliamentary petitions. The forty-one articles in 1327, for example, became a statute of seventeen articles, the twenty-four in 1362 a statute of thirteen, and so on. By 1327, it was felt that any fundamental change in law had to be ratified in parliament. Ratification did not mean that legislation was immutable. The measures in 1336 for summary arrest, cited earlier, were only enacted until the following parliament, when their effectiveness could be evaluated, and were not to be held as a statute. At the end of the parliament in 1363, which enacted the sumptuary legislation, the chancellor charged the lords and commons to uphold the measures and ordered the commons to make them known to the people. He then asked whether they wanted the legislation to be put forward as an ordinance or statute, and they answered that it should be by way of an ordinance so that it could be amended in the next parliament. Indeed, by the following year parliament realized that the legislation did more harm than good and asked the king to repeal it, which he did. There was thus a developing distinction between ordinances and statutes. By 1377 the commons could declare that statutes made in parliament could not be annulled without parliamentary consent. They had groped towards this position after Edward overturned the statute of 1341 but they were only able to make it stick at the end of his reign.

Parliament's increased legislative activity did not force the king and council out of the picture. They determined which items to include and drafted the actual statute, with considerable leeway over the precise language. They decided which laws to enforce. The notably harsh measures of the statute of provisors, for example, were never put into effect. The council may have even had a hand in drafting items in common petitions. Delicate legislation about labourers, judicial procedure, treason, the staple, and papal provisions was largely formulated by the council. The change in legislation was therefore less dramatic than it at first appears. The crown did not give up its role in promulgating laws; as in other areas, it simply opened up the process to include the voice of the representatives of the community of the realm.

The final area of business, taxation, is the best known. The confirmation of the charters in 1297 had asserted the need for consent, and the *Modus* argued for parliamentary consent in the 1320s. Yet great councils occasionally approved taxes and parliament's monopoly was not firmly established until the 1340s, as the incidence of taxation climbed. Only five of seventeen parliaments between 1327 and 1337 discussed taxes, but only five of the remaining thirty-one did *not* deal with taxation. Wool subsidies similarly occupied a central place in parliamentary debates beginning in the 1340s. The commons argued for their right to approve changes in customs duties, which affected the entire community, but did not gain that power until

1356. Continual requests for taxes after 1336 enhanced the prestige of the commons, who were empowered to act on behalf of the mass of taxpayers, the *Modus* noted. The scope of their concerns can be seen in the common petition of 1352. Parliament opened at Westminster on Friday 13 January but was delayed until the following Tuesday because not enough lords had appeared. On Tuesday, Chief Justice William Sharèshull delivered the charge to parliament, which consisted of two points: law and order, and France. The lords and commons deliberated separately and held an intercommuning on Wednesday and Thursday, and then assembled in the white chamber on Friday where Bartholomew de Burghersh again stressed the seriousness of the threat in France. He urged them to consider the request for aid and to draw up their grievances. The commons then presented the king in full parliament a roll containing their consent to a tax for three years as well as a petition that touched the community of the realm (*commune de la terre*).

It contained fifty-three items. It began by asking that the fines from the statute of labourers be applied to tax relief, that the king not demand any more taxes or aids, and that he confirm all reasonable petitions. Other articles treated the problems of justice, purveyance and purveyors, the qualifications of sheriffs and tax collectors, loans to the king, treason, indictments, due process, executors, foresters, military obligations, weights and measures, defence of the Scottish marches, aid for knighting the king's eldest son, disruption of river traffic, sales to foreign merchants, currency and exchange, outlawry and forfeiture, pleas in the Marshalsea court, debts and debtors, customs collection, tithes on wood and underbrush, sheriffs' farms, fees for writs, legal procedure, papal provisions, taxes on cloth, writs of naifty, and the payment of taxes. The clergy presented twelve petitions of their own. The king responded to each item and twenty-three were enshrined in a statute. The king found most of the petitions reasonable, but they did not necessarily end up in the statute. He thus asserted that it was not his intention, nor the lords', to levy another tax, but he did not make that a permanent law. On the other hand, he did not find reasonable the commons' request that no members of the present parliament be appointed to collect the tax that parliament had granted.

Many of these issues came up time and time again. Purveyance, for example, had caused a storm of protest under Edward I and led to renewed complaints in the 1330s. The system of compulsory purchase caused hardships for subjects because it disrupted markets, repayment was uncertain, and purveyors often took more than they were ordered or failed to issue proper receipts (tallies). These ills prompted William of Pagula to compose his sharp critique of purveyance, *De speculo regis Edwardi*. In response to mounting complaints, Edward endorsed legislation on purveyance seven times between 1330 and 1354. Finally, in what came to be known as the great statute of purveyors in 1362, he changed their name to 'buyers' and introduced new reforms. The statute did not end complaints, but it went a long way toward correcting the problem. The commons similarly badgered the king about military service and secured legislation in 1327, 1344, 1346–8, and 1352 that protected subjects from undue royal demands.

The 1352 petition also displayed the commons' sensitivity regarding privilege and special interests. The commons asked that, since taxes were a great and outrageous charge on the community (*commune*), everyone should pay, notwithstanding any charters of exemption, and that lords (*seignurs*) should contribute on account of their demesnes, rents, and tenants just as the gentry (*mesnes gentz*) did on account of their goods. Their logic seems to have been that if taxation was a common necessity borne for the common good, then all should pay. The commons similarly agitated against franchises in 1343, 1344, and 1347, asserting that they oppressed the people. In 1354 they attacked the tenants of liberties, demanding that they contribute, along with all other county residents, to the wages of the knights of the shire, while in the 1370s the government tried to eliminate the tax-exempt status of the Cinque Ports, Chester, and Durham.

The commons focused on guilds in 1363, claiming that they were responsible for high prices. Merchant monopolists likewise came under attack. When Edward's wool monopoly collapsed at Dordrecht in 1337, most of the participants received receipts, the 'Dordrecht bonds', which proved to be virtually worthless. A fortunate few, however, received exemptions from duty on their wool exports. Short of cash, Edward used privilege as collateral in these years, giving creditors a variety of considerations. During the 1340s, English companies composed of a few, select merchants, such as William de la Pole or Walter Chiriton, farmed the customs. The government helped to clear its backlog of debts by allowing these 'contractors' to buy up royal debts at a discount from other merchants and reimburse themselves at full value out of the customs. Edward thus placed a handful of merchants in an advantageous position relative to their competitors. Yet, because everyone in England, peasants and lords, retailers and merchants, depended on wool profits, such favouritism aroused deep resentment. The wool trade was part of the common good. The commons therefore denounced the monopolists in 1347 and 1348 and protested against their privileges in 1352. An ordinance drawn up by a great council in October 1353 prohibited English, Welsh, and Irish merchants from exporting wool and allowed foreigners to dominate the wool trade for the next four years. The commons were taking their role as the watchdog of the community of the realm seriously, and howled loudly whenever they perceived anyone trespassing on the common good. Perhaps emboldened by their

stand, the government systematically brought charges during the 1340s and
1350s against many of the merchants, Pole and Chiriton among them, who
had been at the forefront of its fiscal schemes in the 1330s and 1340s.

Disputes between church and state also came up in parliament. The
clergy drew up their own parliamentary petitions, called *gravamina*, which
addressed their concerns. Freedom from arrest and prosecution in lay courts
was one such issue. For example, Edward's inquests into official misconduct
in 1340–1, which punished abuses by ecclesiastical officials, ignited opposition from Stratford and Grandisson who vigorously defended clerical
privilege. Edward was equally determined that his ministers be justiciable in
his courts and so appointed a lay chancellor and treasurer in place of clerical
officers. Otherwise, lay and ecclesiastical courts established a smooth working relationship regarding criminous clerks, geared to protecting the
interests of both. Stratford, however, also wanted to protect church property from taxation and purveyance and extracted a statute to that end from
Edward during a moment of political weakness in 1340. The clergy also
protested at royal interference in ecclesiastical jurisdiction, business, or
property; the disruption of ecclesiastical processes such as elections, sanctuary, examinations, or excommunication; and the denial of benefit of clergy.
These *gravamina* could be incorporated into statutes, as in 1341, 1344, 1352,
1376, and 1377.

The lower clergy attended parliament throughout the fourteenth century, though only in an advisory capacity. Once the power of convocation
to grant clerical taxes had been established in the 1330s, large numbers of
lower clergy stopped attending parliament. In convocation, the clergy
sometimes tied their consent to the redress of grievances, as did the commons. In May 1351, for example, they granted the king a tenth to be collected in two parts, but made payment of the second conditional on his
approval of their demands. They aired their complaints in twelve petitions
presented in the next parliament in January 1352. These formed the basis of
the nine articles of the ordinance of the clergy.

Parliament also had to deal with the mounting tension between the king,
the clergy, and the papacy over papal provisions. Though, as has been seen,
the practice was not nearly as harmful as critics claimed, it aroused opposition. Parliament targeted the issue in 1307, 1309, 1318, and 1327, but its
anger really exploded in 1343, 1344, and 1346 amid war with France. The
king's rights, however, were more than adequately safeguarded. Favourable
interpretations by royal judges in the 1340s made the action of *quare impedit*
a frightening weapon and deprived the clergy of their own rights. Furthermore, provisions often worked to the king's advantage. Edward thus gained
sweeping authority over benefices and significantly increased his patronage
while eroding the church's power.

The statute of provisors gave him even more authority in 1351. Though in the form of a common petition, it was probably drafted by the crown with the intention of extending its already considerable power. The statute would have denied not only the papacy its powers of provision, but the clergy any legal recourse when a member was ousted from a benefice. The statute, however, was never enforced, even though it was reissued in 1365. In the ordinance of the clergy in 1352, moreover, Edward retreated and offered the clergy legal protection.

Legal conflicts also brewed trouble. The existence within the kingdom of a separate system of church law and courts had been a constant irritant to the monarchy, leading to jurisdictional conflicts. Crown policy straightforwardly aimed at preventing encroachment on its domain and taking cognizance of pleas whenever circumstances gave it the opportunity. The church stoutly resisted these inroads on its legal territory, but it slowly lost ground. The issues were spelled out in Edward I's *Circumspecte agatis* (1285), a writ ordering royal officials to act circumspectly over ecclesiastical jurisdiction and in the *Articuli cleri* (1316), Edward II's response to ecclesiastical complaints. The crown generally conceded the church's competence over morals, marriages, and testaments, though even there the royal courts began to intrude. Suits involving advowsons, lay fees, and debts were controversial and the crown steadily advanced at the expense of the church courts. Furthermore, ecclesiastical officials were not immune from private complaints about corruption or coercion nor from royal inquests into ministerial abuses. In response, the church threatened those who trespassed on its territory with excommunication. It also won a writ of consultation to restore cases taken out of its courts, though it was never as effective as royal measures.

The crown wielded an impressive arsenal in its fight to preserve and extend its jurisdiction. One weapon was the writ of prohibition. A defendant in certain kinds of suits before a church court could obtain from the chancery a writ which brought the issue into a royal court. Another was a general prohibition on taking pleas out of the kingdom. The privilege stemmed from a papal indult (permission to deviate from church law) of 1231, but English monarchs had extended it considerably. The statute of *praemunire* in 1353 supplemented royal prerogative. The process against those taking pleas out of the country could be excruciatingly slow. Between 1343 and 1353, the king, spurred on by parliamentary demands, authorized swifter arrest and outlawry. The statute created new procedures: a warning in the new writ of *praemunire facias*, an order to appear in court supplemented by a writ of arrest, forfeiture for non-appearance, and finally outlawry. They made it even more difficult than before for clergymen to appeal to the papacy if they felt the king had violated their rights. Edward thus manipulated popular sentiment against clerical privileges and papal provisions to bolster his own authority. Royal prerogative expanded enormously, but it did so with parliament's help.

Parliament thus debated an array of issues from virtually every sector of English society and became the primary arena for negotiations between the king and the community of the realm. For the first time in English history, a sustained political discourse emerged. It lacks the dazzle of thirteenth century political rhetoric. The commons, who took the lead in these debates, seldom fired the imagination the way the barons did between Magna Carta and the Ordinances when they acted as spokesmen for the community of the realm. The commons haggled over practical points rather than constitutional principles. Though political negotiation lost some of its lustre, it became more responsive than it had been to individuals and communities as the commons handled the consequences of policies and the interests of the interlinked hierarchies on which the crown depended for success. Their arguments reveal, moreover, a sophisticated use of rhetoric and political reasoning.

The pattern emerges in the issues of war and taxation. Edward had to convince the lords and commons that war was necessary and took every opportunity to assert his 'great necessity' (*la grand necessite*). He put it in terms of his own safety as well as the safety of the realm. While he was at the siege of Calais in 1346, his messengers to parliament dramatically proclaimed that since no one knew, when Edward departed for France 'to recover his rights there and to save and defend his land of England', what would happen to the king, he and the lords who accompanied him along with the council ordered a parliament to be held in his absence. In 1340, messengers spoke of the 'outrageous mischiefs and weighty necessities' and the 'great mischiefs and perils' that beset the king and lords in Flanders. The other side of the coin, as pointed out by Thomas Gray in his *Scalacronica*, was that peace, though the most coveted of earthly possessions, must be honourable. A debasing peace, sought for unbecoming reasons such as indolence, cowardice, or poverty, jeopardizes the kingdom. 'Let him who seeks to stop a war otherwise than it pleases God consider that the dice may turn against him just when he expects to reap advantage.'

Necessity, however, was an assertion, not a fact. Hence, it was negotiable. Faced with this rhetorical bombardment, the commons responded by asserting the common good, though there were no legal criteria for determining either common necessity or good. Political rhetoric, not constitutional arguments, structured bargaining between the king and commons. Their positions crystallized over taxation. By Edward's reign it had been well established that taxes were voluntary contributions from which the community as a whole should benefit. They needed the community's consent to be levied, and so had to be justified anew each time the king needed money. Since none of this was written into law and since memory and custom were so malleable, each request for taxes was a new adventure, opening the door to the airing of grievances if not outright opposition. Even though, as Harriss points out, the commons never withheld their consent until the very end of Edward III's reign, Edward never took it for granted. He bombarded parliament with speeches, newsletters, and propaganda on behalf of his policies. He even made some concessions to win support. The rise of the common petition is inconceivable outside a context in which king and parliament bargained from positions of mutual strength.

The commons had three fears. One was that if they lost the power of consent, taxation would become a customary rent leviable at the king's will. A second was that tax revenues, indeed all royal income, might be appropriated by a narrow clique for its own use rather than for the common good. That concern became acute over the monopoly merchants in 1340s and the court faction in the 1370s. Parliament was equally suspicious of royal creditors. They were often repaid by assignments of tax or customs revenues, which *appeared* to divert tax proceeds from the war to the profit of select individuals. Finally, the commons feared that the burden of taxation would prove intolerable and ignite rebellion. Since popular resistance to taxation was not uncommon (it erupted outside parliament in 1348), the argument was not purely rhetorical.

The commons either had to accept the king's plea of necessity or find ways around it. They suggested, for example, that other perils besides war beset the community. In consenting to a wool tax in 1340, parliament urged the king to adhere to the covenants agreed to by the council and backed by the oaths of the peers, 'because many damages and mischiefs would follow if the covenants were broken'. The commons thus appropriated Edward's language and turned it against him. In 1346, they expressed a forthright scepticism about the war despite the presentation in parliament of the recently discovered plans for a French invasion of England drawn up in 1339. They prefaced their grant of a subsidy with a long lesson on the oppressiveness of wartime demands and hoped that the tax would help speed the war to its conclusion, points they made again in 1352 and 1373.

The commons also bargained. Archbishop Stratford, for example, responding to Edward's complaint in 1341 about the relaxation of royal debts, pointed out that it was done only with 'the assent of the king and the whole parliament on consideration of a greater advantage thereby accruing to you, namely that the community of the land should grant you the ninth [of 1340]; nor would the community have otherwise assented to the subsidy'. The commons built on the exchange inherent in medieval taxation to ask for things besides defence in return for taxes, namely the redress of grievances. Furthermore, the commons made their grants of taxes conditional. The grant of 1344 had four conditions attached, that of 1348 fourteen. Some were repeated: that the tax be used only for war, that the second or third year be not collected if the war ended, and that the proceeds north of the Trent be used for defence against the Scots if they invaded. These items surfaced in 1373 as well. War might be a necessity, but the commons asserted that other aspects of the polity demanded equal attention.

This kind of bargaining, centred on customary ideas of necessity and common good, formed the essence of parliamentary politics in Edward's reign. Negotiations covered a wide array of issues and clarified the powers and policies of the crown. Though sometimes antagonistic, debate was largely peaceful. Edward's willingness to bargain with the lords and commons helps to explain the political peace that prevailed through much of his reign. Nevertheless, it could not altogether prevent confrontation.

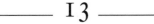

13

POLITICAL CONFLICT

It is eloquent testimony to the wisdom of Edward's use of counsel that serious political conflict erupted on only three occasions: once before Edward was fully in charge, once in his old age, and only once in the prime of his leadership. Otherwise, disagreements were resolved through parliamentary negotiation. Edward was politically fortunate. After his father's disastrous reign, the nobility was wary of political confrontation and civil war. After the Black Death, king, lords, and gentry united over the need to control the peasantry. There was a large measure of support for the war, particularly after the stunning victories at Crécy and Poitiers. Nevertheless, opposition tested Edward's policies. A look at these occasions reveals that relations between the crown and the prelates, lords, and gentry were remarkably resilient. Each refrained from pushing its powers to the fullest, allowing a high degree of trust to build up among them.

Beginning in 1320, England endured a decade of extreme factionalism spawned by the excessive influence that the Despensers exercised over Edward II. It led directly to Edward's deposition in 1327, but any hopes that Mortimer and Isabella's new regime would heal the divisiveness soon faded as its true character revealed itself. Their arrogance was their undoing and they, too, were overthrown in 1330.

The problem facing Edward and his friends was to restore trust between the king and the elite and among members of the nobility and gentry. Edward began the day after the coup by announcing that he was assuming full control of the government, that those who had been responsible for dishonouring him and impoverishing his people would be arrested, and that he would henceforth rule with the consent of the magnates. He followed through by summoning a parliament. The summons pleaded for help in reforming the realm and invited people to bring their grievances to parliament. Furthermore, because in the past knights of the shire had been maintainers of false quarrels and had not allowed the good men of the county to declare the grievances of the common people to be redressed in parliament, Edward ordered the election of loyal and sufficient knights. The returns indeed show a clean sweep. While knights who had previously sat in parliament outnumbered first timers, there were only three who had sat in the immediately preceding parliament. Edward thus used the summoning of parliament to set a new political direction.

The parliament that opened at Westminster on 26 November was crucial in establishing Edward's authority and is worth looking at in a little detail. The main business was Mortimer's trial. Yet Edward also wanted to mend wounds and rebuild trust. The proscriptions, therefore, were not extensive. Only Mortimer, four associates, and two accused murderers of Edward II were condemned. In addition, Oliver de Ingham forfeited his lands for supporting Mortimer, but was pardoned by December. Even John de Maltravers, who was sentenced to hang for his part in the murders of Edward II and Edmund earl of Kent and fled into exile, served Edward overseas in the 1340s and was eventually pardoned in 1351. In contrast to his father's behaviour after Boroughbridge, Edward did not create a party of disaffected nobles. Indeed, he balanced the condemnations with pardons to Lancaster, Kent, and others who had opposed Mortimer. He reached even further back and restored the inheritance of Richard fitz Alan, son and heir of Edmund earl of Arundel who had been tried and executed in 1326 for supporting Edward II. His language was healing: 'for the good of peace and to nourish love and unity between him and his people', or 'our lord the king wishes to do grace to all who deserve it', or 'for the tranquillity and quiet of all the people of the realm'. Parliament was an instrument for conciliation as well as discipline.

Edward, moreover, conscientiously turned to the magnates for advice. The peers rendered the judgements. Petitions were read before the king, earls, barons, and peers. Edward rewarded William de Montagu (1,000 marks), Edward de Bohun (400 marks), Robert de Ufford (300 marks), and John de Nevill (200 marks) for their help in overthrowing Mortimer, but only with the lords' consent. In stark contrast, the peers denounced Mortimer for impoverishing the crown and realm by encroaching on royal power.

Finally, Edward displayed his determination to re-establish justice and order. He removed all sheriffs and replaced them with 'good men knowledgeable in the law'. He called for inquests into conspiracies and oppressions by officials, royal councillors, and malefactors. He demanded that judges provide justice for rich and poor alike and not be persuaded to deviate from doing right to everyone according to the law and custom of the realm. As we know, accomplishing such goals proved far more difficult than merely uttering them. But they set the tone of the new regime.

Over the next decade Edward built on this beginning. He brought parliament and council into consultation with him on his diplomatic and military plans, holding nineteen meetings between 1330 and 1339. He acted decisively, if not conclusively, against the Scots. He distributed favours broadly, the high point occurring in the creations of the 1337 parliament. The lords and commons responded by consenting to taxes in 1332, 1334, 1336, and 1337 for three years.

Edward's generosity and finances led to the first political drama of his rule. Though it can be called a 'crisis', it is vital to make sure that its precise nature is understood. It did not fit the mould of the political crises of the preceding generation, since it lacked military confrontation and questioning of constitutional roles and since there is no evidence of any rupture between Edward and the nobility. Edward's acrimonious quarrel with Stratford should not mislead us into assuming that Stratford either had the backing of the nobility or represented a 'Lancastrian' party dedicated to advancing a particular cause. As has often been remarked, it was the first conflict conducted almost entirely in parliament, and that fact is crucial in understanding what happened.

The roots of the conflict lay in two problems, financial and administrative. Edward was virtually bankrupt by 1341 because of his policy of buying allies and his fruitless campaigning in Flanders. Forced to borrow because tax proceeds did not come in fast enough, Edward was forced to allocate tax revenues to creditors because he had borrowed so much. Though he had extracted more than £400,000 through taxes and other levies since 1337, he had spent it all and was still £400,000 in debt. He may have spent £1 million altogether, with nothing to show for it. Indebtedness was humiliating, as Stratford explained to Parliament in 1339, because English knights and nobles were held as surety for the loans and could not depart until they had been paid. In a fit of pique, Edward had dismissed his treasurer, Robert de Wodehouse, in December 1338, for failing to raise enough money quickly, a portent of things to come. Despite these difficulties, Edward named one of his allies, William of Juliers, earl of Cambridge in 1340 and gave him £1,000 a year to support the dignity. Meanwhile, deflation, brought about in part by these policies, impaired the collection of taxes and impoverished the peasantry, who, critics warned, were on the verge of rebellion. Since the war did not go well, taxpayers did not see their sacrifices producing any results.

Administrative weaknesses exacerbated the situation. Edward set up a regency council under the nominal leadership of his son Edward to administer the realm while he was overseas. The Walton Ordinances, issued on 12 July 1338 just before he departed, gave overall authority to the household. They tried to impose financial stringency by curtailing grants and exemptions, speeding up payments, and carefully auditing accounts. The regency council, however, was in the difficult position of having to enforce unpopular policies without any real power of its own. In an exchange of letters with Edward in 1339, the council explained the problems it was having and pleaded for assistance. At the urging of a delegation of counsellors, Edward made a number of concessions in September 1339. They included pardons of debts and felons' chattels, release from aids for knighting the king's eldest son or marrying his eldest daughter, and an end to 'Englishry' (a fine imposed on communities after the Conquest whenever an unknown homicide occurred unless it could be proved that the victim was English). Most importantly, Edward increased the authority of the regency council. He wanted to keep the war going at any cost.

These concessions form the background to a temporary settlement hammered out in four parliaments between October 1339 and July 1340. Because of the dearth of coin, the lords mooted the idea of a tax in kind, the ninth, in the first parliament. The commons, however, balked and declared that they needed to consult with their communities before making any grant. They also called for concessions on the king's part, echoing those already granted. The second parliament in January 1340 offered Edward 30,000 sacks of wool under certain conditions. The common petition in the third parliament in March 1340 got at the heart of the crisis by trying to delegate financial and administrative supervision to the magnates. It called for inquests into the collection and disbursement of revenues dating back to 1336 and forbade the assignment of tax revenues. The magnates would guarantee that tax proceeds were delivered to the king for the good of the people as parliament had dictated. Parliament requested that all crown lands alienated since Edward I be resumed into the king's hands so that he could live on his own and not have to tax his people. Finally, it called for the appointment of a council of peers with the approval of parliament.

G. L. Harriss and others have pointed out that these provisions recall the Ordinances of 1311. The comparison is useful because it shows how limited the demands of 1340 really were. The election of officials and the resumption of royal grants were key elements of the Ordinances, which were oriented toward baronial control of the king through parliament. But parliament in 1340 did not try to shackle Edward III in quite the same way. It did not demand parliamentary approval to make war or to leave the realm, or remove all royal ministers, or place restrictions on the privy seal. Like any ruler, Edward III disliked the idea of parliament dictating appointments and financial policy. Yet the provisions were not entirely unacceptable. He, too, felt let down by his administration and wanted the speedy receipt of his revenues. In other words, though provocative, the petition was not inflammatory. Most of the provisions, moreover, did not become law.

The negotiations carried out in these parliaments bore fruit when the March 1340 parliament granted Edward the famous ninth, a tax in kind. In order to get the tax approved, Edward agreed to wide ranging legislation issued in four statutes. They embodied, in part, the concessions he had made the year before. He thus pardoned old debts and felons' chattels; abolished Englishry; made improvements to speed judicial process; enacted administrative measures concerning sheriffs, escheators, weights and measures, hundreds, gaols, and clerks of markets; promised to grant wardships to the next of kin and to use the proceeds to pay for the war; placed limits on purveyance; promised that his assumption of the crown of France would not affect his English subjects; and upheld the liberties of the English church. The commons demonstrated that they were a force to be reckoned with, and Edward treated their grievances respectfully. Relations between Edward and parliament, therefore, had not been confrontational. They engaged in hard but peaceful bargaining and the negotiations had been successful for both.

Unfortunately, the tax did not solve Edward's problems. Not only did he assign nearly £190,000 to creditors, but he had trouble collecting the tax because of poor conditions. By the end of 1340, only £15,000 had been collected. In the last of the four parliaments in July 1340, therefore, the lords proposed a grant of wool in place of the first year of the ninth. The proceeds of the second year would be used to pay for the wool. The discussion revealed two points. One was parliament's hatred of assignments. It insisted that the tax proceeds be paid to the wool suppliers, not to creditors. Parliament failed to see the fundamental connection between lending and military campaigning. It only saw its money going to creditors, and hence not to the common good. The second point was the problem of obedience to the tax. Parliament was determined to show a united front to the populace to avoid the difficulties that had plagued the first regency council. The commons demanded that the measure be sealed by all of the lords present and absent, sent around to the knights of the counties, and reported to the local population. Obviously, they feared resistance.

Things did not go smoothly. The shortage of funds forced Edward to call off the siege of Tournai and conclude the truce of Espléchin on 25 September. In December, he stormed back to England, removed his leading ministers, and demanded a sweeping inquiry into the conduct of his officials. He sent a stinging letter to Stratford accusing him of duplicity and disloyalty. Issues finally came to a head in parliament in April and May 1341.

Did events between 1339 and 1341 signal a serious weakening of royal authority in the face of powerful magnate or parliamentary opposition? Was this a constitutional crisis?

To answer such questions, it is essential first to appreciate Edward's position. He wanted political harmony above all so that he could get on with his war. To that end, he had made broad concessions in the summer of 1339 and again the following summer. He had realized the ineffectiveness of the Walton Ordinances, relinquished some personal power, and set up a new regency council with enhanced authority in May 1340. In return, he received a pledge that supplies would be forthcoming. Edward conceded much; his counsellors and parliament promised much in return. His hopes must have soared after his victory at Sluys. When they crashed back to earth because of a lack of funds, he felt utterly betrayed by those in whom he had placed so much trust. Stratford headed the list. The London Chronicle gives the flavour of Edward's anger when it speaks of the 'false' or 'evil traitors' on his council who failed to deliver the money that had been promised.

Three events triggered political conflict. The first was the inquest into royal ministers. Although prompted by popular protests as well as the king's anger, it proved to be oppressive and hateful. Never one to forego an opportunity to raise cash, Edward levied huge communal fines, regardless of culpability. In Essex and Suffolk, for example, fines amounted to 3,000 and 4,000 marks, 69 and 85 per cent greater than their ordinary tax liabilities. The county elites were distressed partly by the misuse of the inquest and partly by the threat it posed to their own power. After all, in many cases, they were the objects of inquiry. In the April parliament, the commons, therefore, rallied against the inquests and the ordinance of Northampton of 1328 on which they were modelled and called for commissions of local men to take their place. The commons' demand that Magna Carta be upheld clearly referred to unjust arrests and seizures of property. Significantly, when the government proposed another inquest in 1343, it was chosen and sworn in parliament.

The second incitement was the arrest of clerical ministers. Vigorously defending clerical privilege, Stratford swiftly excommunicated those making the arrests, though he carefully avoided implicating Edward. Bishop Grandisson in Exeter similarly excommunicated members of the local inquest. The excommunications provoked Edward who swore, according to the London Chronicle, that 'in his time no man of the church would be treasurer or chancellor, or in any other great office pertaining to the king, but only such persons who, if they were convicted of wrongdoing, he could draw, hang, and behead'.

This interchange led to the third problem, the quarrel between Edward and Stratford. Edward was quick-tempered. He focused all his disappointment on Stratford. For his part, Stratford fled London and barricaded himself in Canterbury. He turned away the king's emissaries, declaring that he feared for his life, a fear that may have stemmed from the fact that in recent memory bishop Stapledon had been murdered on the streets of London during political conflict. Edward and Stratford tried to justify their positions through a war of letters, which were given wide publicity. Stratford's were circumstantially more correct than Edward's and provide interesting insight into his assumptions about government. He spent much of his energy protecting the church's liberties and personnel. Edward's letter, the *libellus famosus*, is important, not for the accuracy of its denunciation, but because it reveals his sense of betrayal. Promises and expectations had not been fulfilled, and he heaped all the blame on Stratford.

Matters were temporarily resolved in the parliament that met on 23 April. Stratford acknowledged his summons, but when he tried to enter parliament, Edward's most fervent supporters barred his way. They said he had to answer charges in the exchequer. He maintained his right to be tried by his peers in parliament. The deadlock ended when the earls of Surrey and Arundel intervened, allowed Stratford to take his place among the lords, and forced some 'unworthy' *curiales*, John Darcy and William Kilsby, to withdraw. Stratford's trial never came up, and after some hesitation, Edward and Stratford were superficially reconciled.

Edward was obviously in a weak position and once again forced to make concessions. The commons submitted a petition of eight articles, the lords presented one of their own, and there were seven clerical petitions. Parliament concluded that Edward's initial responses were insufficient. Edward assented to review the matters with a committee of lords and counsellors. The new responses were acceptable and put in a statute. Parliament then consented to a new levy of 30,000 sacks of wool, under strict conditions.

The statute of 1341 was short but important. Among other things, it declared that any violations of Magna Carta or other franchises would be tried in parliament, established that peers should be tried only in parliament, and called for the appointment and swearing in of ministers in parliament. On the one hand, the legislation protected the franchises and rights of the elite. On the other, it gave parliament extraordinary control over royal officials. The idea of strict accountability stretched back to the baronial reforms of the mid-thirteenth century and had even surfaced in the common petition of Edward's first parliament. Nevertheless, it was surely the most objectionable feature in Edward's eyes, accounting for his abrupt revocation of the statute on 1 October. Declaring that he had dissimulated his consent out of fear that if he did not parliament would dissolve in discord without having transacted any important business, Edward voided the statute with the advice of earls, barons, and other wise men of the realm.

The crisis seemed to have passed, but Edward prudently did not summon parliament for another two years, until April 1343. The commons, however, had not forgotten what had happened. Among the thirty-five articles in the common petition of 1343, they asked for the enforcement of the 1341 statute, that legislation passed by the lords and commons not be repealed, that certain conditions be applied to the appointment of the treasurer and chancellor, and that the king retain his lands and income so that he could live on his own. Edward responded that the 1341 statute was contrary to the law of the land and damaging to the crown, that he could appoint any one he pleased as his ministers though he only wanted good and sufficient men, and that he wanted to save his property as his council advised. Relations between Edward and the commons were still unsettled.

Parliamentary bargaining was the hallmark of this crisis. For the first time, parliament was the primary site of political manoeuvring, where the king, lords, and commons haggled over complaints and remedies. The debate raised three critical issues. One was counsel. Stratford played on the theme in his letter to Edward. It also emerged in a stinging protest poem 'Against the king's taxes', probably written around 1339, and underlay the struggle over the appointment of royal ministers. Stratford and the poem agreed that bad policy was the result of bad advice and that the wrong persons had been chosen as counsellors. Their remedies were vague; Stratford called for counsel by the great and wise men of the realm. Parliament conceived the issue narrowly. It concentrated on the accountability and removal of the king's ministers in parliament, echoing the Ordinances but diminishing their emphasis on the baronage. Nor did it go as far as the Ordinances and demand the removal of all of Edward's advisors. The crisis was much more ministerial in nature than the earlier conflict. Nevertheless, by taking control of ministers out of Edward's hands, the statute was an intolerable intrusion into his sovereignty.

Another issue was the common good. Stratford played on this effectively. He identified the common good with the safety of the realm and the king's honour. He contrasted them with private profit, which false counsellors sought. But he never questioned the necessity of Edward's 'enterprise'. The poem hit harder than Stratford's letter and reveals a deeper stratum of discontent. It repeated the Ordinances' demand that the king not leave the realm for war without the consent of the community of the realm and then catalogued a litany of complaints against taxes, wool collection, royal ministers, and the rich. A hint of rebellion by the poor sharpens the poem's critique. From its standpoint, royal policy, advanced by evil counsellors, has nothing to do with the common good.

A final aspect of the crisis was the emergence of political differences between the nobility and the gentry. The intensification of parliamentary negotiation in the first decades of Edward's reign hastened the institutional and social differentiation of the peerage from the commons or gentry. They belonged to a single community that ruled England, but they did not always see eye to eye.

There is no indication that the nobility seriously wavered in support of the king. The lowest point in their relations, according to the London Chronicle, came in the fall of 1340, when the council of lords with Edward overseas recommended that he abandon the campaign. Otherwise, the lords had consistently supported Edward's pleas for taxes. Bertie Wilkinson has argued that the earls' intervention in the 1341 parliament was intended to calm the situation rather than coerce Edward. By 6 June, Edward felt confident enough to summon six earls, twelve barons, and five prelates to a council and relied on council meetings in place of parliament for the next two years. Prestwich has shown, moreover, that during the summer of 1341 Edward planned a new assault on France. It was eventually called off on the advice of his magnates, but he could not have even contemplated it unless he had the backing of the eighteen earls and lords who were supposed to lead the campaign. Edward was careful not to make any arrangements which would irritate the delicate political situation, but he was determined to go ahead with his ambitions. Finally, the fact that Edward revoked the 1341 legislation so quickly shows that he could count on a solid core of baronial support. Their main stake in the 1341 legislation was the upholding of franchises and trial by peers in parliament, which were not particularly threatened by the voidance of the statute.

In contrast, the commons were restless. It was harder for knightly landholders than magnates to equip themselves for war, leave their estates, pay taxes, and face the uncertainties of royal pay. Knightly estates, moreover, demanded close personal supervision because they could not bear the costs of elaborate estate management. The commons, therefore, tended to be more ambivalent about war than the lords. The gentry were also much closer than the magnates to local communities and hence more vulnerable to popular unrest. They were in direct contact with the peasantry, collecting taxes, raising armies, and executing policy. They made their discomfort plain when they demanded to consult with their communities before granting a tax in 1339 and when they pleaded that the lords show their solidarity over the ninth in 1340. They displayed their concern about finances in their cautious responses about the defence of Scotland and the coasts and in the common petition of March 1340 which called for stringent restrictions on the expenditure of tax receipts. The 1339 poem indicates a powerful popular sentiment against the costs of the war and against those responsible for levying taxes. The representatives of the community of the realm must have felt very anxious. Their uneasiness may have increased when the inquests of

1341 revealed the depth of popular anger at royal, ecclesiastical, and private officials. The commons drew together in the face of popular outrage, abolished the inquests, and proposed ones which they might be better able to control. Their laments throughout these years about the burdens and hardships created by wartime demands may have been self-serving, but they reflected an intimate knowledge of the effects of taxation on localities. They may have been genuinely fearful of revolt.

Further evidence of the divergence between nobility and gentry may be found in Thomas Gray's *Scalacronica*. Gray was a member of the county gentry. He went to Flanders in 1338 in William de Montagu's retinue and fought at Neville's Cross in 1346, but was captured by the Scots in 1355 and imprisoned until 1359. During his captivity he began his chronicle. It is important here because of the attitudes it reveals. Gray, for example, was the only chronicler to criticize Edward's creation of the earls in 1337. He declared that because Edward was so liberal in his grants, he had scarcely any lands left to live upon and was therefore forced to levy taxes. He went on to complain about the costs of Edward's policy of enlisting continental allies in 1338 and said that Edward's leading counsellor, William de Montagu, argued against it. The payments brought no profit to England and only satisfied the allies' greed. He complained that Edward and his men did nothing after arriving in Flanders except to joust. His objections dovetail with those of the 1339 protest poem which bemoaned the cost of maintaining the troops abroad, whom Edward was paying at an unusually high rate. The *Scalacronica*'s view was thus congruent with the commons' attitude toward taxation.

The commons continued their criticism through the 1340s. Complaints against taxation produced turbulent meetings in 1343, 1344, 1346, 1348, and 1352. Perhaps the greatest achievement of the 1339–41 crisis was that it brought the commons and gentry directly into the centre of the political arena, where they continued to be an active presence throughout the rest of Edward's reign. Political discourse was now three-cornered, and neither the king nor the lords could afford to ignore the gentry's voice.

Politics in the 1350s and 1360s was quieter than in the 1340s though dissent could still be heard. Edward's great victories provided justification at long last for the wartime sacrifices. The government shifted the tax burden away from direct taxes to customs, which helped abate criticism somewhat. Though the commons finally won the power of consent to wool subsidies, Edward was in a stronger position in these years largely because he was not totally dependent on direct taxes. The issue of wool exports and subsidies was rancorous but not divisive.

Another reason for the relatively smooth relations between king and parliament was the closing of ranks among the nobility and gentry to protect themselves in the face of high wages and peasant resistance after the Black Death. There was broad agreement over the need for labour legislation. The crown even agreed to use labour fines for tax relief. Co-operation, however, should not conceal the fact that the lords and commons remained far apart on some issues. The commons were still finely attuned to differences in status and privilege. As has been seen, in 1352 they called for the elimination of all exemptions from taxation. The political identities that had been forged in the 1330s and 1340s did not disappear. Thus, the issue of privilege would remain a sore point as long as the commons saw themselves as the guardians of the common good.

Political trouble began to brew once again after Edward resumed the title king of France and went to war against Charles V in 1369. The first hint of trouble came in 1371, and it portended problems more for the church than for the monarchy. Parliament called for the removal of clerical ministers and their replacement by able laymen. Edward responded by dismissing the chancellor, treasurer, and keeper of the privy seal and appointing laymen in their places. William Wykeham, chancellor since 1367 and Edward's closest advisor, was thus forced out of government.

The attack was the product of anti-clericalism rather than opposition to Edward. Resentment toward the church had not entirely disappeared since the parliamentary outbursts of the 1340s and 1350s. The lords and commons certainly understood that the resumption of war would mean a resumption of taxation and they may have responded warmly to the suggestion of two Austin friars in parliament that church property be 'nationalized' to meet a national emergency. The idea was not new. William of Ockham had voiced it earlier in the century. In 1371, however, it was aired publicly, outside the sheltered arena of academic disputation. The friars and traditional clergy had argued over property, poverty, dominion, and grace inside the church for over a century. The 1371 fracas brought these issues to the attention of a wider audience, confirmed the prejudices of those with anti-clerical feelings, and supplied them with sophisticated ammunition. It helped in a small way to pave the way for Wycliff and the Lollards.

The storm quickly passed, but serious troubles erupted in the final years of Edward's reign. Five factors underlay the conflict. The first was the costly and futile war in France. Not only did it not bring the kind of victories that England had enjoyed before, but after 1372 it resulted in the loss of almost all of the English lands in France. After several fruitless campaigns, the English agreed to a humiliating truce with the French in June 1375. Despite the truce and negotiations for peace, the English lost two important castles in Normandy and Brittany. Furthermore, the Castilians, who had not been a party to the truce, had a powerful fleet which threatened invasion. England, therefore, still had to prepare for war. Expenses did not let up, and the crown needed support from the community of the realm in a time of official peace.

Diplomatic relations with the papacy were a second ingredient in the gathering political crisis. Pope Gregory XI wanted peace between the kings of England and France so that they could undertake a crusade. He also wanted to return the papacy to Rome from Avignon. At the same time, however, the papacy's deep involvement in Italian politics led to war with Milan, which drove Gregory to ask more from local churches in taxes and fees. The papacy was unpopular in England because of papal provisions, the papacy's connection with France, and its financial demands. The English resisted Gregory's pleas until 1375, when the king's envoys made a concordat with the pope, at the same time that they settled on a truce with France. The concordat proved equally embarrassing. It allowed the pope to tax the English church, but gave the king nothing in return and did not alter papal provisions in the slightest. The agreement reversed a political alignment that had endured over the previous generation. The crown had consistently espoused the commons' cries against the papacy and papal provisions, but now it seemed to ally itself with the church against the commons.

These diplomatic reversals came amidst an economic downturn. The consequences of population loss were beginning to hurt landlords, who had increasing difficulty finding tenants and keeping rents and services intact. The futile military campaigning also jeopardized the finances of the great lords who contracted to be royal captains. They were in precisely the same position as the king: going to war required a huge outlay of cash for wages, equipment, and victuals that could only be raised quickly enough through loans. If the campaign ended too soon, or if the king failed to deliver on the contracts, then the lords could not pay off their own creditors. Furthermore, all the evidence points to a serious decline in trade from 1369 onward. Wars in Gascony and Italy disrupted markets. All aspects of English overseas trade – wool, cloth, and wine, imports and exports alike – suffered. These economic vicissitudes were felt throughout English society and made everyone exceptionally sensitive to financial issues.

Changes at court represented a fourth factor in the changing political climate. After the 1360s, Edward increasingly withdrew from public life. He still hunted and still celebrated the feast of St George at Windsor. Otherwise, he preferred travelling around his royal residences with only a small, personal staff. He was thus disconnected from the government, even the household, for long periods. More fatefully, he lost touch with the political environment. Two interrelated problems cropped up. On the one hand, a small clique of courtiers, centred on the king's mistress, Alice Perrers, exercised power on their own behalf. On the other, the king was not publicly

present to dampen criticism of the court and to provide the unifying cama-
raderie that had been so potent in the past. The government lacked direction. Military campaigns and diplomacy
suffered from the absence of clear-cut goals. Policy was left in the hands of
officials with power in different spheres: John of Gaunt in military and
diplomatic matters, William Latimer as chamberlain of the household, John
Nevill as steward of the household, Richard Lyons in royal finance, and so
on. As a result, the government moved haltingly and indecisively. Furthermore, it had to finance the war through loans, but with Edward detached
from policy making, courtiers manipulated borrowing for their own profit.
They bought up old crown debts at a discount and then settled with the
government at full rates. The court not only seemed distant and aloof, but
self-interested as well. And it began to attract the same kind of criticism that
had been levelled against evil counsellors in the past or against merchant
monopolists in the 1350s.

The concentration of influence at court coincided with a change in the
aristocracy. In many ways, Edward had lost touch with the political world
beyond his immediate circle of favourites. Edward's generation was dying
off. At the beginning of 1376, only two earls, Arundel and Devon, were left
from the glorious years of Crécy and Poitiers. Arundel died in January, and
Devon died the following year. None of those elevated to earldoms in 1337
was still alive. Power shifted to a new generation. Edward was sixty-four in
1376, but the average age of nine titled aristocrats who were not minors was
only thirty-six. Edward's son, the popular Black Prince, was forty-seven.
He would have been the natural leader as his father aged, but he himself
suffered a debilitating disease and died in the course of the Good Parliament.
Edward's two younger sons, Edmund and Thomas, were thirty-five and
twenty-two respectively. Leadership had passed to John of Gaunt, thirty-
seven, an ambitious but neither capable nor popular leader. Without
Edward's energy and charisma, the court was particularly vulnerable.

Finally, there was parliament. Since the 1330s Edward had relied on the
lords and commons to build support for the war. Counsel had been the hallmark of his politics. As a result, parliament had learned to debate royal policy
and finances. This experience had been of great importance for the maturation of the house of commons. From 1339, it had been in the vanguard of
reform and had been the loudest political voice on behalf of the common
good. When viewed in this light, the commons' attack on the court in 1376
is not surprising.

The government was forced to summon parliament to raise money to
fend off the French. The proceedings are well known because the sources
are more abundant than for any other medieval parliament. The narrative
account in *The anonimalle chronicle*, in particular, offers an unprecedented

view of the commons at work. The government originally asked parliament to meet in February but it was prorogued until 28 April. The opening was put off until the next day because of poor attendance. On the 29th, John Knyvet, the chancellor, gave the charge on the king's behalf saying that parliament would advise on government, defence, and war in France. The crown badly needed a subsidy. The lords and commons met separately and the commons vigorously debated the issues for several days. Their main complaint was that while they were ready to do all that they could to support the king and defend the country, the king would not have to ask for taxes were it not for the fact that he had been badly advised by counsellors who sought their private profit at the king's expense. They elected Peter de la Mare as their speaker to convey these sentiments to the lords and council. On 9 May, the lords and commons met in a general assembly. The commons asked for a committee of named lords to join in their discussions and then continued the debate. Latimer, Lyons, and Perrers were charged with moving the Calais staple and arranging loans for their personal profit, with the loss of castles in Normandy and Brittany, and with excessive expenditure. The commons pressed these charges in full parliament by questioning former treasurers and hearing the testimony of other officials and counsellors. As additional evidence turned up, the scope of the accusations widened and other officials came under scrutiny. The commons demanded their ejection and the appointment of a royal council in parliament. After 26 May, the court gave in. The courtiers and their friends were removed and a new council was appointed. Clearly, the old king had lost his sting. In 1327, 1341, and 1343 he had fought off parliamentary attempts to impose its choice of councillors. But the fight had left him, and in 1376 the commons got their way, if only temporarily. Furthermore, they did not grant a direct tax – 'And so the parliament finished without a grant of a tenth and fifteenth' – though they did extend the wool subsidy.

Parliament also presented a common petition of 140 items. A large number dealt with procedural questions in law or administration, whether gaol delivery, the court of the verge, the exchequer, or the work of escheators. Many touched on traditional areas of complaint, such as the conduct of local officers, the forests and foresters, papal provisions, purveyance, and so on. Others aired the grievances or requests of local communities. The towns of Southampton, Winchester, Bath, London, Chichester, Southwark, and Rochester asked for special favours of one kind or another. The petition also linked up with the main business of parliament, forbidding pardons for those impeached or repeals of the impeachments. The commons called for annual parliaments, the election of knights of the shire by the better men of the county, the annual election of sheriffs, and for an end to sheriffs serving as knights of the shire. They asked the king to consider the great costs, charges, and labours that they had willingly borne for the king and his honour since his coronation, to take to heart the pestilences that had affected the realm one after another to the destruction and impoverishment of the people, and to keep the profits from ecclesiastical vacancies, escheats, fines, ransoms, wardships, and marriages in his hands and not grant them away. They professed their willingness to help Edward in the future, *if* they had good and rightful government and due correction of those counsellors who had deceived and impoverished the king and the community of the realm (*commune*).

The petitions and impeachments were consistent with worries that parliament had voiced since the beginning of the century. They reveal apprehension about royal demands and suspicion of those who, like the Despensers or Mortimer, might monopolize influence for their own profit. As the unnamed knight from the south said at the opening of the debate in commons, 'the commons are so weakened and impoverished by various tallages and taxes already paid that they cannot bear such a charge at this time, and, on the other hand, all that we have granted for war for a long time we have lost by malversation because it has been badly wasted and falsely spent'. Their concerns were similar in 1341, though there was no sense then that courtiers had diverted royal income into their own hands. As Stratford had made it an issue of good counsel in his letter to Edward in 1341, so did Thomas Brinton in 1376. In a sermon to convocation on 18 May, Brinton used Augustine's famous dictum that states are nothing but thieves if not ruled by justice to expound on the bad counsel that Edward received. He pointedly stated that it was not decent for all of the keys to hang from the belt of just one woman and declared that royal counsellors should be men not women, adults not youths, nobles not paupers. The system of counsel and negotiation had broken down. For the commons, Brinton, and Stratford the consequences were the same: counsellors seek their private profit, subjects are plundered and impoverished, and the common good is destroyed.

The commons led the attack. When parliament met, there was no procedure for bringing an indictment in parliament, though the lords had sat in judgement in state trials, such as those of Mortimer in 1330 and Thorp in 1351. A procedure for impeachment, moreover, seems to have been evolving within the legal system prior to 1376, in which persons accused of wrongdoing by communities were given a hearing with the crown acting as prosecutor. The commons may have been building on these precedents in 1376, but because the action was so novel and the circumstances so highly charged, their precise legal intentions are not clear. Historians have argued whether commons thought they were acting on the basis of the criminal procedure of indictment by notoriety, as a jury bringing an indictment, or through an appeal. It is clear from the commons' actions and the statements of those involved that everyone realized that a precedent was being established. In those circumstances legal technicalities may have been stretched somewhat. In any case, during the debates in 1376, the commons gradually hammered out a procedure for indicting and trying royal ministers in parliament. The process was limited in scope. The Good Parliament did not attack government in general and there was no change among the higher officials. Yet it was a potent weapon.

The lords and commons successfully worked together in the impeachments, but the commons, as they had in the past, betrayed an ambivalent attitude toward privilege. They did not kowtow to the lords. There were, of course, areas where they found common ground. The petitions, for example, called for the enforcement of the statute of labourers and condemned the sturdy beggars who refused to work and lived off alms in towns (no. x). The petition, however, attacked the farming of hundreds by lords (no. xviii), asked that lords with possessions near the coast stay on them to guard the realm (no. xxii), complained that because the lords and warden of the Scottish marches did not remain in the region the inhabitants were subject to rebellions among the English and to invasion by the Scots (no. xxiii), and, somewhat obscurely, denounced those who, for their own profit and by their demesne authority, levied new impositions and assumed royal power without parliament's consent (no. cxxxiii). They attacked other privileged groups, such as craft guilds (no. iii). Nor did the church escape. Thirteen petitions dealt with the church or clergy. In particular, they singled out the cost of papal exactions. These were not particularly onerous, though they were unusual, since the last two taxes had been levied as long ago as 1362 and 1336. In contrast, the commons pleaded for support for the men-at-arms who had served the king in peacetime and war, naming eight men as well as other knights and squires who languished as prisoners, unable to afford their ransom (no. lxx).

It may be, as Professor Holmes has argued, that in formulating their charges against the courtiers, the commons drew heavily on the complaints of merchants and magnates. And, certainly, the success of the attack depended on the combined support of the prelates and lords. The commons could not have managed by themselves. Yet it is equally clear that they acted out of a tradition stretching back half a century in which they served as the representatives of the community of the realm and the guardians of the common good. The accusations of 1376 fall into line with complaints aired from 1339 onward. That tradition emboldened the commons to take the political initiative. And, as they had throughout Edward's reign, the commons asserted interests that diverged from those of the lords and prelates. They could be expressed only as petitions and their success was never guaranteed. None the less, they show a distrust of privilege that was consistent with the commons' role as the protector of the common good. The commons had travelled far since their first foray into national politics in 1339–41. It is worth reflecting on the similarities and differences between the two episodes to see what changes had occurred. The problems underlying political tension in 1339 and 1376 were much the same. Economic troubles brought on by ineffective military campaigning made people sceptical about the king's pleas for additional taxes. They created tension between royal ministers or favourites and the representatives of the community of the realm. This political distrust led to attacks on royal ministers. Finally, both conflicts were conducted and resolved in parliament with the house of commons playing the leading role in formulating the terms of attack and settlement. On both occasions, moreover, the commons demonstrated a scrupulous concern for 'due process'. In 1341, it was expressed in their questioning of the royal inquests and in 1376 in their efforts to devise a valid procedure for trying the courtiers. Political conflict in each case was less a polarization of king and nobility such as had been the case between 1297 and 1330, even when the nobility addressed issues of general concern, than a disagreement between the king and his subjects over the effect of royal policies.

Within that context, however, there were striking differences between the two affairs. The commons, for example, acted with much greater assurance and sophistication in 1376 than they had in 1341, reflecting their continual participation in negotiations over taxes, administration, and law since 1341. Their attack in 1376, moreover, was selective. They devised the scalpel of impeachment to excise objectionable elements of the court rather than using the bludgeon of ministerial accountability advocated in 1341. It was, as Maurice Keen has observed, a remarkably clever solution to the problem of removing the king's 'evil counsellors' which had bedevilled baronial reformers for over a century. The linkage the commons made between impeachment, consent to taxes, and redress of grievances was a logical outcome of the maturation of the house of commons which had begun in 1339–41. Their attack in 1376 was thus limited to the courtiers who had perverted policy in their own interest, rather than on the royal government in general. Indeed, the use of royal ministers to testify in the proceedings against the courtiers created a sense of solidarity between parliament and royal officers that had also been evident in 1341. Finally, Edward's role differed. In 1341, he initiated the crisis and was active in the political negotiations that followed. His continuing involvement after 1341 created the atmosphere of counsel and dissent that characterized politics to the end of his reign. In 1376, however, Edward was not actively involved in politics. He died a year after the Good Parliament closed and was not a direct party to the events that set the stage for his grandson's turbulent reign.

In practical terms, the aftermath of the Good Parliament was a disappointment. Some, but not all, of the courtiers were removed. A new council was installed. But within a few months, John of Gaunt had recaptured the initiative and rebuilt power at court.

Nevertheless, though success was only temporary, in 1341 as well as 1376, parliament had taken actions which altered the structure of English politics. In the generation between the two crises, the commons had honed their political skills and created a tradition of participation in national affairs. Peers and gentry took up new roles reflecting and sharpening the social distinctions that separated them. In contrast to the previous century, politics did not revolve primarily around relations between the king and the magnates. It centred instead in the house of commons, where gentry and burgesses articulated the anxieties of local elites faced with the problem of enforcing unprecedented royal demands on a sceptical population. The magnates generally united behind Edward. His programme of regaining and cementing their trust had been a stunning success. The knightly ranks, however, were Janus-faced – attracted both toward nobility with whom they shared social values and interests yet also keenly aware of the peasantry behind them. War did not receive their wholehearted support. Furthermore, they were distrustful of privilege, because they did not always share in it and because it caused inequities in financial burdens. Elites in the county, towns, and villages made it possible to go to war because they organized and collected the resources of the country. But they were poised atop a restless population.

Their precarious position prompted them to question royal policy. Economic distress caught the gentry's attention because unrest threatened the foundations of their authority. It goaded the commons to action and underlay political conflict in 1341 and 1376. The gentry, however, did not turn their backs on their class. They rallied with the lords to repress the peasantry in the wake of the Black Death. They consolidated their power over county communities by monopolizing local office-holding. And they clamoured for greater authority for the keepers of the peace. The commons thus became the primary channel of communication between the king and his subjects. Elections, petitions, and proclamations deepened their awareness of and responsiveness to popular opinion.

The commons had thus fashioned a self image, much like the older image of the nobility as the king's 'natural counsellors'. It was partly the creation of war. Edward had to go to parliament time and time again to ask for funding, and the bargaining strengthened the house of commons and polished its image. Yet, Michael Prestwich has shown that the mantle of representing the community of the realm was shifting from the nobility to the commons under Edward II. Edward III, moreover, consciously fostered that process to solidify support for his policies. The self-confidence that the commons displayed in the Good Parliament was not simply the by-product of war. It was the artifact of political interaction between the king, lords, and commons in which the commons took a leading role formulated in terms of counsel, common good, and community of the realm. The political language was limited, but it resonated with medieval ideals of reciprocity and obligation, rights and powers. It gave the commons a weapon against royal extravagance and lordly privilege and created an enduring political tradition.

14

CONCLUSION

———— • ————

In some ways, it was unfortunate that Edward lived as long as he did. For one whose triumphs were so striking, Edward's end was singularly ignominious. By the time of his death in 1377 at the age of sixty-five, the glorious years of his reign had long passed. The last years were engulfed in controversy. In the dispute over Alice Perrers and the courtiers, Edward was portrayed as a victim, not the forceful leader he once was. Depicting Edward's lonely death, the *Chronicon Angliae* captures the sadness of a leader whose time had passed. Deserted by his mistress as well as the knights and squires who had served him, Edward was comforted in his final moments by only a single priest. Another chronicle drew the lesson, saying that before his final years Edward had ruled gloriously and won great victories over the French and Scots, while his people lived in peace and prosperity. But at the end, in the manner of Solomon, his heart was infatuated by women, his body weakened and even annihilated. The poem 'On the Death of Edward III' likewise sensed the passing of an era. It likened the chivalry of England to a stout ship, with Edward the rudder, prince Edward the helmsman, and the commons the mast. When rudder and ship were united, there was nothing that they could not accomplish, but now, bereft of Edward and his son, England could only hope that the young Richard would prove as capable a leader as his father and grandfather had been. Brinton, too, lamented Edward's death and the passing of powerful men and captains. Now, because of the sins of the English, 'God who was wont to be English' had withdrawn from them. Yet, in Edward's heyday, England 'could be called the realm of realms, which had so many victories, captured so many kings and occupied so many lordships'.

Writers thus identified Edward with the incredible achievements of the middle decades of the fourteenth century. What was his actual contribution?

Though Edward has been designated as the maker of royal policy throughout this account, his personal role is difficult to discern for two reasons. The first is a problem of sources. There is no Matthew Paris, Gerald of Wales, or Orderic Vitalis to give insight into Edward's character, habits, and activities. Baker, Murimuth, Knighton, and even Avesbury are usually terse or adulatory. Though garrulous, Froissart largely confined himself to military exploits. There are no accounts of Edward's inner counsel where politics were hatched. Parliamentary sources abound, but debate came *after* policy had been made. Responsibility for particular policies is therefore hard to pinpoint. The second problem is the intractable one of assessing the importance of individual rulers in historical change. By the fourteenth century, the king no longer had a direct hand in day-to-day governing. His will could be exerted only through institutions and within a political framework structured by the interests and expectations of the leading men of the realm. His range of action was narrow. Still, in the small, face-to-face world of medieval administration and politics, the force of the ruler's personality and opinion was much greater than it would be when states became heavily bureaucratized. Personal respect between the king and the governing classes and the king's responsiveness to their ideals and interests went a long way toward determining the short-term success or failure of a medieval state.

Routine business was handled by the king's delegates. Edward always placed enormous confidence in ministers and magnates such as Stratford, Edington, Wykeham, Lancaster, Arundel, Percy, or Wake. Edward's letter to Stratford in 1341, blaming the archbishop for his recent failures, provides some insight into his attitudes. While specific charges can be discarded, Edward's general point that he depended heavily on Stratford's advice rings true. Stratford did not deny it. Edward may have indeed been as pliable as the letter implies, acting at his confidant's urging. At the very least, he delegated to Stratford sweeping responsibility for executing policy. But the letter itself exemplifies the problem at hand. Who wrote it? Certainly not Edward, though he may have approved it.

Another aspect of Edward's leadership that emerges in his clash with Stratford is the companionship of warriors. Like a pack of snarling dogs the Darcys, the Beauchamps, Stafford, and Neville barred Stratford's entry to parliament and faithfully took up Edward's cause. They were not constitutionally motivated nor did they conspire to build an 'anti-Lancastrian' government in the household. Like their master, they strained at the leash, impatient to go to war. Edward liked the company of knights, and his fellowship with warriors was enshrined in the Order of the Garter, tournaments, and campaigns. War was their driving ambition, not recondite theories of household government. Edward largely left administrative details to his ministers. It should not be expected, in other words, that he was a subtle policy maker or that he conceived all the policies for which he was credited. He was a hail-fellow-well-met type who got along supremely well with the nobility and gentry. Yet this ability to inspire loyalty was profoundly important in explaining why England was able to maintain such a prolonged fight.

Edward's attachments, however, could be troublesome. He would shower rewards on those whom he saw as his boon companions or as useful to him in some way. William de Montagu and William de la Pole, two very different examples, thus reaped Edward's bounty. Yet he had an exaggerated sense of obligation and mercilessly turned on those whom he thought had failed him. Overly generous when things were going smoothly, he could be excessively harsh when his plans went awry. He was quick tempered and quick to cast blame. Royal officials found this out when the Scottish campaign in 1335 failed and Edward threatened to punish them for their negligence. The treasurer William Wodehouse learned this lesson when Edward unceremoniously dumped him in 1338, angered by the slow pace of raising funds. A few years later, Stratford and other ministers bore the brunt of Edward's rage and frustration over the futility of the campaign in France. His treatment of de la Pole was especially callous, as the government hounded the financier until he had given up the bulk of the gifts bestowed by Edward in the balmy days before 1341.

The scene with the burghers of Calais, as painted by Froissart, illustrates this pattern of behaviour. Edward took the town's resistance personally: 'The people of Calais have caused him so much trouble and vexation, have cost him so much money and so many lives, that you cannot wonder that he should be enraged against them.' When the town finally capitulated in 1347, six burghers were brought in chains before Edward, who ordered them beheaded at once. His knights and counsellors pleaded for mercy, but he would not budge. Finally, his pregnant queen Philippa flung herself on her knees before him and begged that he relent. Only then did he soften and spare their lives. The scene may only have been Froissart's invention, though it could also have been carefully stage-managed to make a point. Edward did not destroy his opponents, but like the burghers of Calais who dispersed among the towns of Picardy, they faded from prominence. Whether fact or fiction, the story shows a side of Edward's character that was influential in shaping the politics of his reign.

It also underlines Edward's sense of drama. Juliet Vale has shown that Edward seized on any occasion as an excuse for elaborate ceremonies and games. His chivalry was internationally recognized. The French chronicler

Jean le Bel called him the 'noble Edward' and favourably contrasted his character, counsellors, and policies with those of the French king. In October 1350, Thomas de la Marche and John Visconti chose to hold their duel before Edward in Westminster palace because of his chivalric fame. Chivalry in this context was not solely a set of codes internalized by individual knights. The values of court and elite were enacted publicly, to reinforce among the populace and one another commitment to Edward and his policies. As in the Black Prince's progress after Poitiers across southern England and through the streets of London with his captive, king John, pageantry brought the English together and gave even humble subjects a degree of participation, however passive, in the great movements of war and state.

That returns us to the issue of policy making. Was war inevitable? The structural contradictions in England's relations with France, based on the anomalous role of the English king as a vassal of the king of France, made skirmishing highly likely. Short, indecisive conflicts had characterized their relations since 1259, and would have been likely to continue. Three factors changed that pattern. One was the decision to claim the throne of France. Whether the claim was a genuine end in itself or merely a ploy to protect Gascony, the effect was to lay France open to plunder. Another was the studious consultation with parliament. In both respects, policy played into the interests and values of the English elite. So did the third factor: Edward's view of himself. John of Reading reported that at Westminster in 1359 Edward told how he wanted to be buried alongside his three predecessors, Edward the Confessor, Henry III, and Edward I. He mentioned the beatific Confessor and devout Henry, but then extolled his 'nobilissimus' grandfather, Edward I, saying that 'in a whole life of knightly deeds, no one was more illustrious or bold or prudent in leading armies'. He made it clear with whom he identified. Indeed, if battlefield accounts are accurate, Edward did not always display the prudence he praised. Even in 1369, at the age of fifty-seven, he was proposing to lead his armies. Perhaps the most telling image was that of the young prince shedding tears of frustration and humiliation after the fiasco at Stanhope Park in 1327. It reveals that Edward was already keenly sensitive about his honour and military achievement. The memory rankled; perhaps he spent a lifetime of battlefield and tournament exploits to erase it.

Tout condemned Edward for sacrificing everything to this goal. Motivated by a 'shallow opportunism', he 'cheerfully bartered away' royal authority for consent to war. He thus had no 'other general policy than an intelligent pursuit of his own personal interests'. Others have followed Tout's lead, assigning Edward responsibility for the growing power of the commons (in return for taxes), the erosion of the king's feudal powers and the creation of huge palatinates (in return for aristocratic support), and the establishment of the justices of the peace (in return for gentry support). His hand was indeed evident in each, but a medieval ruler's personal role in such changes should not be overestimated. The problems of law and order, for example, had frustrated the government for some time and centralized solutions had proved inadequate. Even when the justices of the peace were established, power was given to them only piecemeal and the council retained directive authority. The great palatinates appeared more powerful than they actually were and none became an independent base of power threatening the crown in the way that Burgundy, for example, did in France. The rise of enfeoffments to use among tenants-in-chief was potentially corrosive to the king's rights as a feudal lord, but they proceeded slowly and usually applied to lands not held of the king. Royal lordship was not destroyed; after all, the Tudors found it profitable. War and taxation were clearly influential in the development of parliament. Yet, the importance of the commons had been increasing from the time of Edward II and bargaining for taxes was only one facet of their business. Intractable problems of national concern such as law and order, legal changes, wages, privilege, and the money supply would have dictated intense parliamentary work whether or not England had invaded France.

Though the 'intelligent pursuit' of his goals demanded that he make accommodations, Edward had no intention of bartering away his monarchical powers. He retained a strong sense of his primacy and fully exercised his sovereignty and suzerainty. True, his generosity and extravagance led him into trouble, particularly in the late 1330s when he recklessly purchased allies. An assessment of the full impact of his patronage will have to await detailed studies. But the problems caused by gifts were largely financial. There is no sign that Edward enfeebled the monarchy to go to war.

While Edward's reign was a turning-point in English history, his pursuit of war was not the sole agency of change and he was not in control of the primary forces directing England's fate. The influence of a single ruler must be assessed within the conjunction of structures, forces, and individuals that constitute society and government at any given time. Edward was successful largely because his personal qualities meshed with the interests of the hierarchies that ruled England. He inspired deep loyalty and projected contemporary ideals of kingship and nobility. He rarely stood on principle alone, and did not hold grudges. He had a clear aim and was willing to make short-term concessions to secure his long-range goals. He was willing to bargain and thus brought the community of the realm into partnership with him. His leadership was crucial at a time when elements even more powerful than war conspired to change the social and economic landscape beyond recognition. Strong medieval lordship was not only the capacity to act decisively, it was also an ineffable quality of personifying the values and aspirations of the dominant classes in society. For most of his reign, Edward did just that. Despite enthusiasm for Edward's victories, however, war sharpened class differences. Even in the period of Edward's greatest successes some were sceptical of war and longed for peace. When asked in 1354 if they would assent to a treaty for perpetual peace, the commons shouted with one voice, 'Yes! Yes!' ('Oil, Oil'). A surprisingly diverse body of literature – sermons, prophecies, protest poems, satires, and moral works – expressed opposition to the hierarchies that made war possible.

Brinton, for example, made wealth and taxation moral issues. He lashed out at lords and ministers, lay and ecclesiastical alike, for seeking their own profit at the expense of the poor and failing to work for the common good. He argued that the sins of the magnates were greater than those of 'mediocres' or the poor, because magnates lived off others with voluptuous expenses, by violence, exactions, and extortions. He cited the *Secreta secretorum* to make the point that kingdoms fell because the expenses of kings and lords exceeded their revenues. Like Robert Mannyng's *Handlyng Synne* and Langland's *Piers Plowman*, the sermons argued that lords must not harm the peasantry under their care. This is a Christian topos but it must have assumed added meaning in a period when the peasants were being pressed hard by the economy, the king, and their lords. Similar points appear in the obscure 'Prophecy' attributed to John of Bridlington. Now thought to have been written around 1349–50, the work excoriates the notorious licentiousness of Edward's court at Calais. More to the point, it condemns Edward's need for money, arising out of either avarice or war. He has betrayed his obligations and destroyed his people through excessive taxation. War itself came under attack in the caustic satire, 'The vows of the Heron'. A fictional account of oaths supposedly taken by Edward and his courtiers on the eve of their embarkation to Flanders, the poem belittles their chivalric pretensions and condemns the reality of war. Although associated with the Low Countries, it none the less demonstrates how widely criticism of the war spread.

The poems 'On the times of Edward II' and 'Against taxes' put these themes in the vernacular of protest. They connected taxes and the greed of the wealthy in accounting for the misery of the peasantry. They complained about the burden of taxes, whether in cash or wool, about the ability of the rich to avoid taxes, and about the misuse of tax proceeds. As Maddicott has demonstrated, such poetry drew on satirical and religious traditions to give voice to common grievances. While they were probably composed by clergymen and while it is not known how widely they circulated, their trenchant criticism and the specificity of their charges indicate that they probably reflect popular opinion.

War alone, in other words, did not create a national identity. A tenuous image of a national community was promoted by Edward's policies and propaganda, but it was the commons which gave it substance. Frequent parliaments, convocations, and assemblies produced a sense of coherence between central and local authority, between the crown and social elites within the country. The commons, speaking time and again on behalf of the community of the realm, gave national voice to the myriad local communities that constituted the English realm. By repeatedly invoking the 'common good' they gave it political reality. Not only did they maintain the war from first to last with their wealth and property, as the poem on Edward's death would have it, they articulated fears and grievances passed up through the hierarchies that governed the people. The idea of English nationhood woven in Edward's reign, therefore, was not simply a bellicose patriotism distinguishing English from French, though that was part of it; it was also a commitment to particular forms of political action.

Language also played a part. In 1362 English was formally used in parliament for the first time and made the language of the courts in order to facilitate pleas. French had long ceased to be the language of the elite. True, the first notable book by a layman, *Le livre du seyntz medicines*, was written in French, but the author had to apologize for its quality. In the meantime, English writers were gaining new confidence that would burst forth in the poetry of Gower and Chaucer toward the end of the century. The use of the vernacular was not unique to England; it was a phenomenon of the growing lay literacy all over Europe in the fourteenth century. It is none the less a strong indication of a growing national culture.

In his *Scalacronica*, Thomas Gray saw the good of the nation in the hands of its lords, who, if they were unified, could accomplish anything. By the end of Edward's reign, the political reality had grown more complex as the commons demonstrated that they too had a crucial part to play in national affairs. Still, the king was the linchpin holding the political nation together. Edward III had shown a remarkable talent for uniting the diverse elements of the English realm in a single cause. In 1377, people worried whether or not his grandson would have the same capabilities.

GLOSSARY

Note
References to money are all in medieval pounds sterling: £1 (libra –
pound) = 20s. (solidi – shillings) = 240d. (denarii – pence); 1s = 12d.;
1 mark = ⅔ pound = 13s. 4d.

absenteeism **benefice** holders not residing in the benefice or performing the
duties attached to the benefice though still collecting the income from the
benefice. An absentee priest would appoint a substitute (vicar) to perform the
duties of the parish and pay him a small stipend.

advowson the right to appoint a priest to a parish church. Advowsons could be
held by laymen and were treated as real property which could be inherited, sold,
exchanged, or even divided between co-heiresses (one appointing on one
occasion, another on the next, and so on).

ancient demesne lands at one time held by the crown. Tenants of the ancient
demesne were privileged and could not be treated as villeins.

annuity an annual cash payment, granted for life or a term of years as stipulated in
a contract between a lord and a retainer.

armigerous those ranks of society, esquires and above, who were entitled to bear
a coat of arms.

banneret a knight of high status entitled to carry a square banner as opposed to
the pennant carried by an ordinary knight.

baronage the leading members of the landed elite, above the bannerets. The title
of baron carried no specific duties or rights, though most were treated as peers.

benefice an ecclesiastical office, such as a parish church or **prebend**, to which
specific duties and revenues are assigned.

chapel of ease a subsidiary chapel of a mother church founded to ease the difficulties of parishioners in worshipping, especially where the parish was very large.

corrody a lifetime payment of food and clothing by a religious house to an individual and sometimes to his wife and children as well.

courts leet hundred courts in private hands, where the lord had the right to conduct the sheriff's **tourn**.

cursitor the lowest grade of clerks in the chancery, probably responsible for writing out standardized writs.

debenture a receipt given to the supplier of goods or services to the crown specifying the payment due to him and redeemable for cash.

demesne that land retained in the landlord's hand and cultivated by himself or leased out, as opposed to tenant land held by hereditary peasant tenants.

Englishry a fine paid by a hundred for an unknown homicide. After the Conquest, Normans were sometimes ambushed and slain by the English. The hundred where the body was found would be fined unless they could prove that the victim was English.

entry fine payment, set at the lord's discretion, by an unfree heir, heiress, or purchaser on entering an unfree tenement.

escheator the royal official responsible for holding inquests on the deaths of tenants-in-chief to determine who should inherit the property and taking custody of any lands coming into the king's custody because of the minority of heirs or the vacancy of a bishopric or monastery. Escheators also conducted inquests into the alienation of lands held of the king and lands granted to the church without royal permission.

eyre a periodic visitation of a county or group of counties by the king's court.

farm a fixed annual payment, a lease.

feoffee one to whom land is granted. In the language of medieval law, a grant of land was an 'enfeoffment' meaning to endow with a fief or knight's fee.

frankpledge the obligation of unfree men twelve years and older, to be sworn into tithings or groups of ten for the purpose of keeping the peace. The members of the tithing were responsible for one another's actions and had to report any crimes that came to their knowledge. Twice a year, the sheriff conducted a **view of frankpledge** to ensure that the tithings were kept full and at which the chief pledges, or heads of the tithings, reported crimes.

fulling mill mill used to process cloth (fulling) in water and with clay earth after it has been woven to make the weave denser and tighter.

hauberk armour of chain mail in the shape of a tunic to protect the body.

heriot obligation of unfree families to give up the best ox or livestock or cash equivalent on the death of the tenant.

high farming practice of landlords whereby **demesne** lands were kept in hand, cultivated with wage or unfree labour, and the produce consumed or sold for profit.

hobelar light horseman armed with knife, sword, and lance. Hobelars were used for reconnoitring and combat, in which they dismounted to fight with the infantry.

merchet a payment by unfree tenants for the right to marry off daughters or other female relatives.

moneyer a minter or maker of coins.

murrain a sheep or livestock disease. Lacking a sophisticated system of classifying animal diseases, contemporaries lumped all outbreaks as murrains.

oyer and terminer commissions issued to a panel of justices to 'hear and determine' specific complaints raised by individuals.

papal provision process by which the pope named an individual to a **benefice**.

pluralism the practice of holding more than one **benefice** at a time, often leading to **absenteeism**.

prebend a **benefice** in a cathedral chapter designed to support one of the members of the chapter with income supplied by a manor belonging to the cathedral.

primogeniture right of the eldest son to inherit his parents' lands.

purveyance the king's right to requisition food and goods in return for payment. Purveyances were made to supply the royal household and households of the royal family members in ordinary times as well as to supply royal armies in wartime.

specie coins.

staple an official site for selling wool. The government decreed that wool could only be sold at certain locations in order to control the trade and to facilitate the collection of customs. Sites often changed as the objectives of royal policy changed.

star chamber building erected next to the exchequer in Westminster where the royal council met, probably called that because stars were painted on the ceiling.

sumptuary legislation laws regulating expenditure on food and dress.

suzerain a feudal overlord. The king as suzerain was the highest feudal lord in the kingdom.

tallage tax levied at the will of the lord on unfree tenants, or tax levied on towns at the king's discretion.

tally a long wooden stick used as a receipt. It was notched to indicate the amount due and then split in half. Tallies were used in the exchequer for accounting and could also be used to assign revenues. The exchequer could issue half a tally to a creditor who took it to a revenue officer such as a tax or customs collector and exchanged the tally for cash. The official would then take the tally to the exchequer when he accounted for his receipts and get credit for the payment when it was matched with the exchequer's portion.

temporalities the non-spiritual holdings of the church such as lands, markets, and liberties.

tithe a tax of one-tenth levied by the church on harvests and animals for the support of the parish priest.

tithing see **frankpledge**.

tourn visitation carried out by the sheriff twice a year of all the hundreds in the county not in private hands. In the tourn, he held a view of the **frankpledges** and conducted a searching inquest into crime in the hundred.

trailbaston periodic commissions of justices instituted after 1304 to investigate a wide range of crimes and corruption in a particular area. The name derived from the club or staff wielded by criminals.

vill the smallest unit of government covering the village, or township, and the surrounding countryside. It was roughly equivalent to the parish, the smallest unit in ecclesiastical administration.

 •

BIBLIOGRAPHY

 •

Like all surveys, this study is built out of the work of many different scholars. Two notable historiographic traditions have been brought together: one political and constitutional and the other economic and social.

The political history of the first three-quarters of the fourteenth century has been viewed in several different ways. An older generation of historians, Davies and Tout, saw the factional politics of Edward II's reign primarily through the lens of constitutional or administrative conflict. Recent historians have preferred to view it through the eyes of the participants, through biography. From Maddicott's magisterial *Thomas of Lancaster* through Phillips, Denton (cited under Chapter 9), Haines (Chapter 9), and most recently Hamilton, the attitudes and interests of the leading figures in the drama, with the exception of Edward himself, have been laid bare, emphasizing the force of personality in shaping politics (see, notably, Phillips' comments in 'Leake').

There have been three important approaches to Edward III's reign. One has been through war and military organization. It has produced superb analyses of armies, obligations, and combat, as well as biographies of the Black Prince, Henry of Lancaster, and others. Good summaries of this tradition can be found in Allmand and in Hewitt (Chapter 10). Another approach has been the exploration of relations between the king, nobility, and parliament. May McKisack sounded this call in her paper on 'Edward III and the historians', in which she tried to rescue Edward from both critics and apologists by arguing for a more realistic portrait based on contemporary expectations of monarchs. She emphasized the high degree of co-operation between Edward and the landed elite. Finally, there has been a constitutional/administrative approach. Tout, too, was impressed by the political harmony of Edward's reign but attributed it to slightly different causes. According to Tout, Edward on the one hand made excessive concessions to the nobility and on the other was blessed with a highly competent clerical corps who worked well with the king.

Ormrod (Chapter 11) has followed this lead and argued even more forcefully for a revival of monarchical government after 1341 based on the framework created by the Walton Ordinances (1338) and carried out by a tightly knit group of administrators working in the household and central ministries. Harriss has focused on relations between Edward and parliament as part of a broader study of finance. His concern has been to show the respective rights and responsibilities of king and subjects in regard to taxation, as they grew out of a tradition of Roman and canon law, and the way they shaped the development of parliament. Guenée and Kaeuper help place English developments in a broader European context.

Edward III still awaits a good modern biographer, though Johnson and Packe are both useful. Joshua Barnes' history of Edward's reign is still helpful because of its extensive translations of documents and chronicles. Biographies of other figures in Edward's reign, notably by Barber, Fowler, and Haines (Chapter 9), help to flesh out the political events.

Other scholars have conducted penetrating investigations of the English economy and society, producing a comparably rich harvest of excellent scholarship. The most influential template was drawn by M. M. Postan. In a number of studies, he laid out an explanation for the economic ups and downs of the fourteenth century based on demographic change. Many of his theses have been confirmed by studies of individual estates. Of course, his work has not gone unchallenged, and the comments of Bridbury and Harvey, in particular, have stimulated new discussion. Most recently, economic and social studies have been pushed in four different directions. One has been the intensive study of local communities, families, and markets. Smith's volume on *Land, kinship, and life-cycle* is representative of this analysis and contains work by some of the leading practitioners. A fruitful and interesting offshoot of this trend has been the study of women in villages and towns. Studies by Bennett (Chapter 3), Hanawalt (Chapter 3), Kowaleski (Chapter 4), and others have considerably broadened our understanding of local societies as well as relations between men and women in the household and at work. Another productive area of research has been the study of currency and monetary policy. Mate, Mayhew, Munro, and Prestwich (Chapter 6) have convincingly argued for the fundamental importance of money supply in determining the course of the medieval economy. Population change was not the only determining factor in the late medieval economy. In this respect, Robert Brenner has added another challenge to the demographic explanation by arguing forcefully for the primacy of social relations in explaining economic change.

This bibliography is arranged by chapter, each section listing those works on which the material in the chapter is based. Many findings, of course, have been used throughout the book; as a general rule, a book or article is cited only once under the chapter in which reference to it is first made. The bibliography is not intended to be exhaustive but it is hoped that it suggests the scope of current research as well as indicating scholarly debts.

The first section lists the works consulted for Chapters 1 and 2 in particular and the rest of the book generally. The first part contains general overviews of the period, biographies, and political surveys (additional works on politics can be found under Chapter 13). The second part covers surveys of society and economics. For convenience, part three provides full references to collections of articles or papers which are cited under particular chapters (though if only one article is cited, the collection is cited along with it). The leading chronicles for the period are given in part four. Chronicles provide invaluable guidance for the course of events, but do have several drawbacks. First, they do not offer much insight into Edward III's personality or the character of those around him. Secondly, after about 1340, they are concerned primarily with military events, often reciting verbatim the newsletters that Edward issued to keep his subjects informed about the war, and only refer to domestic affairs in passing. Finally, very few have been translated. Those translations which are available have been noted. The last section deals with general sources useful for Edward's reign and referred to throughout the book.

Abbreviations

AgHR	*Agricultural History Review*
BHRS	*Bedfordshire Historical Records Society*
BIHR	*Bulletin of the Institute of Historical Research*
BJRL	*Bulletin of the John Rylands Library*
EAH	*Essex Archaeology and History*
EcHR	*Economic History Review*
EGW	Dunham et al., *The English Government at Work*
EHR	*English Historical Review*
JBS	*Journal of British Studies*
JEcH	*Journal of Economic History*
JEH	*Journal of Ecclesiastical History*
JMH	*Journal of Medieval History*
JRH	*Journal of Religious History*
LHR	*Law and History Review*
MH	*Midland History*
MS	*Mediaeval Studies*
NC	*Numismatic Chronicle*
NH	*Northern History*
NMS	*Nottingham Medieval Studies*
SAC	*Sussex Archaeological Collections*
SH	*Southern History*
SMRH	*Studies in Medieval and Renaissance History*
TBGAS	*Transactions of the Bristol and Gloucestershire Archaeological Society*
THSLC	*Transactions of the Historical Society of Lancashire and Cheshire*
TNNAS	*Transactions of the Norfolk and Norwich Archaeological Society*
TRHS	*Transactions of the Royal Historical Society*
UBHJ	*University of Birmingham Historical Journal*

1. Biographies and political surveys

Allmand, Christopher. *The Hundred Years War: England and France at war c. 1300–c. 1450* (Cambridge, 1988).

Armitage-Smith, Sydney. *John of Gaunt, king of Castile and Leon, duke of Aquitaine and Lancaster, Earl of Derby, Lincoln, and Leicester, seneschal of England.* Reprinted (New York, 1964).

Barber, Richard W. *Edward, prince of Wales and Aquitaine: a biography of the Black Prince* (London, 1978).

Barnes, Joshua. *The history of that most victorious monarch Edward III king of England and France and lord of Ireland* (Cambridge, 1699).

Campbell, James. 'England, Scotland and the Hundred Years War in the fourteenth century'. In Hale, J. R., J. R. L. Highfield, and B. Smalley, eds., *Europe in the late middle ages* (London, 1963).

Davies, James Conway. *The baronial opposition to Edward II, its character and policy. A study in administrative history* (Cambridge, 1918).

Fryde, Natalie. *The tyranny and fall of Edward II, 1321–1326* (Cambridge, 1977).

Guenée, Bernard. *States and rulers in later medieval Europe.* Trans. Juliet Vale (Oxford, 1985).

Hamilton, J. S. *Piers Gaveston, earl of Cornwall, 1307–1312: politics and patronage in the reign of Edward II* (Detroit and London, 1988).

Harriss, G. L. *King, parliament and public finance in medieval England to 1369* (Oxford, 1975).

Johnson, Paul. *The life and times of Edward III* (London, 1973).

Johnstone, Hilda. 'Isabella, the she-wolf of France'. *History* 21 (1936): 208–18.

Kaeuper, Richard W. *War, justice, and public order: England and France in the late middle ages* (Oxford, 1988).

Keen, Maurice. *England in the later middle ages: a political history* (London and New York, 1973).

Le Patourel, John. 'Edward III and the kingdom of France'. *History* 43 (1958): 173–89.

Lucas, Henry S. *The Low Countries and the Hundred Years War, 1326–1347* (Ann Arbor, 1929).

McKisack, May. *The fourteenth century, 1307–1399* (Oxford, 1959).
　'Edward III and the historians'. *History* 45 (1960), 1–15.

Maddicott, J. R. *Thomas of Lancaster, 1307–1322. A study in the reign of Edward II* (Oxford, 1970).

Nicholson, Ranald. *Edward II and the Scots: the formative years of a military career, 1327–1335* (Oxford, 1965).

Packe, Michael. *King Edward III* (London, 1983).

Perroy, Edouard. *The Hundred Years War* (New York, 1965).

Phillips, J. R. S. *Aymer de Valence, earl of Pembroke, 1307–1324. Baronial politics in the reign of Edward II* (Oxford, 1972).
　'The "middle party" and the negotiating of the treaty of Leake, August 1318: a reinterpretation'. *BIHR* 46 (1973): 11–27.

Prestwich, Michael. *The three Edwards: war and state in England 1272–1377* (New York, 1980).

Tout, Thomas F. *Chapters in the administrative history of medieval England: the wardrobe, the chamber and the small seals.* Vol. III (Manchester, 1928).

The place of the reign of Edward II in English history. 2nd edn (Manchester, 1936).

Tuck, Anthony. *Crown and nobility, 1272–1461: political conflict in late medieval England* (London, 1985).

2. Social and economic surveys

Aston, T. H. and C. H. E. Philpin, *The Brenner debate: agrarian class structure and economic development in pre-industrial Europe* (Cambridge, 1985).

Bolton, J. L. *The medieval English economy, 1150–1500* (London and Totowa, 1980).

Hallam, H. E. *Rural England 1066–1348* (Brighton and Atlantic Heights, 1981).

Hallam, H. E., ed. *The agrarian history of England and Wales*. Vol. II, 1042–1350 (Cambridge, 1988).

Hatcher, John. *Plague, population and the English economy 1348–1530* (London, 1977).

Hatcher, John and Edward Miller. *Medieval England: rural society and economic change, 1086–1348* (London and New York, 1978).

Postan, M. M. *The medieval economy and society. An economic history of Britain in the middle ages* (London, 1972).

'Medieval agrarian society in its prime: England', in M. M. Postan, ed., *The Cambridge economic history of Europe*, vol. II, 2nd edn (Cambridge, 1966).

Power, Eileen. *Medieval women*. Ed. M. M. Postan (Cambridge, 1975).

Titow, J. Z. *English rural society 1200–1350* (London, 1969).

3. Collections of articles, papers, or studies

Allmand, C. T., ed. *War, literature, and politics in the late middle ages* (New York, 1976).

Aston, T. H., P. R. Coss, C. Dyer, and J. Thirsk, eds. *Social relations and ideas: essays in honour of R. H. Hilton* (Cambridge, 1983).

Aston, T. H. and R. H. Hilton, eds. *The English Rising of 1381* (Cambridge, 1984).

Baker, Derek. *Sanctity and secularity: the church and the world*. Studies in Church History, vol. IX (Oxford, 1973).

Bonfield, Lloyd, Richard M. Smith, and Keith Wrightson, eds. *The world we have gained: histories of population and social structure. Essays presented to Peter Laslett on his seventieth birthday* (Oxford, 1986).

Cam, Helen M. *Law-finders and law-makers in medieval England* (London, 1962).

Liberties and communities in medieval England: collected studies in local administration and topography (Cambridge, 1944; reprinted London, 1963).

Charles, Lindsey and Lorna Duffin, eds. *Women and work in pre-industrial England* (London, 1985).

Coleman, D. C. and A. H. John, eds. *Trade, government and economy in pre-industrial England: essays presented to F. J. Fisher* (London, 1976).

Crittall, Elizabeth, ed. *VCH: Wiltshire*. Vol. IV (London, 1959).

Crittall, Elizabeth and R. B. Pugh, eds. *VCH: Wiltshire*. Vol. V (London, 1957).

Darby, H. C., ed. *A new historical geography of England* (Cambridge, 1973).

Davies, R. G. and J. H. Denton, eds. *The English parliament in the middle ages* (Manchester, 1981).

Dunham, William H., William A. Morris, Joseph R. Strayer, and James F. Willard, eds. *The English government at work, 1327–1336.* 3 vols. (Cambridge, Mass., 1940–50).

Dyer, Christopher. *Standards of living in the later middle ages: social change in England c. 1200–1520* (Cambridge, 1989).

Edwards, J. G., V. H. Galbraith, E. F. Jacob, eds. *Historical essays in honour of James Tait* (Manchester, 1933).

Eler, Mary and Maryanne Kowaleski, eds. *Women and power in the middle ages* (Athens and London, 1988).

Fowler, K. ed. *The Hundred Years War* (London, 1971).

Fryde, E. B. and Edward Miller, eds. *Historical studies of the English parliament.* Vol. I: origins to 1399 (Cambridge, 1970).

Goody Jack, Joan Thirsk, and E. P. Thompson, eds. *Family and inheritance: rural society in western Europe 1200–1800* (Cambridge, 1976).

Hanawalt, Barbara A., ed. *Women and work in preindustrial Europe* (Bloomington, 1986).

Harvey, P. D. A., ed. *The peasant land market in medieval England* (Oxford, 1984).

Herbert, N. M., ed. *VCH: Gloucestershire.* Vol. IV (London, 1988).

Hilton, R. H. *The English peasantry in the later middle ages* (Oxford, 1975).

Class conflict and the crisis of feudalism: essays in medieval social history (London, 1985).

Hoskins, W. G. and R. A. McKinley, eds. *VCH: Leicestershire.* Vol. II (London, 1954).

VCH: Leicestershire. Vol. III (London, 1955).

Hudson, Anne and Michael Wilks, eds. *From Ockham to Wyclif.* Studies in Church History, *Subsidia* 5 (Oxford, 1987).

Hunnisett, R. F. and J. B. Post, eds. *Medieval legal records edited in memory of C. A. F. Meekings* (London, 1978).

LaMonte, John L. and Charles H. Taylor, eds. *Anniversary essays in mediaeval history by students of Charles Homer Haskins* (Boston, 1929).

Levy, Bernard S. and Paul E. Szarmach, eds. *The fourteenth century.* Acta. Vol. IV (Binghampton, 1978).

McKinley, R. A., ed. *VCH: Leicestershire.* Vol. IV, *The city of Leicester* (London, 1958).

Mayhew, N. J., ed. *Edwardian monetary affairs.* British Archaeological Reports 36 (Oxford, 1977).

Coinage in the Low Countries. British Archaeological Reports 54 (Oxford, 1979).

Ormrod, W. M., ed. *England in the fourteenth century: proceedings of the 1985 Harlaxton Symposium* (Woodbridge and Dover, 1986).

Powicke, Michael R. and Thayron R. Sanquist, eds. *Essays in English history presented to Bertie Wilkinson* (Toronto, 1969).

Raftis, J. A., ed. *Pathways to medieval peasants* (Toronto, 1981).

Richardson, H. G. and G. O. Sayles. *The English parliament in the middle ages* (London, 1981).

Scattergood, V. J. and J. W. Sherborne, eds. *English court culture in the later middle ages* (London, 1983).

Smith, Richard M., ed. *Land, kinship and life-cycle* (Cambridge, 1984).

Tout, Thomas F. *The collected papers of Thomas Frederick Tout with a memoir and bibliography.* Vol. III (Manchester, 1934).

Unwin, George, ed. *Finance and trade under Edward III* (Manchester, 1918).

Victoria history of the counties of England. Ed. Herbert A. Doubleday, William Page, Louis Salzman, and Ralph B. Pugh (London, 1900– in progress).

Wilkinson, Bertie. *Studies in the constitutional history of the thirteenth and fourteenth centuries.* 2nd edn (Manchester, 1952).

4. Chronicles

Annales Paulini, 1307–1344. In vol. II of Stubbs, *Chronicles*, q.v.

The anonimalle chronicle, 1333 to 1381. Ed. V. H. Galbraith (Manchester, 1927).

Avesbury, Robert de. *De gestis mirabilibus regis Edwardi tertii.* Ed. Edward Maunde Thompson. Rolls Series, 93 (London, 1889).

Baker, Geoffrey le. *Chronicon Galfridi le Baker de Swynebroke.* Ed. Edward Maunde Thompson (Oxford, 1889).

Bel, Jean le. *Les vrayes chroniques de messire Jehan le Bel.* Ed. M. L. Polain. 2 vols. (Brussels, 1863).

The Brut, or chronicles of England. Ed. Friedrich W. D. Brie. 2 vols. Early English Text Society, Original Series, 131, 136 (London, 1906–8).

Chandos, Herald of. *Life of the Black Prince.* Ed. and trans. M. K. Pope and Eleanor C. Lodge (Oxford, 1910).

Chronica Johannis de Reading et anonymi Cantuariensis, 1346–1367. Ed. James Tait (Manchester, 1914).

Chronicon Angliae, 1328–1388 auctore monacho quodam sancti Albani. Ed. Edward Maunde Thompson. Rolls Series, 64 (London, 1874). A translation for the years 1376–7 can be found in Thomas Amyot, 'Transcript of a chronicle in the Harleian Library of Mss. No. 6217, entitled "An historicall relation of certain passages about the end of king Edward the Third and of his death"'. *Archaeologia* 22 (1829): 204–84.

Chronicon de Lanercost, 1201–1346. Ed. Joseph Stevenson. Bannatyne Club (Edinburgh, 1839). Maxwell, Herbert, trans. *Chronicle of Lanercost, 1272–1346* (Glasgow, 1913).

Chroniques de London depuis l'an 44 Hen. III. jusqu'à l'an 17 Edw. III. Ed. George James Aungier. Camden Society Publications, Old Series, 28 (London, 1844).

Froissart, Jean. *Chroniques.* Ed. Kervyn de Lettenhove. 25 vols. (Brussels, 1867–1877). Various translations are available, e.g. Thomas Johnes, trans. *Chronicles of England, France, Spain, and the adjoining countries.* 2 vols. (London, 1844); Brereton, Geoffrey, trans. and ed. *Chronicles* (Harmondsworth, 1968).

Gesta Edwardi de Carnarvan auctore canonico Bridlingtoniensi, cum continuatione AD 1377. In vol. II of Stubbs, *Chronicles*, q.v.

Gransden, Antonia. *Historical writing in England II: c. 1307 to the early sixteenth century* (London and Henley, 1982).

Gray, Thomas. *Scalacronica.* Ed. Joseph Stevenson. Maitland Club (Edinburgh, 1836). Maxwell, Herbert, trans. *Scalacronica, the reigns of Edward I, Edward II, and Edward III as recorded by Sir Thomas Gray* (Glasgow, 1907).

Higden, Ranulf. *Polychronicon Radulphi Higden monachi Cestrensis.* Ed. Churchill Babington and J. R. Lumby, 9 vols. Rolls Series, 41 (London, 1865–86).

Knighton, Henry. *Chronicon Henrici Knighton vel Cnitthon monachi Leycestrensis.* Ed. Joseph Rawson Lumby. 2 vols. Rolls Series, 92 (1889–95).

Murimuth, Adam. *Continuatio chronicarum.* Ed. Edward Maunde Thompson. Rolls Series, 93 (London, 1889).

Stubbs, William, ed. *Chronicles of the reigns of Edward I and Edward II.* 2 vols. Rolls Series, 76 (London, 1882–3).

Taylor, John. *English historical literature in the fourteenth century* (Oxford, 1987).

Vita Edwardi II, Monachi cuiusdam Malmesberiensis. Ed. and trans. N. Denholm-Young (London, 1957).

5. Miscellaneous sources

A good short debate between Winner and Waster. Ed. I. Gollanz (London, 1920).

Anglo-Norman political songs. Ed. Isabel S. T. Aspin. Anglo-Norman Text Society, Texts 11 (Oxford, 1953).

Brinton, Thomas. *The sermons of Thomas Brinton, bishop of Rochester (1373–1389).* Ed. Sister Mary Aquinas Devlin. 2 vols. Camden Society Publications, 3rd series, 85, 86 (London, 1954).

Calendar of inquisitions miscellaneous (chancery), Henry III–Henry V. 7 vols. to date (London: HMSO, 1916–68).

Calendar of the charter rolls, 1226–1516. 6 vols. (London: HMSO, 1903–27).

Calendar of the close rolls (1272–1485). 45 vols. (London: HMSO, 1892–1954).

Calendar of the fine rolls. 22 vols. (London: HMSO, 1911–62).

Calendar of the patent rolls (1232–1509). 52 vols. (London: HMSO, 1891–1916).

Chaucer, Geoffrey. *The Canterbury Tales.* Trans. Nevill Coghill (Harmondsworth, 1977).

Cockayne, George E. *The complete peerage of England.* Ed. Vicary Gibbs, Herbert A. Doubleday, Duncan Warrand, Geoffrey White, et al. 12 vols. in 13 (London, 1910–59).

English historical documents. Ed. David C. Douglas. Vol. III, 1189–1327, ed. Harry Rothwell (London, 1974). Vol. IV, 1327–1485, ed. A. R. Myers (London, 1969).

Foedera, conventiones, litterae, et cujuscunque generis acta publica, etc. Ed. Thomas Rymer. New edn by John Caley, Adam Clarke, and Frederic Holbrooke. 4 vols. in 7 (London: Record Commission, 1816–69).

Foss, Edward. *The judges of England; with sketches of their lives.* 9 vols. (London, 1848–64).

Handbook of British chronology. Ed. E. B. Fryde, D. E. Greenway, S. Porter, and I. Roy. 3rd edn (London, 1986).

L'histoire de Guillaume le Marechal, comte de Striguil et de Pembroke, regent d'Angleterre de 1216 a 1219. Ed. Paul Meyer. 3 vols. Société de l'histoire de France (Paris 1891–1901).

Lancaster, Henry of. *Le livre de seyntz medicines: the unpublished devotional treatise of Henry of Lancaster.* Ed. E. J. Arnould. Anglo-Norman Text Society, Texts 2 (Oxford, 1940).

Langland, William. *Piers Plowman.* Ed. J. A. W. Bennett (Oxford, 1972). Translated by J. F. Goodridge (Harmondsworth, 1966).

The lay subsidy of 1334. Ed. Robin E. Glasscock (London, 1975).

'Ministers' accounts of the manor of Petworth, 1347–1353'. Ed. L. F. Salzman. *Sussex Record Society* 55 (1955).

Political poems and songs relating to English history, composed during the period from the accession of Edward III to that of Richard III. Ed. Thomas Wright. 2 vols. Rolls Series, 14 (London, 1859–61).

The register of John de Grandisson, bishop of Exeter (A.D. 1327–1369). Ed. F. C. Hingeston-Randolph. 3 vols. (London, 1894–9).

Reports from the lords' committees touching the dignity of a peer. 5 vols. (London, 1820–9).

Rotuli parliamentorum anglie hactenus inediti, MCCLXXIX–MCCCLXXII. Ed. Henry G. Richardson and George O. Sayles. Camden Society Publications. 3rd series 51 (1935).

Rotuli parliamentorum; ut et petitiones, et placita in parliamento. 6 vols. (London: Record Commission, 1832).

Second report of the deputy keeper of the public records (London, 1841).

The song of Lewes. Ed. and trans. Charles L. Kingsford (Oxford, 1890).

De speculo regis Edwardi III. Ed. Joseph Moisant (Paris, 1891).

Statutes of the realm, 1101–1713. Ed. Alexander Luders, Thomas E. Tomlins, John Raithby, et al. 11 vols. (London: Record Commission, 1810–28).

Thomas of Erceldoune. Part 1, ed. Ingebord Nixon. Publications of the Department of English, University of Copenhagen. Vol. IX (Copenhagen, 1980).

Walter of Henley and other treatises on estate management and accounting. Ed. Dorothea Oschinsky (Oxford, 1971).

The wardrobe book of William de Norwell, 12 July 1338 to 27 May 1340. Ed. Henry S. Lucas, Bryce Lyon, Mary Lyon, and Jean de Sturler (Brussels, 1983).

6. Sources for Chapter 3

There have been two important and complementary avenues into the study of the medieval English countryside. One is the estate study, based on an exhaustive exploration of all the materials of a particular manor or estate. The other is the reconstruction of village life. Modern work on the village community using manorial court rolls dates from Homans' masterful study, and has been greatly expanded in recent years by Raftis and his students as well as by Campbell, Razi, and Smith. Hanawalt gives a good introduction to the topic and historiography. Bennett has used this approach to cast new light on the role of women in the family and village community.

Concentration on peasant households has recently overshadowed work on manorial lordship and its impact on villages and peasants. Beginning with Hatcher's revisionist article, some historians have played down the differences between freedom and villeinage. It is crucial, therefore, to refer to studies by Hilton, Searle, and others who have placed lordship at the centre of their conceptions of rural society. Estate studies constitute a remarkable historiographic tradition. Only a few, which have been used directly in the text, are mentioned here and under Chapters 6 and 7.

Ault, Warren O. *Open-field farming in medieval England: a study of village by-laws* (London, 1972).
'The village church and the village community in medieval England'. *Speculum* 45 (1970): 197–215.
Baker, A. R. H. and R. A. Butlin, eds. *Studies of field systems in the British Isles* (Cambridge, 1973).
Bennett, Judith M. *Women in the medieval English countryside: gender and household in Brigstock before the plague* (Oxford, 1987).
'The tie that binds: peasant marriages and peasant families in late medieval England'. *Journal of Interdisciplinary History* 15 (1984): 111–29.
'Medieval peasant marriage: an examination of marriage licence fines in the *Liber Gersumarum*'. In Raftis, *Pathways*, 193–246, q.v.
'The village ale-wife: women and brewing in fourteenth-century England'. In Hanawalt, *Women and work*, 30–6, q.v.
'Public power and authority in the medieval English countryside'. In Eler and Kowaleski, *Women and power*, 18–36, q.v.
Blanchard, Ian. 'Industrial employment and the rural market 1380–1520'. In Smith, *Land, kinship and life-cycle*, 227–76, q.v.
Brandon, P. F. 'Cereal yields on the Sussex estates of Battle abbey during the later middle ages', *EcHR*, 2nd series, 25 (1972), 403–20.
Britnell, R. H. 'Finchingfield Park under the plough, 1341–2', *EAH* 9 (1977): 107–12.
'Agriculture in a region of ancient enclosure, 1185–1500', *NMS* 27 (1983): 37–55.
Britton, Edward. *The community of the vill: a study in the history of the family and village life in fourteenth-century England* (Toronto, 1977).
'The peasant family in fourteenth-century England'. *Peasant Studies* 5 (1976): 2–7.
Campbell, Bruce M. S. 'Population pressure, inheritance and the land market in a fourteenth-century peasant community'. In Smith, *Land, kinship and life-cycle*, 87–134, q.v.
'Population change and the genesis of commonfields on a Norfolk manor'. *EcHR*, 2nd series, 33 (1980): 174–92.
'The regional uniqueness of English field systems? Some evidence from eastern Norfolk'. *AgHR* 29 (1981): 16–28.
'Arable productivity in medieval England: some evidence from Norfolk', *JEcH* 43 (1983): 379–404.
'Agricultural progress in medieval England: some evidence from eastern Norfolk'. *EcHR*, 2nd series, 36 (1983): 26–46.

Clark, Elaine. 'Debt litigation in a late medieval English vill'. In Raftis, *Pathways*, 247–79, q.v.

'Some aspects of social security in medieval England'. *JEH* 7 (1984): 307–20.

'The custody of children in English manor courts'. *LHR* 3 (1985): 333–48.

De Windt, Anne. 'Peasant power structures in fourteenth-century King's Ripton'. *MS* 38 (1976): 236–67.

'A peasant land market and its participants: King's Ripton, 1280–1400'. *MH* 4 (1978): 142–59.

De Windt, Edwin Brezette. *Land and people in Holywell-cum-Needingworth. Structure of tenure and patterns of social organization in an East Midlands village, 1252–1457* (Toronto, 1972).

Dodwell, B. 'Holdings and inheritance in medieval East Anglia'. *EcHR*, 2nd series, 20 (1967): 53–66.

Dyer, Christopher. 'English diet in the later middle ages'. In Aston, *Social relations*, 191–216, q.v.

Faith, R. J. 'Peasant families and inheritance customs in medieval England'. *AgHR* 14 (1966): 77–95.

'Berkshire: fourteenth and fifteenth centuries'. In Harvey, *Peasant land market*, 107–77, q.v.

'The "Great Rumour" of 1377 and peasant ideology'. In Aston, *The English Rising*, 43–74, q.v.

Farmer, D. L. 'Grain yields on the Winchester manors in the later middle ages'. *EcHR*, 2nd series, 30 (1977): 555–66.

'Grain yields on Westminster abbey manors, 1276–1410'. *Canadian Journal of History* 18 (1983): 331–47.

Finberg, H. P. R. *Tavistock abbey: a study in the social and economic history of Devon*. 2nd edn (Newton Abbot, 1969).

Fox, H. S. A. 'The chronology of enclosure and economic development in medieval Devon'. *EcHR*, 2nd series, 28 (1975): 181–202.

'The alleged transformation from two-field to three-field systems in medieval England'. *EcHR*, 2nd series, 39 (1986): 526–48.

Franklin, Peter. 'Peasant widows' "liberation" and remarriage before the Black Death'. *EcHR*, 2nd series, 39 (1986): 184–204.

Hanawalt, Barbara A. *The ties that bound: peasant families in medieval England* (Oxford, 1986).

'Peasant women's contribution to the home economy in late medieval England'. In Hanawalt, *Women and work*, 3–19, q.v.

Harvey, Barbara. *Westminster abbey and its estates in the middle ages* (Oxford, 1977).

Harvey, P. D. A. *A medieval Oxfordshire village: Cuxham, 1240 to 1400* (Oxford, 1965).

'Introduction' and 'Conclusion'. In Harvey, *Peasant land market*, 1–28, 328–56, q.v.

Hatcher, J. 'English serfdom and villeinage: towards a reassessment'. *Past and Present* 90 (1981): 3–39.

Hilton, R. H. *A medieval society: the West Midlands at the end of the thirteenth century* (London, 1966).

'Medieval agrarian history'. In Hoskins, *VCH: Leicestershire*, 145–98, q.v.

'Reasons for inequality among medieval peasants'. *Journal of Peasant Studies* 5 (1977/8): 271–84.

Hogan, M. Patricia. 'The labour of their days: work in the medieval village'. *SMRH*, 2nd series, 8 (1986): 75–186.

Holt, Richard. 'Whose were the profits of corn milling? An aspect of the changing relationship between the abbots of Glastonbury and their tenants 1086–1350'. *Past and Present* 116 (1987): 3–23.

Homans, George C. *English villagers of the thirteenth century* (Cambridge, Mass., 1941).

Howell, Cicely. 'Peasant inheritance customs in the Midlands, 1280–1700'. In Goody, *Family and inheritance*, 112–55, q.v.

Hyams, Paul. *King, lords and peasants in medieval England: the common law of villeinage in the twelfth and thirteenth centuries* (Oxford, 1980).

Jones, Andrew. 'Caddington, Kensworth, and Dunstable in 1297'. *EcHR*, 2nd series, 32 (1979): 316–27.

King, Edmund. *Peterborough abbey 1086–1310: a study in the land market* (Cambridge, 1973).

Kosminsky, E. A. *Studies in the agrarian history of England in the thirteenth century*. Ed. R. H. Hilton, trans. Ruth Kisch (Oxford, 1956).

Langdon, John. *Horses, oxen and technological innovation: the use of draught animals in English farming from 1066 to 1500* (Cambridge, 1986).

Long, W. Harwood. 'The low corn yields of medieval England'. *EcHR*, 2nd series, 32 (1979): 464–9.

McIntosh, Marjorie K. 'Land, tenure, and population in the royal manor of Havering, Essex, 1251–1352/3'. *EcHR*, 2nd series, 33 (1980): 17–31.

Mate, Mavis. 'Medieval agrarian practices: the determining factors?' *AgHR* 33 (1985): 22–31.

Middleton, Christopher. 'The sexual division of labour in feudal England'. *New Left Review* 113–14 (1979): 147–68.

North, Tim. 'Legerwite in the thirteenth and fourteenth centuries'. *Past and Present* 111 (1986): 3–16.

Penn, Simon A. G. 'Female wage-earners in late fourteenth-century England'. *AgHR* 35 (1987): 1–14.

Pimsler, Martin. 'Solidarity in the medieval village? The evidence of personal pledging at Elton, Huntingdonshire'. *JBS* 17 (1977): 1–11.

Platts, Graham. *Land and people in medieval Lincolnshire. History of Lincolnshire*. Ed. Maurice Barley. Vol. IV (Lincoln, 1985).

Raftis, J. Ambrose. *Tenure and mobility. Studies in the social history of the mediaeval English village* (Toronto, 1964).

Warboys: two hundred years in the life of an English mediaeval village (Toronto, 1974).

'Social structures in five East Midland villages'. *EcHR*, 2nd series, 18 (1965): 83–99.

Ravensdale, Jack. 'Population changes and the transfer of customary land on a Cambridgeshire manor in the fourteenth century'. In Smith, *Land, kinship and life-cycle*, 197–226, q.v.

Razi, Zvi. *Life, marriage and death in a medieval parish. Economy, society and demography in Halesowen 1270–1400* (Cambridge, 1980).

'The struggles between the abbots of Halesowen and their tenants in the thirteenth and fourteenth centuries'. In Aston, *Social relations*, 151–67, q.v.

Roden, D. 'Demesne farming in the Chiltern Hills'. *AgHR* 17 (1969): 9–23.

'Fragmentation of farms and fields in the Chiltern Hills, thirteenth century and later'. *MS* 31 (1969): 225–38.

Searle, Eleanor. *Lordship and community: Battle abbey and its banlieu 1066–1538* (Toronto, 1974).

'Seigneurial control of women's marriage: the antecedents and function of merchet in England'. *Past and Present* 82 (1979): 3–43.

Slota, Leon. 'Law, land transfer and lordship on the estates of St Albans abbey in the thirteenth and fourteenth centuries'. *LHR* 6 (1988): 119–38.

Smith, Richard M. 'Kin and neighbours in a thirteenth-century Suffolk community'. *JFH* 4 (1979): 219–56.

'Some thoughts on "hereditary" and "proprietary" rights in land under customary law in thirteenth and early fourteenth century England'. *LHR* 1 (1983): 95–128.

'Women's property rights under customary law: some developments in the thirteenth and fourteenth centuries'. *TRHS*, 5th series, 36 (1986): 165–94.

'Some issues concerning families and their property in rural England 1250–1800'. In Smith, *Land, kinship and life-cycle*, 1–86, q.v.

'Families and their land in an area of partible inheritance: Redgrave, Suffolk, 1260–1320'. In Smith, *Land, kinship and life-cycle*, 135–96, q.v.

'Marriage processes in the English past: some continuities'. In Bonfield, *World we have gained*, 43–99, q.v.

Stinson, Marie. 'Assarting and poverty in early fourteenth-century West Yorkshire', *Landscape History* 5 (1983): 53–67.

Titow, J. Z. *Winchester yields: a study in medieval agricultural productivity* (Cambridge, 1972).

'Some differences between manors and their effects on the condition of the peasant in the thirteenth century'. *AgHR* 10 (1962): 1–13.

Wales, Tim. 'Poverty, poor relief and the life-cycle: some evidence from seventeenth-century Norfolk'. In Smith, *Land, kinship and life-cycle*, 351–404, q.v.

Waugh, Scott L. 'The confiscated lands of the Contrariants in Gloucestershire and Herefordshire, in 1322: an economic and social study'. Ph.D. thesis, University of London, 1975.

Williamson, Janet. 'Norfolk: thirteenth century'. In Harvey, *Peasant land market*, 31–105, q.v.

7. Sources for Chapter 4

In recent years, studies of English towns have swung away from the legal/institutional tradition founded by Stevenson and Tait toward the kind of investigation of social and economic conditions pioneered by Sylvia Thrupp. Work by Britnell,

Kowaleski, Platt, and others has done much to delineate the structure of town life outside London. As in village studies, an important and revealing area of new research is the role of women in urban work and society (see Bennett and Kowaleski, Goldberg, Hilton, Hutton, and Lacey). Hilton has done much to reclassify English towns and focus attention on the vital role of small towns in the rural economy. Biddick, Britnell, Kowaleski, and others are just beginning to show how pervasive market relations were in country life and the lives of peasants. This familiarity with markets has sometimes been used to argue for the 'individualism' of the English peasantry or nascent capitalism in the medieval economy, but the nature of peasant engagement in buying and selling and the relationship between markets and lordship argue that the phenomena were integral aspects of the seigneurial economy and much less modern than they are sometimes made out to be.

Astill, G. G. 'Archaeology and the smaller medieval town'. *Urban History Yearbook* (1985): 46–53.

Bartlett, J. N. 'The expansion and decline of York in the later middle ages'. *EcHR*, 2nd series, 12 (1959–60): 17–33.

Bennett, Judith M. and Maryanne Kowaleski. 'Crafts, guilds, and women in the middle ages: fifty years after Marian K. Dale'. *Signs* 14 (1989): 474–88.

Bennett, Michael J. *Community, class and careerism: Cheshire and Lancashire society in the age of Sir Gawain and the Green Knight* (Cambridge, 1983).

Beresford, Maurice W. *New towns of the middle ages: town plantation in England, Wales, and Gascony* (London, 1967).

Beresford, Maurice W. and H. P. R. Finburg. *English medieval boroughs: a handlist* (Newton Abbot, 1973).

Biddick, Kathleen. 'Medieval English peasants and market involvement'. *JEcH* 45 (1985): 823–31.

'Missing links: taxable wealth, markets, and stratification among medieval English peasants'. *Journal of Interdisciplinary History* 18 (1987): 277–98.

Bridbury, A. R. 'English provincial towns in the later middle ages'. *EcHR*, 2nd series, 34 (1981): 1–24.

Britnell, R. H. *Growth and decline in Colchester, 1300–1525* (Cambridge, 1986).

'*Avantagium mercatoris*: a custom in medieval English trade'. *NMS* 24 (1980): 37–50.

'Burghal characteristics of market towns in medieval England'. *Durham University Journal*, NS, 42 (1981): 147–51.

'Essex markets before 1350'. *EAH* 13 (1981): 15–21.

'The proliferation of markets in England, 1200–1349'. *EcHR*, 2nd series, 34 (1981): 209–21.

'The fields and pastures of Colchester, 1280–1350'. *EAH* 19 (1988): 159–65.

Butcher, A. F. 'Rent and the urban economy: Oxford and Canterbury in the later middle ages'. *Southern History* 1 (1979): 11–43.

Coates, B. E. 'The origin and distribution of markets and fairs in medieval Derbyshire'. *Derbyshire Archaeological Journal* 85 (1965): 92–111.

Curtis, Margaret. 'The London lay subsidy of 1332'. In Unwin, *Finance and trade*, 35–60, q.v.

Dale, Marian K. 'Social and economic history, 1066–1509'. In McKinley, *Leicester*, 31–54, q.v.

Dobson, R. B. 'Admissions to the freedom of the city of York in the later middle ages'. *EcHR*, 2nd series, 26 (1973): 1–22.

Dyer, Christopher. 'The consumer and the market in the later middle ages'. *EcHR*, 2nd series, 42 (1989): 305–27.

Ekwall, E. *Studies on the population of medieval London* (Stockholm, 1956).

Erskine, Audrey M. 'Political and administrative history, 1066–1509'. In McKinley, *Leicester*, 1–30, q.v.

Fraser, Constance M. 'The pattern of trade in the north-east of England, 1265–1350'. *NH* 4 (1969): 44–66.

Goldberg, P. J. P. 'Female labour, service and marriage in the late medieval urban north'. *NH* 22 (1986): 18–38.

'Marriage, migration, servanthood and life-cycle in Yorkshire towns of the later middle ages: some York cause paper evidence'. *Continuity and Change* 1 (1986): 141–69.

Gooder, Arthur and Eileen Gooder. 'Coventry before 1355: unity or division? The importance of the earl's half'. *MH* 6 (1981): 1–38.

Gottfried, Robert S. *Bury St Edmunds and the urban crisis: 1250–1539* (Princeton, 1982).

Herbert, N. M. 'Medieval Gloucester, 1066–1327', in Herbert, *VCH: Gloucestershire*, 13–72, q.v.

Hill, J. F. W. *Medieval Lincoln* (Cambridge, 1948).

Hilton, R. H. 'Lords, burgesses and hucksters'. *Past and Present* 97 (1982): 1–15.

'The small town and urbanisation – Evesham in the middle ages'. *MH* 7 (1982): 1–8.

'Towns in societies – medieval England'. *Urban History Yearbook* (1982): 9–13.

'Small town society in England before the Black Death'. *Past and Present* 105 (1984): 53–78.

'Medieval market towns'. *Past and Present* 109 (1985): 3–23.

'Towns in English feudal society'. In Hilton, *Class conflict*, 175–86, q.v.

'Women traders in medieval England'. In Hilton, *Class conflict*, 205–15, q.v.

Hutton, Diane. 'Women in fourteenth-century Shrewsbury'. In Charles, *Women and work*, 83–99, q.v.

Keene, Derek. 'A new study of London before the great fire'. *Urban History Yearbook* (1984): 11–21.

Knoop, D. and G. P. Jones. *The mediaeval mason: an economic history of English stone building in the later middle ages and early modern times*. 3rd edn revised (Manchester, 1967).

Kowaleski, Maryanne. 'The commercial dominance of a medieval provincial oligarchy: Exeter in the late fourteenth century'. *MS* 46 (1984): 355–84.

'Women's work in a market town: Exeter in the late fourteenth century'. In Hanawalt, *Women and work*, 145–64, q.v.

'Local markets and merchants in late fourteenth-century Exeter'. Ph.D. thesis, University of Toronto, 1982.

Lacey, Kay E. 'Women and work in fourteenth- and fifteenth-century London'. In Charles, *Women and work*, 24–82, q.v.

Lloyd, T. H. *Some aspects of the building industry in medieval Stratford-upon-Avon. Dugdale Society, Occasional Papers* 14 (1961).

Lobel, Mary D. *The borough of Bury St Edmunds: a study in the government and development of a monastic town* (Oxford, 1935).

'A detailed account of the 1327 rising at Bury St Edmunds and the subsequent trial'. *Suffolk Institute of Archaeology* 21 (1933): 215–31.

McClure, Peter. 'Patterns of migration in the late middle ages: the evidence of English place-name surnames'. *EcHR*, 2nd series, 32 (1979): 167–82.

McIntosh, Marjorie K. *Autonomy and community: the royal manor of Havering 1200–1500* (Cambridge, 1986).

Maitland, Frederic W. *Township and borough* (Cambridge, 1898).

Miller, Edward. 'Medieval York'. In Tillot, P. M., ed. *VCH Yorkshire: the city of York* (London, 1961): 25–116.

Moore, Ellen Wedermeyer. *The fairs of medieval England: an introductory study* (Toronto, 1985).

'Medieval English fairs: evidence from Winchester and St Ives'. In Raftis, *Pathways*, 283–99, q.v.

Ogle, Octavius, ed. *The Oxford market.* Oxford Historical Society 16, *Collectanea*, 2 (1890).

Penn, Simon A. C. 'The origins of Bristol migrants in the early fourteenth century: the surname evidence'. *TBGAS* 101 (1984): 123–30.

'A fourteenth-century Bristol merchant'. *TBGAS* 104 (1986): 183–6.

Platt, Colin. *Medieval Southampton: the port and trading community, A.D. 1000–1600* (London and Boston, 1973).

The English medieval town (London, 1976).

Raftis, J. A. *A small town in late medieval England: Godmanchester, 1278–1400* (Toronto, 1982).

'Geographical mobility in lay subsidy rolls'. *MS* 38 (1976): 385–403.

Reynolds, Susan. *An introduction to the history of English medieval towns* (Oxford, 1977).

Richardson, H. G. *The medieval fairs and markets of York. St Anthony's Hall Publications* 20 (1961).

Rosser, A. G. 'The essence of medieval urban communities: the vill of Westminster 1200–1540'. *TRHS*, 5th series, 34 (1984): 91–112.

Russell, J. C. 'Medieval midland and northern migration to London, 1100–1365'. *Speculum* 34 (1959): 641–5.

Rutledge, Elizabeth. 'Immigration and population growth in early fourteenth-century Norwich: evidence from the tithing roll'. *Urban History Yearbook* (1988): 15–30.

Salzman, L. F. *English trade in the middle ages* (Oxford, 1931).

Saul, A. 'Great Yarmouth and the Hundred Years War in the fourteenth century'. *BIHR* 52 (1979): 105–15.

Scarfe, Norman. *Suffolk in the middle ages* (Woodbridge, 1986).
Slater, T. R. 'The urban hierarchy in medieval Staffordshire'. *Journal of Historical Geography* 11 (1985): 115–37.
Swanson, Heather. *Building craftsmen in late medieval York. Borthwick Papers* 63 (1983).
'The illusion of economic structure: craft guilds in late medieval English towns'. *Past and Present* 121 (1988): 29–48.
Thrupp, Sylvia L. *The merchant class of medieval London (1300–1500)* (Ann Arbor, 1948).
Titow, J. Z. 'The decline of the fair of St Giles, Winchester, in the thirteenth and fourteenth centuries'. *NMS* 31 (1987): 58–75.
Tupling, G. H. 'The origin of markets and fairs in medieval Lancashire'. *Transactions of the Lancashire and Cheshire Antiquarian Society* 99 (1933): 75–94.
'Markets and fairs in medieval Lancashire'. In Edwards, *Historical essays*, 345–56, q.v.
Unwin, George. 'Social evolution in mediaeval London'. In Unwin, *Finance and trade*, 1–18, q.v.
'London tradesmen and their creditors'. In Unwin, *Finance and trade*, 19–34, q.v.
The guilds and companies of London. 4th edn (London, 1963).
Unwin, Tim. 'Rural marketing in medieval Nottinghamshire'. *Journal of Historical Geography* 7 (1981): 231–51.
Veale, Elspeth M. 'Craftsmen and the economy of London in the fourteenth century'. In Hollaender, A. E. J. and W. Kellaway, eds. *Studies in London history* (London, 1969): 133–51.
Wood, H. G. *Medieval Tamworth* (Tamworth, 1972).

8. Sources for Chapter 5

Wool has dominated studies of England's overseas trade in the fourteenth century. The subject is complicated by Edward's financial manipulations of the wool trade as well as by cyclical changes in the trade itself. This account relies heavily on the findings of Lloyd, Munro, and Power. For the politics of wool, one should consult, besides Unwin, Harriss (Chapter 1) and Fryde (Chapters 10, 13). Other aspects of overseas trade can be found in Carus-Wilson, Hatcher, and James.

Baker, Alan R. H. 'Changes in the later middle ages'. In Darby, *New historical geography*, 186–247, q.v.
Blake, J. B. 'The medieval coal trade of north east England: some fourteenth century evidence'. *NH* 2 (1967): 1–26.
Bridbury, A. R. *England and the salt trade in the later middle ages* (Oxford, 1955).
'Before the Black Death'. *EcHR*, 2nd series, 30 (1977): 393–410.
Carus-Wilson, E. M. *Medieval merchant venturers.* 2nd edn (London, 1967).
'Trends in the export of English woollens in the fourteenth century'. *EcHR*, 2nd series, 3 (1950): 162–79.
'The woollen industry before 1550'. In Crittall, *VCH: Wiltshire*, 115–47, q.v.
Carus-Wilson, E. M. and Olive Coleman. *England's export trade, 1275–1547* (Oxford, 1963).

Childs, Wendy R. *Anglo-Castilian trade in the later middle ages* (Manchester, 1978).

Chorley, Patrick. 'English cloth exports during the thirteenth and early fourteenth centuries: the continental evidence'. *BIHR* 61 (1988): 1–10.

Dyer, Christopher. *Lords and peasants in a changing society: the estates of the bishopric of Worcester, 680–1540* (Cambridge, 1980).

Fryde, E. B. *The wool accounts of William de la Pole. St Anthony's Hall Publications* 25 (York, 1964).

Some business transactions of York merchants, John Goldbeter, William Acastre and partners, 1336–1349. Borthwick Papers 29 (York, 1966).

'Edward III's wool monopoly of 1337: a fourteenth-century royal trading venture'. *History* 37 (1952): 8–24.

'The English farmers of customs, 1343–51'. *TRHS*, 5th series, 9 (1969): 1–17.

Glasscock, R. E. 'England *circa* 1334'. In Darby, *New historical geography*, 136–85, q.v.

Gras, N. S. B. *The evolution of the English corn market, from the twelfth to the eighteenth century* (Cambridge, Mass., 1915).

Gray, H. L. 'The production and exportation of English woollens in the fourteenth century'. *EHR* 39 (1924): 13–35.

Hatcher, John. *English tin production and trade before 1550* (Oxford, 1973).

James, M. K. 'The fluctuations of the Anglo-Gascon wine trade during the fourteenth century'. *EcHR*, 2nd series, 4 (1951): 170–96.

Kershaw, Ian. *Bolton priory: the economy of a northern monastery, 1286–1325* (Oxford, 1973).

Lloyd, T. H. *The movement of wool prices in medieval England. EcHR* Supplement 6 (Cambridge, 1973).

The English wool trade in the middle ages (Cambridge, 1977).

Alien merchants in England in the high middle ages (Sussex and New York, 1982).

'Overseas trade and the English money supply in the fourteenth century'. In Mayhew, *Monetary affairs*, 96–124, q.v.

Mate, Mavis. 'The estates of Canterbury cathedral priory before the Black Death 1315–1348'. *SMRH*, NS 8 (1986): 3–31.

'Agrarian economy after the Black Death: the manors of Canterbury cathedral priory'. *EcHR*, 2nd series, 37 (1984): 341–54.

Miskimin, Harry A. *The economy of early renaissance Europe, 1300–1460* (Englewood-Cliffs, 1969).

Munro, J. H. *Wool, cloth, and gold: the struggle for bullion in Anglo-Burgundian trade, 1370–1478* (Toronto, 1972).

'Wool-price schedules and the qualities of English wools in the later middle ages, c. 1270–1499'. *Textile History* 9 (1978): 118–69.

'Monetary contraction and industrial change in the late medieval low countries, 1335–1500'. In Mayhew, *Coinage*, 95–161, q.v.

Nicholas, David M. 'Town and countryside: social and economic tensions in fourteenth-century Flanders'. *Comparative Studies in Society and History* 10 (1967/8): 458–85.

'The English trade at Bruges in the last years of Edward III'. *JMH* 5 (1979): 23–61.

Pelham, R. A. 'The distribution of sheep in Sussex in the early fourteenth century'. *SAC* 75 (1934): 128–34.

Postan, M. M. *Medieval trade and finance* (Cambridge, 1973).

'Partnership in English medieval commerce'. In idem, *Medieval trade*, 65–91.

'The trade of medieval Europe: the north'. In M. M. Postan and E. E. Rich, eds. *The Cambridge economic history of Europe*. Vol. II (Cambridge, 1952). Reprinted in idem, *Medieval trade*, 92–231.

'The medieval wool trade'. In idem, *Medieval trade*, 342–52.

Power, Eileen. *The wool trade in English medieval history* (Oxford, 1941).

Russell, Ephraim. 'The societies of the Bardi and the Peruzzi and their dealings with Edward III, 1327–1345'. In Unwin, *Finance and trade*, 93–135, q.v.

Ryder, M. L. 'Medieval sheep and wool types'. *AgHR* 32 (1984): 15–28.

Saul, Nigel. *Scenes from provincial life: knightly families in Sussex, 1280–1400* (Oxford, 1986).

Sayles, G. O. 'The "English company" of 1343 and a merchant's oath'. *Speculum* 6 (1931): 177–205.

Scott, Richenda. 'Medieval agriculture'. In Crittall, *VCH: Wiltshire*, 7–42, q.v.

Sergeant, Frank. 'The wine trade with Gascony'. In Unwin, *Finance and trade*, 257–311, q.v.

Stephenson, M. J. 'Wool yields in the medieval economy'. *EcHR*, 2nd series, 41 (1988): 368–91.

Unwin, George. 'The estate of merchants, 1336–1365'. In Unwin, *Finance and trade*, 179–255, q.v.

9. Sources for Chapter 6

Our knowledge about economic changes in the early fourteenth century is rapidly changing under the impact of intensive studies of local agricultural conditions, population, and prices. The respective roles of money and population in determining prices have been hotly debated. The account here relies heavily on the findings of Mate, Mayhew, Munro, and Prestwich (see, also, works by Lloyd, Mate, Mayhew, Munro cited in Chapter 5 and Farmer in Chapter 3). Bridbury offers an alternative explanation. References to Edward's financial problems can be found under Chapter 13. Fryde, Nash, Poos, and others have refined the understanding of population trends through careful demographic and local studies. Thanks to Dyer, Mate, and others, conditions in the crucial period between the Black Death and the Peasants' Revolt (1381) are becoming clearer.

Twigg presents a challenging argument against plague as the cause of the massive loss of life in 1348–50, based on a zoological assessment of rats and population density. He offers an anthrax epidemic as an alternative explanation. His book has the virtue of bringing new ideas to bear on the subject and stimulating debate. It certainly shows the shortcomings of many historical assumptions, but his conclusion is not very convincing. (Because of the specialized nature of Twigg's argument, it is useful to consult reviews in the *Journal of the History of Medicine* 41 (1986): 485–6, *Medical History* 29 (1986): 326–8, *Perspectives in Biology and Medicine* 29 (1986): 631–2,

Quarterly Review of Biology 62 (1987): 124, and *Journal of Historical Geography* 11 (1985): 313–14.)
The costs and benefits of war have been debated by Bridbury, McFarlane, Maddicott, Miller, Postan, and others. It has involved a consideration of the impact of taxation, the destination of tax proceeds, the loss of manpower, income from ransoms and booty, and losses from war and ransoms. Drawing up an accurate balance sheet has proved very difficult, all arguments depending on a certain amount of conjecture. Conclusive evidence has been elusive. The issue of social mobility is considered in Chapter 8.

Ames, Edward. 'The sterling crisis of 1337–1339'. *JEcH* 25 (1965): 496–522.

Astill, G. G. 'Economic change in later medieval England: an archaeological review'. In Aston, *Social relations*, 217–47, q.v.

Baker, Alan R. H. 'Evidence in the "Nonarum Inquisitiones" of contracting arable lands in England during the early fourteenth century'. *EcHR*, 2nd series, 19 (1966): 518–32.

'Some evidence of a reduction in the acreage of cultivated lands in Sussex during the early fourteenth century'. *SAC* 109 (1966): 1–5.

Benedictow, O. J. 'Morbidity in historical plague epidemics'. *Population Studies* 41 (1987): 401–43.

Beresford, Maurice and John G. Hurst. *Deserted medieval villages* (London, 1971).

Brent, Judith A. 'Alciston manor in the later middle ages'. *SAC* 106 (1968): 89–102.

Bridbury, A. R. 'The Black Death'. *EcHR*, 2nd series, 26 (1973): 577–92.

'Before the Black Death'. *EcHR*, 2nd series, 30 (1977): 393–410.

'Thirteenth-century prices and the money supply'. *AgHR* 33 (1985): 1–21.

'The hundred years war: costs and profits'. In Coleman, *Trade*, 80–95, q.v.

Davies, R. A. 'The effect of the Black Death on the parish priests of the medieval diocese of Coventry and Lichfield'. *BIHR* 62 (1989): 85–90.

Dyer, Christopher. *Warwickshire farming 1349–c. 1520: preparations for agricultural revolution. Dugdale Society, Occasional Papers* 27 (Oxford, 1981).

'Population and agriculture on a Warwickshire manor in the late middle ages'. *UBHJ* 11 (1968): 114–27.

'Deserted villages in the West Midlands'. *EcHR*, 2nd series, 35 (1982): 19–34.

'The rise and fall of a medieval village: Little Aston (in Aston Blank), Gloucestershire'. *TBGAS* 105 (1987): 165–81.

Farmer, D. L. 'Crop yields, prices and wages in medieval England'. *SMRH*, ns 6 (1983): 117–55.

Feaveryear, A. E. *The pound sterling: a history of English money*. 2nd edn by E. Victor Morgan (Oxford, 1963).

Fryde, E. B. 'The tenants of the bishops of Coventry and Lichfield and of Worcester after the plague of 1348–9'. In Hunnisett, *Medieval records*, 224–66, q.v.

Harvey, Barbara. 'The population trend in England between 1300 and 1348'. *TRHS*, 5th series, 16 (1966): 23–42.

Hatcher, John. *Rural economy and society in the duchy of Cornwall 1300–1500* (Cambridge, 1970).

'A diversified economy: later medieval Cornwall'. *EcHR*, 2nd series, 22 (1969): 208–27.

Holt, Richard. 'Gloucester in the century after the Black Death'. *TBGAS* 103 (1985): 149–62.

Kershaw, Ian. 'The great famine and agrarian crisis in England 1315–1322'. *Past and Present* 59 (1973): 3–50.

McFarlane, K. B. 'War, the economy and social change: England and the Hundred Years War'. *Past and Present* 22 (1962): 3–13.

Maddicott, J. R. 'The English peasantry and the demands of the crown, 1294–1341'. *Past and Present*, Supplement 1 (1975).

Mate, Mavis. 'High prices in early fourteenth-century England'. *EcHR*, 2nd series, 28 (1975): 1–16.

'The estates of Canterbury cathedral priory before the Black Death 1315–1348'. *SMRH*, ns, 8 (1986): 3–31.

'The role of gold coinage in the English economy, 1338–1400'. *NC*, 7th series, 18 (1978): 126–41.

'Agrarian economy after the Black Death: the manors of Canterbury cathedral priory'. *EcHR*, 2nd series, 37 (1984): 341–54.

Mayhew, N. J. 'Numismatic evidence and falling prices in the fourteenth century'. *EcHR*, 2nd series, 27 (1974): 1–25.

'Money and prices in England from Henry II to Edward III'. *AgHR* 35 (1987): 121–32.

Miller, Edward. 'War, taxation and the English economy in the late thirteenth and early fourteenth centuries'. In Winter, J. M., ed. *War and economic development: essays in memory of David Joslin* (Cambridge, 1975): 11–31.

Miskimin, H. A. 'Monetary movements and market structure – forces for contraction in fourteenth- and fifteenth-century England'. *JEcH* 24 (1964): 470–90.

Morris, Colin. 'The plague in Britain'. *Historical Journal* 14 (1971): 205–15. Review of Shrewsbury, *Bubonic plague*, q.v.

Nash, A. E. 'The mortality pattern of the Wiltshire lords of the manor, 1242–1377'. *SH* 2 (1980): 31–43.

Poos, L. R. 'The rural population of Essex in the later middle ages'. *EcHR,* 2nd series, 38 (1985): 515–30.

'Population turnover in medieval Essex: the evidence of some early fourteenth-century tithing lists'. In Bonfield, *World we have gained*, 1–22, q.v.

Postan, M. M. 'Some social consequences of the Hundred Years War'. *EcHR* 12 (1942): 1–12.

'Some economic evidence of declining population in the later middle ages'. *EcHR*, 2nd series, 2 (1950): 221–46.

'The costs of the Hundred Years War'. *Past and Present* 27 (1964): 34–53.

'Note'. To Robinson, 'Money, population and economic change', 77–82, q.v.

Postan, M. M. and J. Z. Titow. 'Heriots and prices on Winchester manors'. *EcHR*, 2nd series, 11 (1959): 392–411.

Potter, W. J. W. 'The gold coinages of Edward III'. *NC*, 7th series, 3 (1963): 105–28.

Prestwich, Michael. 'Early fourteenth-century exchange rates'. *EcHR*, 2nd series, 32 (1979): 470–82.

'The crown and the currency: the circulation of money in later thirteenth- and early fourteenth-century England'. *NC*, 7th series, 22 (1982): 51–65.

'Currency and the economy of early fourteenth-century England'. In Mayhew, *Monetary affairs*, 45–58, q.v.

Raftis, J. A. 'Changes in an English village after the Black Death'. *MS* 24 (1962): 158–77.

Reddaway, T. F. 'The king's mint and exchange in London 1343–1543'. *EHR* 82 (1967): 1–23.

Robinson, W. C. 'Money, population and economic change in late medieval Europe'. *EcHR*, 2nd series, 12 (1959): 63–75.

Robo, E. 'The Black Death in the hundred of Farnham'. *EHR* 44 (1929): 560–72.

Russell, Josiah C. *British medieval population* (Albuquerque, 1948).

'The pre-plague population of England'. *JBS* 5 (1966): 1–21.

Shrewsbury, J. F. D. *A history of the bubonic plague in the British Isles* (Cambridge, 1970).

Smith, C. T. 'Population'. In Hoskins, *VCH: Leicestershire*, Vol. III: 129–55, q.v.

Spufford, Peter. *Money and its use in medieval Europe* (Cambridge, 1988).

Thompson, A. Hamilton. 'Registers of John Gynewell, bishop of Lincoln, for the years 1347–1350'. *Archaeological Journal* 68 (1911): 300–60.

'The pestilences of the fourteenth century in the diocese of York'. *Archaeological Journal* 71 (1914): 97–154.

Thrupp, Sylvia L. 'The problem of replacement rates in late medieval English population'. *EcHR*, 2nd series, 18 (1965): 101–19.

Titow, J. Z. 'Evidence of weather in the account rolls of the bishopric of Winchester, 1209–1350'. *EcHR*, 2nd series, 12 (1960): 360–407.

'Histoire et climat dans l'évêché de Winchester, 1350–1450'. *Annales ESC* 25 (1970): 312–50.

Twigg, Graham. *The Black Death: a biological reappraisal* (London, 1984).

Watson, Andrew M. 'Back to gold – and silver'. *EcHR*, 2nd series, 20 (1967): 1–34.

Watts, D. G. 'A model for the early fourteenth century'. *EcHR*, 2nd series, 20 (1967): 543–7.

Ziegler, Philip. *The Black Death* (London, 1969).

10. Sources for Chapters 7 and 8

Materials for Chapters 7 and 8 belong together. Changes in estate management, charted in Chapter 7, are controversial, but the aggregate evidence points to the continuity of seigneurial policies from the 1340s until the late 1370s when landlords began to feel the effects of plague most strongly. The post-plague period, the 1350s to the 1370s, has become much clearer than it was before, thanks to the insightful contributions of Bridbury and Mate and the gradual accumulation of estate studies (see also Bennett on Cheshire and Lancashire, Bridbury on the effects of the Black Death, Dyer on Worcester, Hatcher on Cornwall, Hilton on Leicestershire,

Kershaw on Bolton, Maddicott on Thomas of Lancaster, Roden on the Chilterns, and Saul on Sussex, cited in earlier chapters). While the Peasants' Revolt or English Rising of 1381 lies outside the scope of this study, the analyses of the revolt by Dobson, Dyer, Hilton, and others help illuminate conditions in the post-plague era which fostered rebellion, especially the so-called seigneurial reaction. The works by Given-Wilson, McFarlane, Orme, and Rosenthal are essential to understanding noble society in this period. The emphasis placed by Bennett, Maddicott, and Saul on 'horizontal' ties among county gentry, strengthening the county community, should be tempered by the findings of Cherry, Goodman, Lewis, and Walker which stress the power of the 'vertical' ties of lord/client relations, to obtain a well-rounded picture of the gentry. Information about specific retinues can also be found in Maddicott and Phillips (Chapters 1 and 2) while biographical material on knights of the shires is listed under Chapter 12. Although published too late to be used in this work, the comprehensive survey of indentured retaining by Bean and the speculative reworking of McFarlane's thesis on bastard feudalism by Coss are now essential to understanding social relations in the later middle ages.

Altschul, Michael. *A baronial family in medieval England: the Clares, 1217–1314* (Baltimore, 1965).

Baldwin, Frances Elizabeth. *Sumptuary legislation and personal regulation in England* (Baltimore, 1926).

Barnie, John. *War in medieval English society: social values in the Hundred Years War 1337–1399* (Ithaca, 1974).

Bean, John M. W. *The estates of the Percy family, 1416–1537* (Oxford, 1958).

The decline of English feudalism, 1215–1540 (Manchester, 1968).

'The Percies' acquisition of Alnwick'. *Archaeologia Aeliana*, 4th series, 32 (1954): 309–19.

From lord to patron: lordship in late medieval England (Philadelphia, 1989).

Bell, Susan Groag. 'Medieval women book owners: arbiters of lay piety and ambassadors of culture'. In Eler and Kowaleski, *Women and power*, 149–87, q.v.

Bennett, Michael J. 'A county community: social cohesion amongst the Cheshire gentry, 1400–1425'. *NH* 8 (1973): 24–44.

'Sources and problems in the study of social mobility: Cheshire in the later middle ages'. *THSLC* 128 (1979): 59–95.

'Provincial gentlefolk and legal education in the reign of Edward II'. *BIHR* 57 (1984): 203–8.

Booth, P. H. W. *The financial administration of the lordship and county of Chester, 1272–1377*. Chetham Society, 3rd series, 28 (Manchester, 1981).

Boulton, D'Arcy J. D. *The knights of the crown: the monarchical orders of knighthood in later medieval Europe 1325–1525* (Woodbridge, Suffolk; Dover, N.H., 1987).

Brewer, Derek. 'Class distinction in Chaucer'. *Speculum* 43 (1968): 290–305.

Britnell, R. H. 'Production for the market on a small fourteenth-century estate'. *EcHR*, 2nd series, 19 (1969): 380–7.

Cherry, M. 'The Courtenay earls of Devon: the formation and disintegration of a late medieval aristocratic affinity'. *SH* 1 (1979): 71–97.

Clark, Elaine. 'Medieval labour law and English local courts'. *American Journal of Legal History* 27 (1983): 330–53.

Coss, P. R. 'Aspects of cultural diffusion in medieval England: the early romances, local society and Robin Hood'. *Past and Present* 108 (1985): 35–79.

'Literature and social terminology: the vavasour in England'. In Aston, *Social relations*, 109–50, q.v.

'Bastard feudalism revised'. *Past and Present* 125 (1989): 27–64.

Denholm-Young, Noël. *Seignorial administration in England* (Oxford, 1937).

The country gentry in the fourteenth century (Oxford, 1969).

'Feudal society in the thirteenth century: the knights'. *History* 29 (1944): 107–19.

Dobson, R. B. *The Peasants' Revolt of 1381* (London and New York, 1970).

Douch, Robert. 'The career, lands and family of William Montagu, earl of Salisbury, 1301–1344'. *BIHR* 24 (1951): 85–8.

DuBoulay, F. R. H. *The lordship of Canterbury: an essay on medieval society* (London, 1966).

Dyer, Christopher. 'The social and economic background to the rural revolt of 1381'. In Aston, *English Rising*, 9–42, q.v.

Faith, Rosamond. 'The "great rumour" of 1377 and peasant ideology'. In Aston, *English Rising*, 43–73, q.v.

Feiling, K. G. 'An Essex manor in the fourteenth century'. *EHR* 26 (1911): 333–8.

Fowler, Kenneth. *The king's lieutenant: Henry of Grosmont first duke of Lancaster 1310–1361* (London, 1969).

Given-Wilson, Chris. *The English nobility in the late middle ages: the fourteenth-century political community* (London and New York, 1987).

'The king and the gentry in fourteenth-century England'. *TRHS*, 5th series, 37 (1987): 87–102.

Goheen, R. B. 'Social ideals and social structure: rural Gloucestershire, 1450–1500'. *Histoire Sociale – Social History* 12 (1979): 262–80.

Goodman, Anthony. 'John of Gaunt: paradigm of the late fourteenth-century crisis'. *TRHS*, 5th series, 37 (1987): 133–48.

'John of Gaunt'. In Ormrod, *England in the fourteenth century*, 67–87, q.v.

Goose, Nigel R. 'Wage labour on a Kentish manor: Meopham 1307–75', *Archaeologia Cantiana* 92 (1976): 203–23.

Halcrow, E. M. 'The decline of demesne farming on the estates of Durham cathedral priory'. *EcHR*, 2nd series, 7 (1955): 345–56.

Harte, N. B. 'State control of dress and social change in pre-industrial England'. In Coleman, *Trade*, 132–65, q.v.

Hilton, R. H. *The economic development of some Leicestershire estates in the fourteenth and fifteenth centuries* (Oxford, 1947).

The decline of serfdom in medieval England (London and New York, 1969).

Bond men made free: medieval peasant movements and the English rising of 1381 (New York, 1973).

'Rent and capital formation in feudal society'. *Proceedings of the second International Conference of Economic History 1962* (1965), reprinted in idem, *The English peasantry*, 174–214, q.v.

'Lord and peasant in Staffordshire in the middle ages'. *North Staffordshire Journal of Field Studies* 10 (1970): 1–20, reprinted in idem, *The English peasantry*, 215–43, q.v.

Hodgett, G. A. J. 'Feudal Wiltshire'. In Crittall, *VCH: Wiltshire*, 5: 44–71, q.v.

Holmes, George A. *The estates of the higher nobility in fourteenth-century England* (Cambridge, 1957).

Jefferies, Peggy. 'The medieval use as family law and custom: the Berkshire gentry in the fourteenth and fifteenth centuries'. *SH* 1 (1979): 45–69.

Keen, Maurice. *Chivalry* (New Haven and London, 1984).

'Brotherhood in arms'. *History* 47 (1962): 1–17.

'Chivalry, nobility, and the man-at-arms'. In Allmand, *War*, 57–72, q.v.

'Chaucer's knight, the English aristocracy and the crusade'. In Scattergood, *English court culture*, 45–62, q.v.

Kosminsky, E. A. *Studies in the agrarian history of England in the thirteenth century.* Ed. R. H. Hilton, trans. Ruth Kisch (Oxford, 1956).

Lewis, N. B. 'The organization of indentured retinues in fourteenth-century England'. *TRHS*, 4th series, 27 (1945): 29–39.

Lomas, R. A. 'The priory of Durham and its demesnes in the fourteenth and fifteenth century'. *EcHR*, 2nd series, 31 (1978): 339–53.

McFarlane, Kenneth B. *The nobility of later medieval England* (Oxford, 1973).

'Bastard feudalism'. *BIHR* 20 (1945): 161–80.

Maddicott, J. R. 'Law and lordship: royal justices as retainers in thirteenth- and fourteenth-century England'. *Past and Present*, Supplement 4 (Oxford, 1978).

Mason, Emma. '*Maritagium* and the changing law'. *BIHR* 49 (1976): 286–9.

Mate, Mavis. 'The farming out of manors: a new look at the evidence from Canterbury cathedral priory'. *JMH* 9 (1983): 331–43.

'Property investment by Canterbury cathedral priory 1250–1400'. *JBS* 23 (1984): 1–21.

'Labour and labour services on the estates of Canterbury cathedral priory in the fourteenth century'. *SH* 7 (1985): 55–67.

Mertes, Kate. *The English noble household 1250–1600: good governance and politic rule* (Oxford, 1988).

Naughton, Katherine S. *The gentry of Bedfordshire in the thirteenth and fourteenth centuries. Leicester University, Department of English Local History, Occasional Papers* 2 (Leicester, 1976).

Newton, Stella M. *Fashion in the age of the Black Prince: a study of the years 1340–1365* (Woodbridge and Totowa, 1980).

Nicolas, Nicholas Harris. 'Observations on the institution of the most noble Order of the Garter'. *Archaeologia* 31 (1846): 1–163.

Orme, Nicholas. *From childhood to chivalry: the education of the English kings and aristocracy 1066–1530* (London and New York, 1984).

'The education of the courtier'. In Scattergood, *English court culture*, 63–86, q.v.

Ormrod, W. M. 'Edward III and his family'. *JBS* 26 (1987): 398–422.

Palmer, Robert C. *The Whilton dispute, 1264–1380: a social–legal study of dispute settlement in medieval England* (Princeton, 1984).

Payling, S. J. 'Inheritance and local politics in the later middle ages: the case of Ralph, Lord Cromwell, and the Heriz inheritance'. *NMS* 30 (1986): 67–96.

Poos, L. R. 'The social context of the statute of labourers enforcement'. *LHR* 1 (1983): 27–52.

Postan, M. M. 'Investment in medieval agriculture'. *JEcH* 27 (1967): 576–87.

Postles, David. 'Problems in the administration of small manors: three Oxfordshire glebe-demesnes, 1278–1345'. *MH* 4 (1977): 1–14.

'The perception of profit before the leasing of demesnes'. *AgHR* 34 (1986): 12–28.

Powell, J. Enoch and Keith Wallis. *The house of lords in the middle ages: a history of the English house of lords to 1540* (London, 1968).

Powicke, Michael. *Military obligation in medieval England: a study in liberty and duty* (Oxford, 1962).

Putnam, Bertha H. *The enforcement of the statutes of labourers during the first decade after the Black Death, 1349–1359* (New York, 1908).

Raban, Sandra. *Mortmain legislation and the English church, 1279–1500* (Cambridge, 1982).

Raftis, J. A. *The estates of Ramsey abbey: a study in economic growth and organization* (Toronto, 1957).

'The structure of commutation in a fourteenth-century village'. In Powicke, *Essays*, 282–300, q.v.

Razi, Zvi. 'The struggles between the abbots of Halesowen and their tenants in the thirteenth and fourteenth centuries'. In Aston, *Social relations*, 151–68, q.v.

Rees, Una. 'The leases of Haughmond abbey, Shropshire'. *MH* 8 (1983): 13–28.

Rosenthal, Joel. *The purchase of paradise: gift-giving and the aristocracy, 1307–1485* (London and Toronto, 1972).

Nobles and the noble life 1295–1500 (London and New York, 1976).

Saul, Nigel. *Knights and esquires: the Gloucestershire gentry in the fourteenth century* (Oxford, 1981).

'A "rising" lord and a "declining" esquire: Sir Thomas de Berkeley III and Geoffrey Gascelyn of Sheldon'. *BIHR* 61 (1988): 345–56.

Sitwell, George R. 'The English gentleman'. *The Ancestor* 1 (1902): 58–103.

Smith, Llinos Beverley. 'Seignorial income in the fourteenth century: the Arundels in Chirk'. *Bulletin of the Board of Celtic Studies* 28 (1979): 443–57.

Smyth, John. *The Berkeley Manuscripts*. Vol. 1: *The Lives of the Berkeleys*. Ed. John Maclean. Bristol and Gloucestershire Archaeological Society (Gloucester, 1883).

Stretton, Grace. 'The travelling household of the middle ages'. *Journal of the British Archaeological Association*, NS, 50 (1935): 75–103.

Tuck, J. A. 'Northumbrian society in the fourteenth century'. *NH* 6 (1971): 22–39.

'The emergence of a northern nobility, 1250–1400'. *NH* 22 (1986): 1–17.

Vale, Juliet. *Edward III and chivalry: chivalric society and its context 1270–1350* (Woodbridge, 1982).

Walker, Simon K. 'Lancaster v. Dallingridge: a franchisal dispute in fourteenth-century Sussex'. *SAC* 121 (1983): 87–94.

'Profit and loss in the Hundred Years War: the subcontracts of Sir John Strother, 1374'. *BIHR* 58 (1985): 100–6.

'Lordship and lawlessness in the palatinate of Lancaster, 1370–1400'. *JBS* 28 (1989): 325–48.

'John of Gaunt and his retainers, 1361–1399'. Ph.D. thesis, Oxford University, 1986.

Watson, G. W. 'Marriage settlements'. *Genealogist*, NS, 36 (1920): 198–204.

Willis, Dorothy. 'The estate book of Henry de Bray of Harlestone, Northampton-shire (1289–1340)'. *TRHS*, 3rd series, 4 (1910): 117–39.

11. Sources for Chapter 9

Church and religion are huge topics with a massive bibliography. Only a sample is given here. Pantin has provided an excellent general framework covering all aspects of the church, though some points have been corrected by Highfield and others. Literacy, schooling, and scholasticism have received new and penetrating attention in the works of Courtenay, Moran, and Orme. The somewhat more intractable issue of religious attitudes has been explored by Rosenthal (Chapter 7), Saul, and Vale. No attempt has been made here to tackle the problems of Wycliff or the Lollards, though some studies, such as McFarlane's, provide useful background material that relates to conditions in the church during Edward's reign. The studies of the parish clergy by Bennett, Bill, Boyle, Owen, Robinson, and Thompson add a crucial dimension to our understanding of the church hierarchy.

The world of doctrinal debate, philosophy, and theology has been left out of this account. The magnificent survey of scholastic changes in the fourteenth century coupled with what might be called a sociology of higher learning by Courtenay, along with studies by Wilks and others, provides the best summary of the topic.

Bennett, Michael J. 'The Lancashire and Cheshire clergy in 1379'. *THSLC* 124 (1973): 1–30.

Bill, P. A. *The Warwickshire parish clergy in the later middle ages*. Dugdale Society, Occasional Papers 17 (1967).

'Five aspects of the medieval parochial clergy of Warwickshire'. *UBHJ* 10 (1966): 95–116.

Boyle, Leonard E. 'Aspects of clerical education in fourteenth-century England'. In Levy, *The fourteenth century*, 19–32, q.v.

Bray, Jennifer R. 'Concepts of sainthood in fourteenth-century England'. *BJRL* 66 (1984): 40–77.

Butler, L. H. 'Archbishop Melton, his neighbours, and his kinsmen, 1317–1340'. *JEH* 2 (1951): 54–67.

Cannon, Henry Lewin. 'The poor priests: a study in the rise of English lollardy'. *Annual Report of the American Historical Association for the Year 1899*. Vol. 1 (Washington, 1900): 449–82.

Catto, Jeremy. 'Religion and the English nobility in the later fourteenth century'.

In Lloyd-Jones, Hugh, Valerie Pearl, and Blair Worden, eds. *History and imagination: essays in honour of H. R. Trevor-Roper* (London, 1981), 43–55.

Courtenay, William J. *Schools and scholars in fourteenth-century England* (Princeton, 1987).

Dawson, James Doyne. 'Richard FitzRalph and the fourteenth-century poverty controversies'. *JEH* 34 (1983): 315–43.

Deanesley, Margaret. *A history of the medieval church*. Revised edn (London, 1947).

Denton, J. H. *Robert Winchelsey and the crown, 1294–1313: a study in the defence of ecclesiastical liberty* (Cambridge, 1980).

'The "communitas cleri". in the early fourteenth century'. *BIHR* 51 (1978): 72–8.

Dickinson, J. C. *An ecclesiastical history of England: the later middle ages from the Norman Conquest to the eve of the reformation* (London, 1979).

Erickson, Carolly. 'The fourteenth-century Franciscans and their critics: I. The order's growth and character'. *Franciscan Studies* 35 (1975): 107–35. II. 'Poverty, jurisdiction, and internal change'. *Franciscan Studies* 36 (1976): 108–47.

Godfrey, C. J. 'Pluralists in the province of Canterbury in 1366'. *JEH* 11 (1960) 23–40.

Haines, Roy Martin. *The church and politics in fourteenth-century England: the career of Adam Orleton, c. 1275–1345* (Cambridge, 1978).

Archbishop John Stratford: political revolutionary and champion of the liberties of the English church ca. 1275/80–1348 (Toronto, 1986).

'The education of the English clergy in the later middle ages: some observations on the operation of Pope Boniface VIII's constitution *Cum ex eo*'. *Canadian Journal of History* 4 (1969): 1–22.

Harper, Richard I. 'A note on corrodies in the fourteenth century'. *Albion* 15 (1983): 95–101.

Hay, Denys. 'The church of England in the later middle ages'. *History* 53 (1968): 35–50.

Highfield, J. R. L. 'The promotion of William of Wickham to the see of Winchester'. *JEH* 4 (1953): 37–54.

'The English hierarchy in the reign of Edward III'. *TRHS*, 5th series, 6 (1956): 115–38.

Hill, Rosalind M. T. *The labourer in the vineyard: the visitations of archbishop Melton in the archdeaconry of Richmond*. *Borthwick Papers* 35 (1968).

Hodgetts, M. 'Adam of Harvington, prelate and politician'. *Transactions of the Worcestershire Archaeological Society* 36 (1959): 33–41.

Jennings, Margaret. 'Higden's minor writings and the fourteenth-century church'. *Proceedings of the Leeds Philosophical and Literary Society* 16 (1977): 149–58.

Jones, E. D. 'The church and "bastard feudalism": the case of Crowland abbey from the 1320s to the 1350s'. *JRH* 10 (1978): 142–50.

Jones, W. R. 'Patronage and administration: the king's free chapels in medieval England'. *JBS* 9 (1969): 1–23.

'Relations of the two jurisdictions: conflict and co-operation in England during the thirteenth and fourteenth centuries'. *SMRH* 7 (1970): 77–210.

Knowles, David. *The religious orders in England.* Vol. II: *The end of the middle ages* (Cambridge, 1955).

Little, A. C. 'A royal inquiry into property held by the mendicant friars in England in 1349 and 1350'. In Edwards, *Historical essays*, 179–88, q.v.

McFarlane, Kenneth. B. *John Wycliffe and the beginnings of English nonconformity* (London, 1952).

McHardy, A. K. 'The Lincolnshire clergy in the later fourteenth century'. In Ormrod, *Fourteenth century*, 145–51, q.v.

Manning, Bernard L. *The people's faith in the time of Wyclif.* 2nd edn (Hassocks and Totowa, N.J., 1975).

Mason, Emma. 'The role of the English parishioner, 1100–1500'. *JEH* 27 (1976): 17–29.

Moran, JoAnn Hoeppner. *Education and learning in the city of York 1300–1560. Borthwick Papers* 55 (1979).

The growth of English schooling 1340–1548: learning, literacy, and laicization in pre-reformation York diocese (Princeton, 1985).

Olson, Sharon L. 'Perpetrators of vice or perpetuators of prerogatives: an analysis and assessment of the bishop's role in late fourteenth-century England, 1356–1405'. M.A. thesis, California State University, Long Beach, 1986.

Orme, Nicholas. *English schools in the middle ages* (London, 1973).

Ormrod, W. M. 'The personal religion of Edward III'. *Speculum* 64 (1989): 849–77.

Owen, Dorothy M. *Church and society in medieval Lincolnshire. History of Lincolnshire.* Ed. Joan Thirsk. Vol. V (Lincoln, 1971).

Pantin, William A. *The English church in the fourteenth century* (Cambridge, 1955).

Richardson, H. G. 'The parish clergy in the thirteenth and fourteenth centuries'. *TRHS*, 3rd series, 6 (1912): 89–128.

Robinson, D. *Beneficed clergy in Cleveland and the East Riding, 1306–1340. Borthwick Papers* 37 (1970).

Saul, Nigel E. 'The religious sympathies of the gentry in Gloucestershire, 1200–1500'. *TBGAS* 98 (1981): 99–112.

Scammell, Jean. 'The rural chapter in England from the eleventh to the fourteenth century'. *EHR* 86 (1971): 1–21.

Thompson, A. Hamilton. *The English clergy and their organization in the later middle ages* (Oxford, 1947).

'William Bateman bishop of Norwich 1344–55'. *TNNAS* 25 (1933): 102–37.

'Diocesan organization in the middle ages: archdeacons and rural deans'. *Proceedings of the British Academy* 29 (1943): 153–94.

Thomson, J. A. F. 'Piety and charity in late medieval London'. *JEH* 16 (1965): 178–95.

Tillotson, John H. 'Pensions, corrodies and religious houses: an aspect of the relations of crown and church in early fourteenth-century England'. *JRH* 8 (1974): 127–43.

Vale, M. G. A. *Piety, charity and literacy among the Yorkshire gentry, 1370–1480. Borthwick Papers* 50 (1976).

Warren, W. L. 'A reappraisal of Simon Sudbury, bishop of London (1361–75) and
    archbishop of Canterbury (1375–81)'. *JEH* 10 (1959): 139–53.
Wilks, Michael. 'Royal patronage and anti-papalism from Ockham to Wyclif'. In
    Hudson, *Ockham to Wyclif*, 135–63, q.v.
Wood-Legh, K. L. *Studies in church life in England under Edward III* (Cambridge,
    1934).
    Perpetual chantries in Britain (Cambridge, 1965).
Wright, J. Robert. *The church and the English crown 1305–1334: a study based on the
    register of archbishop Walter Reynolds* (Toronto, 1980).

12. Sources for Chapters 10 and 11

The local and central work of the royal government, discussed in Chapters 10 and
11, has prompted a large number of expert studies which are cited together here.
Chrimes and Brown provide general surveys of the topic.

For the most part, local administration in the fourteenth century has been well
researched, though there are no specialized studies of the sheriff or escheator for the
fourteenth century. The articles in the volumes of *The English Government at Work*
usefully summarize the main branches of government. Pugh (for Wiltshire) and Saul
(for Gloucestershire, Chapter 7) give good overviews of county government. Crime
has received a great deal of attention. Bellamy, Hanawalt, and Post survey the problem, while Crook, Harding, Kaeuper, McLane, and Sutherland explore the efforts
at law enforcement. The rise of the justices of the peace can be followed in Putnam's
studies and in the introductions to collections of local cases (e.g. Taylor).

As is the case for local administration, *The English Government at Work* provides a
good survey of the central government in the 1330s. Tout and Ormrod offer a more
intensive look at the central government, Tout concentrating on the household and
Ormrod considering broadly all the offices. The most pressing concerns of government under Edward III were military organization and finance. Hewitt and
Powicke (Chapter 7) summarize the former while Fryde's studies (Chapter 13) and
Harriss' broad monograph explore the latter in great detail. Taxation has likewise
received considerable attention, notably from Harriss and Willard. Law is the one
aspect of central government that has not been well studied. The works by Sayles
and Sutherland, along with those of Jones and Neilson, offer some coverage of these
issues.

Baker, Robert L. *The English customs service, 1307–1343: a study of medieval adminis-
    tration*. *Transactions of the American Philosophical Society*, NS, 51 (Philadelphia,
    1961).
Bellamy, J. G. *The law of treason in England in the later middle ages* (Cambridge, 1970).
    Crime and public order in England in the later middle ages (London, 1973).
    Criminal law and society in late medieval and Tudor England (Gloucester and New
    York, 1984).
    'The Coterel gang: an anatomy of a band of fourteenth-century criminals'. *EHR*
    79 (1964): 698–717.

Booth, P. H. W. 'Taxation and public order: Cheshire in 1353'. *NH* 12 (1976): 16–31.

Brand, Paul. 'Courtroom and schoolroom: the education of lawyers in England prior to 1400'. *BIHR* 60 (1987): 147–65.

Broome, Dorothy M. and T. F. Tout. 'A national balance sheet for 1362–3'. *EHR* 39 (1924): 404–19.

Brown, A. L. *The governance of late medieval England 1272–1461* (London and Stanford, 1989).

Bryant, William N. 'The financial dealings of Edward III with the county communities, 1330–1360'. *EHR* 83 (1968): 760–71.

Buck, M. C. 'The reforms of the exchequer, 1316–1326'. *EHR* 98 (1983): 241–60.

Burley, S. J. 'The victualling of Calais, 1347–65'. *BIHR* 31 (1958): 49–57.

Cam, Helen M. *The hundred and the hundred rolls* (London, 1930).
'The general eyres of 1329–10'. *EHR* 39 (1924). Reprinted in *Liberties and communities*, 150–62, q.v.
'Shire officials: coroners, constables, and bailiffs'. In *EGW*, 3: 143–83.

Chalkin, C. W. and H. A. Hanley, eds. 'The Kent lay subsidy of 1334/5'. In DuBoulay, F. R. H., ed. *Documents illustrative of medieval Kentish society. Kent Records* 18 (1964): 58–172.

Chrimes, S. B. *An introduction to the administrative history of mediaeval England* (Oxford, 1966).

Colvin, H. M. 'The "court style" in medieval English architecture: a review'. In Scattergood, *English court culture*, 141–62, q.v.

Crook, David. 'The later eyres'. *EHR* 97 (1982): 241–68.

Crowley, D. A. 'The later history of frankpledge'. *BIHR* 48 (1975): 1–15.

Doyle, A. I. 'English books in and out of court from Edward III to Henry VII'. In Scattergood, *English court culture*, 163–82, q.v.

Elrington, Christopher R. 'Assessments of Gloucestershire: fiscal records in local history'. *TBGAS* 103 (1985): 5–15.

Fowler, G. H., ed. 'Rolls from the office of sheriff of Bedfordshire and Buckinghamshire'. *BHRS*. Quarto Memoirs 3 (1929).

Fryde, E. B. 'Dismissal of Robert de Wodehouse from the office of treasurer, December 1338'. *EHR* 67 (1952): 74–8.
'Loans to the English crown, 1328–1331'. *EHR* 70 (1955): 198–211.
'Materials for the study of Edward III's credit operations, 1327–1348'. *BIHR* 22 (1949): 105–38, 23 (1950): 1–30.
'The last trials of Sir William de la Pole'. *EcHR*, 2nd series, 15 (1962): 75–88.

Fryde, Natalie. 'A medieval robber baron: Sir John Molyns of Stoke Poges, Buckinghamshire'. In Hunnisett, *Medieval legal records*, 192–222, q.v.

Given-Wilson, Chris. *The royal household and the king's affinity: service, politics and finance in England 1360–1413* (New Haven and London, 1986).
'Purveyance for the royal household, 1362–1413'. *BIHR* 56 (1983): 145–64.

Goodman, A. 'The military subcontracts of Sir Hugh Hastings, 1380'. *EHR* 95 (1979): 114–20.

Hadwin, J. F. 'The medieval lay subsidies and economic history'. *EcHR*, 2nd series, 36 (1983): 200–17.

Hall, G. D. G. 'Three courts of the hundred of Penwith, 1333'. In Hunnisett, *Medieval legal records*, 169–96, q.v.

Hammer, Carl I. 'Patterns of homicide in a medieval university town: fourteenth-century Oxford'. *Past and Present* 78 (1978): 3–23.

Hanawalt, Barbara A. *Crime and conflict in English communities 1300–1348* (Cambridge, Mass., 1979).

Harding, Alan. *The law courts of medieval England* (London, 1973).
    'The origins of conspiracy'. *TRHS*, 5th series, 33 (1983): 89–105.
    'The revolt against the judges'. In Aston, *The English Rising*, 165–93, q.v.
    'Early trailbaston proceedings from the Lincoln roll of 1305'. In Hunnisett, *Medieval legal records*, 144–68, q.v.

Harriss, G. L. 'Preference at the medieval exchequer'. *BIHR* 30 (1957): 17–40.

Hewitt, H. J. *The organization of war under Edward III, 1338–1362* (Manchester, 1966).

Holt, James C. *Robin Hood* (London, 1982).

Hudson, W. 'The Norwich militia in the fourteenth century'. *TNNAS* 14 (1901): 263–320.

Hunnisett, R. F. *The medieval coroner* (Cambridge, 1961).

Jenkinson, H. and D. Broome. 'An exchequer statement of receipts and issues, 1339–1340'. *EHR* 58 (1943): 210–16.

Jewell, Helen M. *English local administration in the middle ages* (Newton Abbot, 1972).

Johnson, Charles. 'The collectors of lay taxes'. In *EGW*, 2: 201–26.

Johnson, J. H. 'The king's wardrobe and household'. In *EGW*, 1: 206–49.

Johnstone, Hilda. 'The queen's household'. In *EGW*, 1: 250–99.
    'The queen's exchequer under the three Edwards'. In Edwards, *Historical essays*, 143–54, q.v.

Jones, Michael. 'Sir John de Hardreshull, king's lieutenant in Brittany, 1343–5'. *NMS* 31 (1987): 76–97.

Jones, W. R. 'The court of the verge: the jurisdiction of the steward and marshal of the household in later medieval England'. *JBS* 10 (1970): 1–29.

Kaeuper, Richard W. 'Law and order in fourteenth-century England: the evidence of special commissions of oyer and terminer'. *Speculum* 54 (1979): 734–84.

Keen, M. H. *The outlaws of medieval legend*. 2nd edn (London, 1977).

Lewis, N. B. 'An early fourteenth-century contract for military service'. *BIHR* 20 (1944): 111–18.
    'The recruitment and organization of a contract army, May to November 1337'. *BIHR* 37 (1964): 1–19.
    'The summons of the English feudal levy, 5 April 1327'. In Powicke, *Essays*, 236–49.

McLane, Bernard William. 'A case study of violence and litigation in the early fourteenth century: the disputes of Robert Godsfield of Sutton-Le-Marsh'. *NMS* 28 (1984): 22–44.
    'Changes in the court of king's bench, 1291–1340: the preliminary view from Lincolnshire'. In Ormrod, *Fourteenth century*, 152–60, q.v.

'Juror attitudes toward local disorder: the evidence of the 1328 Lincolnshire trailbaston proceedings'. In J. S. Cockburn and Thomas A. Green, eds. *Twelve good men and true: the criminal trial jury in England, 1200–1800* (Princeton, 1988), 36–64.

Maddicott, J. R. 'The county community and the making of public opinion in fourteenth-century England'. *TRHS*, 5th series, 28 (1978): 27–43.

'The birth and setting of the ballads of Robin Hood'. *EHR* 93 (1978): 276–99.

May, Teresa. 'The Cobham family in the administration of England'. *Archaeologia Cantiana* 82 (1967): 1–31.

Mills, Mabel H. 'The collectors of customs'. In *EGW*, 2: 168–200.

Moberly, George Herbert. *The life of William of Wykeham sometime bishop of Winchester and lord high chancellor of England* (Winchester and London, 1887).

Morris, Arnold S., ed. 'Introduction'. In *Select cases of trespass from the king's courts 1307–1399*. Vol. 1. Selden Society Publications 100 (London, 1985).

Morris, William A. 'The sheriff'. In *EGW*, 2: 41–108.

Neilson, N. 'The forests'. In *EGW*, 1: 394–467.

'The court of common pleas'. In *EGW*, 3: 259–85.

Ormrod, William M. 'Edward III's government of England c. 1346–1356'. Ph.D. thesis, Oxford University, 1984.

'Edward III and the recovery of royal authority in England, 1340–60'. *History* 72 (1987): 4–19.

'The English crown and the customs, 1349–63'. *EcHR*, 2nd series, 40 (1987): 27–40.

'An experiment in taxation: the English parish subsidy of 1371'. *Speculum* 63 (1988): 58–82.

'The origins of the *sub pena* writ'. *BIHR* 61 (1988): 11–20.

'The English government and the Black Death of 1348–49'. In Ormrod, *Fourteenth century*, 175–88, q.v.

Palmer, Robert C. *The county courts of medieval England 1150–1350* (Princeton, 1982).

Post, J. B. 'Some limitations of the medieval peace rolls'. *Journal of the Society of Archivists* 4 (1973): 633–9.

'Local jurisdictions and judgement of death in later medieval England'. *Criminal Justice History* 4 (1983): 1–21.

'The justice of criminal justice in late fourteenth-century England'. *Criminal Justice History* 7 (1986): 33–49.

Prestwich, Michael. 'English armies in the early stages of the Hundred Years War: a scheme in 1341'. *BIHR* 56 (1983): 102–13.

Prince, Albert E. 'The strength of English armies in the reign of Edward III'. *EHR* 46 (1931): 353–71.

'The payment of army wages in Edward III's reign'. *Speculum* 19 (1944): 137–60.

'The army and navy'. In *EGW*, 1: 332–93.

'The indenture system under Edward III'. In Edwards, *Historical essays*, 283–98, q.v.

Pugh, R. B. 'The king's government in the middle ages'. In Crittall, *VCH: Wiltshire*, 1–43, q.v.

Putnam, Bertha H. *Proceedings before the justices of the peace in the fourteenth and fifteenth centuries* (London, 1938).

The place in legal history of Sir William Shareshull, chief justice of the King's Bench 1350–1361: a study of judicial and administrative methods in the reign of Edward III (Cambridge, 1950).

'The transformation of the keepers of the peace into the justices of the peace 1327–1380'. *TRHS*, 4th series, 12 (1929): 19–48.

'Records of the keepers of the peace and their supervisors, 1307–1327'. *EHR* 45 (1930): 435–44.

'Chief justice Shareshull and the economic and legal codes of 1351–1352'. *The University of Toronto Law Journal* 5 (1944): 251–81.

'Records of the courts of common law, especially of the sessions of the justices of the peace: sources for the economic history of England in the fourteenth and fifteenth centuries'. *Proceedings of the American Philosophical Society* 91 (1947): 258–73.

'Shire officials: keepers of the peace and justices of the peace'. In *EGW* 3: 185–217.

Salzman, L. F. 'Early taxation in Sussex'. *SAC* 98 (1960): 29–43, and 99 (1961): 1–19.

Sayles, G. O. 'Introduction'. In *Select cases in the court of king's bench*. Vol. IV. Ed. G. O. Sayles. Selden Society Publications 74 (London, 1957).

'Introduction'. In *Select cases in the court of king's bench*. Vol. V. Ed. G. O. Sayles. Selden Society Publications 76 (London, 1958).

'Introduction'. In *Select cases in the court of king's bench*. Vol. VI. Ed. G. O. Sayles. Selden Society Publications 82 (London, 1965).

Sharpe, J. A. 'The history of crime in late medieval and early modern England: a review of the field'. *Social History* 7 (1982): 187–203.

Sherborne, J. W. 'Indentured retinues and English expeditions to France, 1369–1380'. *EHR* 79 (1964): 718–46.

'The cost of English warfare with France in the later fourteenth century'. *BIHR* 50 (1977): 135–50.

'Aspects of English court culture in the later fourteenth century'. In Scattergood, *English court culture*, 1–28, q.v.

Stevenson, E. R. 'The escheator'. In *EGW*, 2: 109–67.

Stones, E. L. G. 'The Folvilles of Ashby-Folville, Leicestershire, and their associates in crime, 1326–1347'. *TRHS*, 5th series, 7 (1957): 117–36.

'Sir Geoffrey le Scrope (c. 1280–1340), chief justice of the king's bench'. *EHR* 69 (1954): 1–17.

Strayer, Joseph R. 'Introduction'. In *EGW*, 2: 3–40.

Sutherland, Donald W. 'Introduction'. In *The eyre of Northamptonshire 3–4 Edward III A.D. 1329–1330*. Vol. I. Ed. Donald W. Sutherland. Selden Society Publications 97 (London, 1983).

Taylor, Mary Margaret. *Some sessions of the peace in Cambridgeshire in the fourteenth century, 1340, 1380–83*. Cambridge Antiquarian Society. Octavo Publications 55 (Cambridge, 1942).

'The justices of the assize'. In *EGW*, 3: 219–57.

Tout, T. F. T. *Chapters in the administrative history of medieval England: the wardrobe, the chamber, and the small seals.* Vol. IV (Manchester, 1928).

'The English civil service in the fourteenth century'. *BJRL* 3 (1916–17): 185–214. Reprinted in *Collected papers*, 3: 191–222, q.v.

'The beginnings of a modern capital: London and Westminster in the fourteenth century'. *Proceedings of the British Academy* 10 (1921–3): 487–511. Reprinted in *Collected papers*, 3: 249–75, q.v.

'Some conflicting tendencies in English administrative history during the fourteenth century'. *BJRL* 8 (1924): 82–106. Reprinted in *Collected papers*, 3: 223–47, q.v.

Wilkinson, Bertie. *The chancery under Edward III* (Manchester, 1929).

'A letter of Edward III to his chancellor and treasurer'. *EHR* 42 (1927): 248–51.

'The seals of the two benches under Edward III'. *EHR* 42 (1927): 397–401.

'The chancery'. In *EGW*, 1: 162–205.

'The development of the council'. In idem, *Studies*, 108–79, q.v.

'The council and the origins of the equitable jurisdiction of chancery'. In idem, *Studies*, 196–215, q.v.

Willard, James F. *Parliamentary taxes on personal property, 1290 to 1334: a study in mediaeval English financial administration* (Cambridge, Mass., 1934).

'The English church and the lay taxes of the fourteenth century'. *The University of Colorado Studies* 4 (1906/7): 217–25.

'The Scotch raids and the fourteenth-century taxation of northern England'. *The University of Colorado Studies* 5 (1907/8): 237–42.

'Side-lights upon the assessment and collection of the mediaeval subsidies'. *TRHS*, 3rd series, 7 (1913): 167–89.

'Taxes on movables in the reign of Edward III'. *EHR* 30 (1915): 69–74.

'The crown and its creditors, 1327–1333'. *EHR* 42 (1927): 12–19.

'The collectors of clerical subsidies'. In *EGW*, 2: 227–80.

'Taxation boroughs and parliamentary boroughs, 1294–1336'. In Edwards, *Historical essays*, 447–36.

13. Sources for Chapter 12

There is no single, modern survey of parliament in the fourteenth century. Richardson and Sayles' discussion of Edward's parliaments forms a good starting point. Plucknett's article is very informative, though chronologically restricted. Sayles devotes most of his attention to the early foundations of parliament with an interesting chapter on later trends. Harriss (Chapter 1) focuses exclusively on finance and taxation, though his shorter survey is more inclusive. Edwards' lectures are wide-ranging, though also very general. Maddicott gives a refreshing local perspective on parliamentary development that should be read in conjunction with his work on the county community (Chapter 7). Finally, in an important article, Prestwich explores the changing political relationship between the nobility and commons.

Material for the development of the peerage, especially Powell and Wallis on the house of lords, cited under Chapter 7.

Baldwin, James F. *The king's council in England during the middle ages.* (Oxford, 1913). 'The king's council'. In *EGW*, 1: 129–61.

Basset, Margery. *Knights of the shire for Bedfordshire during the middle ages.* BHRS 29 (1949).

Blair, C. H. Hunter. 'Members of parliament for Northumberland'. *Archaeologia Aeliana*, 4th series, 10 (1933): 140–77; 11 (1934): 21–82.

Bryant, W. N. 'Some earlier examples of intercommuning in parliament, 1340–1348'. *EHR* 85 (1970): 54–8.

Cam, Helen M. 'The legislators of medieval England'. *Proceedings of the British Academy* 21 (1945): 127–50. Reprinted in *Law-finders*, 132–58, q.v.

'The theory and practice of representation in medieval England'. *History*, NS, 28 (1931): 11–26. Reprinted in *Law-finders*, 159–75, q.v.

'The relation of English members of parliament to their constituencies in the fourteenth century: a neglected text'. In *Liberties and communities*, 223–35, q.v.

'The community of the shire and the payment of its representatives in parliament'. In *Liberties and communities*, 236–50, q.v.

Cave-Brown, J. 'Knights of the shire for Kent 1275–1831'. *Archaeologia Cantiana* 21 (1985): 198–243.

Cheyette, Fredric. 'Kings, courts, cures, and sinecures: the statute of provisors and the common law'. *Traditio* 19 (1963): 295–349.

Clarke, M. V. *Representation and consent* (London, 1936).

Clementi, Dionna. 'That the statute of York of 1322 is no longer ambiguous'. In *Album Helen Maude Cam: studies presented to the international commission for the history of representative and parliamentary institutions* (Louvain and Paris, 1961): 93–100.

Cuttino, G. P. 'King's clerks and the community of the realm'. *Speculum* 29 (1954): 395–409.

'Medieval parliament reinterpreted'. *Speculum* 41 (1966): 681–7.

'A reconsideration of the *modus tenendi parliamentum*'. In Utley, Francis Lee, ed. *The forward movement of the fourteenth century* (Columbus, 1961): 31–60.

Davies, Cecily. 'The statute of provisors of 1351'. *History* 38 (1953): 116–33.

Denton, J. H. 'The clergy and parliament in the thirteenth and fourteenth centuries'. In Davies and Denton, *English parliament*, 88–108, q.v.

Denton, J. H. and J. P. Dooley. *Representatives of the lower clergy in parliament 1295–1340* (Woodbridge, Suffolk and Wolfeboro, N.H., 1987).

Edwards, J. Goronwy. *The commons in medieval English parliaments.* Creighton lecture in history, 1957 (London, 1958).

The second century of the English parliament (Oxford, 1979).

'Taxation and consent in the court of common pleas, 1338'. *EHR* 57 (1942): 473–80.

'"Justice" in early English parliaments'. *BIHR* 27 (1954). Reprinted in Fryde and Miller, *Studies*, 280–97, q.v.

Gooder, A. *The parliamentary representation of the county of York 1258–1832*. Vol. 1. *Yorkshire Archaeological Society* 91 (1935).

Graves, Edgar B. 'The legal significance of the statute of praemunire of 1353'. In LaMonte, *Anniversary essays*, 57–80, q.v.

Harriss, G. L. 'War and the emergence of the English parliament'. *JMH* 2 (1976): 35–56.

'The formation of parliament, 1272–1377'. In Davies and Denton, *English parliament*, 29–60, q.v.

Jones, W. R. 'Bishops, politics, and the two laws: the *gravamina* of the English clergy, 1237–1399'. *Speculum* 41 (1966): 209–45.

'Purveyance for war and the community of the realm in late medieval England'. *Albion* 7 (1975): 300–16.

Kemp, Eric W. 'The origins of Canterbury convocation'. *JEH* 3 (1952): 132–43.

Latham, L. C. 'Collection of the wages of knights of the shire in the fourteenth and fifteenth centuries'. *EHR* 48 (1933): 455–64.

Levett, A. E. 'Clerical proctors in parliament and knights of the shire, 1280–1374'. *EHR* 48 (1933): 443–55.

McHardy, A. K. 'The representation of the English lower clergy in parliament during the later fourteenth century'. In Brewer, *Sanctity and secularity*, 97–107, q.v.

McKisack, May. *The parliamentary representation of the English boroughs during the middle ages* (Oxford, 1932).

'The parliamentary representation of King's Lynn before 1500'. *EHR* 42 (1927): 583–9.

Maddicott, John R. 'Parliament and the constituencies, 1272–1377'. In Davies and Denton, *English parliament*, 61–87, q.v.

Miller, Edward. 'Medieval English parliaments'. *Parliamentary History* 1 (1982): 217–20.

'Introduction'. In Fryde and Miller, *Studies*, 1–30, q.v.

Morris, William A. 'Magnates and community of the realm in parliament 1264–1327'. *Medievalia et Humanistica* 1 (1943): 58–94.

'Introduction'. In *EGW*, 1: 3–81.

Ormrod, W. M. 'Agenda for legislation, 1322–c. 1340'. *EHR* 105 (1990): 1–33.

Owen, L. V. D. 'The representation of Nottingham and Nottinghamshire in the early parliaments'. *Thoroton Society* 47 (1944): 20–8.

Plucknett, Theodore F. T. *Statutes and their interpretation in the first half of the fourteenth century* (Cambridge, 1922).

'Parliament'. In *EGW*, 1: 82–128. Reprinted in Fryde and Miller, *Studies*, 195–241, q.v.

Post, Gaines. 'The two laws and the statute of York'. *Speculum* 29 (1954): 417–32.

Prestwich, Michael. 'Parliament and the community of the realm in fourteenth-century England'. In Cosgrove, Art and J. I. McGuire, eds. *Parliament and community*. Irish Historical Studies 14 (Belfast, 1983): 5–24.

'The *modus tenendi parliamentum*'. *Parliamentary History* 1 (1982): 221–5.

'Magnate summonses in England in the later years of Edward I'. _Parliaments, estates and representation_ 5 (1985): 97–101.

Pronay, Nicholas and John Taylor, eds. _Parliamentary texts of the later middle ages_ (Oxford, 1980).

Pugh, R. B. 'The commons of Wiltshire in medieval parliaments'. In Crittall, _VCH: Wiltshire_, 72–9, q.v.

Rayner, Doris. 'The forms and machinery of the "commune petition" in the fourteenth century'. _EHR_ 46 (1931): 198–233, 549–70.

Richardson, H. G. 'John of Gaunt and the parliamentary representation of Lancashire'. _BJRL_ 22 (1938): 175–222.

Richardson, H. G. and G. O. Sayles. 'The parliaments of Edward II'. _BIHR_ 6 (1928): 71–88. Reprinted in idem, _English parliament_.

'The parliaments of Edward III'. _BIHR_ 8 (1930): 65–77, and 9 (1931): 1–18. Reprinted in idem, _English parliament_.

'The king's ministers in parliament, 1307–1327'. _EHR_ 47 (1932): 194–203. Reprinted in idem, _English parliament_.

'The king's ministers in parliament, 1327–1377'. _EHR_ 47 (1932): 377–97. Reprinted in idem, _English parliament_.

'Parliaments and great councils in medieval England'. _Law Quarterly Review_ 77 (1961): 213–36, 401–26. Reprinted in idem, _English parliament_.

Riess, Ludwig. _The history of the English electoral law in the middle ages_. Ed. and trans. K. L. Wood-Legh (Cambridge, 1940).

Roskell, J. S. _The commons and their speakers in English parliaments 1376–1523_ (Manchester, 1965).

'The problem of the attendance of the lords in medieval parliaments'. _BIHR_ 29 (1956): 153–204.

'A consideration of certain aspects and problems of the English _modus tenendi parliamentum_'. _BJRL_ 50 (1967–8): 411–42.

Sayles, G. O. _The king's parliament of England_ (New York, 1974).

Strayer, Joseph R. 'The statute of York and the community of the realm'. _AgHR_ 47 (1941): 1–22.

Taylor, Mary M. 'Parliamentary elections in Cambridgeshire, 1322–8'. _BIHR_ 18 (1940/1): 21–6.

Templeman, Geoffrey. 'The history of parliament to 1400 in the light of modern research'. _UBHJ_ 1 (1948): 202–31.

Trueman, John H. 'The statute of York and the Ordinances of 1311'. _Medievalia et Humanistica_ 10 (1956): 64–81.

Wedgewood, Josiah C. _Staffordshire parliamentary history from the earliest times to the present day_. Vol. 1. _William Salt Archaeological Society_ 42 (1919).

Weske, Dorothy Bruce. _Convocation of the clergy: a study of its antecedents and its rise with special emphasis upon its growth and activities in the thirteenth and fourteenth centuries_ (London, 1937).

Whitley, T. W. _The parliamentary representation of the city of Coventry from the earliest times_ (Coventry, 1894).

Wilkinson, Bertie. '"Plenum parliamentum" and the council in parliament'. In idem, *Studies*, 1–14, q.v.

'The nature of parliament'. In idem, *Studies*, 15–54, q.v.

'The beginnings of parliamentary control over the custom on wool'. In idem, *Studies*, 55–81, q.v.

'The development of the council'. In idem, *Studies*, 108–79, q.v.

Wood-Legh, K. L. 'Sheriffs, lawyers, and belted knights in the parliaments of Edward III'. *EHR* 46 (1931): 372–88.

'The knight's attendance in the parliaments of Edward III'. *EHR* 47 (1932): 398–413.

14. Sources for Chapters 13 and 14

Historians generally agree about the overall shape of political history in Edward III's reign, but political studies have been overshadowed by investigations of the economy and war. The crises of 1341 and 1376 have come under the most intense scrutiny, while periods of relative calm in the 1330s, 1350s, and 1360s have been neglected. This is unfortunate because few historians – Ormrod is an exception – have investigated why Edward was so politically successful. As a result, the 'crisis' of 1341 is sometimes blown out of proportion. In addition to the works here, those cited in Chapter 1 should also be consulted.

Bellamy, J. G. 'Appeal and impeachment in the Good Parliament'. *BIHR* 39 (1966): 35–46.

Bestul, Thomas H. *Satire and Allegory in Wynnere and Wastoure* (Lincoln, 1974).

Blackley, F. D. 'Isabella and the bishop of Exeter'. In Powicke, *Essays*, 220–35, q.v.

Clarke, Maude V. 'The origin of impeachment'. In idem, *Fourteenth-century studies*. Ed. L. S. Sutherland and M. McKisack (Oxford, 1937), 242–71.

'Committees of estates and the deposition of Edward II'. In Edwards, *Historical essays*, 27–46, q.v.

Coleman, Janet. *English literature in history 1350–1400: medieval readers and writers* (London, 1981).

Crump, C. G. 'The arrest of Roger Mortimer and Queen Isabella'. *EHR* 26 (1911): 331–2.

Emerson, Oliver Farrar. 'English or French in the time of Edward III'. *Romantic Review* 7 (1916): 127–43.

Fryde, E. B. 'Financial resources of Edward III in the Netherlands, 1337–40'. *Revue Belge de Philologie et d'Histoire* 40 (1962): 1168–87; and 45 (1967): 1142–216.

'Parliament and the French war, 1336–40'. In Powicke, *Essays*, 250–69, q.v.

Fryde, Natalie M. 'Edward III's removal of his ministers and judges, 1340–1'. *BIHR* 48 (1975): 149–61.

Galbraith, V. H. 'Articles laid before the parliament of 1371'. *EHR* 34 (1919): 579–82.

'Nationality and language in medieval England'. *TRHS*, 4th series, 23 (1941): 113–28.

Galway, Margaret. 'Joan of Kent and the Order of the Garter'. *UBHJ* 1 (1947): 13–50.

Gransden, Antonia. 'The alleged rape by Edward III of the countess of Salisbury'. *EHR* 87 (1972): 333–44.

Harriss, G. L. 'The commons' petitions of 1340'. *EHR* 78 (1963): 625–54.

Holmes, George. *The Good Parliament* (Oxford, 1975).

'The rebellion of the earl of Lancaster, 1328–9'. *BIHR* 28 (1955): 84–9.

Hughes, Dorothy. *A study of social and constitutional tendencies in the early years of Edward III as illustrated more especially by the events connected with the ministerial inquiries of 1340 and the following years* (London, 1915).

Jones, W. R. '*Rex et ministri*: English local government and the crisis of 1341'. *JBS* 13 (1973): 1–20.

Lambrick, G. 'The impeachment of the abbot of Abingdon in 1368'. *EHR* 82 (1967): 250–76.

Lapsley, G. T. 'Archbishop Stratford and the crisis of 1341'. *EHR* 30 (1915): 6–18, 193–215.

McLane, Bernard William, ed. *The 1341 royal inquest in Lincolnshire*. Lincoln Record Society 78 (Woodbridge and Wolfeboro, 1988).

Maddicott, John R. 'Poems of social protest in early fourteenth-century England'. In Ormrod, *Fourteenth century*, 130–44, q.v.

Mannyng, Robert of Brunne. *Handlyng Synne*. Ed. Idelle Sullens (Binghampton, 1983).

Myers, A. R. 'The wealth of Richard Lyons'. In Powicke, *Essays*, 301–29, q.v.

Owst, G. R. *Literature and the pulpit in medieval England: a neglected chapter in the history of English letters and of the English people*. 2nd edn revised (New York, 1961).

Plucknett, Theodore F. T. 'The origin of impeachment'. *TRHS*, 4th series, 24 (1942): 47–71.

'The impeachments of 1376'. *TRHS*, 5th series, 1 (1951): 153–64.

Redstone, V. B. 'Some mercenaries of Henry of Lancaster, 1327–1330'. *TRHS*, 3rd series, 7 (1913): 151–66.

Rigg, A. G. 'John of Bridlington's *Prophecy*: a new look'. *Speculum* 63 (1988): 596–613.

Roskell, J. S. 'Sir Peter de la Mare, speaker for the commons in parliament in 1376 and 1377'. *NMS* 2 (1955): 24–37.

Ross, Thomas W. 'On the evil times of Edward II. A new version from Ms Bodley 48'. *Anglia* 75 (1957): 173–93.

Rothwell, William. 'The teaching of French in medieval England'. *Modern Language Review* 63 (1968): 37–46.

'The role of French in thirteenth-century England'. *BJRL* 58 (1975/6): 445–66.

Stones, E. L. G. 'The treaty of Northampton, 1328'. *History* 38 (1953): 54–61.

Tout, Thomas F. 'Literature and learning in the English civil service in the four-teenth century'. *Speculum* 4 (1929): 365–89.

Wentersdorf, Karl P. 'The clandestine marriages of the fair maid of Kent'. *JMH* 5 (1979): 203–31.

Whiting, B. J. 'The vows of the Heron'. *Speculum* 20 (1945): 261–78.

Wilkinson, Bertie. *The constitutional history of England, 1216–1399, with selected documents.* Vol. II: *Politics and the constitution* (London and New York, 1952).

'The protest of the earls of Arundel and Surrey in the crisis of 1341'. *EHR* 46 (1931): 177–93.

'English politics and politicians of the thirteenth and fourteenth centuries'. *Speculum* 30 (1955): 37–48.

'Latimer's impeachment and parliament in the fourteenth century'. In idem, *Studies*, 82–107, q.v.

Wilson, R. M. 'English and French in England 1100–1300'. *History* 25 (1943): 37–60.

Woodbine, George E. 'The language of English law'. *Speculum* 18 (1943): 395–436.

INDEX